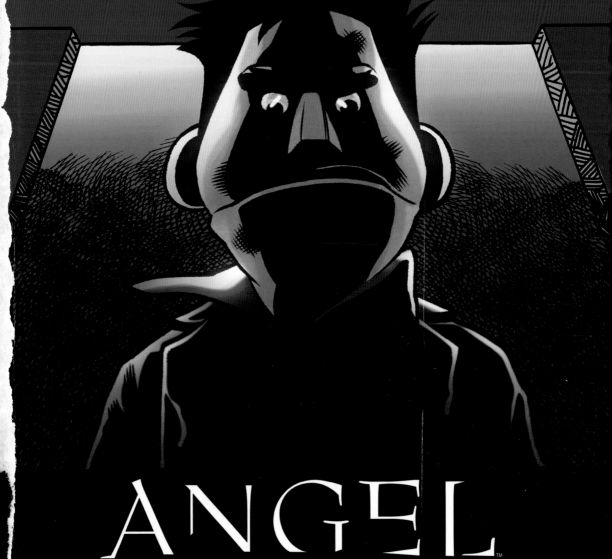

ANGEL™

SMILE TIME

Original Series Edits by Chris Ryall

Collection Edits by Justin Eisinger

Collection Design by Neil Uyetake

® Angel created by Joss Whedon and David Greenwalt.
Special thanks to our Watcher, Joss Whedon, and Fox Worldwide
Publishing's Debbie Olshan for their invaluable assistance.

ANGEL: SMILE TIME HC. AUGUST 2009. FIRST PRINTING. Angel is © 2009 Twentieth Century Fox Film Corporation. All Rights Reserved. © 2009 Idea and Design
Works, LLC. IDW Publishing, a division of Idea and Design Works, LLC. Editorial offices: 5080 Santa Fe St., San Diego, CA 92109. All Rights Reserved. The IDW logo
is registered in the U.S. Patent and Trademark Office. All Rights Reserved. Any similarities to persons living or dead are purely coincidental. With the exception of artwork
used for review purposes, none of the contents of this publication may be reprinted without the permission of Idea and Design Works, LLC. Printed in Korea.
IDW Publishing does not read or accept unsolicited submissions of ideas, stories, or artwork.

Originally published as ANGEL: SMILE TIME Issues #1-3, ANGEL: MASKS. and ANGEL: SHADOW PUPPETS #1-4.

ANGEL

SMILE TIME

www.IDWPUBLISHING.com   ISBN: 978-1-60010-481-7   12 11 10 09   1 2 3 4

Operations: Ted Adams, Chief Executive Officer • Greg Goldstein, Chief Operating Officer • Matthew Ruzicka, CPA, Chief Financial Officer • Alan Payne, VP of Sales • Lorelei Bunjes, Dir. of Digital Services • AnnaMaria White, Marketing & PR Manager • Marci Hubbard, Executive Assistant • Alonzo Simon, Shipping Manager • Angela Loggins, Staff Accountant • Editorial: Chris Ryall, Publisher/Editor-in-Chief • Scott Dunbier, Editor, Special Projects • Andy Schmidt, Senior Editor • Justin Eisinger, Editor • Kris Oprisko, Editor/Foreign Lic. • Denton J. Tipton, Editor • Tom Waltz, Editor • Mariah Huehner, Associate Editor • Carlos Guzman, Editorial Assistant • Design: Robbie Robbins, EVP/Sr. Graphic Artist • Neil Uyetake, Art Director • Chris Mowry, Graphic Artist • Amauri Osorio, Graphic Artist • Gilberto Lazcano, Production Assistant

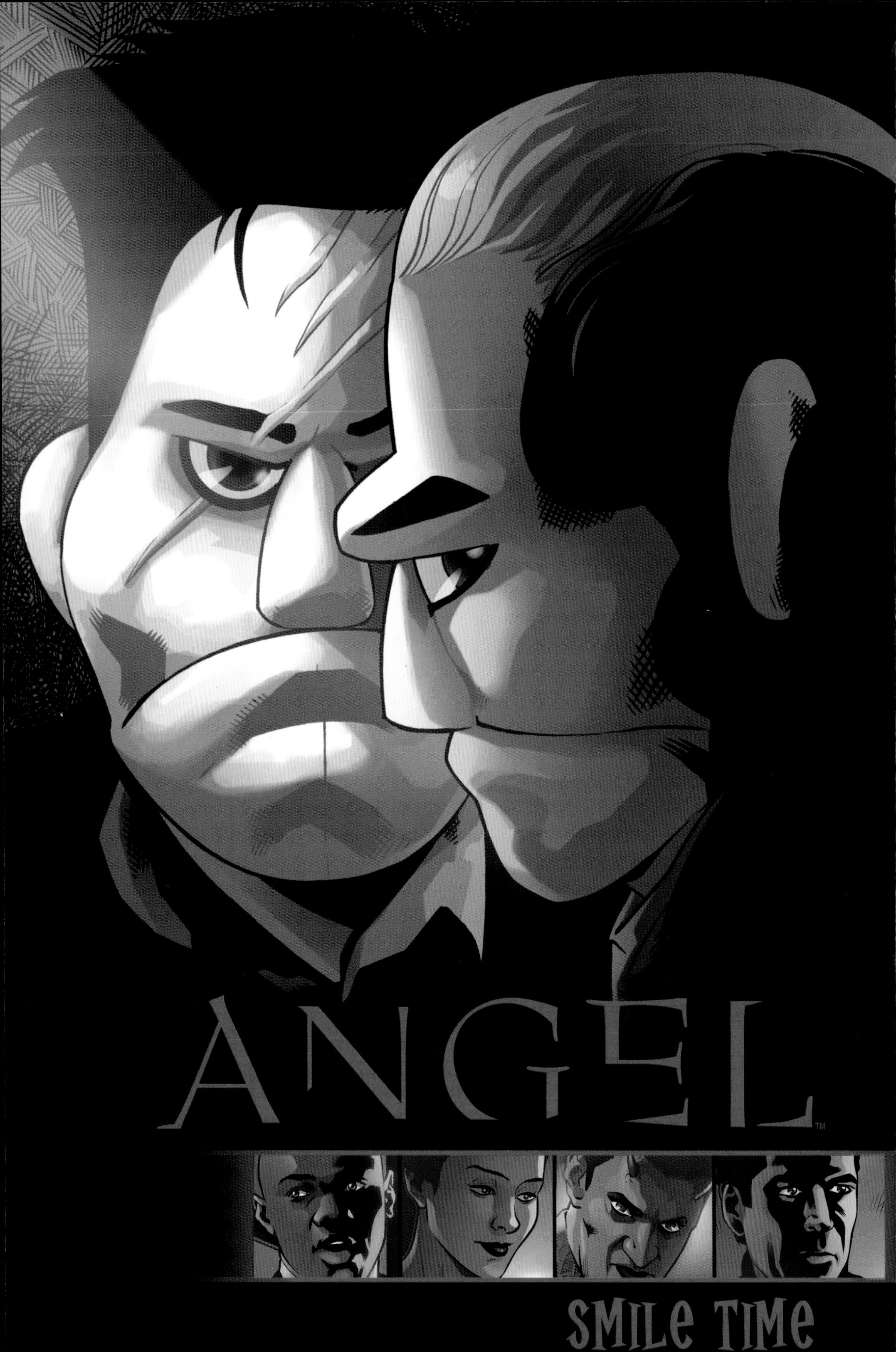
ANGEL™
SMILE TIME

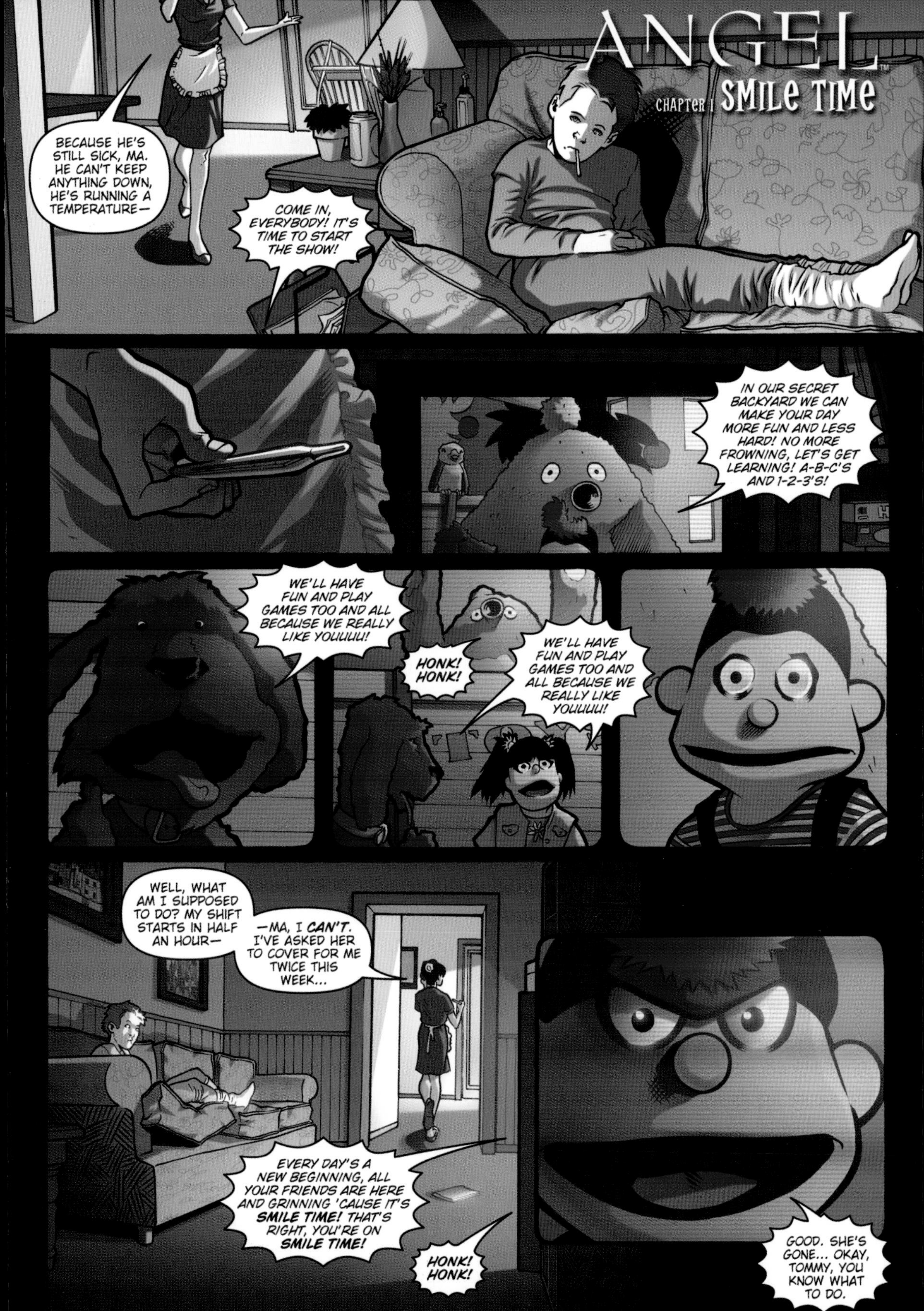
ANGEL
CHAPTER 1 SMILE TIME
BECAUSE HE'S STILL SICK, MA. HE CAN'T KEEP ANYTHING DOWN, HE'S RUNNING A TEMPERATURE—
COME IN, EVERYBODY! IT'S TIME TO START THE SHOW!
IN OUR SECRET BACKYARD WE CAN MAKE YOUR DAY MORE FUN AND LESS HARD! NO MORE FROWNING, LET'S GET LEARNING! A-B-C'S AND 1-2-3'S!
WE'LL HAVE FUN AND PLAY GAMES TOO AND ALL BECAUSE WE REALLY LIKE YOUUUU!
HONK! HONK!
WE'LL HAVE FUN AND PLAY GAMES TOO AND ALL BECAUSE WE REALLY LIKE YOUUUU!
WELL, WHAT AM I SUPPOSED TO DO? MY SHIFT STARTS IN HALF AN HOUR—
—MA, I CAN'T. I'VE ASKED HER TO COVER FOR ME TWICE THIS WEEK...
EVERY DAY'S A NEW BEGINNING, ALL YOUR FRIENDS ARE HERE AND GRINNING 'CAUSE IT'S SMILE TIME! THAT'S RIGHT, YOU'RE ON SMILE TIME!
HONK! HONK!
GOOD. SHE'S GONE... OKAY, TOMMY, YOU KNOW WHAT TO DO.

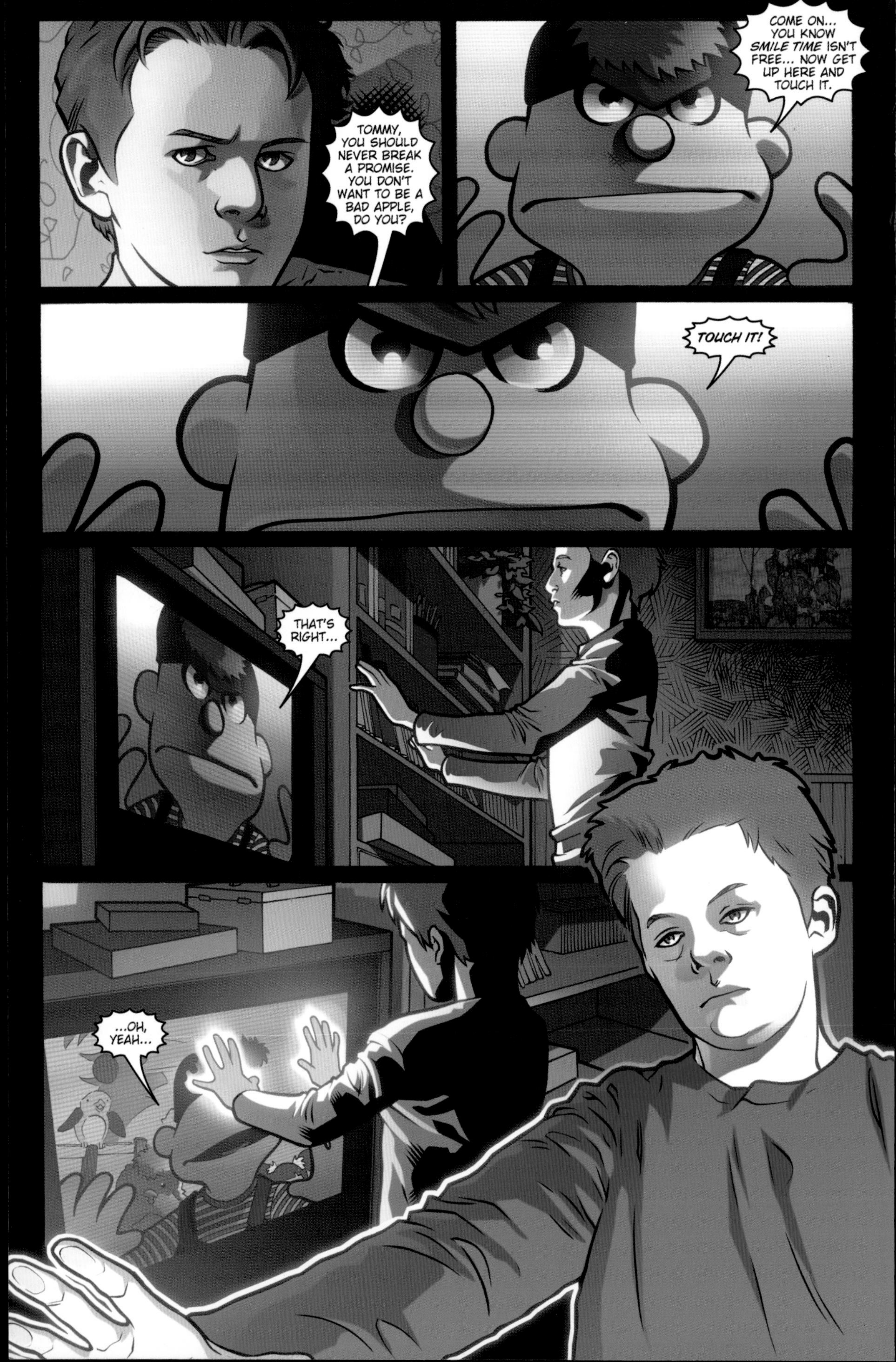
TOMMY, YOU SHOULD NEVER BREAK A PROMISE. YOU DON'T WANT TO BE A BAD APPLE, DO YOU?
COME ON... YOU KNOW *SMILE TIME* ISN'T FREE... NOW GET UP HERE AND TOUCH IT.
TOUCH IT!
THAT'S RIGHT...
...OH, YEAH...

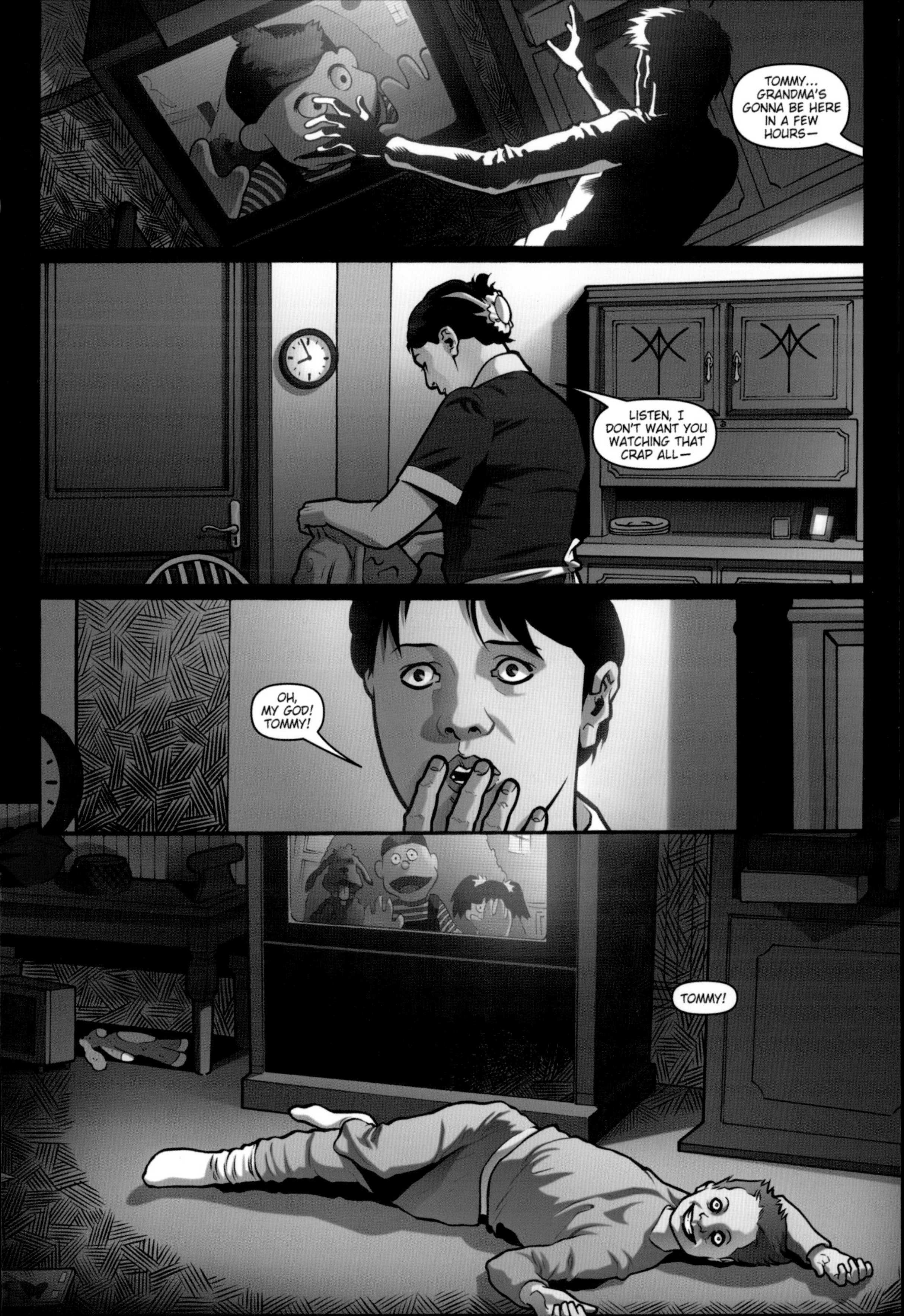
TOMMY... GRANDMA'S GONNA BE HERE IN A FEW HOURS—
LISTEN, I DON'T WANT YOU WATCHING THAT CRAP ALL—
OH, MY GOD! TOMMY!
TOMMY!

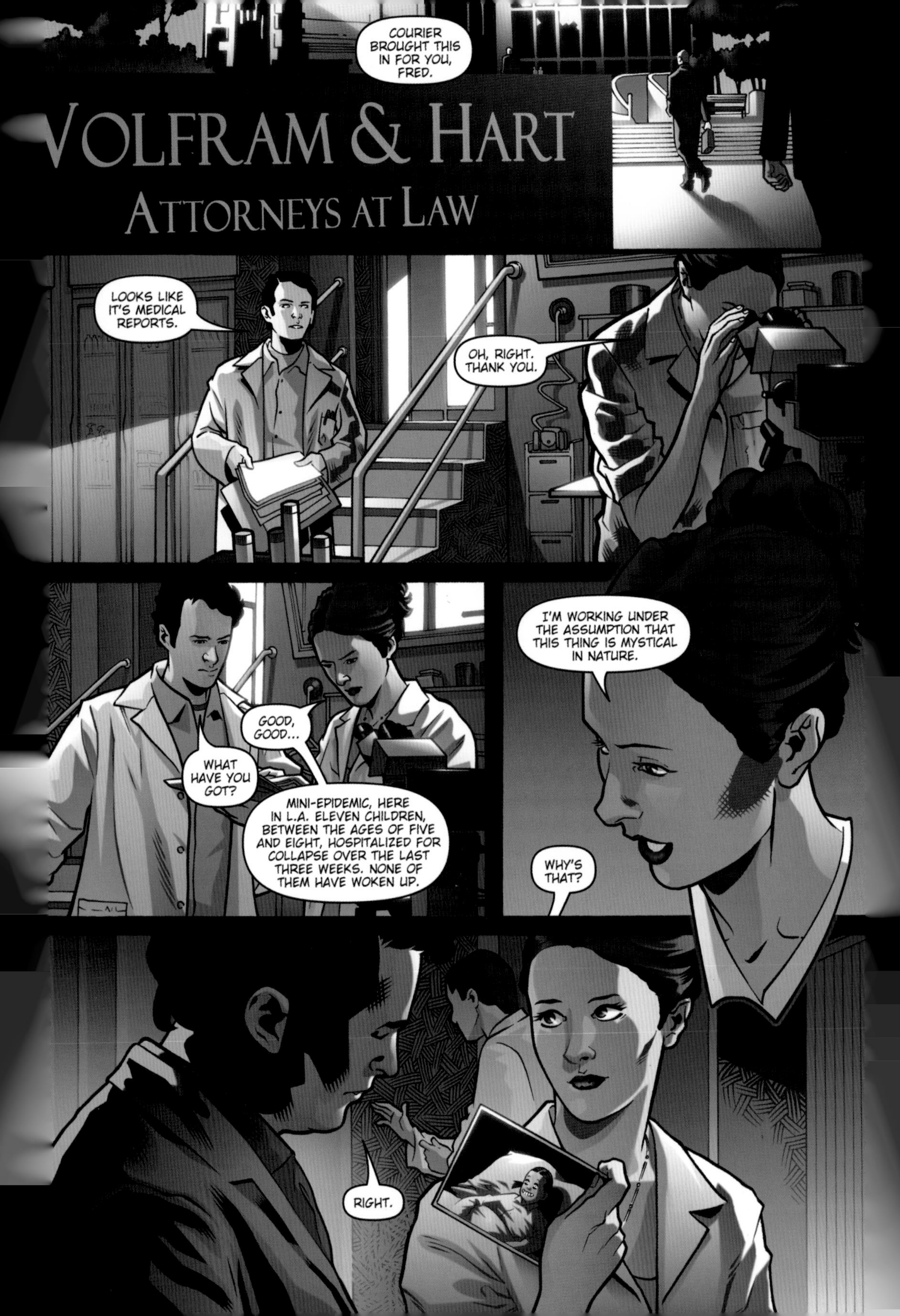

COURIER BROUGHT THIS IN FOR YOU, FRED.
WOLFRAM & HART
ATTORNEYS AT LAW
LOOKS LIKE IT'S MEDICAL REPORTS.
OH, RIGHT. THANK YOU.
WHAT HAVE YOU GOT?
GOOD, GOOD...
MINI-EPIDEMIC, HERE IN L.A. ELEVEN CHILDREN, BETWEEN THE AGES OF FIVE AND EIGHT, HOSPITALIZED FOR COLLAPSE OVER THE LAST THREE WEEKS. NONE OF THEM HAVE WOKEN UP.
I'M WORKING UNDER THE ASSUMPTION THAT THIS THING IS MYSTICAL IN NATURE.
WHY'S THAT?
RIGHT.

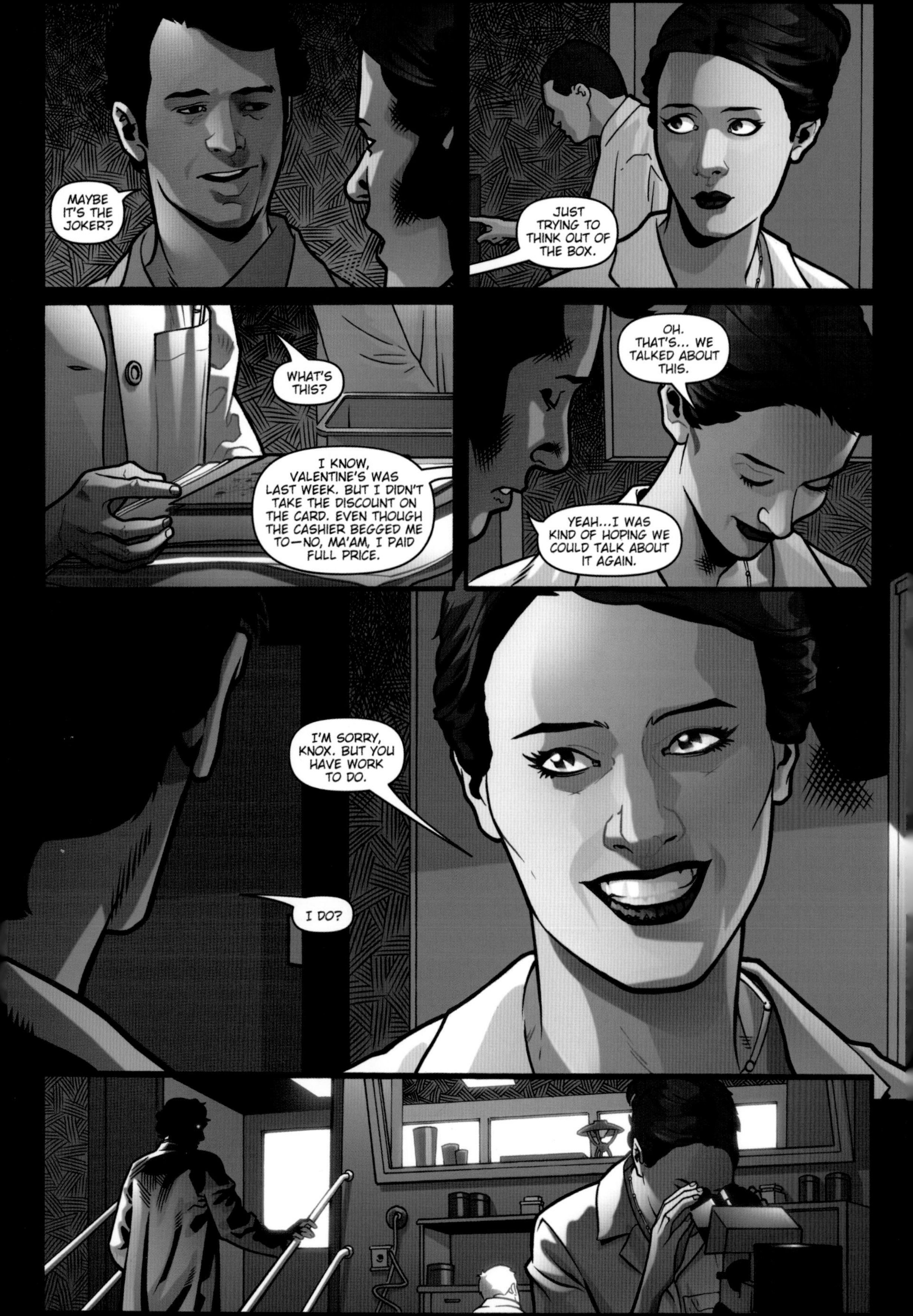
MAYBE IT'S THE JOKER?
JUST TRYING TO THINK OUT OF THE BOX.
WHAT'S THIS?
I KNOW, VALENTINE'S WAS LAST WEEK. BUT I DIDN'T TAKE THE DISCOUNT ON THE CARD. EVEN THOUGH THE CASHIER BEGGED ME TO—NO, MA'AM, I PAID FULL PRICE.
OH. THAT'S... WE TALKED ABOUT THIS.
YEAH...I WAS KIND OF HOPING WE COULD TALK ABOUT IT AGAIN.
I'M SORRY, KNOX. BUT YOU HAVE WORK TO DO.
I DO?

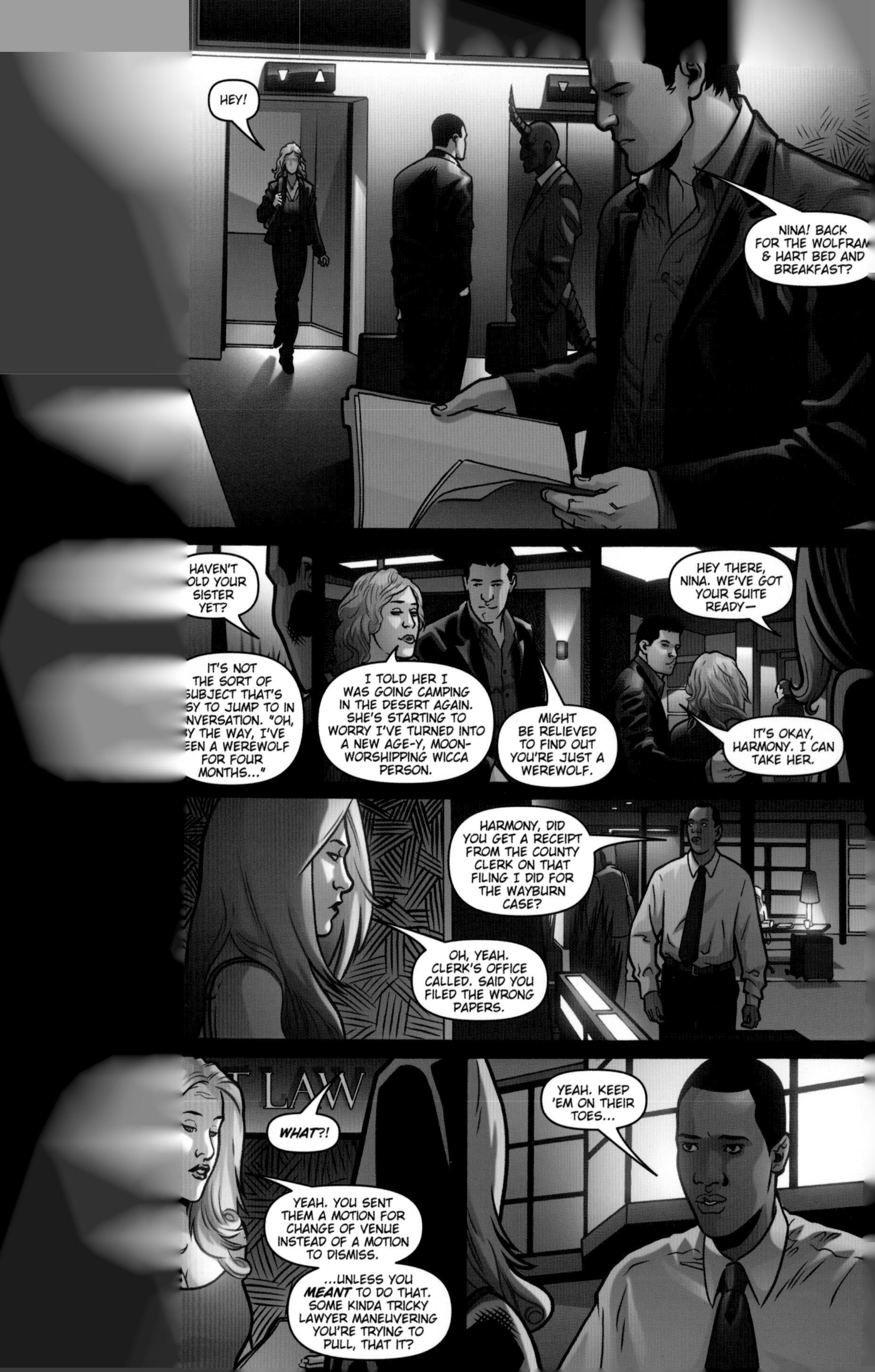
HEY!
NINA! BACK FOR THE WOLFRAM & HART BED AND BREAKFAST?
HAVEN'T OLD YOUR SISTER YET?
IT'S NOT THE SORT OF SUBJECT THAT'S SY TO JUMP TO IN NVERSATION. "OH, Y THE WAY, I'VE EEN A WEREWOLF FOR FOUR MONTHS..."
I TOLD HER I WAS GOING CAMPING IN THE DESERT AGAIN. SHE'S STARTING TO WORRY I'VE TURNED INTO A NEW AGE-Y, MOON-WORSHIPPING WICCA PERSON.
MIGHT BE RELIEVED TO FIND OUT YOU'RE JUST A WEREWOLF.
HEY THERE, NINA. WE'VE GOT YOUR SUITE READY—
IT'S OKAY, HARMONY. I CAN TAKE HER.
HARMONY, DID YOU GET A RECEIPT FROM THE COUNTY CLERK ON THAT FILING I DID FOR THE WAYBURN CASE?
OH, YEAH. CLERK'S OFFICE CALLED. SAID YOU FILED THE WRONG PAPERS.
WHAT?!
YEAH. YOU SENT THEM A MOTION FOR CHANGE OF VENUE INSTEAD OF A MOTION TO DISMISS.
...UNLESS YOU MEANT TO DO THAT. SOME KINDA TRICKY LAWYER MANEUVERING YOU'RE TRYING TO PULL, THAT IT?
YEAH. KEEP 'EM ON THEIR TOES...

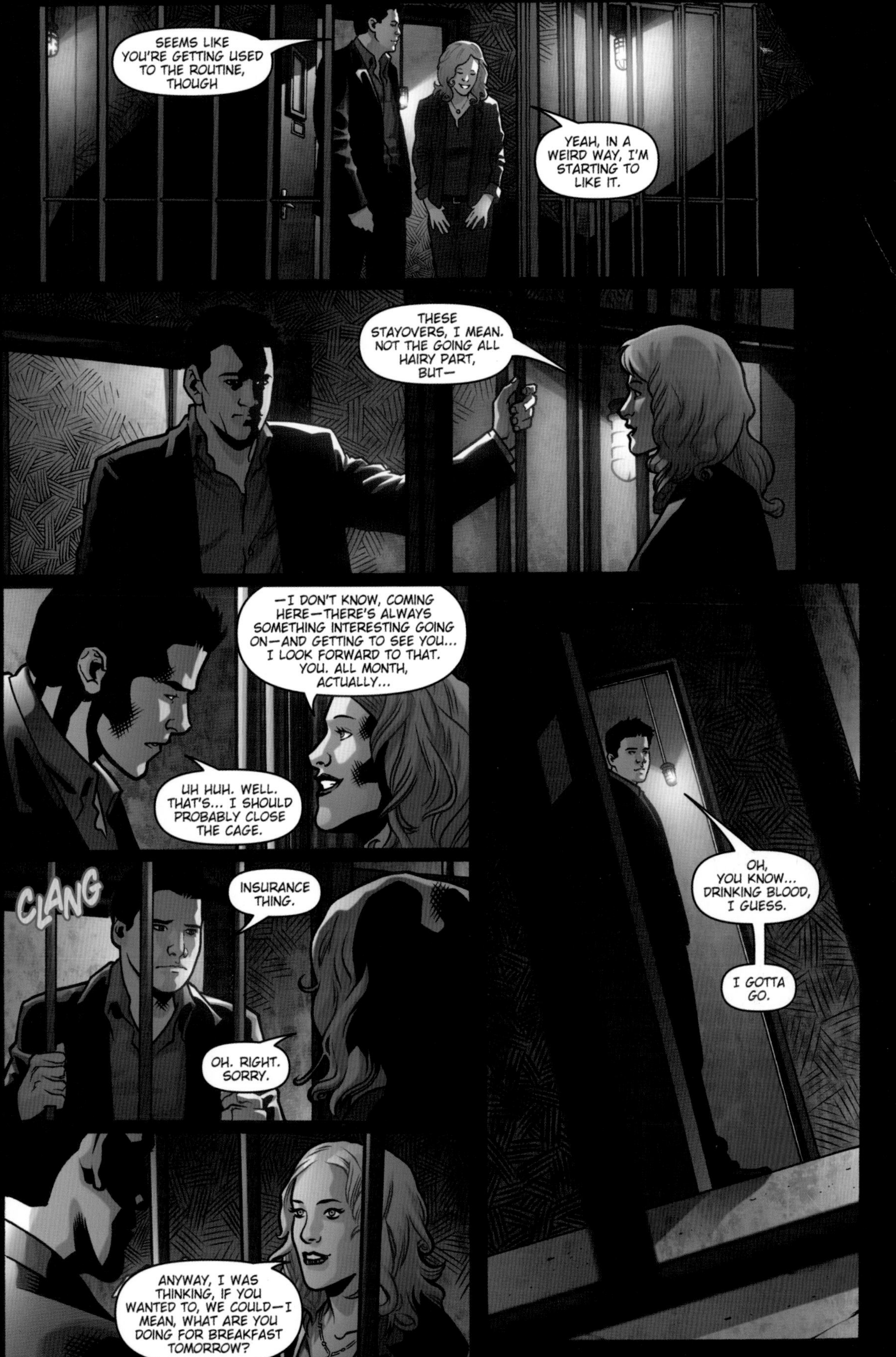
SEEMS LIKE YOU'RE GETTING USED TO THE ROUTINE, THOUGH
YEAH, IN A WEIRD WAY, I'M STARTING TO LIKE IT.
THESE STAYOVERS, I MEAN. NOT THE GOING ALL HAIRY PART, BUT—
—I DON'T KNOW, COMING HERE—THERE'S ALWAYS SOMETHING INTERESTING GOING ON—AND GETTING TO SEE YOU... I LOOK FORWARD TO THAT. YOU. ALL MONTH, ACTUALLY...
UH HUH. WELL. THAT'S... I SHOULD PROBABLY CLOSE THE CAGE.
CLANG
INSURANCE THING.
OH. RIGHT. SORRY.
ANYWAY, I WAS THINKING, IF YOU WANTED TO, WE COULD—I MEAN, WHAT ARE YOU DOING FOR BREAKFAST TOMORROW?
OH, YOU KNOW... DRINKING BLOOD, I GUESS.
I GOTTA GO.

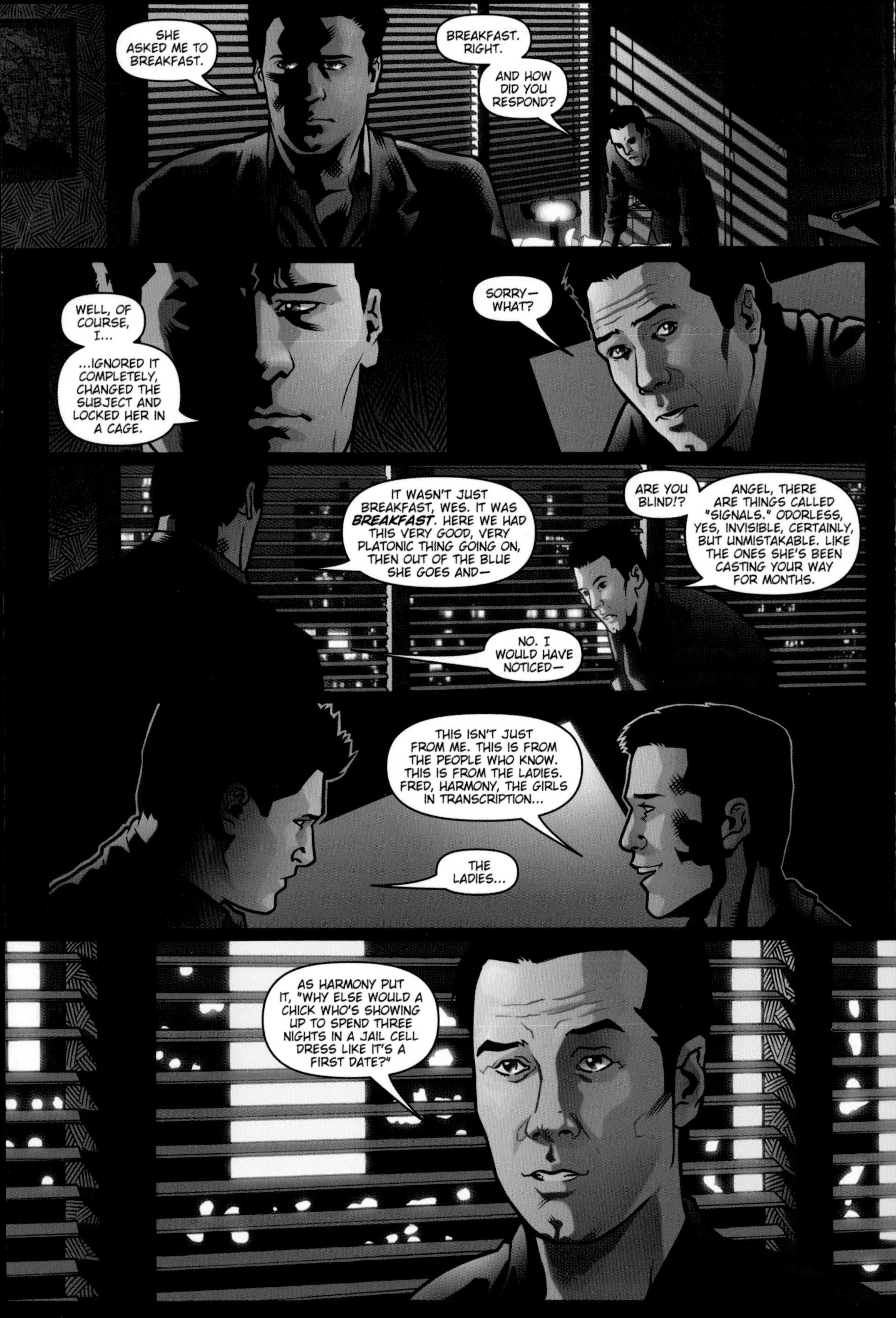
SHE ASKED ME TO BREAKFAST.
BREAKFAST. RIGHT.
AND HOW DID YOU RESPOND?
WELL, OF COURSE, I...
...IGNORED IT COMPLETELY, CHANGED THE SUBJECT AND LOCKED HER IN A CAGE.
SORRY—WHAT?
IT WASN'T JUST BREAKFAST, WES. IT WAS BREAKFAST. HERE WE HAD THIS VERY GOOD, VERY PLATONIC THING GOING ON, THEN OUT OF THE BLUE SHE GOES AND—
ARE YOU BLIND!?
ANGEL, THERE ARE THINGS CALLED "SIGNALS." ODORLESS, YES, INVISIBLE, CERTAINLY, BUT UNMISTAKABLE. LIKE THE ONES SHE'S BEEN CASTING YOUR WAY FOR MONTHS.
NO. I WOULD HAVE NOTICED—
THIS ISN'T JUST FROM ME. THIS IS FROM THE PEOPLE WHO KNOW. THIS IS FROM THE LADIES. FRED, HARMONY, THE GIRLS IN TRANSCRIPTION...
THE LADIES...
AS HARMONY PUT IT, "WHY ELSE WOULD A CHICK WHO'S SHOWING UP TO SPEND THREE NIGHTS IN A JAIL CELL DRESS LIKE IT'S A FIRST DATE?"

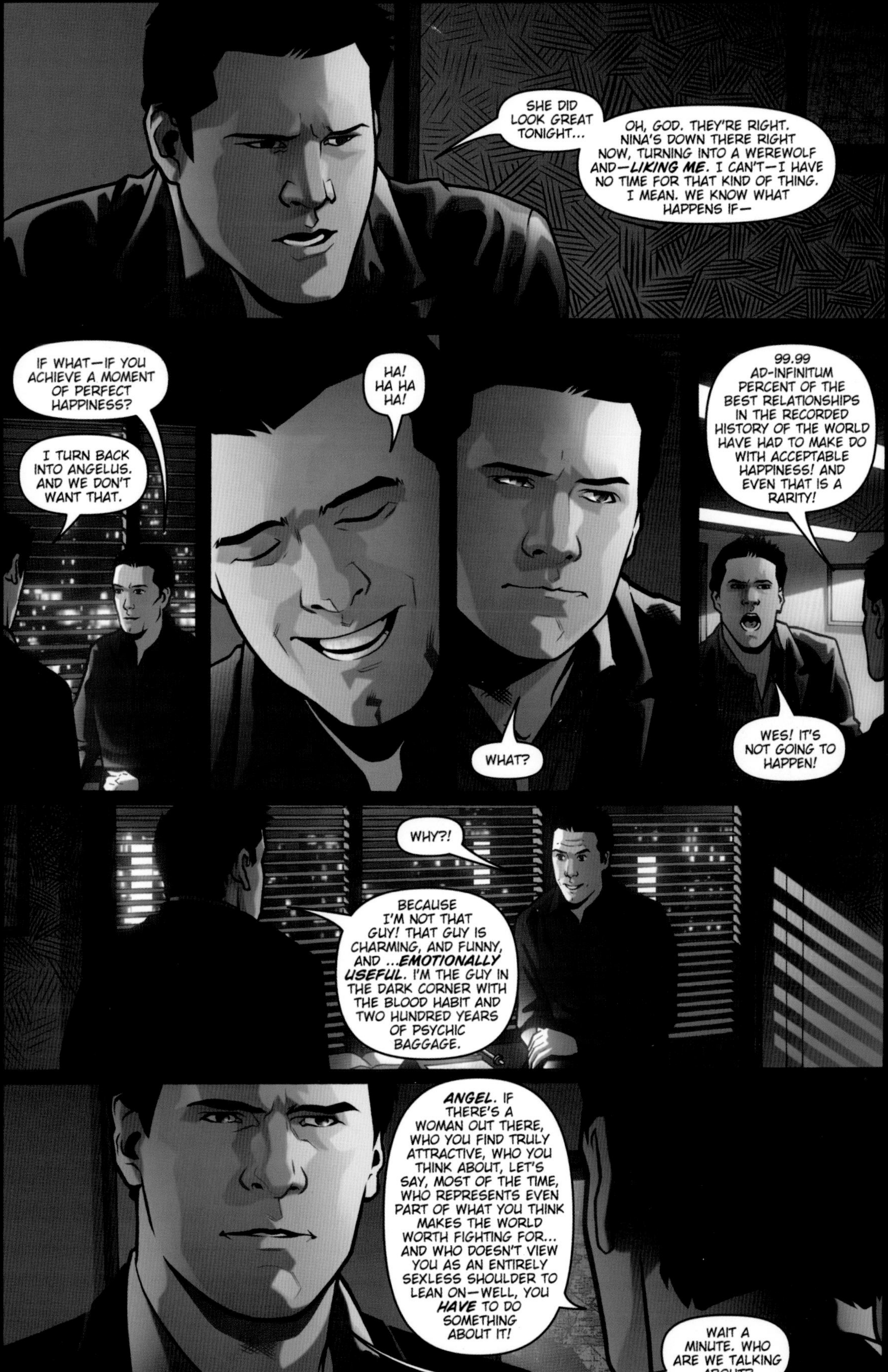
SHE DID LOOK GREAT TONIGHT...
OH, GOD. THEY'RE RIGHT. NINA'S DOWN THERE RIGHT NOW, TURNING INTO A WEREWOLF AND—LIKING ME. I CAN'T—I HAVE NO TIME FOR THAT KIND OF THING. I MEAN. WE KNOW WHAT HAPPENS IF—
IF WHAT—IF YOU ACHIEVE A MOMENT OF PERFECT HAPPINESS?
I TURN BACK INTO ANGELUS. AND WE DON'T WANT THAT.
HA! HA HA HA!
WHAT?
99.99 AD-INFINITUM PERCENT OF THE BEST RELATIONSHIPS IN THE RECORDED HISTORY OF THE WORLD HAVE HAD TO MAKE DO WITH ACCEPTABLE HAPPINESS! AND EVEN THAT IS A RARITY!
WES! IT'S NOT GOING TO HAPPEN!
WHY?!
BECAUSE I'M NOT THAT GUY! THAT GUY IS CHARMING, AND FUNNY, AND ...EMOTIONALLY USEFUL. I'M THE GUY IN THE DARK CORNER WITH THE BLOOD HABIT AND TWO HUNDRED YEARS OF PSYCHIC BAGGAGE.
ANGEL. IF THERE'S A WOMAN OUT THERE, WHO YOU FIND TRULY ATTRACTIVE, WHO YOU THINK ABOUT, LET'S SAY, MOST OF THE TIME, WHO REPRESENTS EVEN PART OF WHAT YOU THINK MAKES THE WORLD WORTH FIGHTING FOR... AND WHO DOESN'T VIEW YOU AS AN ENTIRELY SEXLESS SHOULDER TO LEAN ON—WELL, YOU HAVE TO DO SOMETHING ABOUT IT!
WAIT A MINUTE. WHO ARE WE TALKING ABOUT?

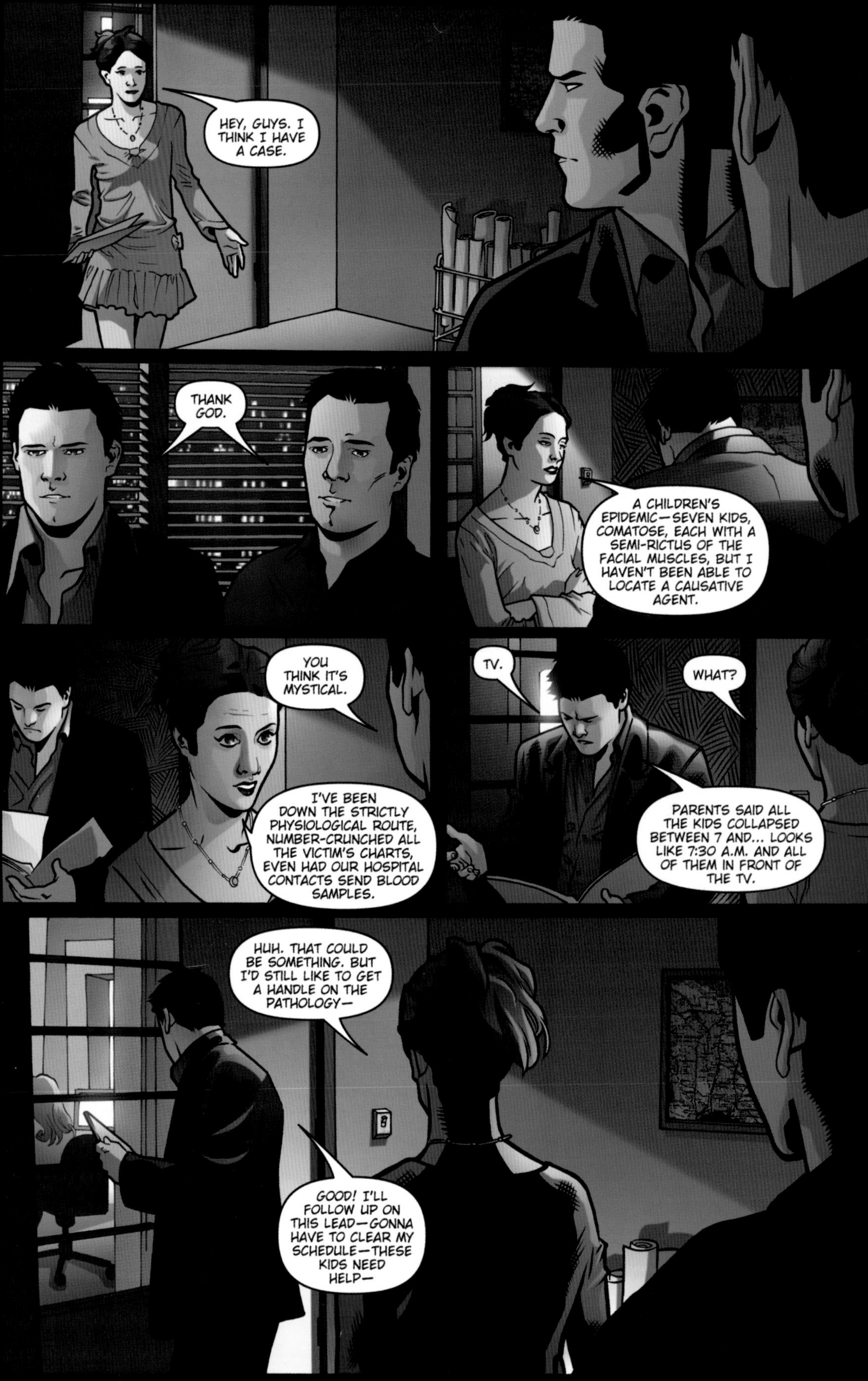

HEY, GUYS. I THINK I HAVE A CASE.
THANK GOD.
A CHILDREN'S EPIDEMIC—SEVEN KIDS, COMATOSE, EACH WITH A SEMI-RICTUS OF THE FACIAL MUSCLES, BUT I HAVEN'T BEEN ABLE TO LOCATE A CAUSATIVE AGENT.
YOU THINK IT'S MYSTICAL.
I'VE BEEN DOWN THE STRICTLY PHYSIOLOGICAL ROUTE, NUMBER-CRUNCHED ALL THE VICTIM'S CHARTS, EVEN HAD OUR HOSPITAL CONTACTS SEND BLOOD SAMPLES.
TV.
WHAT?
PARENTS SAID ALL THE KIDS COLLAPSED BETWEEN 7 AND... LOOKS LIKE 7:30 A.M. AND ALL OF THEM IN FRONT OF THE TV.
HUH. THAT COULD BE SOMETHING. BUT I'D STILL LIKE TO GET A HANDLE ON THE PATHOLOGY—
GOOD! I'LL FOLLOW UP ON THIS LEAD—GONNA HAVE TO CLEAR MY SCHEDULE—THESE KIDS NEED HELP—

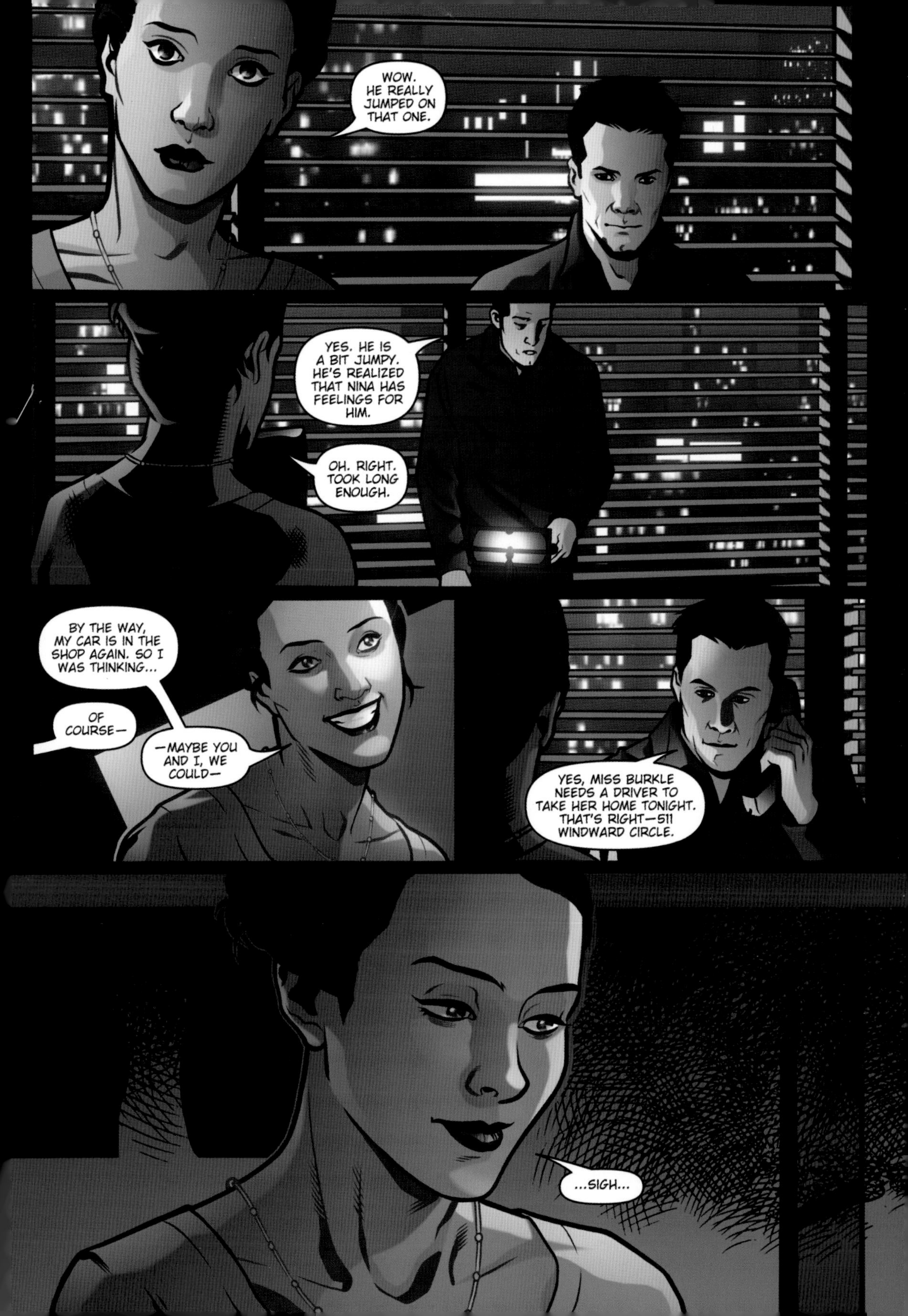
WOW. HE REALLY JUMPED ON THAT ONE.
YES. HE IS A BIT JUMPY. HE'S REALIZED THAT NINA HAS FEELINGS FOR HIM.
OH. RIGHT. TOOK LONG ENOUGH.
BY THE WAY, MY CAR IS IN THE SHOP AGAIN. SO I WAS THINKING...
OF COURSE—
—MAYBE YOU AND I, WE COULD—
YES, MISS BURKLE NEEDS A DRIVER TO TAKE HER HOME TONIGHT. THAT'S RIGHT—511 WINDWARD CIRCLE.
...SIGH...

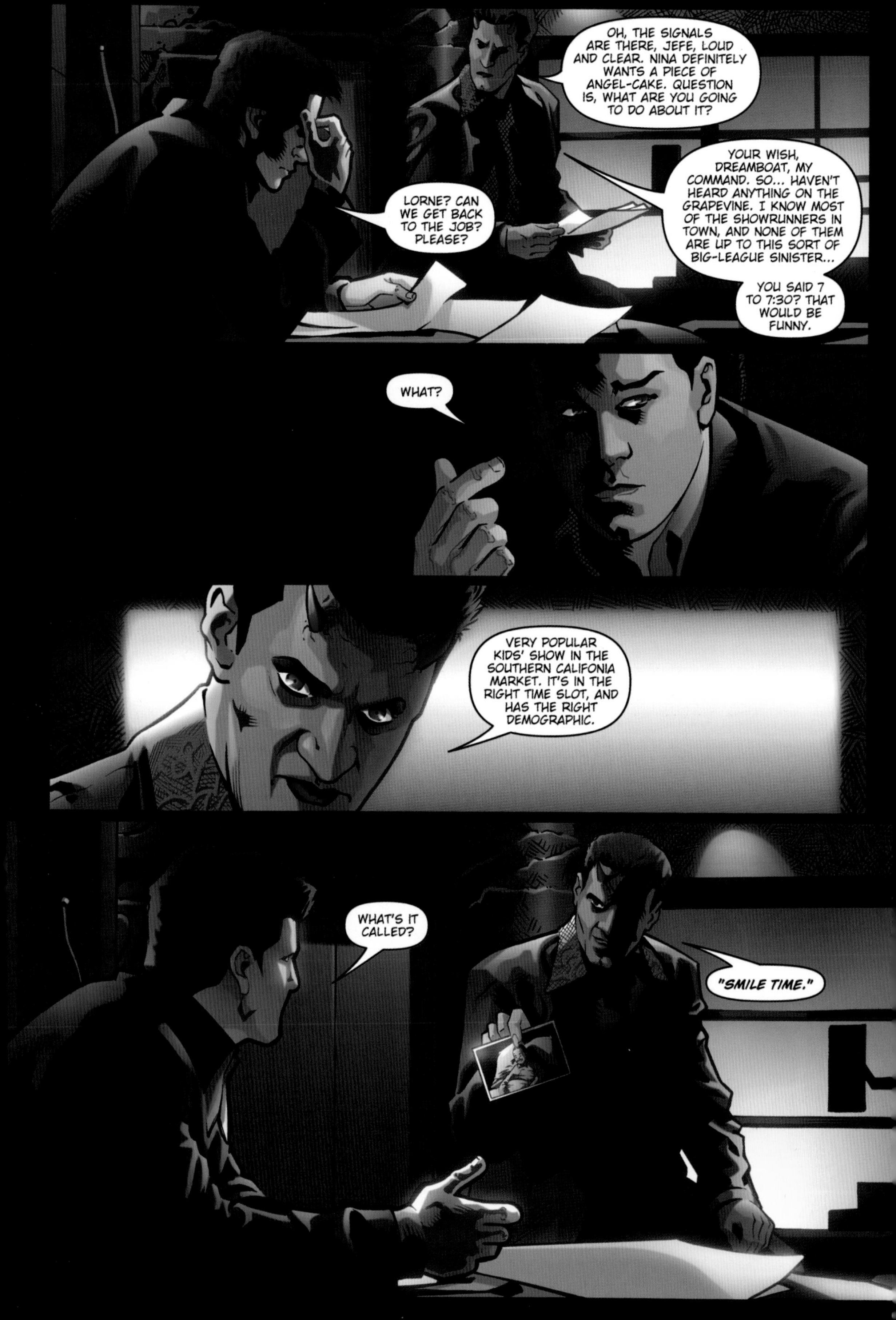
OH, THE SIGNALS ARE THERE, JEFE, LOUD AND CLEAR. NINA DEFINITELY WANTS A PIECE OF ANGEL-CAKE. QUESTION IS, WHAT ARE YOU GOING TO DO ABOUT IT?
LORNE? CAN WE GET BACK TO THE JOB? PLEASE?
YOUR WISH, DREAMBOAT, MY COMMAND. SO... HAVEN'T HEARD ANYTHING ON THE GRAPEVINE. I KNOW MOST OF THE SHOWRUNNERS IN TOWN, AND NONE OF THEM ARE UP TO THIS SORT OF BIG-LEAGUE SINISTER...
YOU SAID 7 TO 7:30? THAT WOULD BE FUNNY.
WHAT?
VERY POPULAR KIDS' SHOW IN THE SOUTHERN CALIFONIA MARKET. IT'S IN THE RIGHT TIME SLOT, AND HAS THE RIGHT DEMOGRAPHIC.
WHAT'S IT CALLED?
"SMILE TIME."

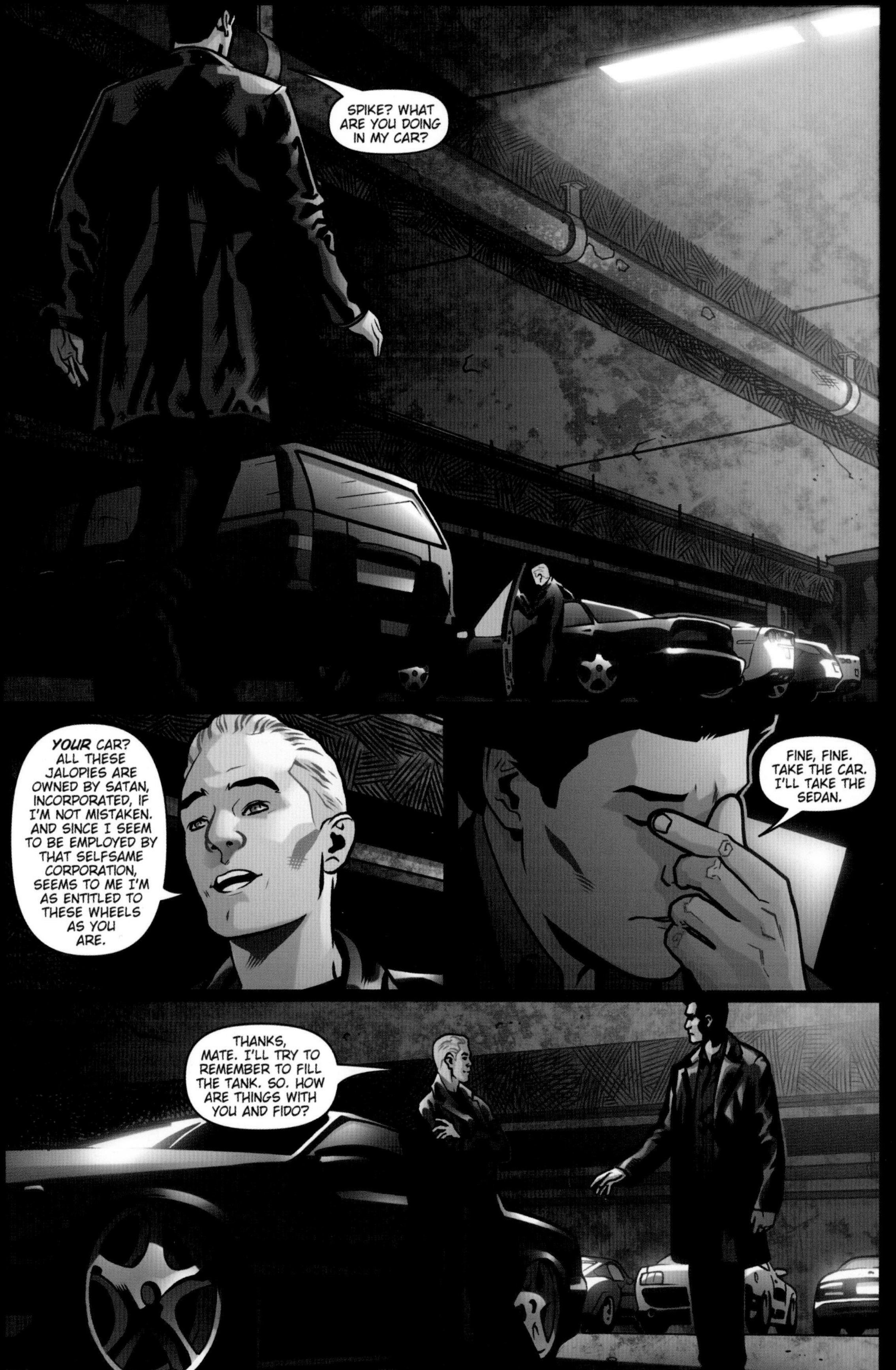
SPIKE? WHAT ARE YOU DOING IN MY CAR?
YOUR CAR? ALL THESE JALOPIES ARE OWNED BY SATAN, INCORPORATED, IF I'M NOT MISTAKEN. AND SINCE I SEEM TO BE EMPLOYED BY THAT SELFSAME CORPORATION, SEEMS TO ME I'M AS ENTITLED TO THESE WHEELS AS YOU ARE.
FINE, FINE. TAKE THE CAR. I'LL TAKE THE SEDAN.
THANKS, MATE. I'LL TRY TO REMEMBER TO FILL THE TANK. SO. HOW ARE THINGS WITH YOU AND FIDO?

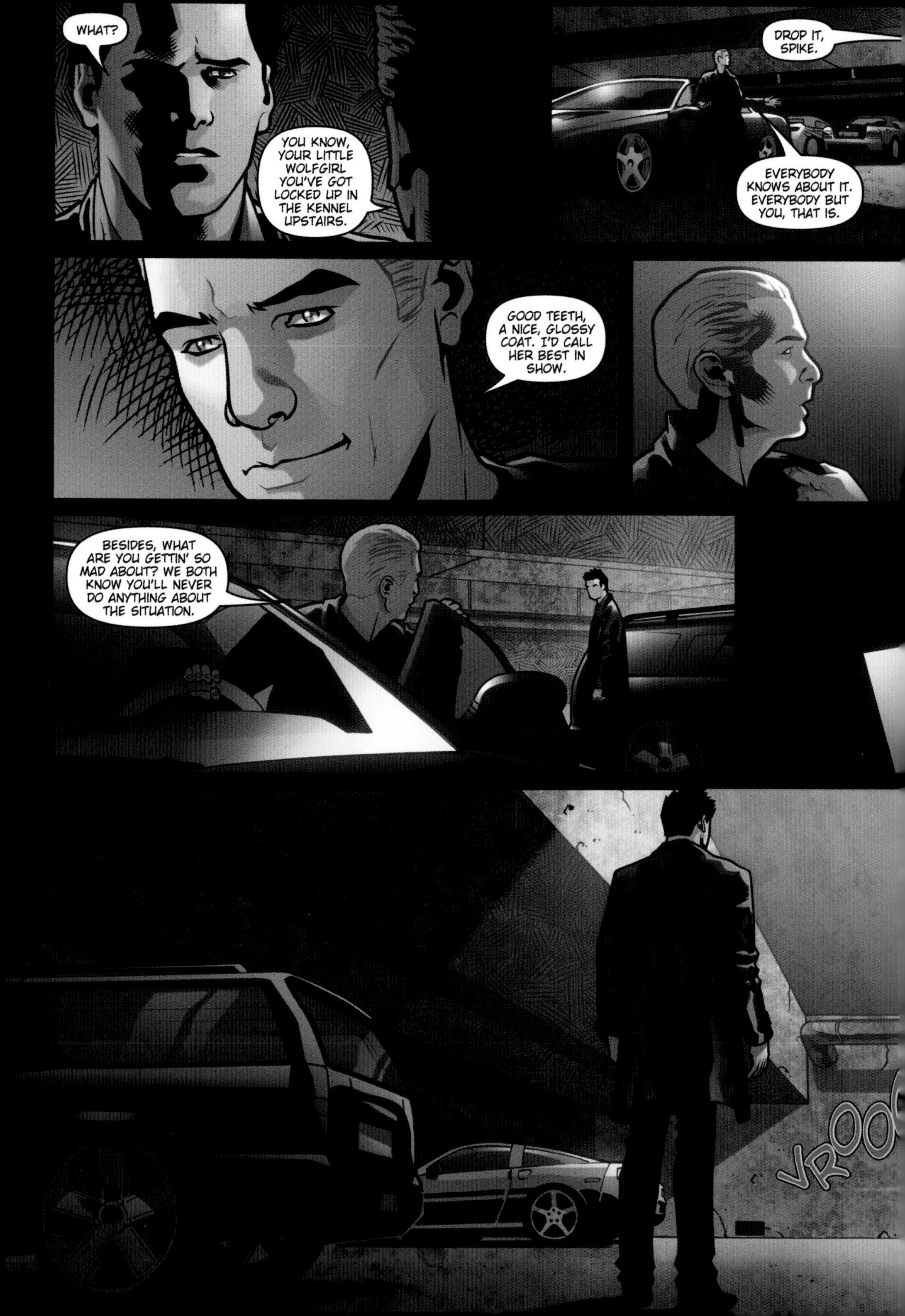
WHAT?
YOU KNOW, YOUR LITTLE WOLFGIRL YOU'VE GOT LOCKED UP IN THE KENNEL UPSTAIRS.
DROP IT, SPIKE.
EVERYBODY KNOWS ABOUT IT. EVERYBODY BUT YOU, THAT IS.
GOOD TEETH, A NICE, GLOSSY COAT. I'D CALL HER BEST IN SHOW.
BESIDES, WHAT ARE YOU GETTIN' SO MAD ABOUT? WE BOTH KNOW YOU'LL NEVER DO ANYTHING ABOUT THE SITUATION.
VROOO

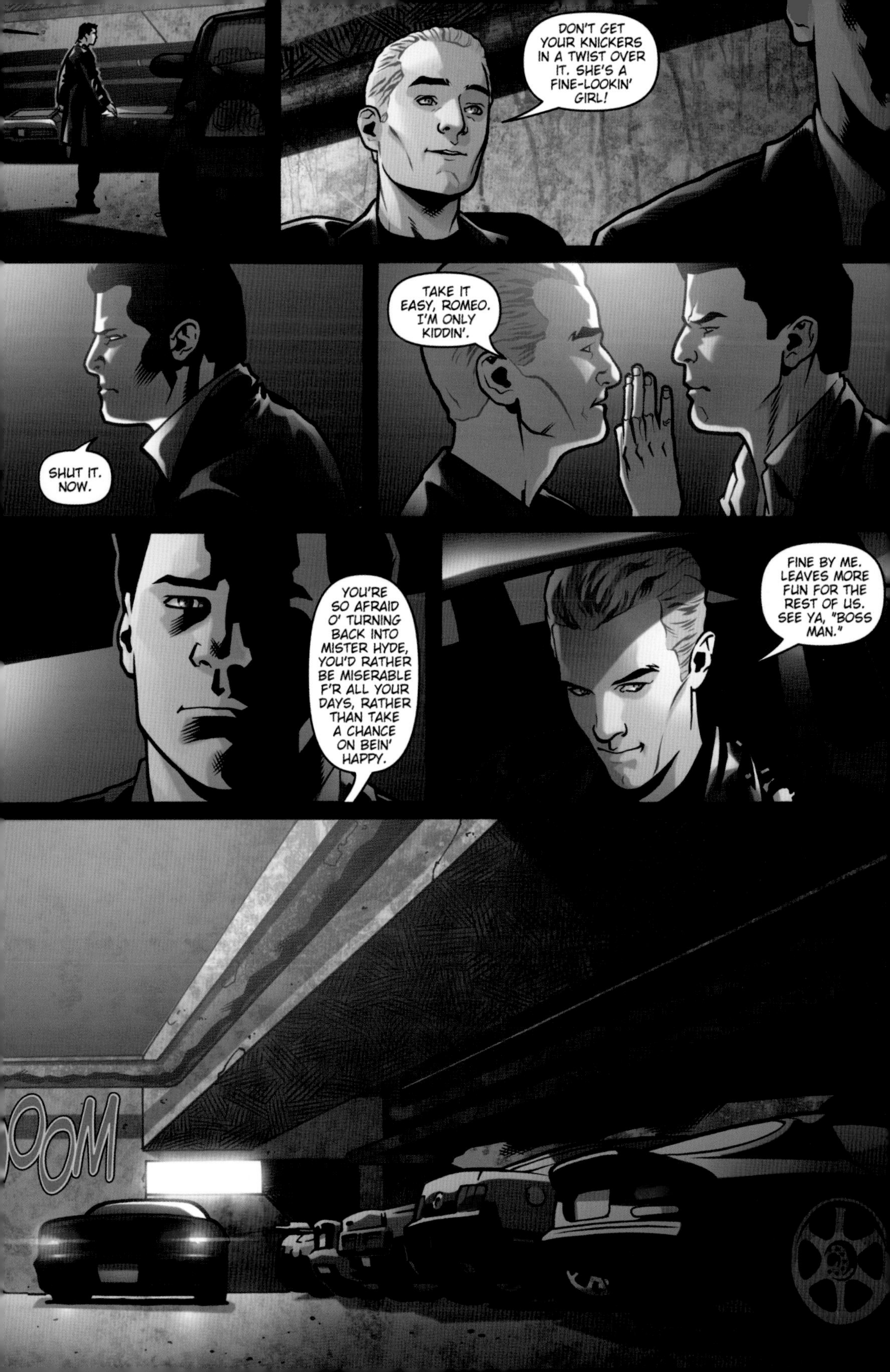
DON'T GET YOUR KNICKERS IN A TWIST OVER IT. SHE'S A FINE-LOOKIN' GIRL!
SHUT IT. NOW.
TAKE IT EASY, ROMEO. I'M ONLY KIDDIN'.
YOU'RE SO AFRAID O' TURNING BACK INTO MISTER HYDE, YOU'D RATHER BE MISERABLE F'R ALL YOUR DAYS, RATHER THAN TAKE A CHANCE ON BEIN' HAPPY.
FINE BY ME. LEAVES MORE FUN FOR THE REST OF US. SEE YA, "BOSS MAN."
OOM

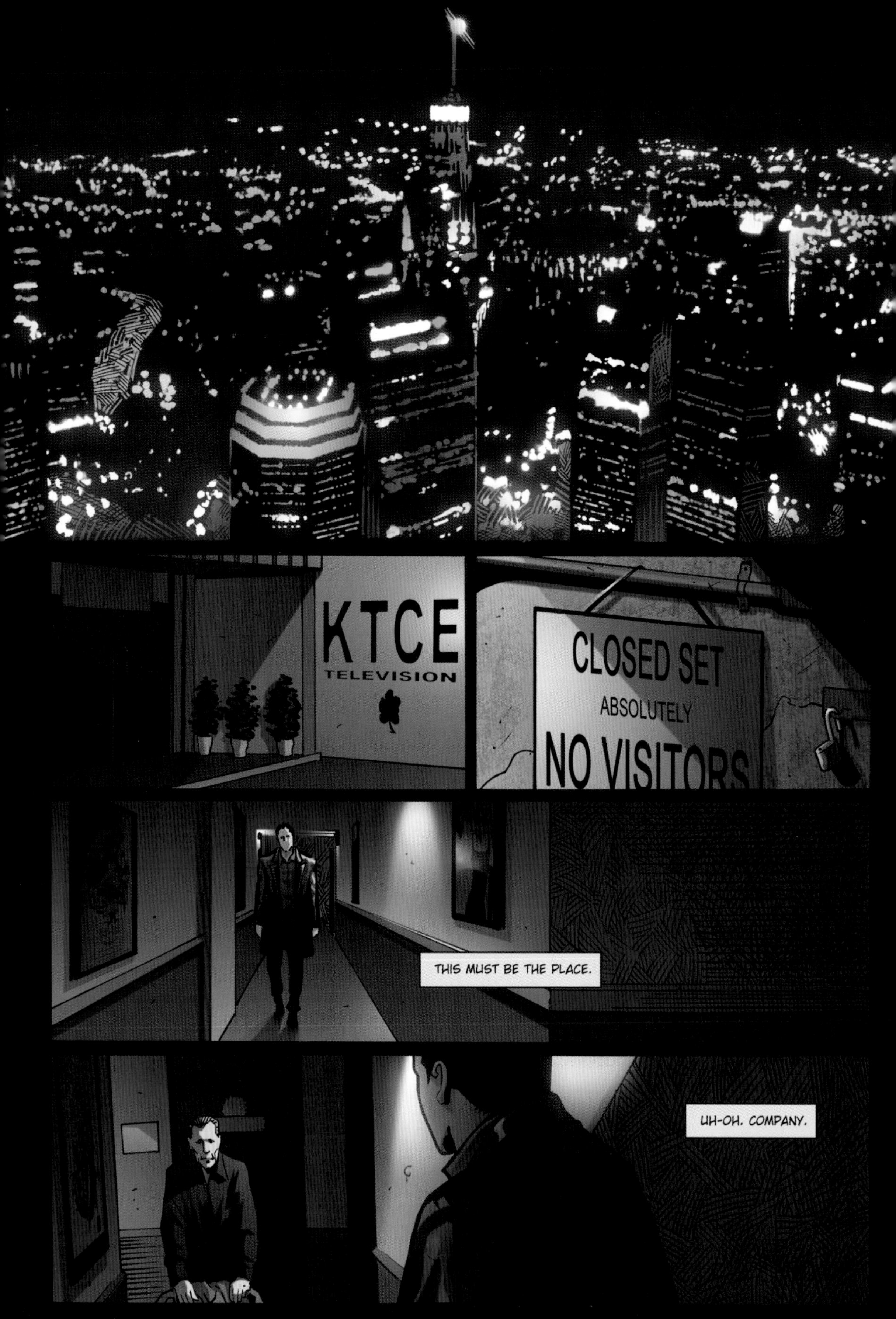
KTCE
TELEVISION
CLOSED SET
ABSOLUTELY
NO VISITORS
THIS MUST BE THE PLACE.
UH-OH. COMPANY.

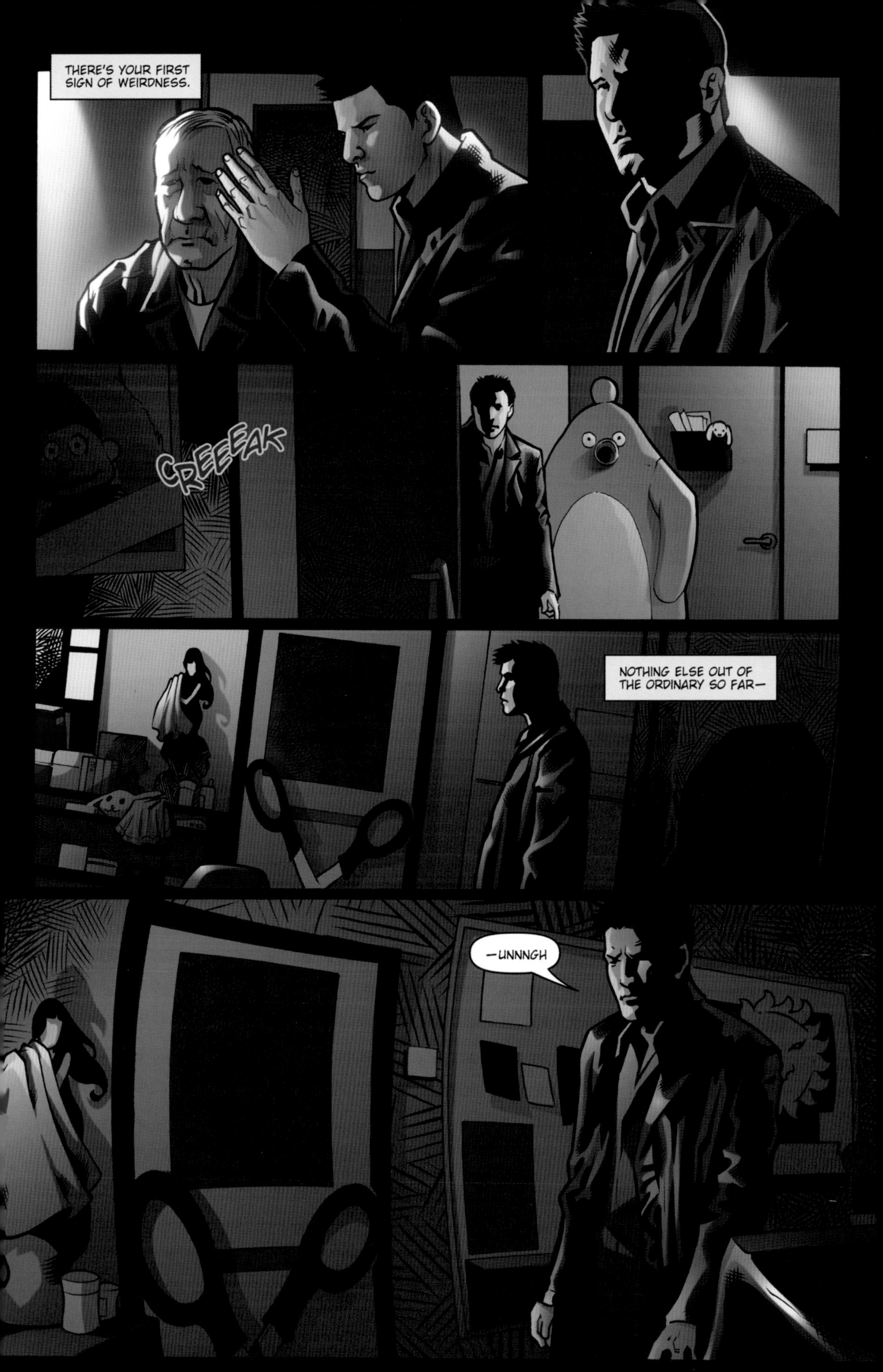

THERE'S YOUR FIRST SIGN OF WEIRDNESS.
CREEEAK
NOTHING ELSE OUT OF THE ORDINARY SO FAR—
—UNNNGH

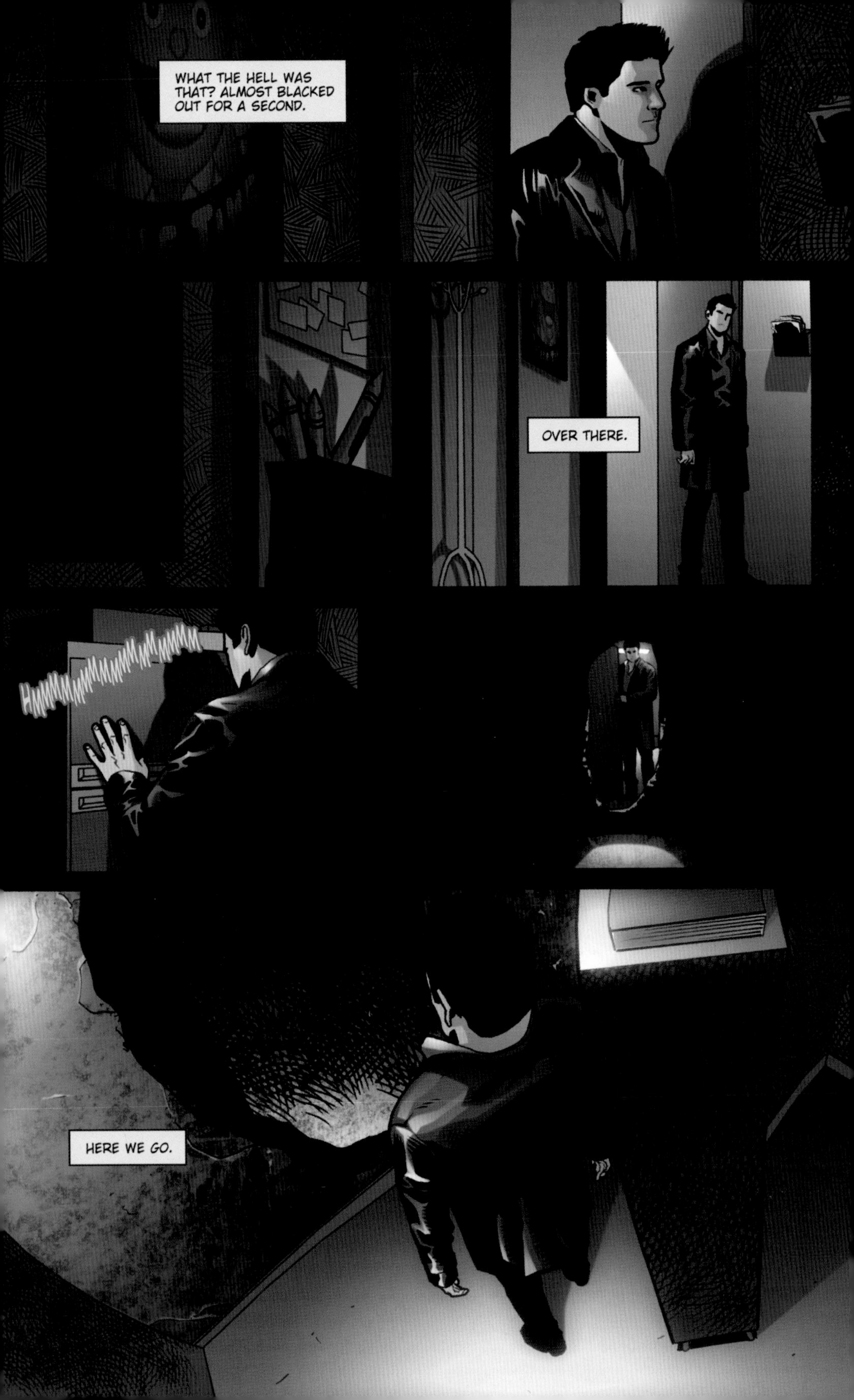
WHAT THE HELL WAS THAT? ALMOST BLACKED OUT FOR A SECOND.
OVER THERE.
HMMMMMMMMMMMMMMM
HERE WE GO.

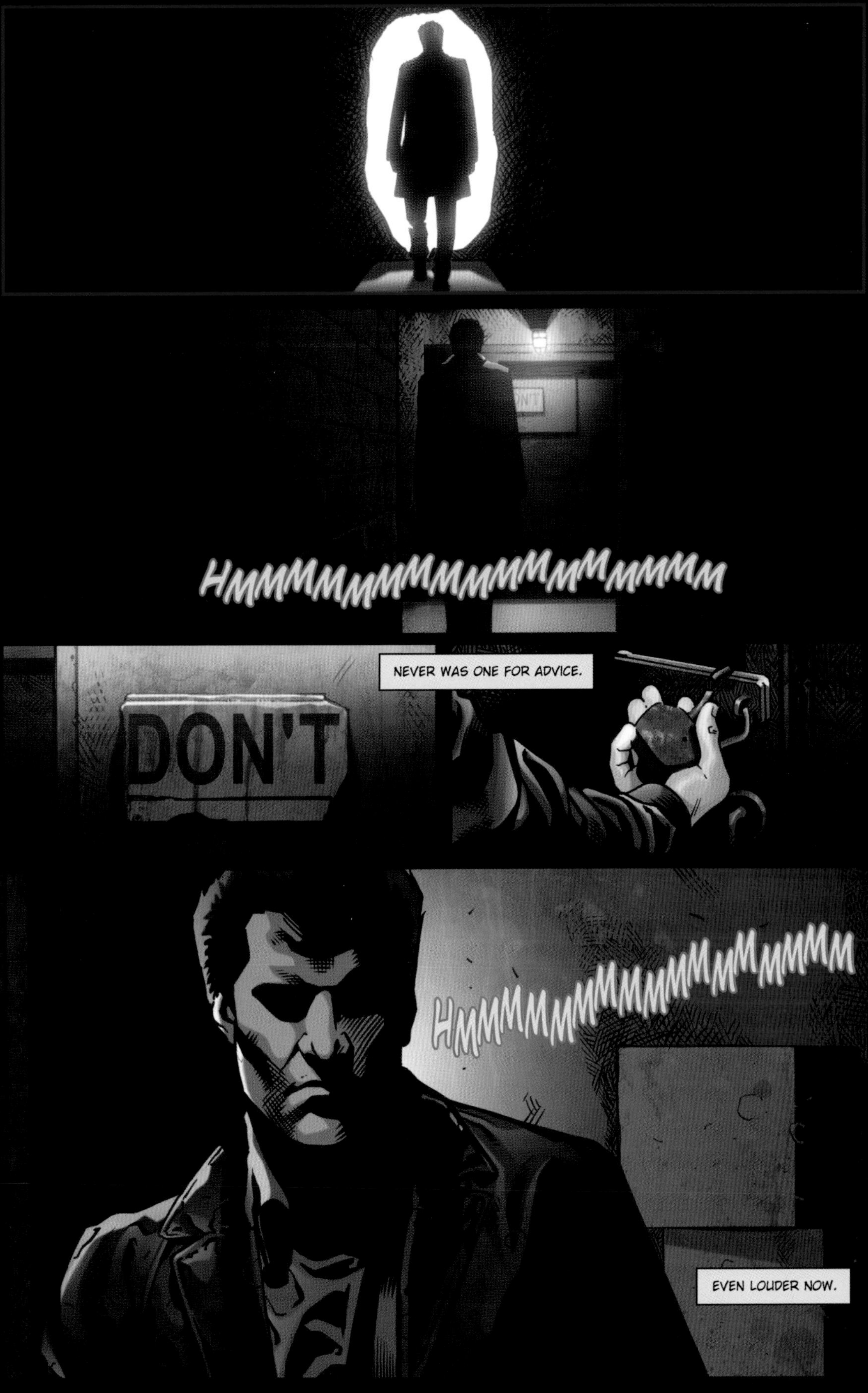
DON'T
HMMMMMMMMMMMMMMMMMMMMMM
DON'T
NEVER WAS ONE FOR ADVICE.
HMMMMMMMMMMMMMMMMMMMMMMM
EVEN LOUDER NOW.

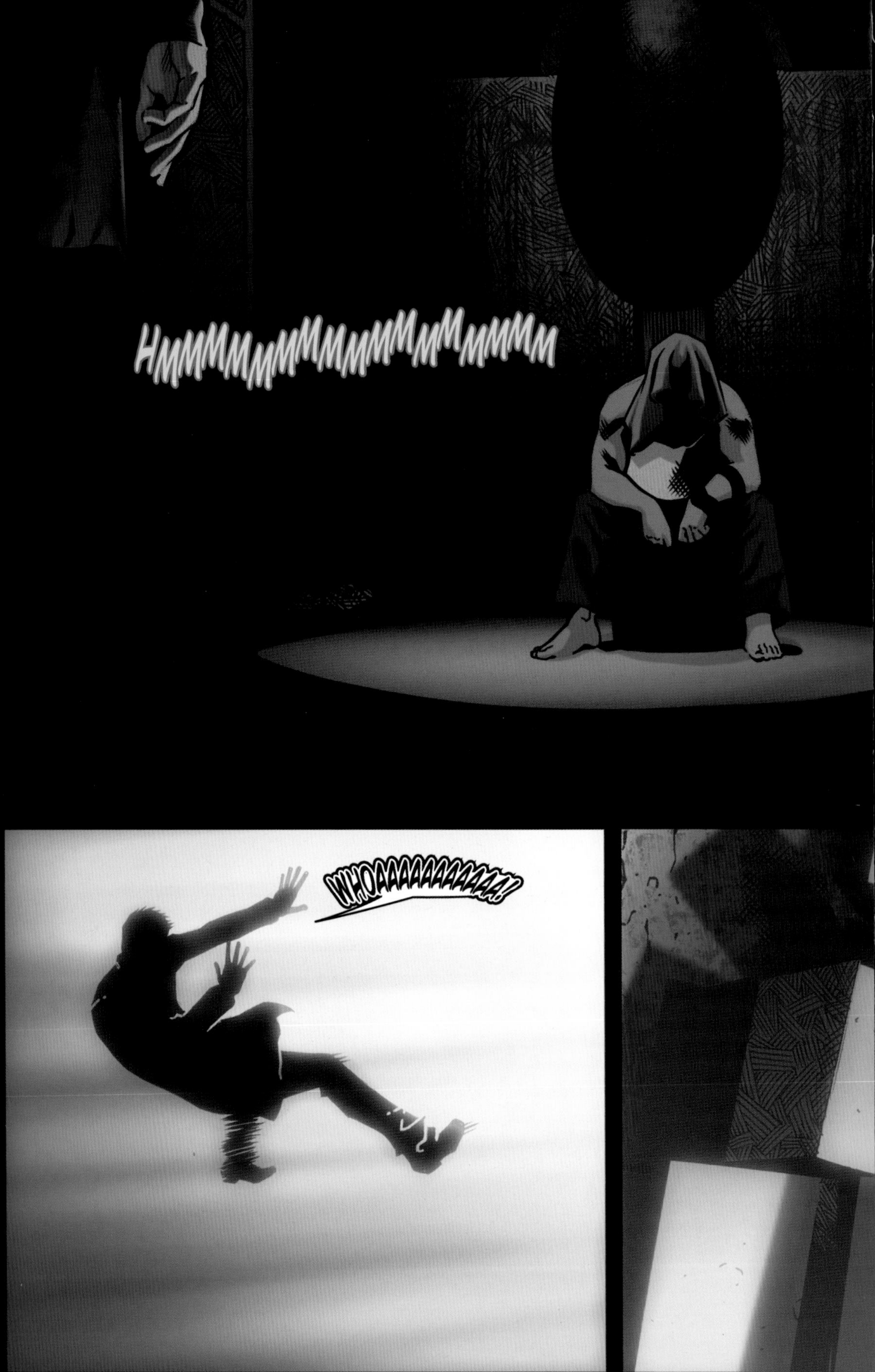
HMMMMMMMMMMMMMMMMMMMM
WHOAAAAAAAAAAAA!

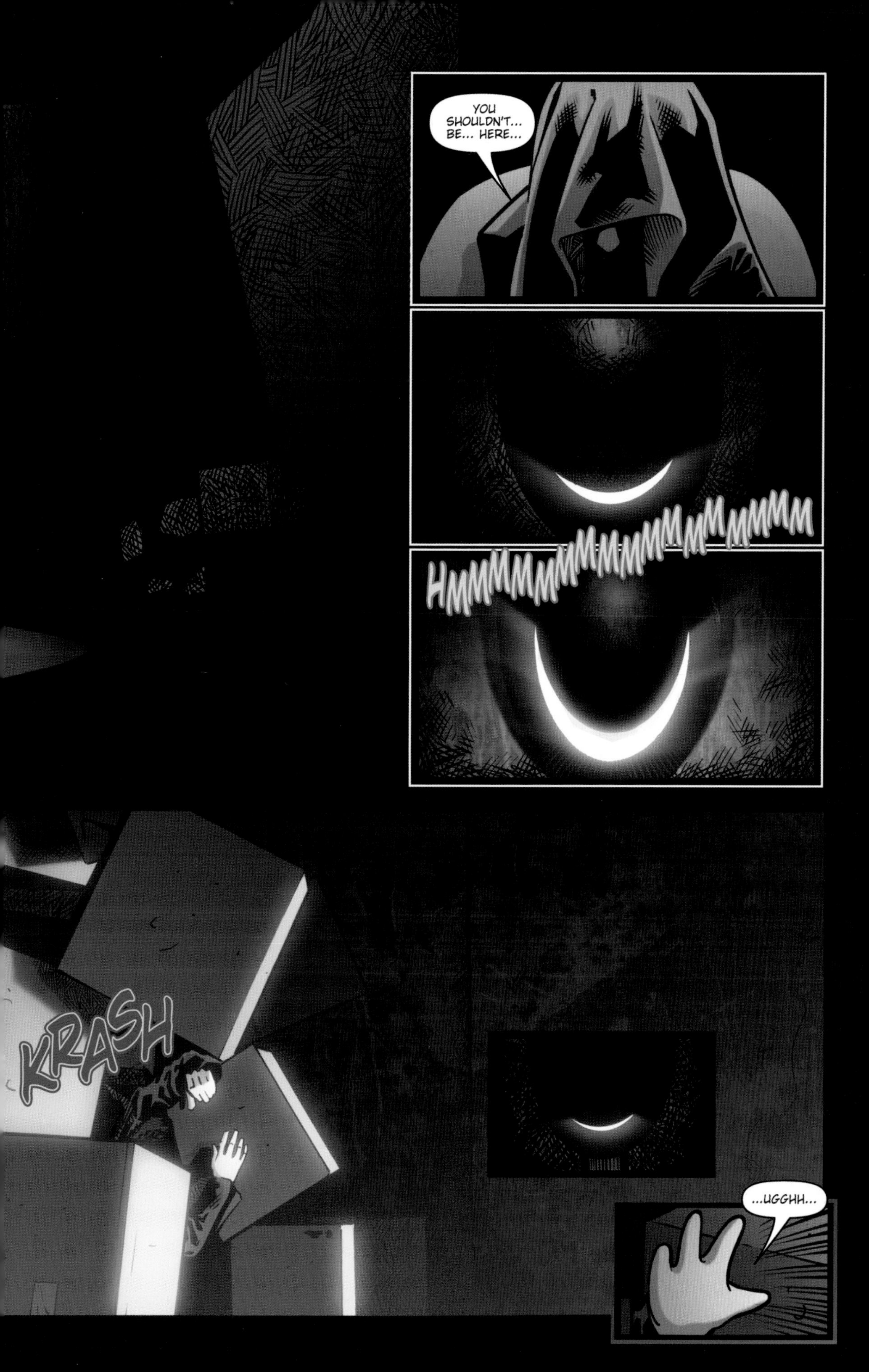

YOU SHOULDN'T... BE... HERE...
HMMMMMMMMMMMMMMMMMMMMMMMM
KRASH
...UGGHH...

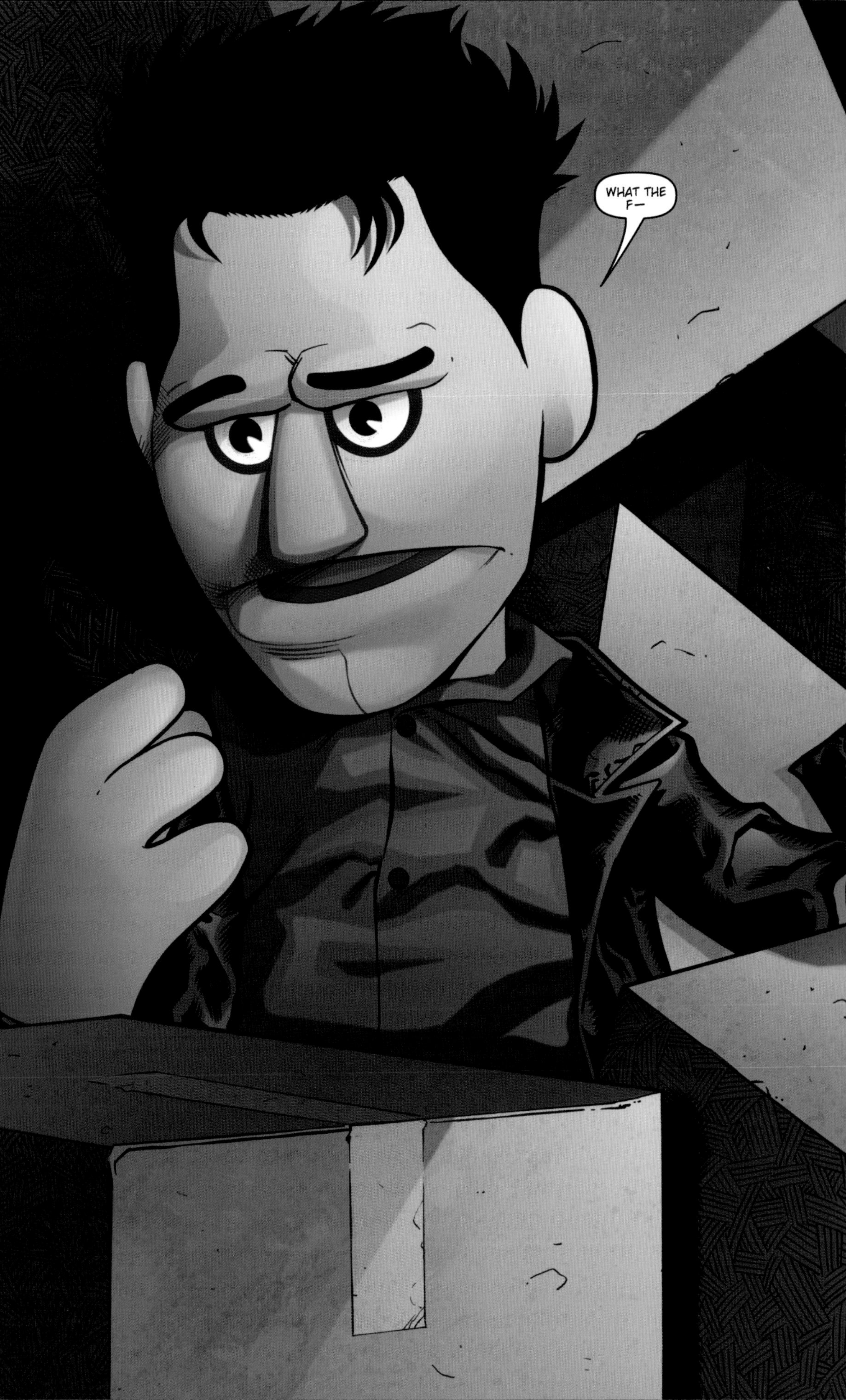
WHAT THE F—

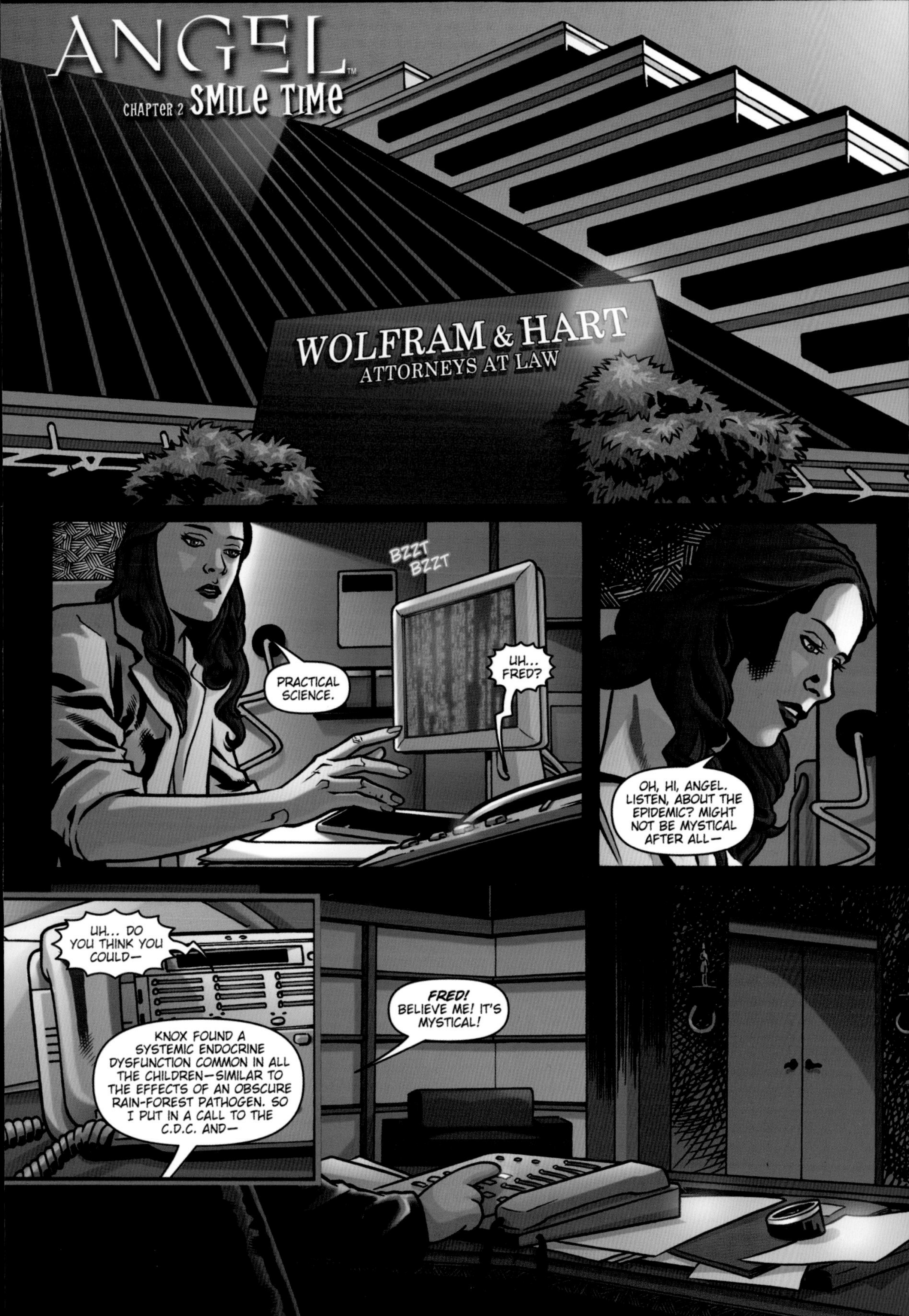
ANGEL™
CHAPTER 2 SMILE TIME
WOLFRAM & HART
ATTORNEYS AT LAW
BZZT
BZZT
PRACTICAL SCIENCE.
UH... FRED?
OH, HI, ANGEL. LISTEN, ABOUT THE EPIDEMIC? MIGHT NOT BE MYSTICAL AFTER ALL—
UH... DO YOU THINK YOU COULD—
KNOX FOUND A SYSTEMIC ENDOCRINE DYSFUNCTION COMMON IN ALL THE CHILDREN—SIMILAR TO THE EFFECTS OF AN OBSCURE RAIN-FOREST PATHOGEN. SO I PUT IN A CALL TO THE C.D.C. AND—
FRED! BELIEVE ME! IT'S MYSTICAL!

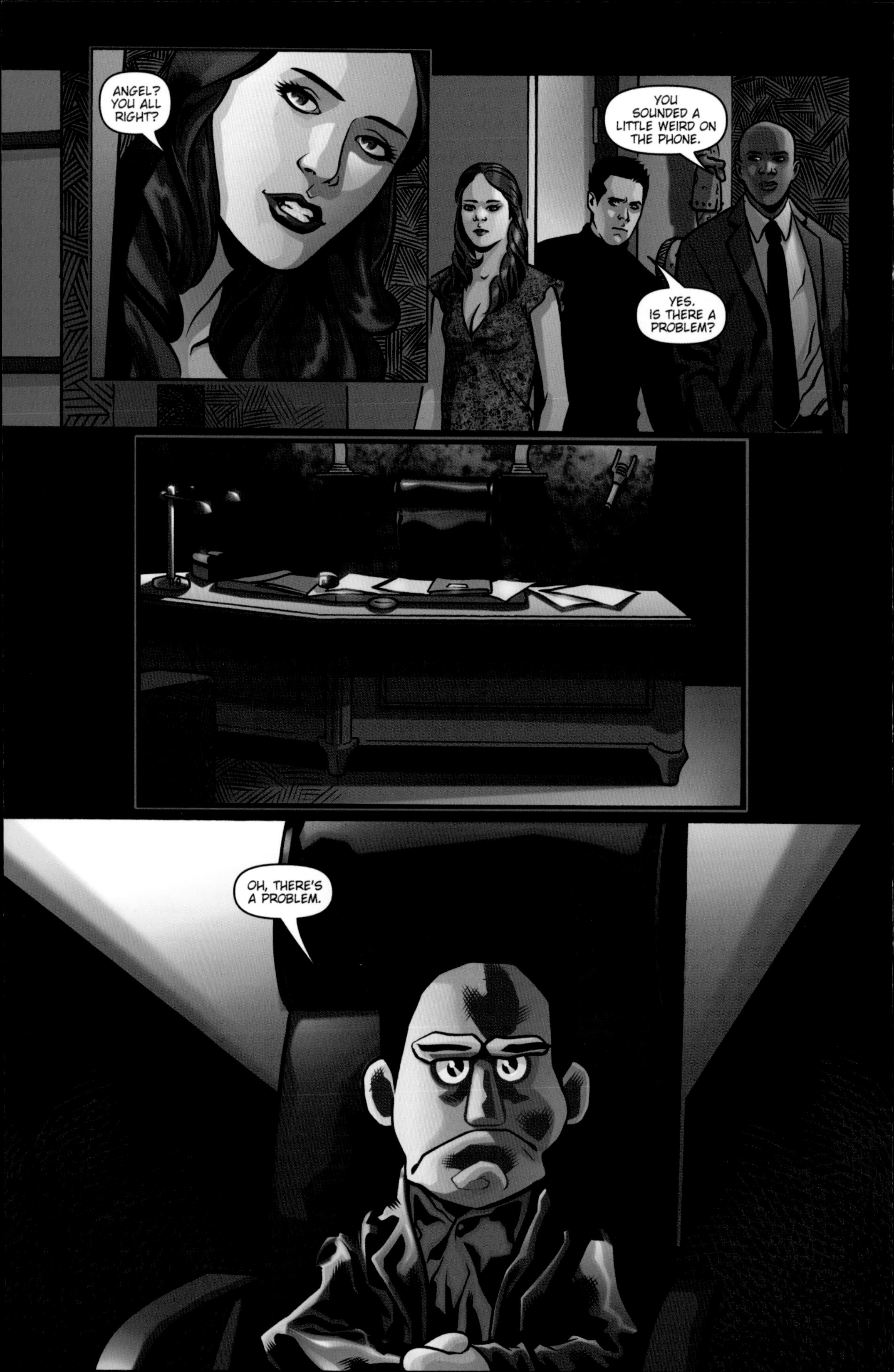
ANGEL? YOU ALL RIGHT?
YOU SOUNDED A LITTLE WEIRD ON THE PHONE.
YES. IS THERE A PROBLEM?
OH, THERE'S A PROBLEM.

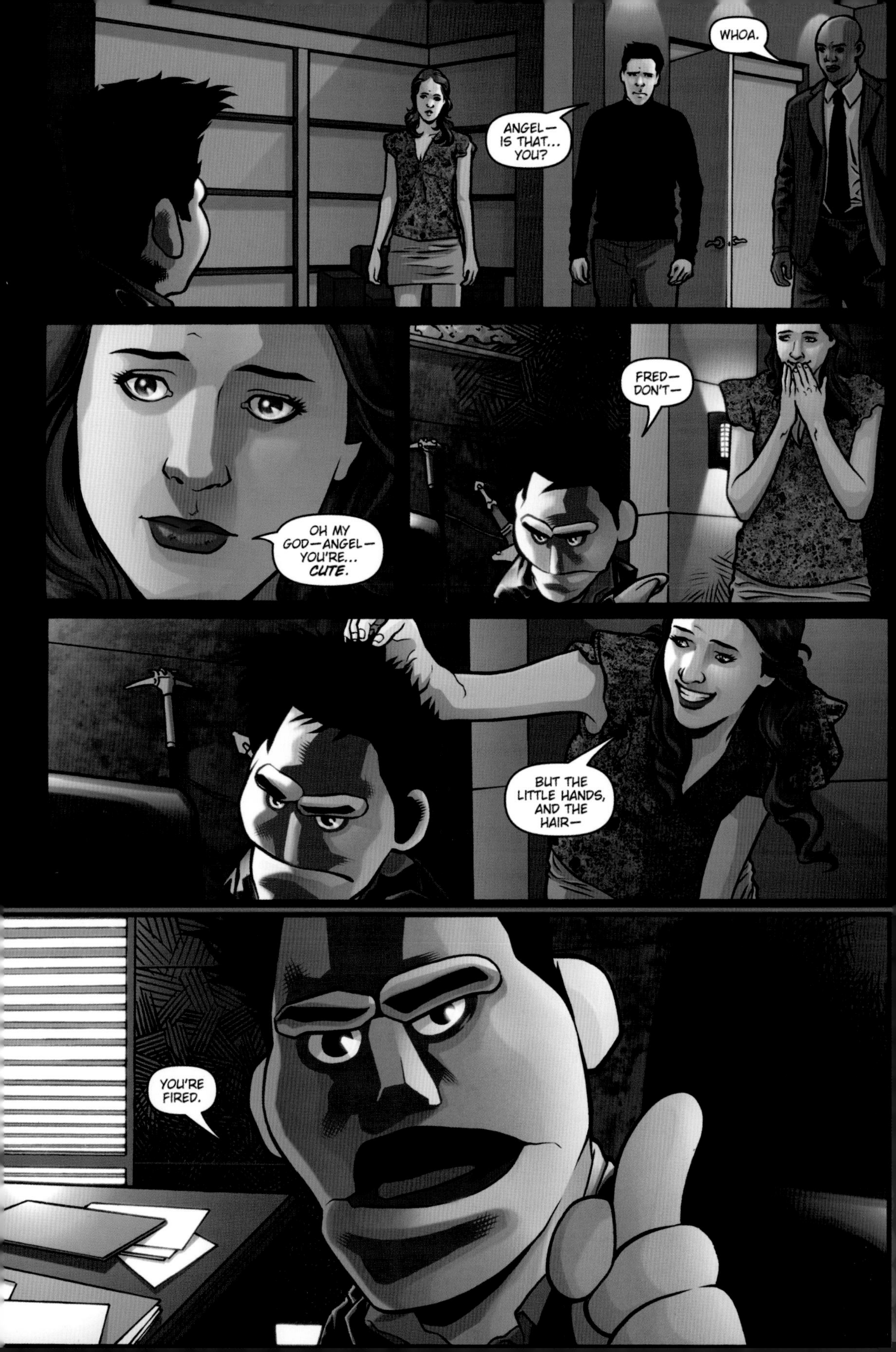
WHOA.
ANGEL— IS THAT... YOU?
OH MY GOD—ANGEL— YOU'RE... *CUTE*.
FRED— DON'T—
BUT THE LITTLE HANDS, AND THE HAIR—
YOU'RE FIRED.

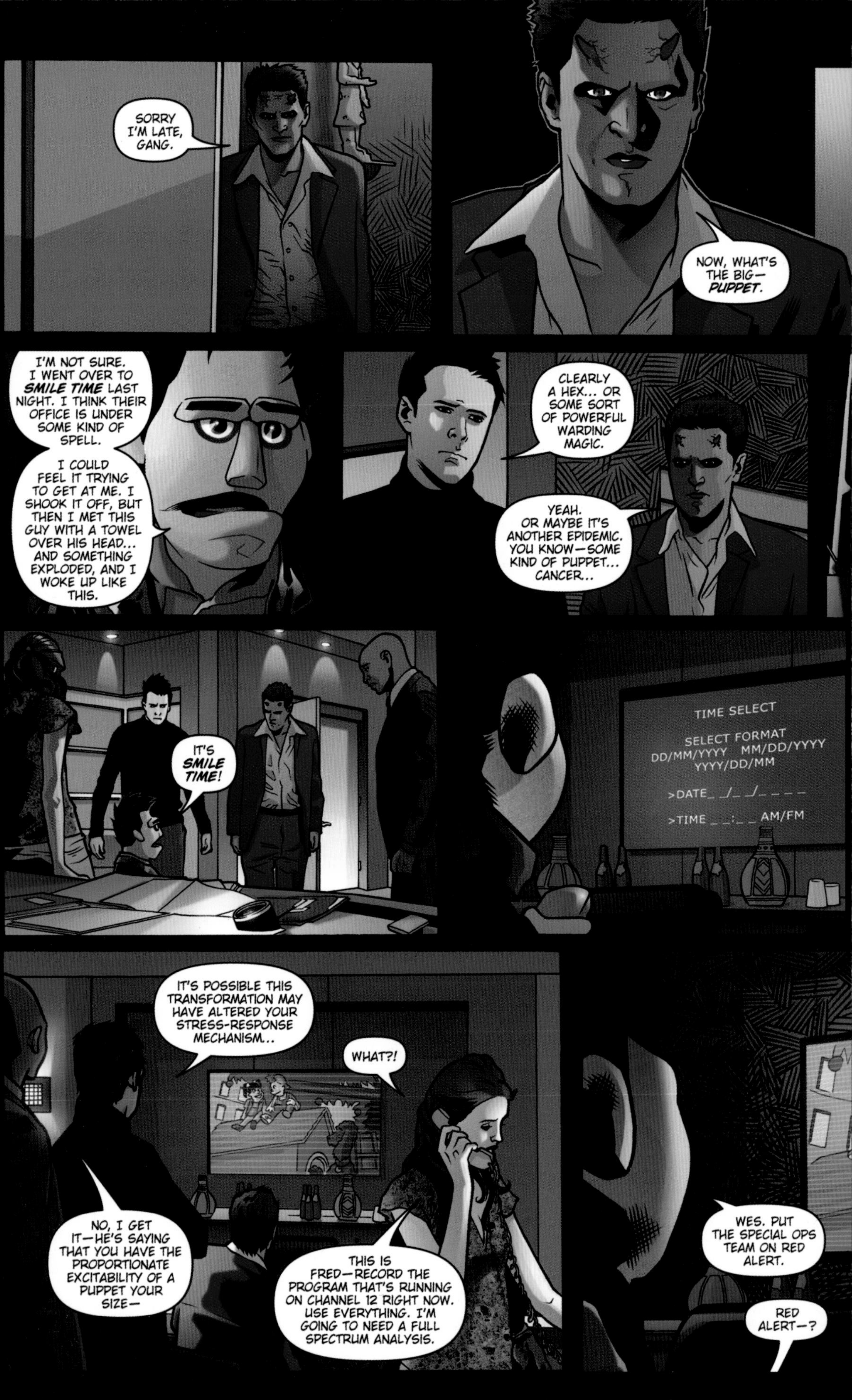
SORRY I'M LATE, GANG.
NOW, WHAT'S THE BIG— PUPPET.
I'M NOT SURE. I WENT OVER TO SMILE TIME LAST NIGHT. I THINK THEIR OFFICE IS UNDER SOME KIND OF SPELL.
I COULD FEEL IT TRYING TO GET AT ME. I SHOOK IT OFF, BUT THEN I MET THIS GUY WITH A TOWEL OVER HIS HEAD... AND SOMETHING EXPLODED, AND I WOKE UP LIKE THIS.
CLEARLY A HEX... OR SOME SORT OF POWERFUL WARDING MAGIC.
YEAH. OR MAYBE IT'S ANOTHER EPIDEMIC. YOU KNOW—SOME KIND OF PUPPET... CANCER...
IT'S SMILE TIME!
TIME SELECT
SELECT FORMAT
DD/MM/YYYY MM/DD/YYYY
YYYY/DD/MM
>DATE _ _/_ _/_ _ _ _
>TIME _ _:_ _ AM/FM
IT'S POSSIBLE THIS TRANSFORMATION MAY HAVE ALTERED YOUR STRESS-RESPONSE MECHANISM...
WHAT?!
NO, I GET IT—HE'S SAYING THAT YOU HAVE THE PROPORTIONATE EXCITABILITY OF A PUPPET YOUR SIZE—
THIS IS FRED—RECORD THE PROGRAM THAT'S RUNNING ON CHANNEL 12 RIGHT NOW. USE EVERYTHING. I'M GOING TO NEED A FULL SPECTRUM ANALYSIS.
WES. PUT THE SPECIAL OPS TEAM ON RED ALERT.
RED ALERT—?

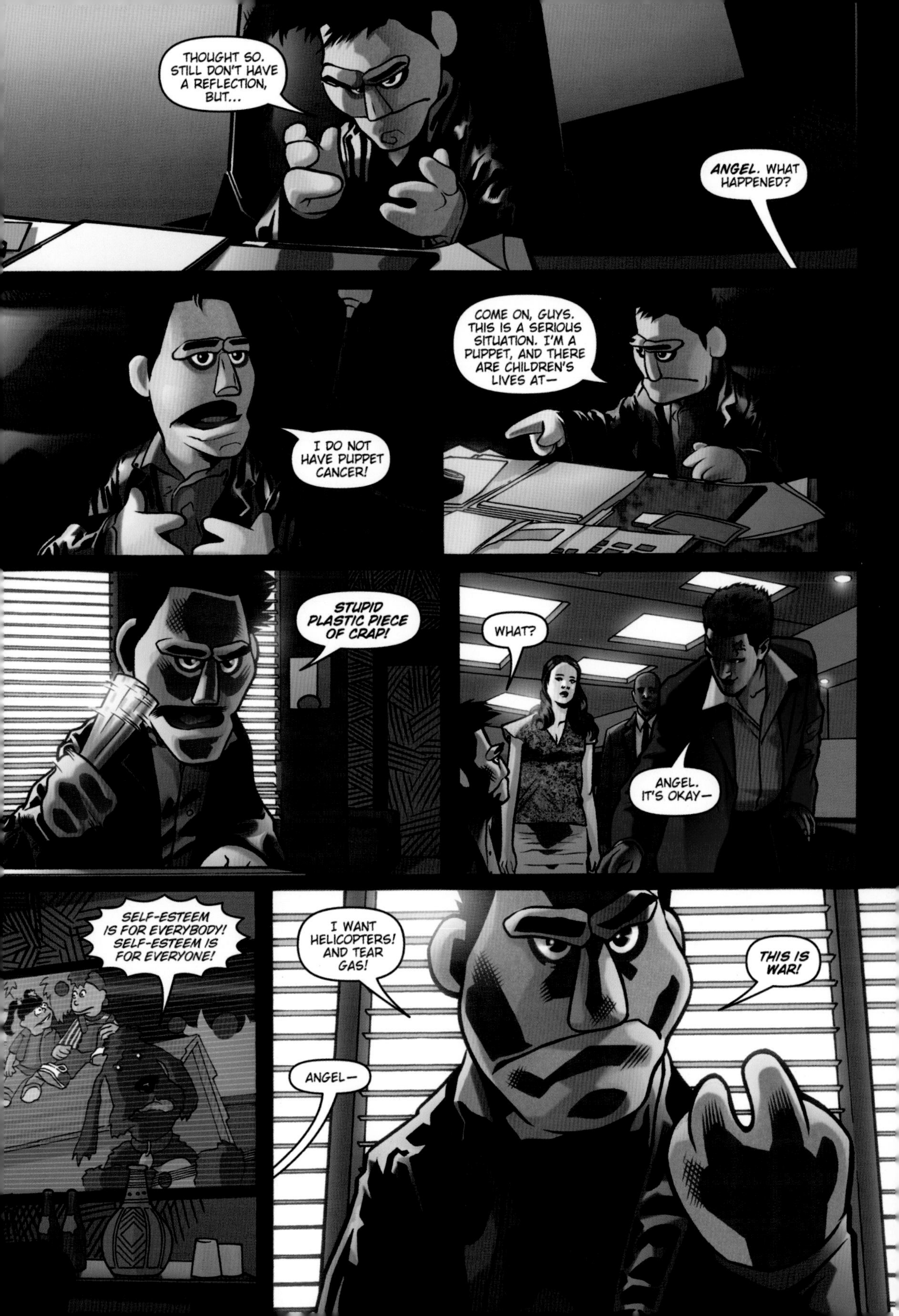

THOUGHT SO. STILL DON'T HAVE A REFLECTION, BUT...
ANGEL. WHAT HAPPENED?
I DO NOT HAVE PUPPET CANCER!
COME ON, GUYS. THIS IS A SERIOUS SITUATION. I'M A PUPPET, AND THERE ARE CHILDREN'S LIVES AT—
STUPID PLASTIC PIECE OF CRAP!
WHAT?
ANGEL. IT'S OKAY—
SELF-ESTEEM IS FOR EVERYBODY! SELF-ESTEEM IS FOR EVERYONE!
I WANT HELICOPTERS! AND TEAR GAS!
ANGEL—
THIS IS WAR!

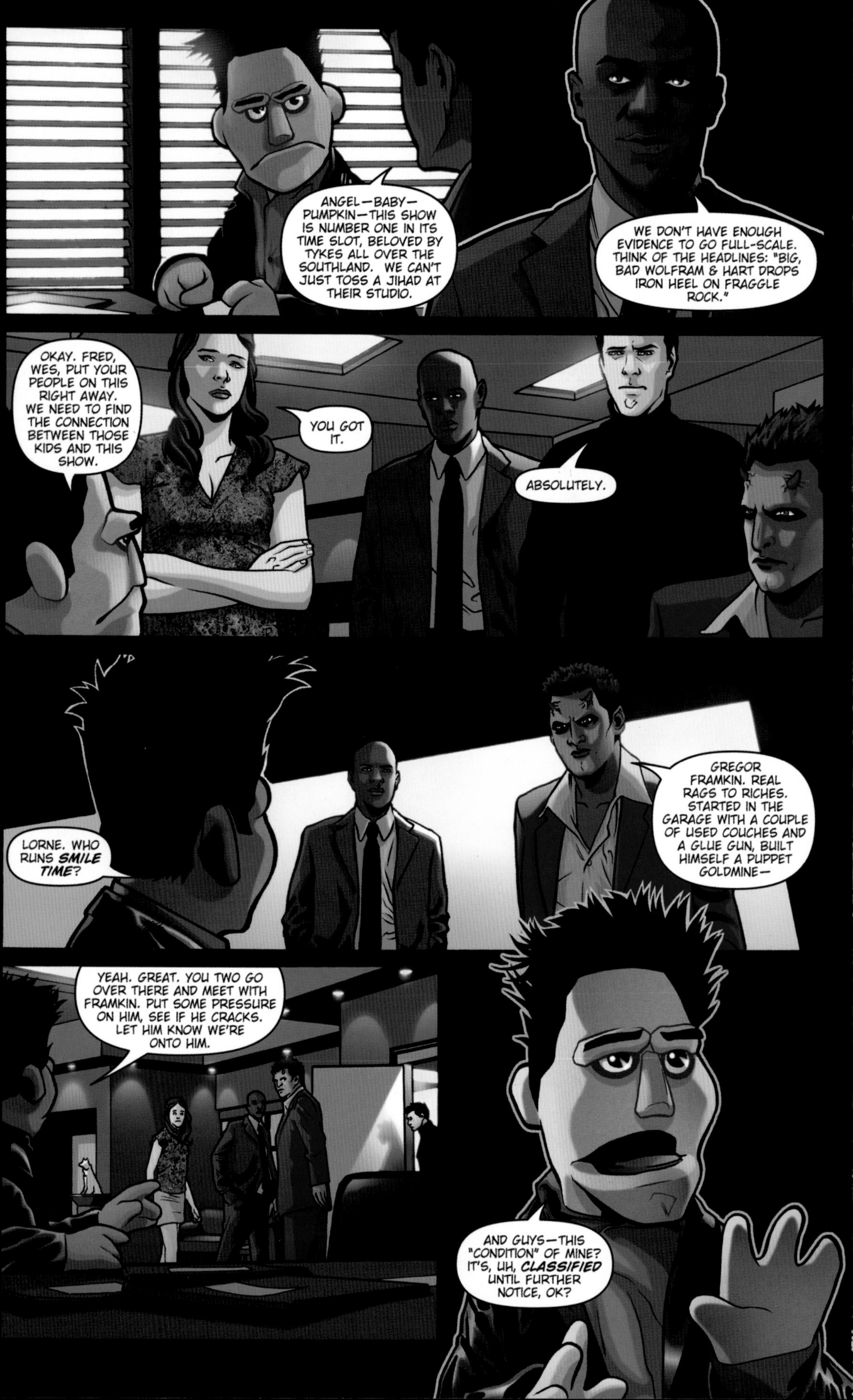
ANGEL—BABY—PUMPKIN—THIS SHOW IS NUMBER ONE IN ITS TIME SLOT, BELOVED BY TYKES ALL OVER THE SOUTHLAND. WE CAN'T JUST TOSS A JIHAD AT THEIR STUDIO.
WE DON'T HAVE ENOUGH EVIDENCE TO GO FULL-SCALE. THINK OF THE HEADLINES: "BIG, BAD WOLFRAM & HART DROPS IRON HEEL ON FRAGGLE ROCK."
OKAY. FRED, WES, PUT YOUR PEOPLE ON THIS RIGHT AWAY. WE NEED TO FIND THE CONNECTION BETWEEN THOSE KIDS AND THIS SHOW.
YOU GOT IT.
ABSOLUTELY.
LORNE. WHO RUNS *SMILE TIME*?
GREGOR FRAMKIN. REAL RAGS TO RICHES. STARTED IN THE GARAGE WITH A COUPLE OF USED COUCHES AND A GLUE GUN, BUILT HIMSELF A PUPPET GOLDMINE—
YEAH. GREAT. YOU TWO GO OVER THERE AND MEET WITH FRAMKIN. PUT SOME PRESSURE ON HIM, SEE IF HE CRACKS. LET HIM KNOW WE'RE ONTO HIM.
AND GUYS—THIS "CONDITION" OF MINE? IT'S, UH, *CLASSIFIED* UNTIL FURTHER NOTICE, OK?

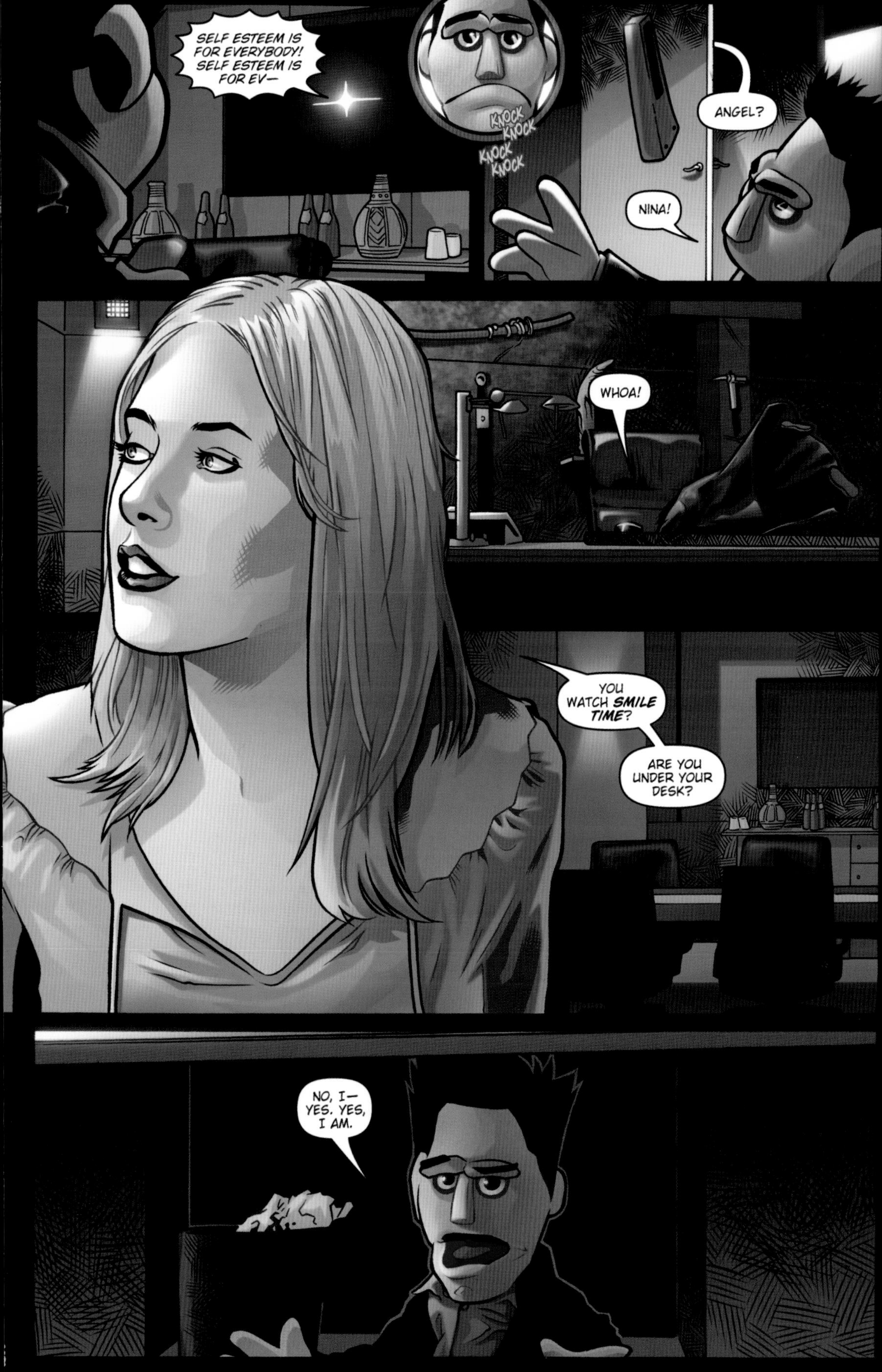

SELF ESTEEM IS FOR EVERYBODY! SELF ESTEEM IS FOR EV—
KNOCK KNOCK
KNOCK KNOCK
ANGEL?
NINA!
WHOA!
YOU WATCH SMILE TIME?
ARE YOU UNDER YOUR DESK?
NO, I— YES. YES, I AM.

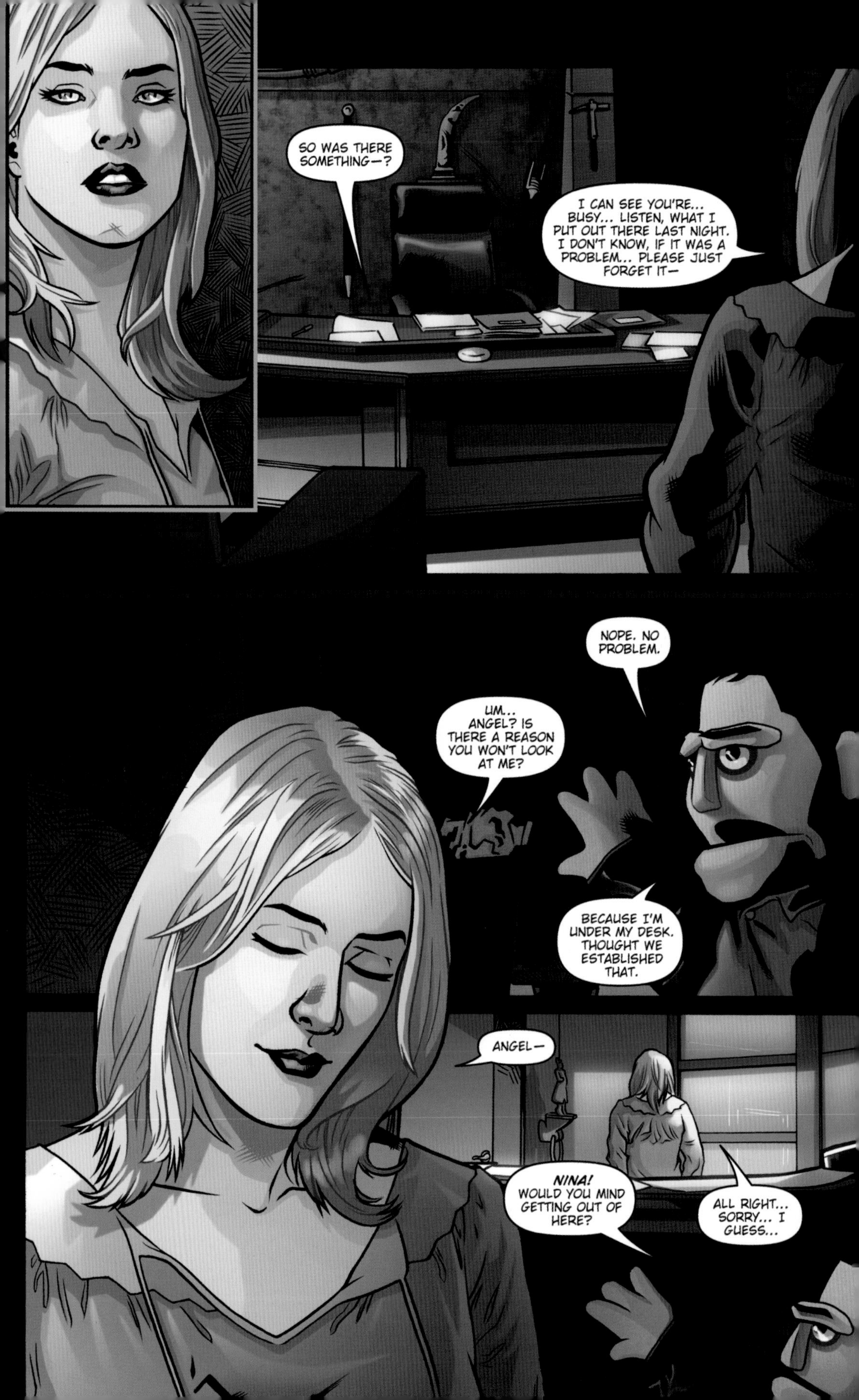
SO WAS THERE SOMETHING—?
I CAN SEE YOU'RE... BUSY... LISTEN, WHAT I PUT OUT THERE LAST NIGHT. I DON'T KNOW, IF IT WAS A PROBLEM... PLEASE JUST FORGET IT—
NOPE. NO PROBLEM.
UM... ANGEL? IS THERE A REASON YOU WON'T LOOK AT ME?
BECAUSE I'M UNDER MY DESK. THOUGHT WE ESTABLISHED THAT.
ANGEL—
NINA! WOULD YOU MIND GETTING OUT OF HERE?
ALL RIGHT... SORRY... I GUESS...

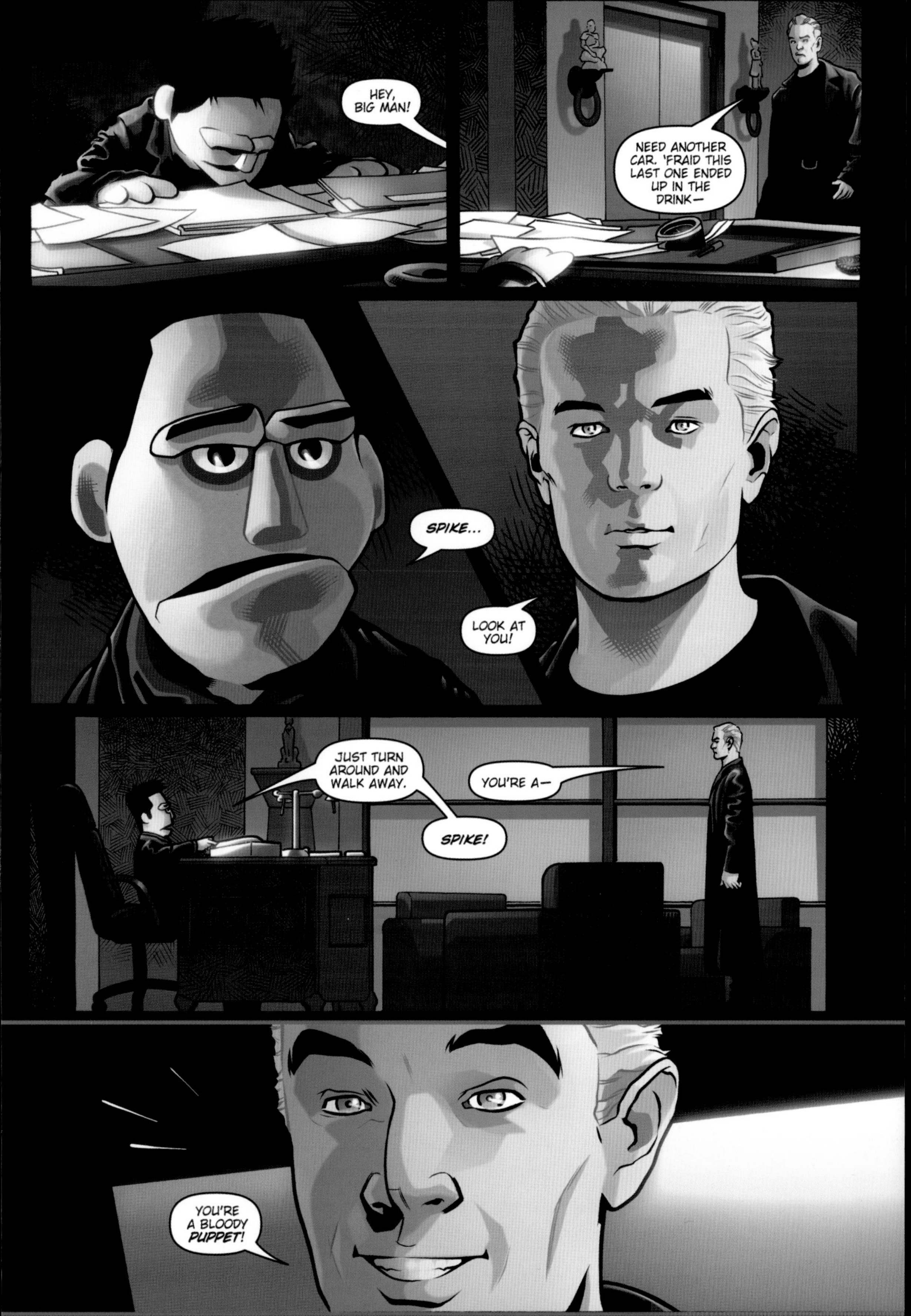
HEY, BIG MAN!
NEED ANOTHER CAR. 'FRAID THIS LAST ONE ENDED UP IN THE DRINK—
SPIKE...
LOOK AT YOU!
JUST TURN AROUND AND WALK AWAY.
YOU'RE A—
SPIKE!
YOU'RE A BLOODY PUPPET!

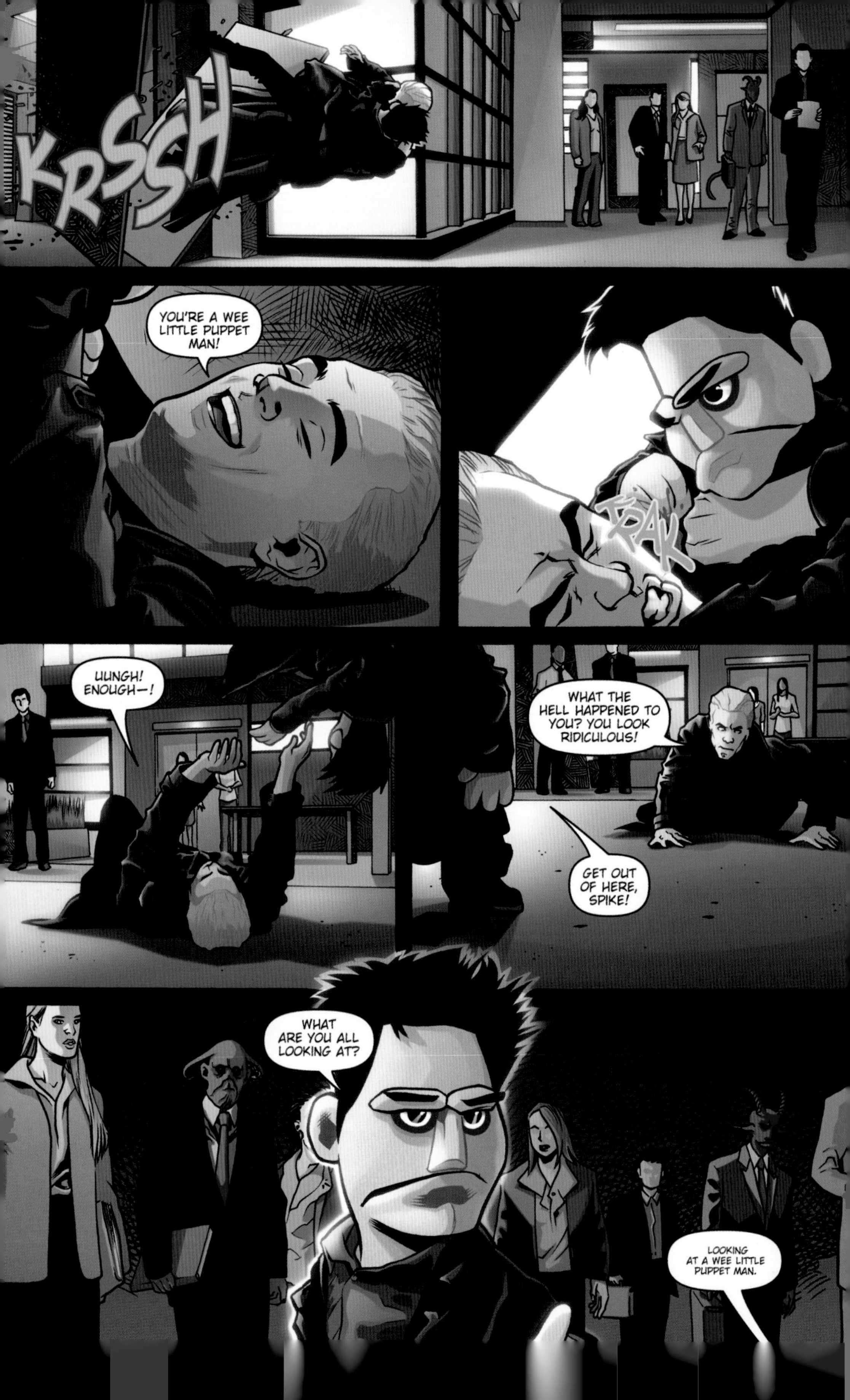
KRSSH
YOU'RE A WEE LITTLE PUPPET MAN!
TRAK
UUNGH! ENOUGH—!
WHAT THE HELL HAPPENED TO YOU? YOU LOOK RIDICULOUS!
GET OUT OF HERE, SPIKE!
WHAT ARE YOU ALL LOOKING AT?
LOOKING AT A WEE LITTLE PUPPET MAN.

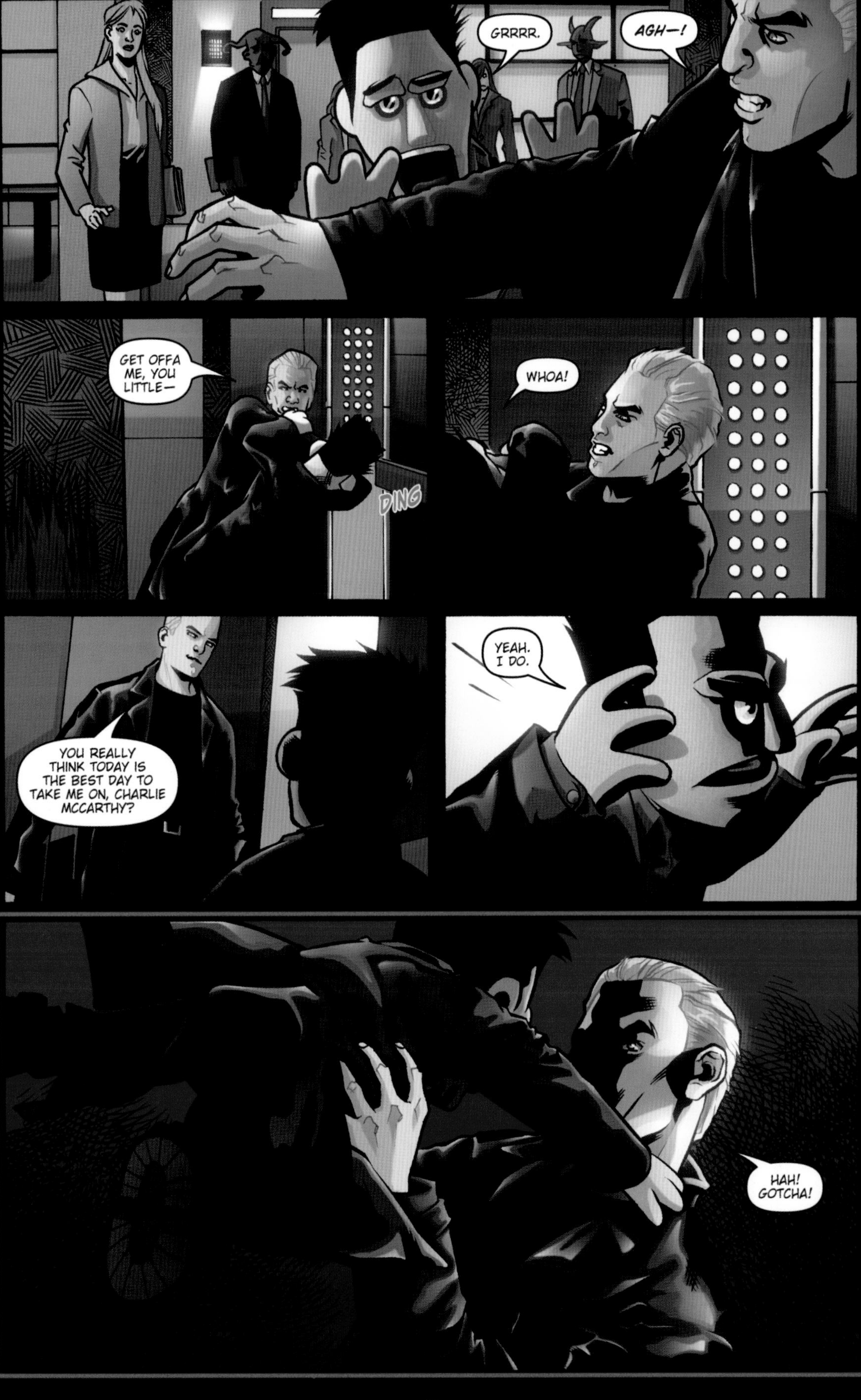
GRRRR.
AGH—!
GET OFFA ME, YOU LITTLE—
DING
WHOA!
YOU REALLY THINK TODAY IS THE BEST DAY TO TAKE ME ON, CHARLIE MCCARTHY?
YEAH. I DO.
HAH! GOTCHA!

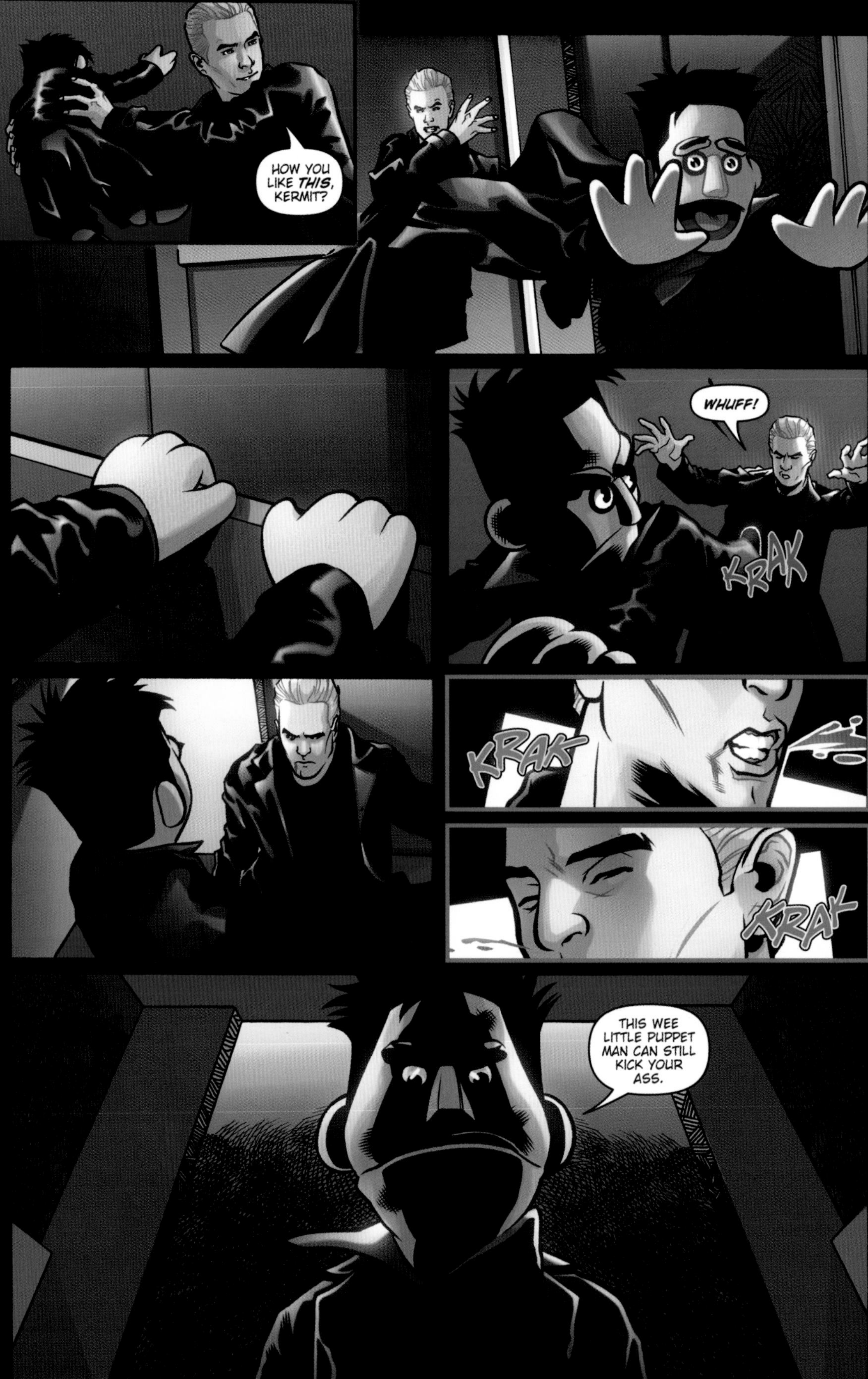
HOW YOU LIKE *THIS*, KERMIT?
WHUFF!
KRAK
KRAK
KRAK
THIS WEE LITTLE PUPPET MAN CAN STILL KICK YOUR ASS.

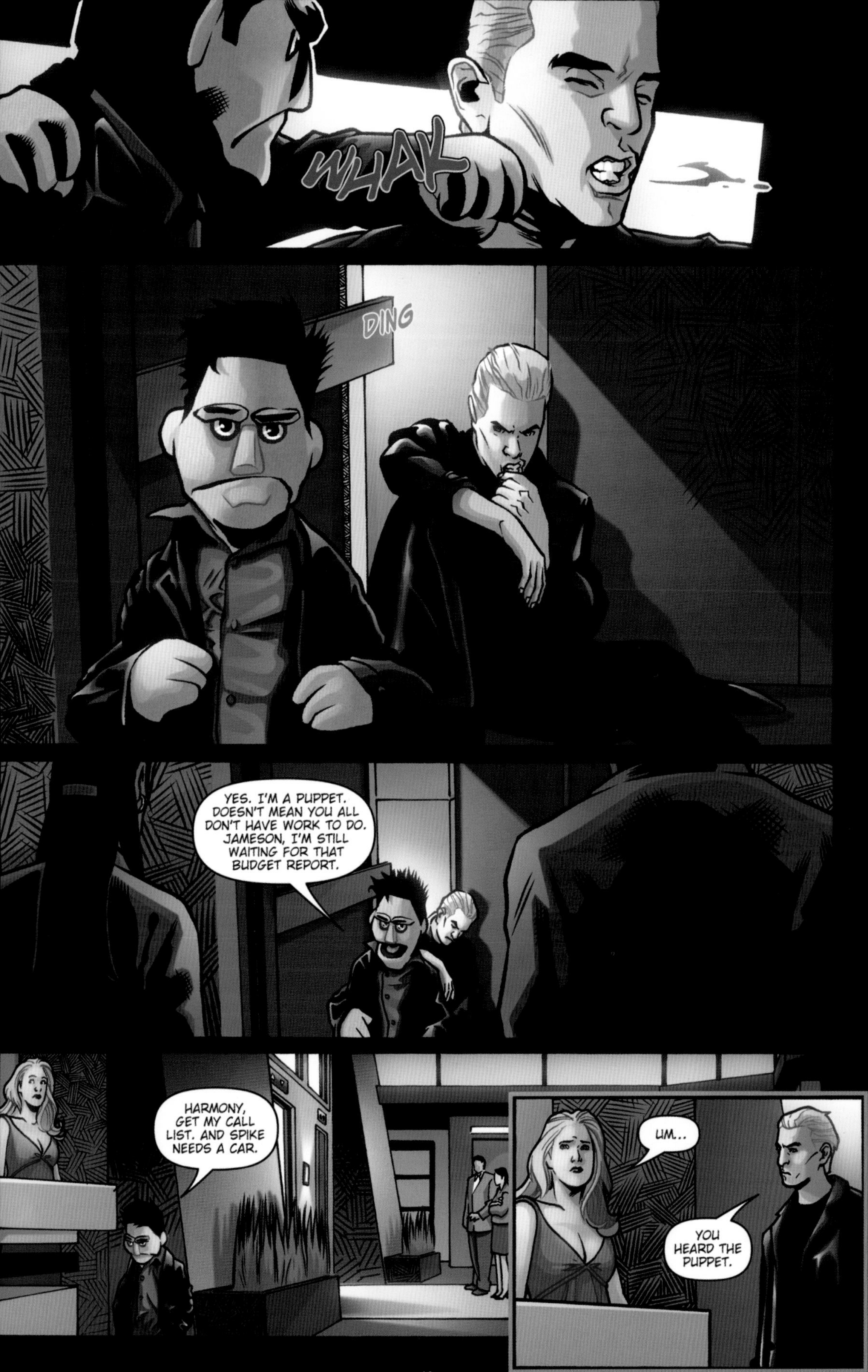
WHAK
DING
YES. I'M A PUPPET. DOESN'T MEAN YOU ALL DON'T HAVE WORK TO DO. JAMESON, I'M STILL WAITING FOR THAT BUDGET REPORT.
HARMONY, GET MY CALL LIST. AND SPIKE NEEDS A CAR.
UM...
YOU HEARD THE PUPPET.

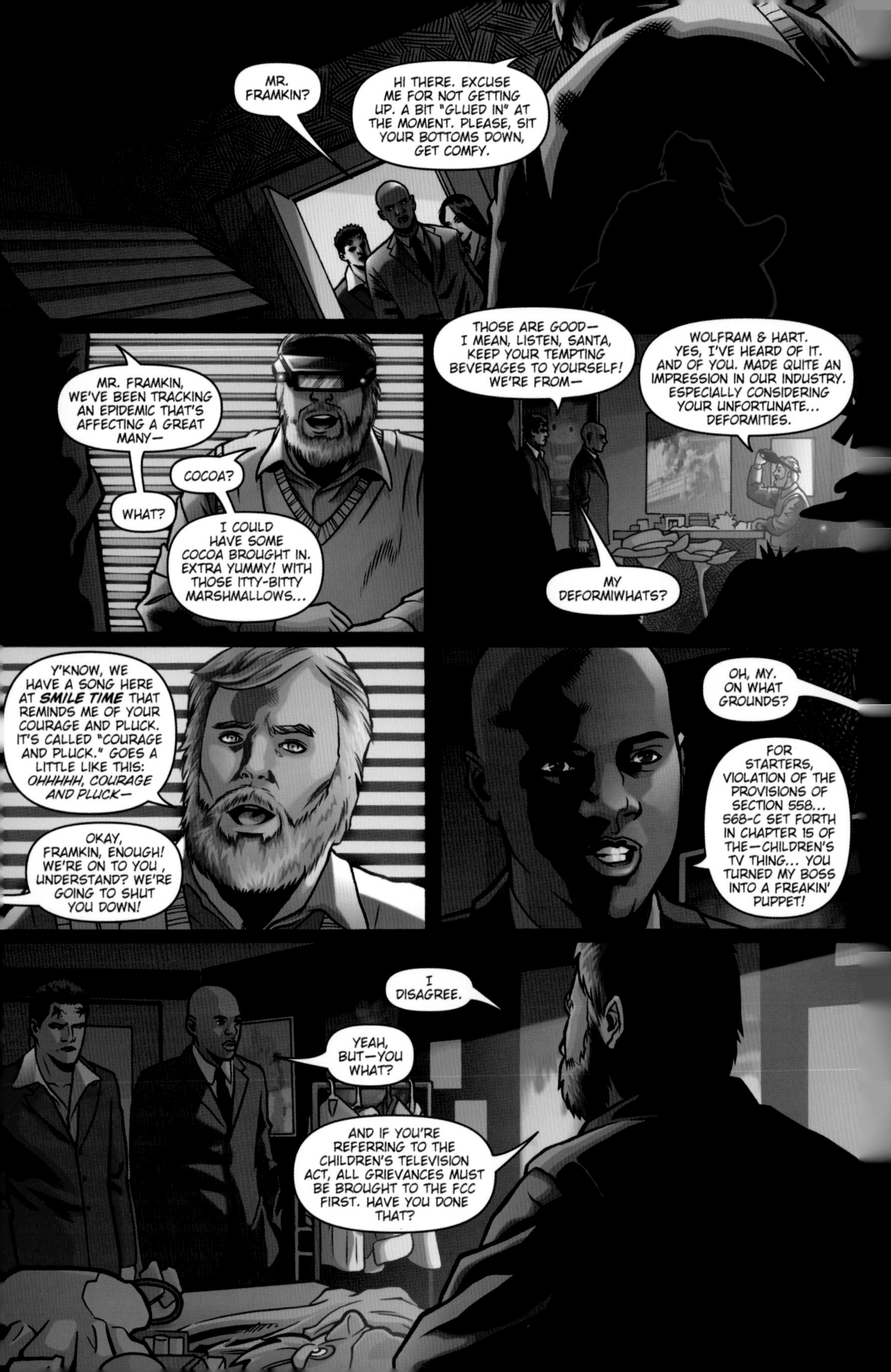
MR. FRAMKIN?
HI THERE. EXCUSE ME FOR NOT GETTING UP. A BIT "GLUED IN" AT THE MOMENT. PLEASE, SIT YOUR BOTTOMS DOWN, GET COMFY.
MR. FRAMKIN, WE'VE BEEN TRACKING AN EPIDEMIC THAT'S AFFECTING A GREAT MANY—
COCOA?
WHAT?
I COULD HAVE SOME COCOA BROUGHT IN. EXTRA YUMMY! WITH THOSE ITTY-BITTY MARSHMALLOWS...
THOSE ARE GOOD— I MEAN, LISTEN, SANTA, KEEP YOUR TEMPTING BEVERAGES TO YOURSELF! WE'RE FROM—
WOLFRAM & HART. YES, I'VE HEARD OF IT. AND OF YOU. MADE QUITE AN IMPRESSION IN OUR INDUSTRY. ESPECIALLY CONSIDERING YOUR UNFORTUNATE... DEFORMITIES.
MY DEFORMIWHATS?
Y'KNOW, WE HAVE A SONG HERE AT SMILE TIME THAT REMINDS ME OF YOUR COURAGE AND PLUCK. IT'S CALLED "COURAGE AND PLUCK." GOES A LITTLE LIKE THIS: OHHHHH, COURAGE AND PLUCK—
OKAY, FRAMKIN, ENOUGH! WE'RE ON TO YOU, UNDERSTAND? WE'RE GOING TO SHUT YOU DOWN!
OH, MY. ON WHAT GROUNDS?
FOR STARTERS, VIOLATION OF THE PROVISIONS OF SECTION 558... 568-C SET FORTH IN CHAPTER 15 OF THE—CHILDREN'S TV THING... YOU TURNED MY BOSS INTO A FREAKIN' PUPPET!
I DISAGREE.
YEAH, BUT—YOU WHAT?
AND IF YOU'RE REFERRING TO THE CHILDREN'S TELEVISION ACT, ALL GRIEVANCES MUST BE BROUGHT TO THE FCC FIRST. HAVE YOU DONE THAT?

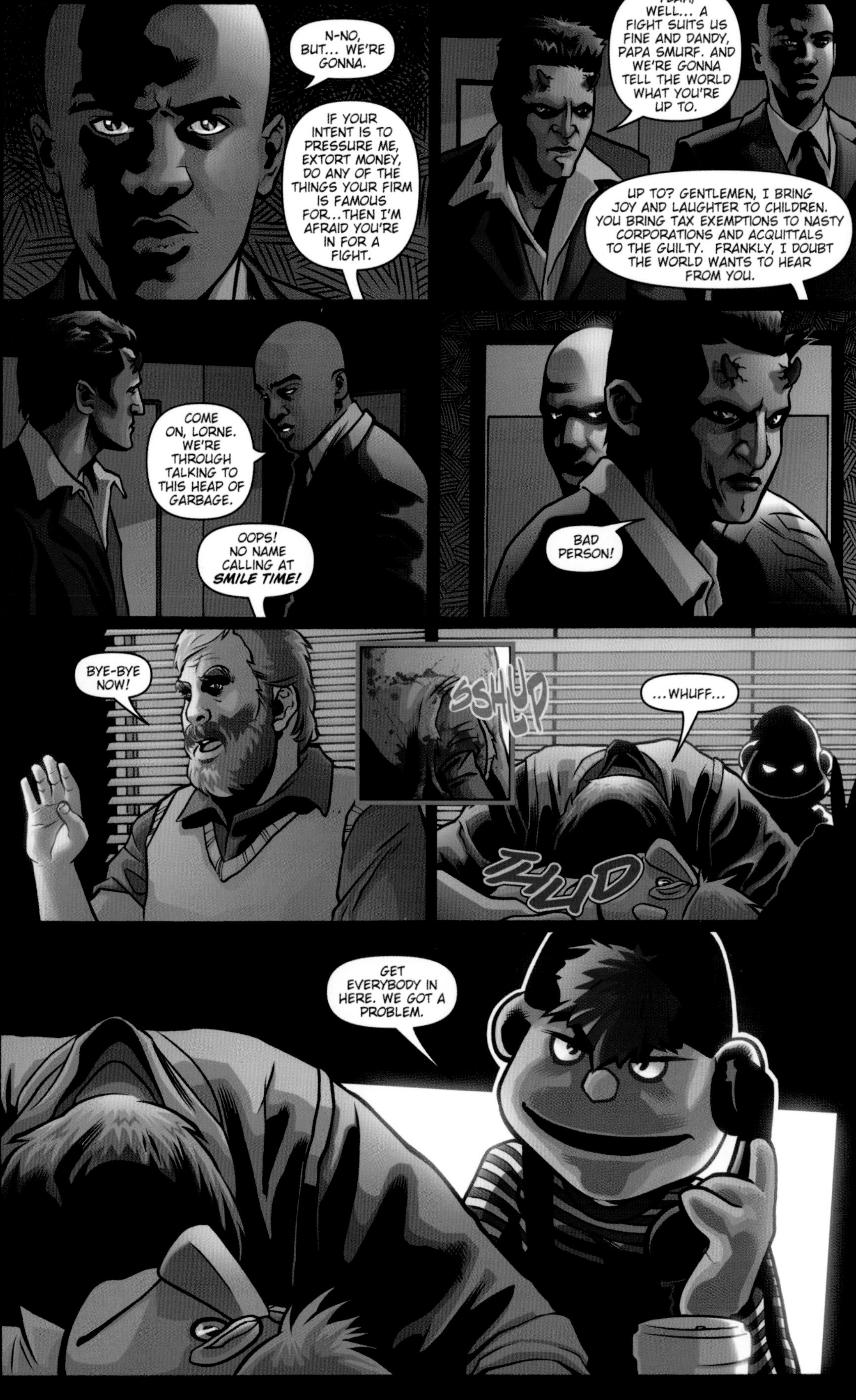
N-NO, BUT... WE'RE GONNA.
IF YOUR INTENT IS TO PRESSURE ME, EXTORT MONEY, DO ANY OF THE THINGS YOUR FIRM IS FAMOUS FOR...THEN I'M AFRAID YOU'RE IN FOR A FIGHT.
YEAH, WELL... A FIGHT SUITS US FINE AND DANDY, PAPA SMURF. AND WE'RE GONNA TELL THE WORLD WHAT YOU'RE UP TO.
UP TO? GENTLEMEN, I BRING JOY AND LAUGHTER TO CHILDREN. YOU BRING TAX EXEMPTIONS TO NASTY CORPORATIONS AND ACQUITTALS TO THE GUILTY. FRANKLY, I DOUBT THE WORLD WANTS TO HEAR FROM YOU.
COME ON, LORNE. WE'RE THROUGH TALKING TO THIS HEAP OF GARBAGE.
OOPS! NO NAME CALLING AT *SMILE TIME!*
BAD PERSON!
BYE-BYE NOW!
SSHLUP
...WHUFF...
THUD
GET EVERYBODY IN HERE. WE GOT A PROBLEM.

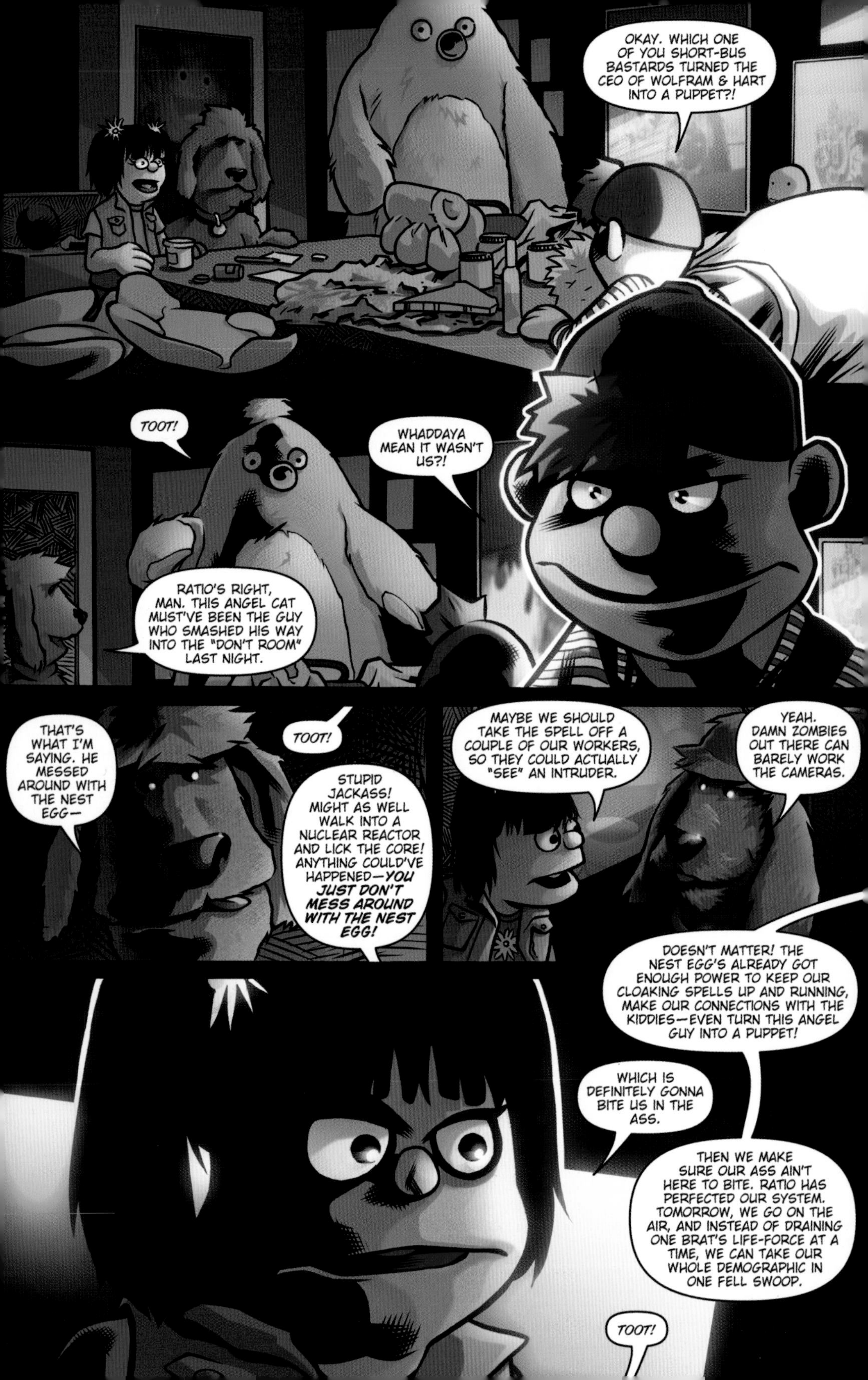
OKAY. WHICH ONE OF YOU SHORT-BUS BASTARDS TURNED THE CEO OF WOLFRAM & HART INTO A PUPPET?!
TOOT!
WHADDAYA MEAN IT WASN'T US?!
RATIO'S RIGHT, MAN. THIS ANGEL CAT MUST'VE BEEN THE GUY WHO SMASHED HIS WAY INTO THE "DON'T ROOM" LAST NIGHT.
THAT'S WHAT I'M SAYING. HE MESSED AROUND WITH THE NEST EGG—
TOOT!
STUPID JACKASS! MIGHT AS WELL WALK INTO A NUCLEAR REACTOR AND LICK THE CORE! ANYTHING COULD'VE HAPPENED—YOU JUST DON'T MESS AROUND WITH THE NEST EGG!
MAYBE WE SHOULD TAKE THE SPELL OFF A COUPLE OF OUR WORKERS, SO THEY COULD ACTUALLY "SEE" AN INTRUDER.
YEAH. DAMN ZOMBIES OUT THERE CAN BARELY WORK THE CAMERAS.
DOESN'T MATTER! THE NEST EGG'S ALREADY GOT ENOUGH POWER TO KEEP OUR CLOAKING SPELLS UP AND RUNNING, MAKE OUR CONNECTIONS WITH THE KIDDIES—EVEN TURN THIS ANGEL GUY INTO A PUPPET!
WHICH IS DEFINITELY GONNA BITE US IN THE ASS.
THEN WE MAKE SURE OUR ASS AIN'T HERE TO BITE. RATIO HAS PERFECTED OUR SYSTEM. TOMORROW, WE GO ON THE AIR, AND INSTEAD OF DRAINING ONE BRAT'S LIFE-FORCE AT A TIME, WE CAN TAKE OUR WHOLE DEMOGRAPHIC IN ONE FELL SWOOP.
TOOT!

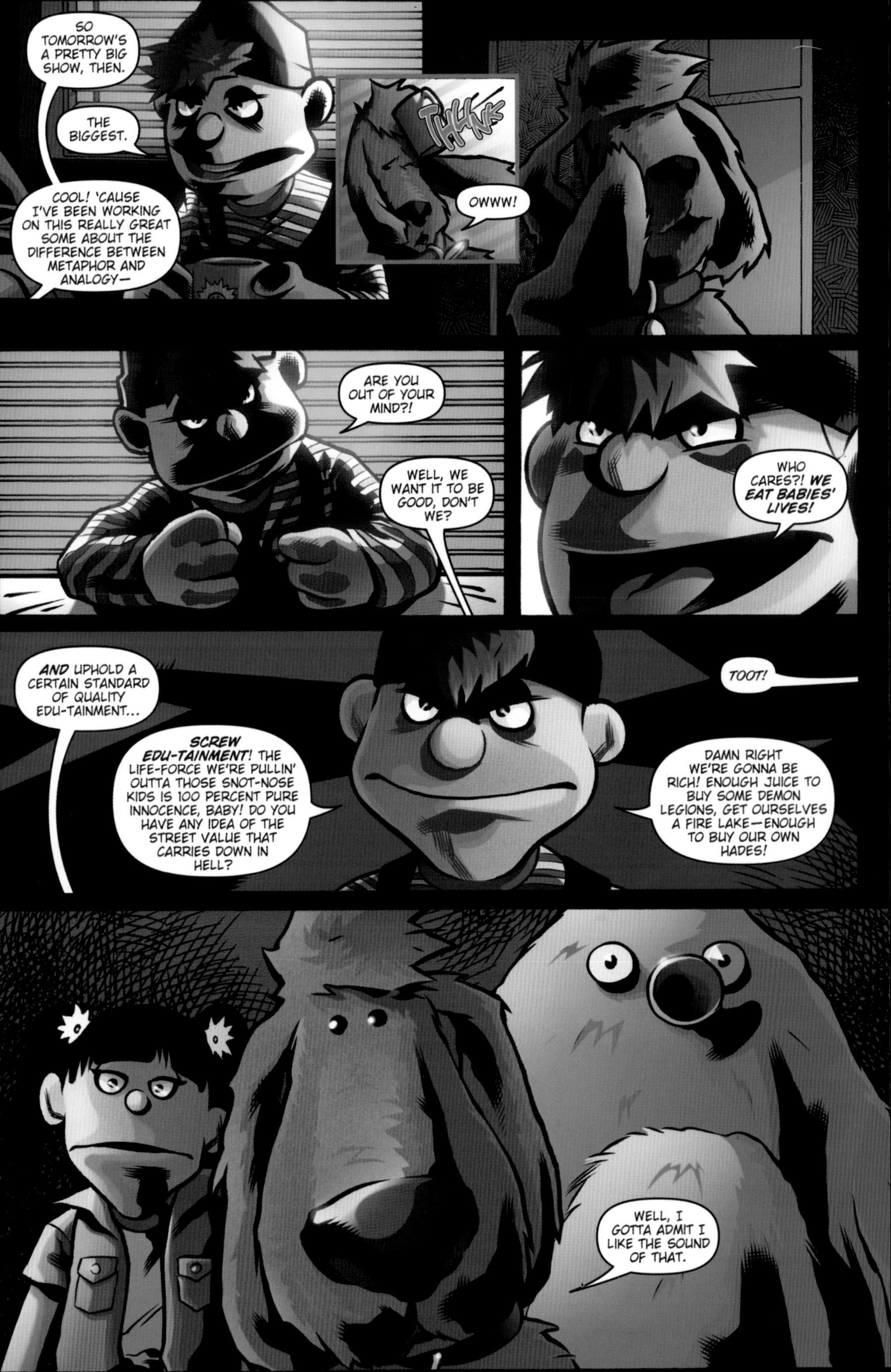
SO TOMORROW'S A PRETTY BIG SHOW, THEN.
THE BIGGEST.
COOL! 'CAUSE I'VE BEEN WORKING ON THIS REALLY GREAT SOME ABOUT THE DIFFERENCE BETWEEN METAPHOR AND ANALOGY—
THUNK
OWWW!
ARE YOU OUT OF YOUR MIND?!
WELL, WE WANT IT TO BE GOOD, DON'T WE?
WHO CARES?! WE EAT BABIES' LIVES!
AND UPHOLD A CERTAIN STANDARD OF QUALITY EDU-TAINMENT...
SCREW EDU-TAINMENT! THE LIFE-FORCE WE'RE PULLIN' OUTTA THOSE SNOT-NOSE KIDS IS 100 PERCENT PURE INNOCENCE, BABY! DO YOU HAVE ANY IDEA OF THE STREET VALUE THAT CARRIES DOWN IN HELL?
TOOT!
DAMN RIGHT WE'RE GONNA BE RICH! ENOUGH JUICE TO BUY SOME DEMON LEGIONS, GET OURSELVES A FIRE LAKE—ENOUGH TO BUY OUR OWN HADES!
WELL, I GOTTA ADMIT I LIKE THE SOUND OF THAT.

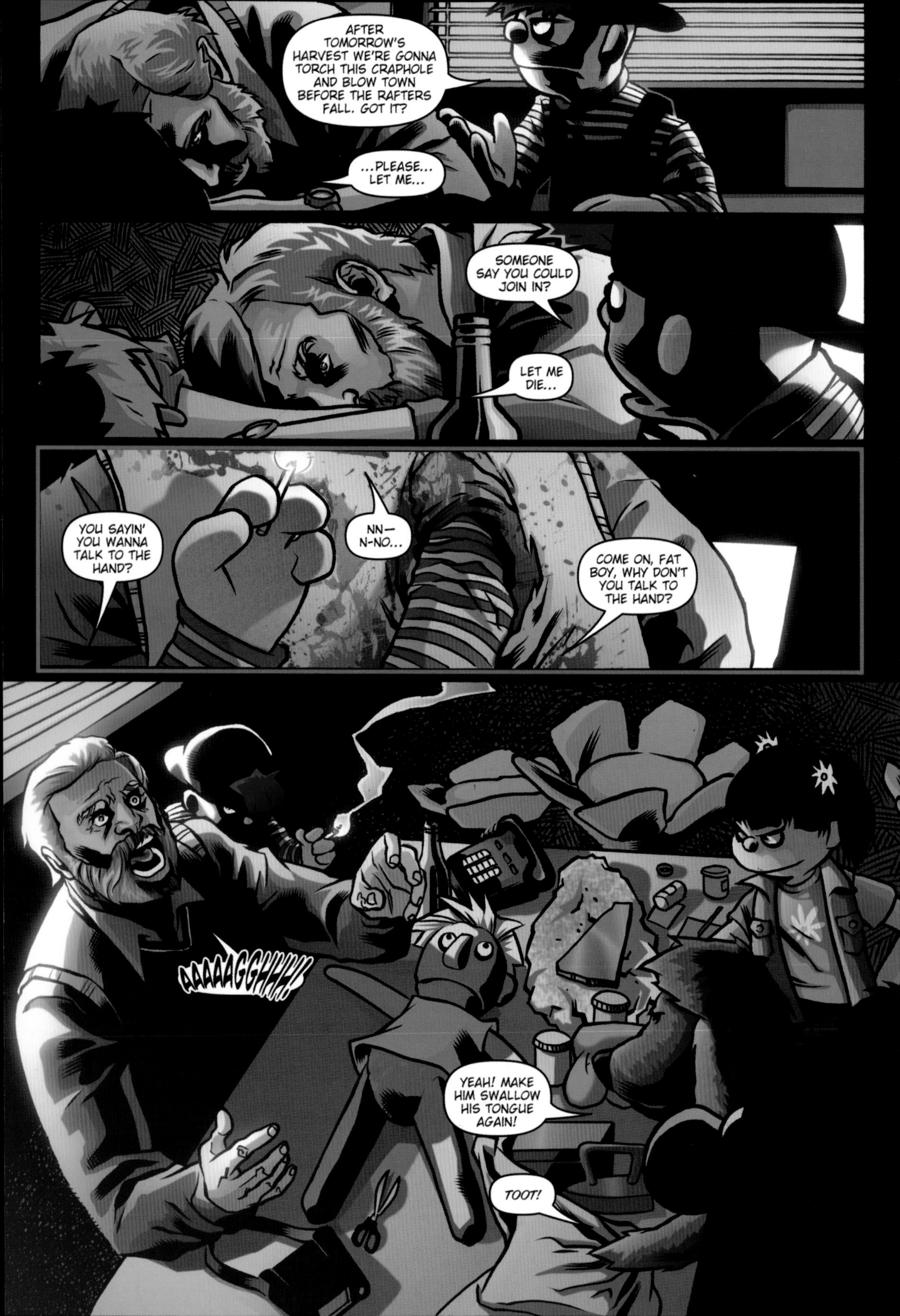
AFTER TOMORROW'S HARVEST WE'RE GONNA TORCH THIS CRAPHOLE AND BLOW TOWN BEFORE THE RAFTERS FALL. GOT IT?
...PLEASE... LET ME...
SOMEONE SAY YOU COULD JOIN IN?
LET ME DIE...
YOU SAYIN' YOU WANNA TALK TO THE HAND?
NN— N-NO...
COME ON, FAT BOY, WHY DON'T YOU TALK TO THE HAND?
AAAAAGGHH!!
YEAH! MAKE HIM SWALLOW HIS TONGUE AGAIN!
TOOT!

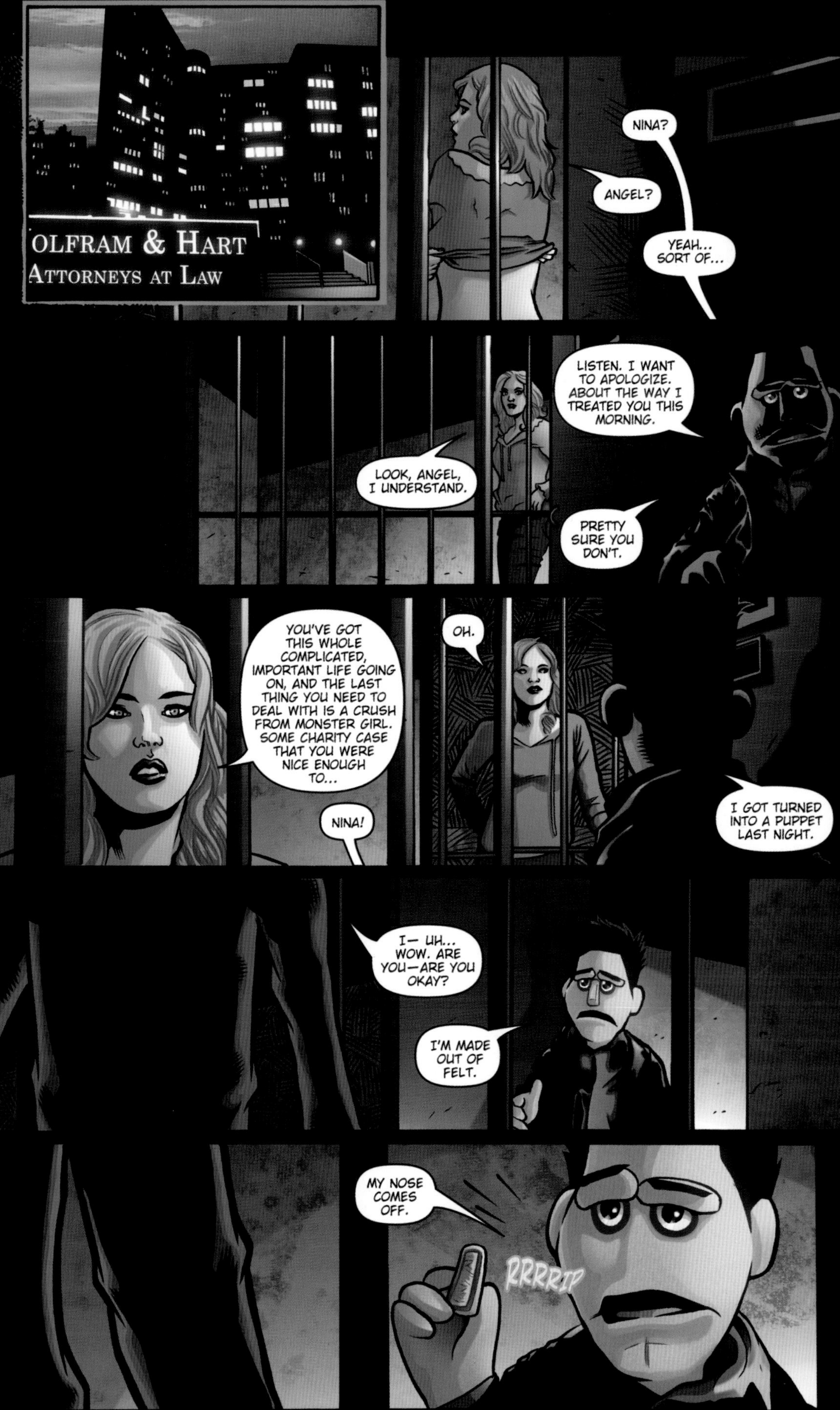

OLFRAM & HART
ATTORNEYS AT LAW
NINA?
ANGEL?
YEAH... SORT OF...
LISTEN. I WANT TO APOLOGIZE. ABOUT THE WAY I TREATED YOU THIS MORNING.
LOOK, ANGEL, I UNDERSTAND.
PRETTY SURE YOU DON'T.
YOU'VE GOT THIS WHOLE COMPLICATED, IMPORTANT LIFE GOING ON, AND THE LAST THING YOU NEED TO DEAL WITH IS A CRUSH FROM MONSTER GIRL. SOME CHARITY CASE THAT YOU WERE NICE ENOUGH TO...
NINA!
OH.
I GOT TURNED INTO A PUPPET LAST NIGHT.
I— UH... WOW. ARE YOU—ARE YOU OKAY?
I'M MADE OUT OF FELT.
MY NOSE COMES OFF.
RRRRIP

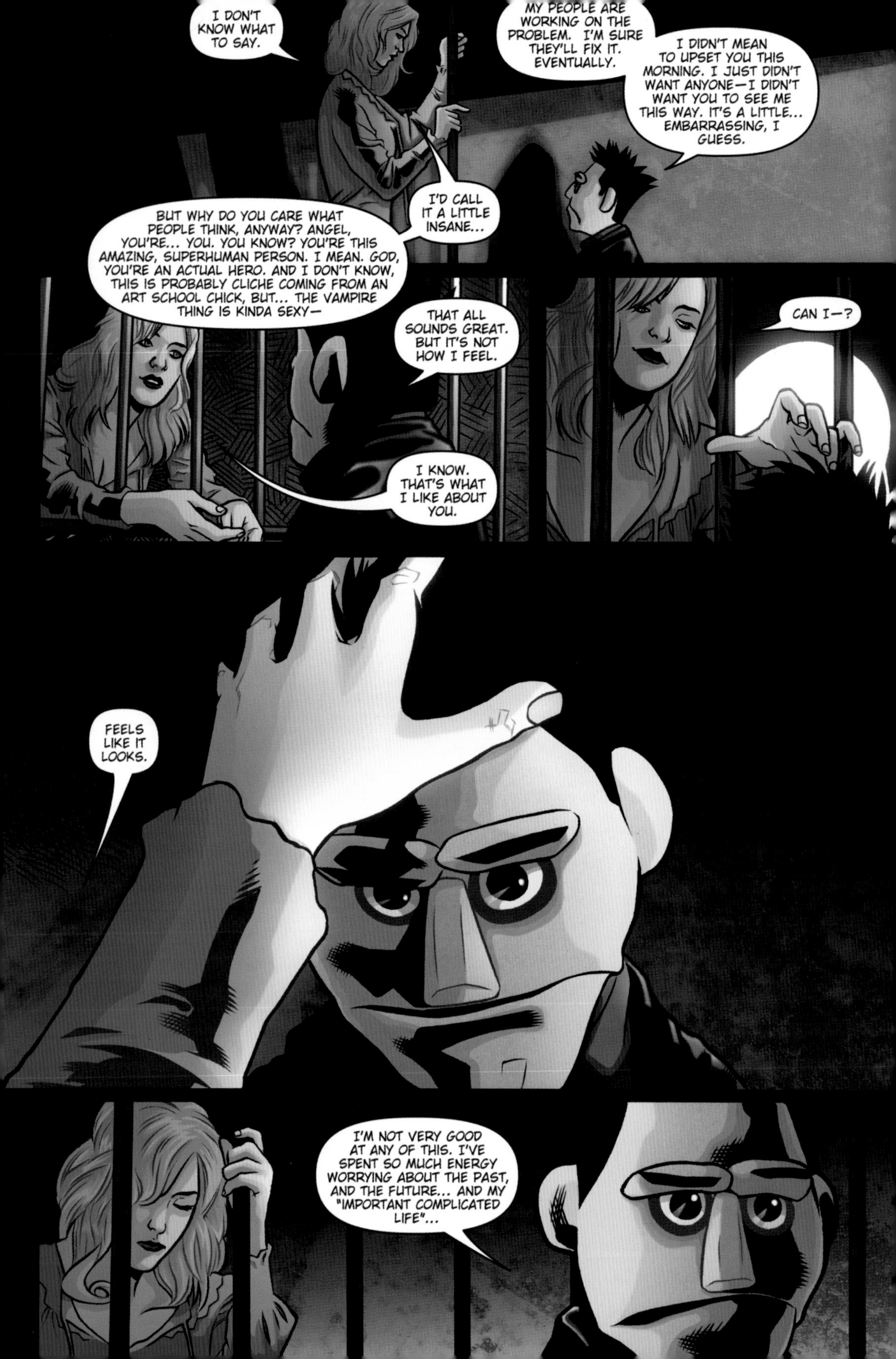
I DON'T KNOW WHAT TO SAY.
MY PEOPLE ARE WORKING ON THE PROBLEM. I'M SURE THEY'LL FIX IT. EVENTUALLY.
I DIDN'T MEAN TO UPSET YOU THIS MORNING. I JUST DIDN'T WANT ANYONE—I DIDN'T WANT YOU TO SEE ME THIS WAY. IT'S A LITTLE... EMBARRASSING, I GUESS.
I'D CALL IT A LITTLE INSANE...
BUT WHY DO YOU CARE WHAT PEOPLE THINK, ANYWAY? ANGEL, YOU'RE... YOU. YOU KNOW? YOU'RE THIS AMAZING, SUPERHUMAN PERSON. I MEAN. GOD, YOU'RE AN ACTUAL HERO. AND I DON'T KNOW, THIS IS PROBABLY CLICHE COMING FROM AN ART SCHOOL CHICK, BUT... THE VAMPIRE THING IS KINDA SEXY—
THAT ALL SOUNDS GREAT. BUT IT'S NOT HOW I FEEL.
I KNOW. THAT'S WHAT I LIKE ABOUT YOU.
CAN I—?
FEELS LIKE IT LOOKS.
I'M NOT VERY GOOD AT ANY OF THIS. I'VE SPENT SO MUCH ENERGY WORRYING ABOUT THE PAST, AND THE FUTURE... AND MY "IMPORTANT COMPLICATED LIFE"...

IT'S BEEN A WHILE SINCE I LOOKED UP AND REALLY SAW WHAT WAS GOING ON AROUND ME.

IT'S NOT MY STRONG SUIT, YOU KNOW? BUT I'M WORKING ON IT, ON PAYING BETTER ATTENTION TO—

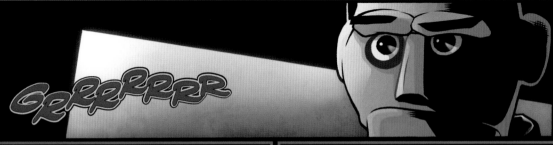

GRRRRRRR

NINA! NO! NO!

GRRRRRRR

BAD NINA! BAD!

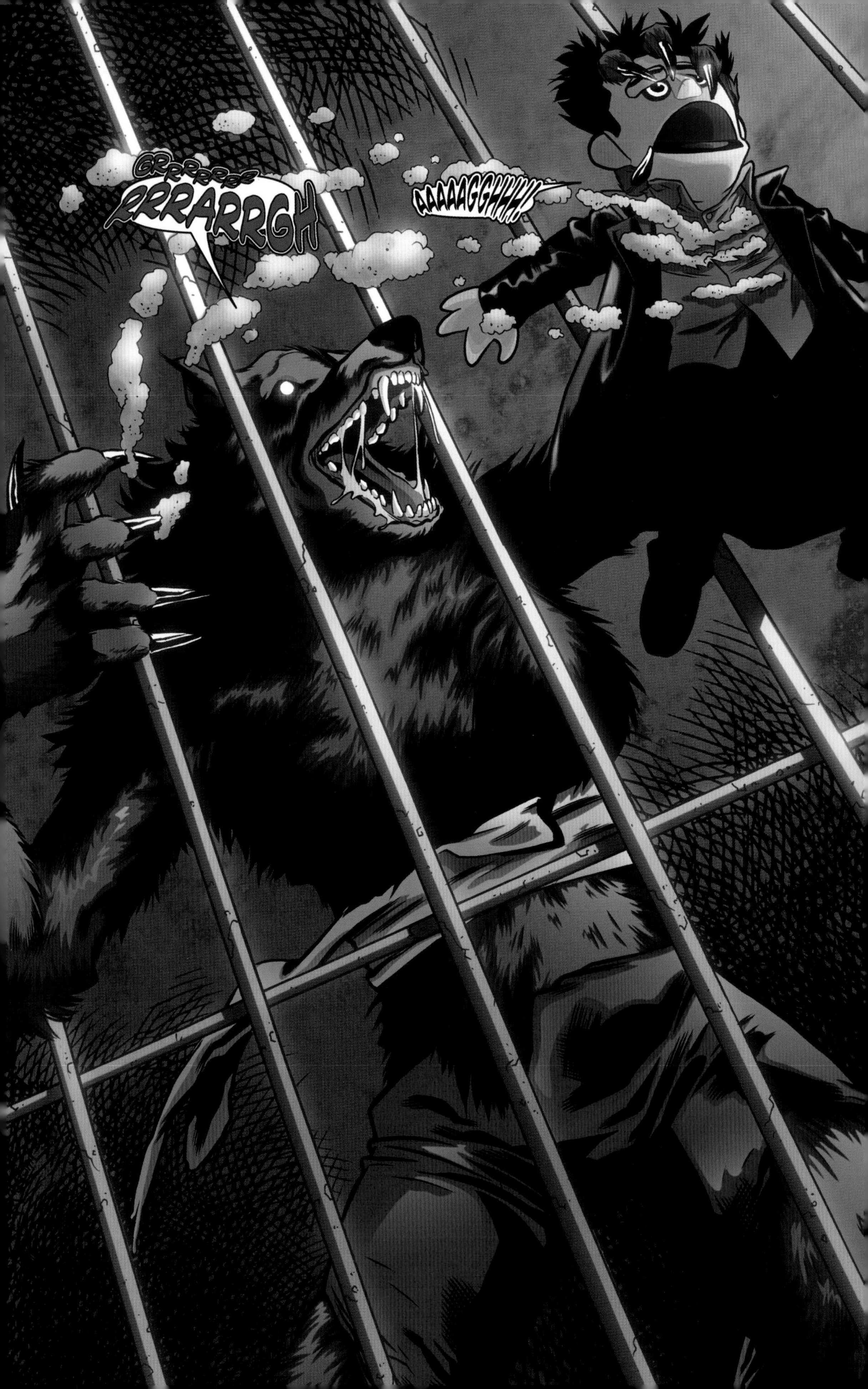
GRRRRRRR RRRARRRGH
AAAAAGGHHH!

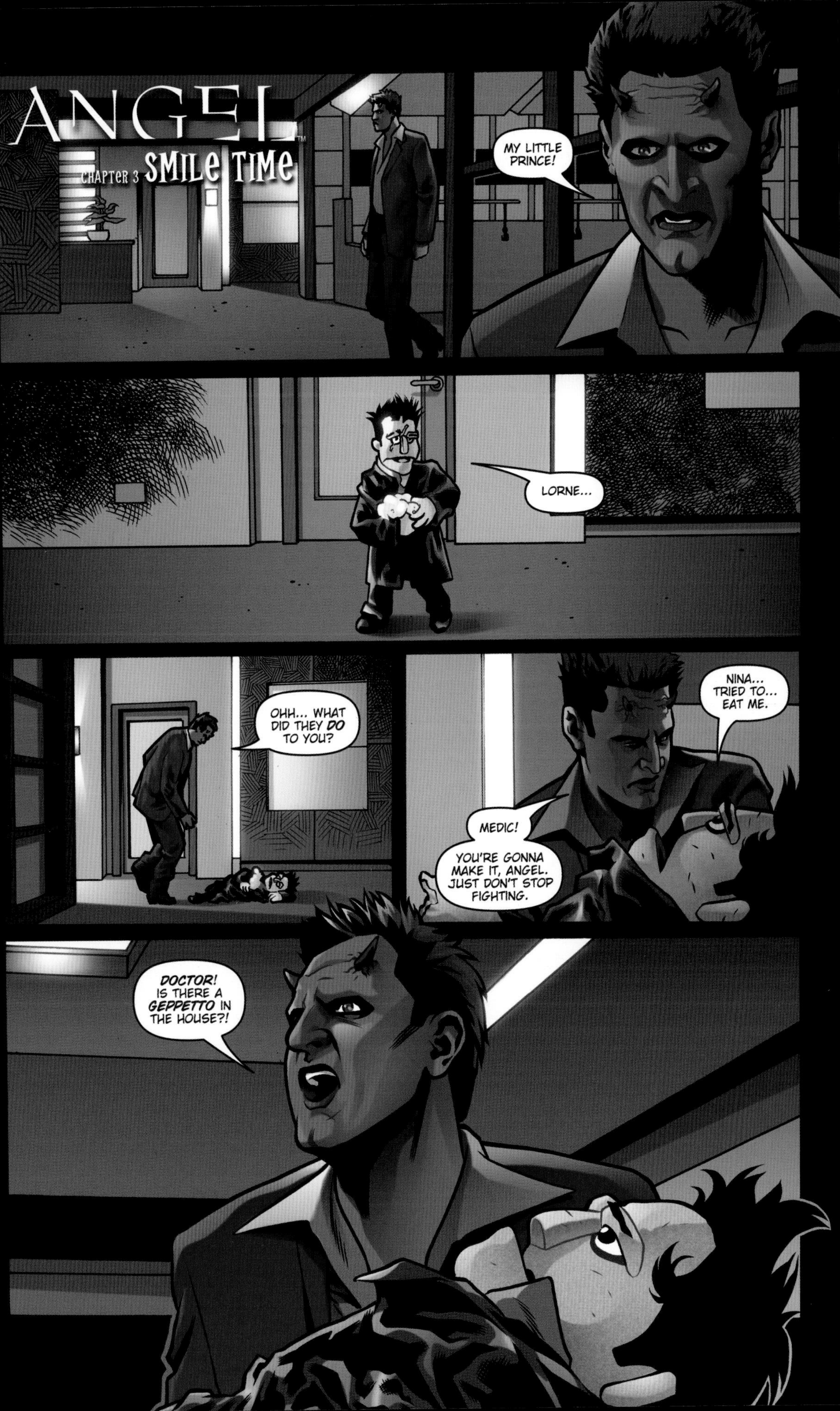

ANGEL™
CHAPTER 3 SMILE TIME
MY LITTLE PRINCE!
LORNE...
OHH... WHAT DID THEY DO TO YOU?
NINA... TRIED TO... EAT ME.
MEDIC!
YOU'RE GONNA MAKE IT, ANGEL. JUST DON'T STOP FIGHTING.
DOCTOR! IS THERE A GEPPETTO IN THE HOUSE?!

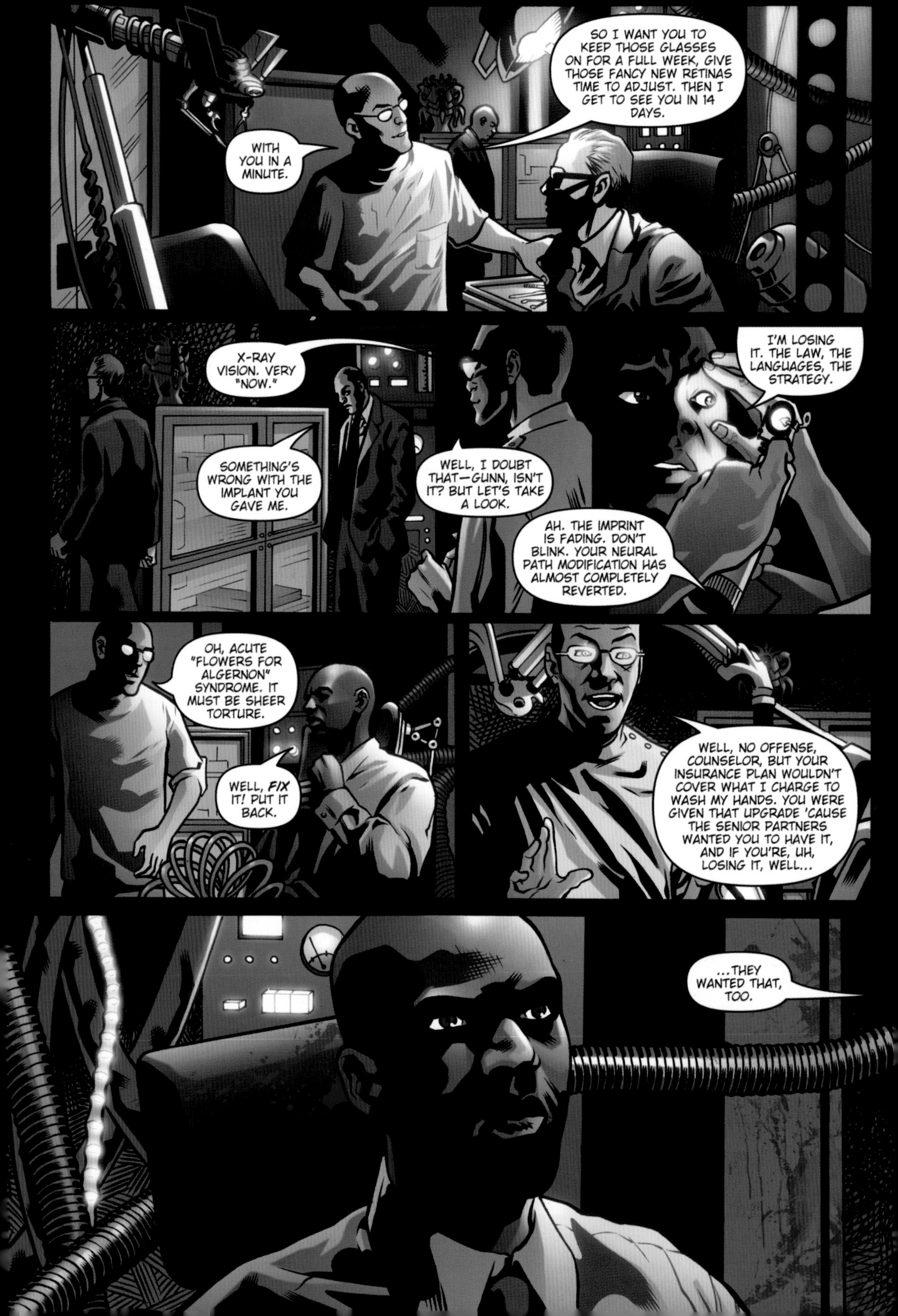
SO I WANT YOU TO KEEP THOSE GLASSES ON FOR A FULL WEEK, GIVE THOSE FANCY NEW RETINAS TIME TO ADJUST. THEN I GET TO SEE YOU IN 14 DAYS.
WITH YOU IN A MINUTE.
X-RAY VISION. VERY "NOW."
SOMETHING'S WRONG WITH THE IMPLANT YOU GAVE ME.
WELL, I DOUBT THAT—GUNN, ISN'T IT? BUT LET'S TAKE A LOOK.
I'M LOSING IT. THE LAW, THE LANGUAGES, THE STRATEGY.
AH. THE IMPRINT IS FADING. DON'T BLINK. YOUR NEURAL PATH MODIFICATION HAS ALMOST COMPLETELY REVERTED.
OH, ACUTE "FLOWERS FOR ALGERNON" SYNDROME. IT MUST BE SHEER TORTURE.
WELL, FIX IT! PUT IT BACK.
WELL, NO OFFENSE, COUNSELOR, BUT YOUR INSURANCE PLAN WOULDN'T COVER WHAT I CHARGE TO WASH MY HANDS. YOU WERE GIVEN THAT UPGRADE 'CAUSE THE SENIOR PARTNERS WANTED YOU TO HAVE IT, AND IF YOU'RE, UH, LOSING IT, WELL...
...THEY WANTED THAT, TOO.

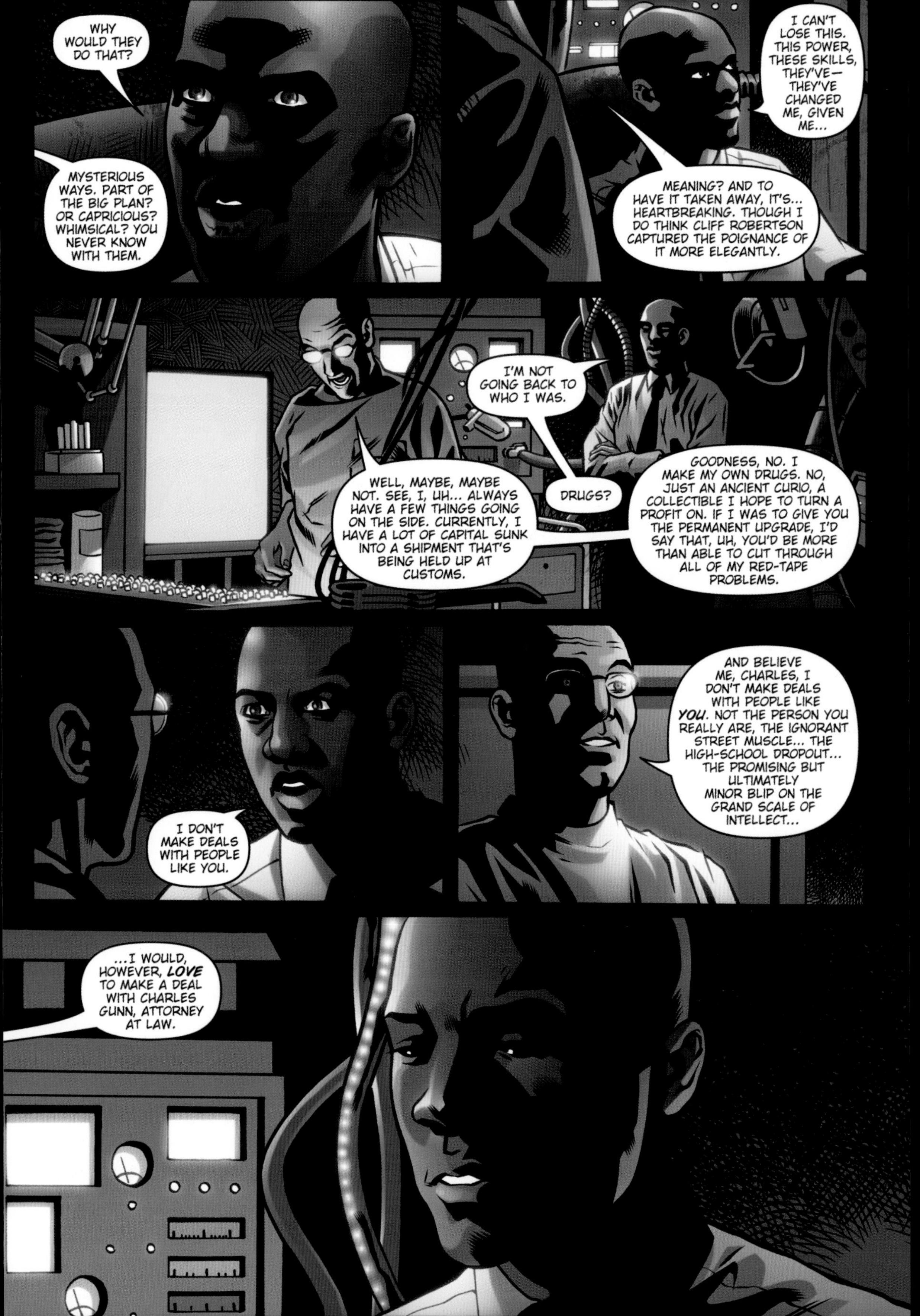

WHY WOULD THEY DO THAT?
MYSTERIOUS WAYS. PART OF THE BIG PLAN? OR CAPRICIOUS? WHIMSICAL? YOU NEVER KNOW WITH THEM.
I CAN'T LOSE THIS. THIS POWER, THESE SKILLS, THEY'VE— THEY'VE CHANGED ME, GIVEN ME...
MEANING? AND TO HAVE IT TAKEN AWAY, IT'S... HEARTBREAKING. THOUGH I DO THINK CLIFF ROBERTSON CAPTURED THE POIGNANCE OF IT MORE ELEGANTLY.
I'M NOT GOING BACK TO WHO I WAS.
WELL, MAYBE, MAYBE NOT. SEE, I, UH... ALWAYS HAVE A FEW THINGS GOING ON THE SIDE. CURRENTLY, I HAVE A LOT OF CAPITAL SUNK INTO A SHIPMENT THAT'S BEING HELD UP AT CUSTOMS.
DRUGS?
GOODNESS, NO. I MAKE MY OWN DRUGS. NO, JUST AN ANCIENT CURIO, A COLLECTIBLE I HOPE TO TURN A PROFIT ON. IF I WAS TO GIVE YOU THE PERMANENT UPGRADE, I'D SAY THAT, UH, YOU'D BE MORE THAN ABLE TO CUT THROUGH ALL OF MY RED-TAPE PROBLEMS.
I DON'T MAKE DEALS WITH PEOPLE LIKE YOU.
AND BELIEVE ME, CHARLES, I DON'T MAKE DEALS WITH PEOPLE LIKE *YOU*. NOT THE PERSON YOU REALLY ARE, THE IGNORANT STREET MUSCLE... THE HIGH-SCHOOL DROPOUT... THE PROMISING BUT ULTIMATELY MINOR BLIP ON THE GRAND SCALE OF INTELLECT...
...I WOULD, HOWEVER, *LOVE* TO MAKE A DEAL WITH CHARLES GUNN, ATTORNEY AT LAW.

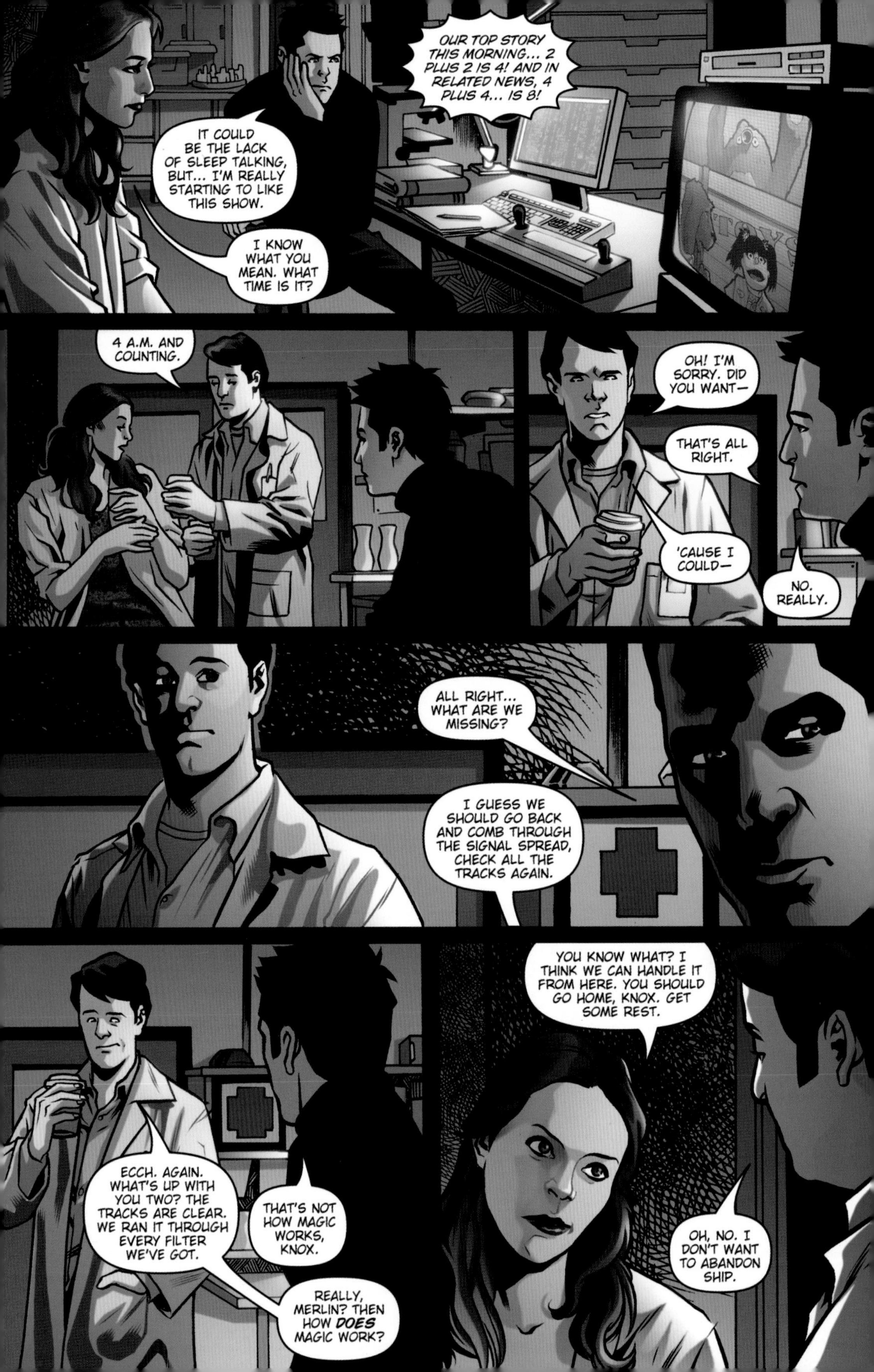
OUR TOP STORY THIS MORNING... 2 PLUS 2 IS 4! AND IN RELATED NEWS, 4 PLUS 4... IS 8!
IT COULD BE THE LACK OF SLEEP TALKING, BUT... I'M REALLY STARTING TO LIKE THIS SHOW.
I KNOW WHAT YOU MEAN. WHAT TIME IS IT?
4 A.M. AND COUNTING.
OH! I'M SORRY. DID YOU WANT—
THAT'S ALL RIGHT.
'CAUSE I COULD—
NO. REALLY.
ALL RIGHT... WHAT ARE WE MISSING?
I GUESS WE SHOULD GO BACK AND COMB THROUGH THE SIGNAL SPREAD, CHECK ALL THE TRACKS AGAIN.
ECCH. AGAIN. WHAT'S UP WITH YOU TWO? THE TRACKS ARE CLEAR. WE RAN IT THROUGH EVERY FILTER WE'VE GOT.
THAT'S NOT HOW MAGIC WORKS, KNOX.
REALLY, MERLIN? THEN HOW *DOES* MAGIC WORK?
YOU KNOW WHAT? I THINK WE CAN HANDLE IT FROM HERE. YOU SHOULD GO HOME, KNOX. GET SOME REST.
OH, NO. I DON'T WANT TO ABANDON SHIP.

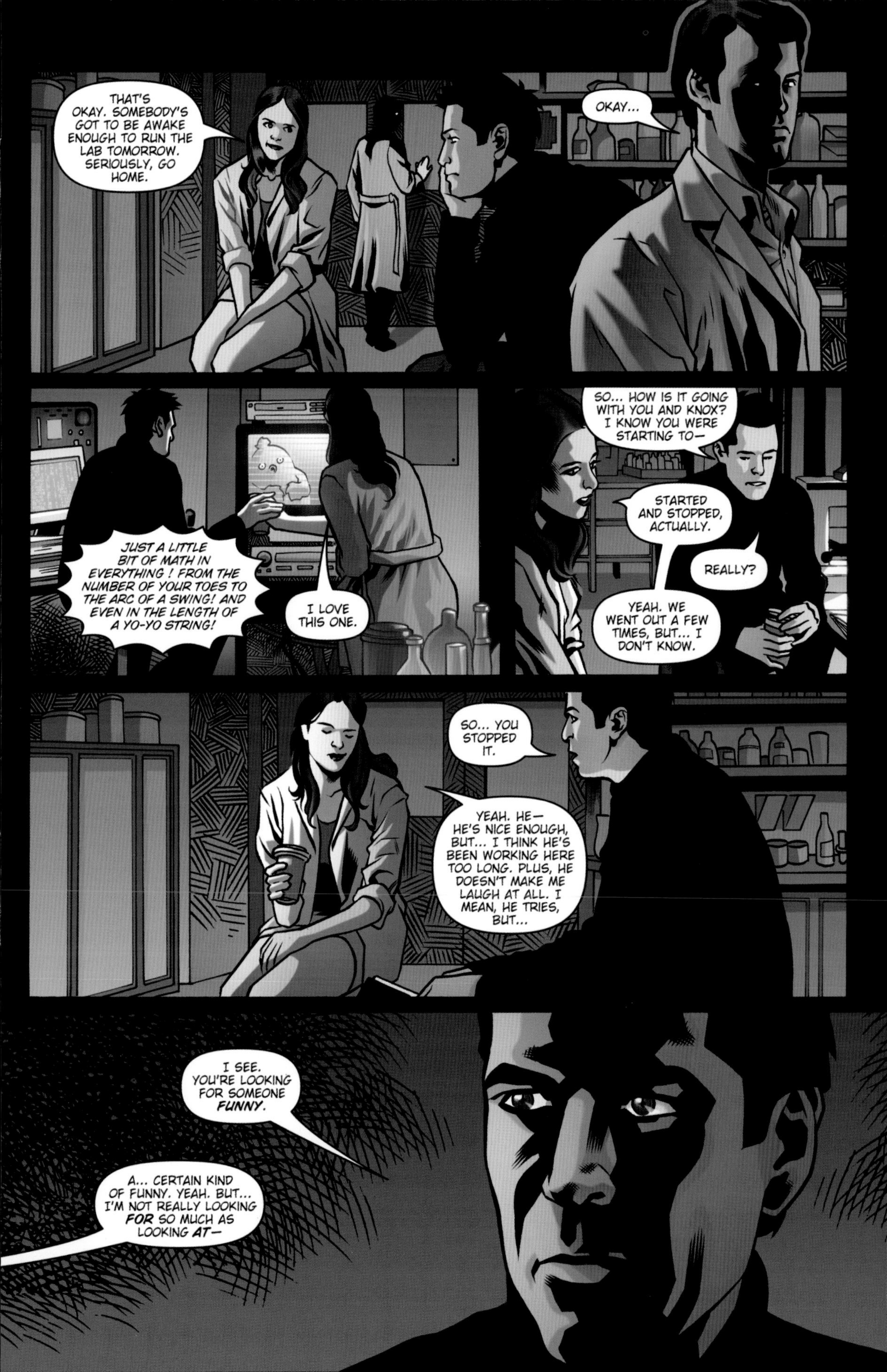
THAT'S OKAY. SOMEBODY'S GOT TO BE AWAKE ENOUGH TO RUN THE LAB TOMORROW. SERIOUSLY, GO HOME.
OKAY...
JUST A LITTLE BIT OF MATH IN EVERYTHING ! FROM THE NUMBER OF YOUR TOES TO THE ARC OF A SWING! AND EVEN IN THE LENGTH OF A YO-YO STRING!
I LOVE THIS ONE.
SO... HOW IS IT GOING WITH YOU AND KNOX? I KNOW YOU WERE STARTING TO—
STARTED AND STOPPED, ACTUALLY.
REALLY?
YEAH. WE WENT OUT A FEW TIMES, BUT... I DON'T KNOW.
SO... YOU STOPPED IT.
YEAH. HE— HE'S NICE ENOUGH, BUT... I THINK HE'S BEEN WORKING HERE TOO LONG. PLUS, HE DOESN'T MAKE ME LAUGH AT ALL. I MEAN, HE TRIES, BUT...
I SEE. YOU'RE LOOKING FOR SOMEONE ***FUNNY***.
A... CERTAIN KIND OF FUNNY. YEAH. BUT... I'M NOT REALLY LOOKING ***FOR*** SO MUCH AS LOOKING ***AT***—

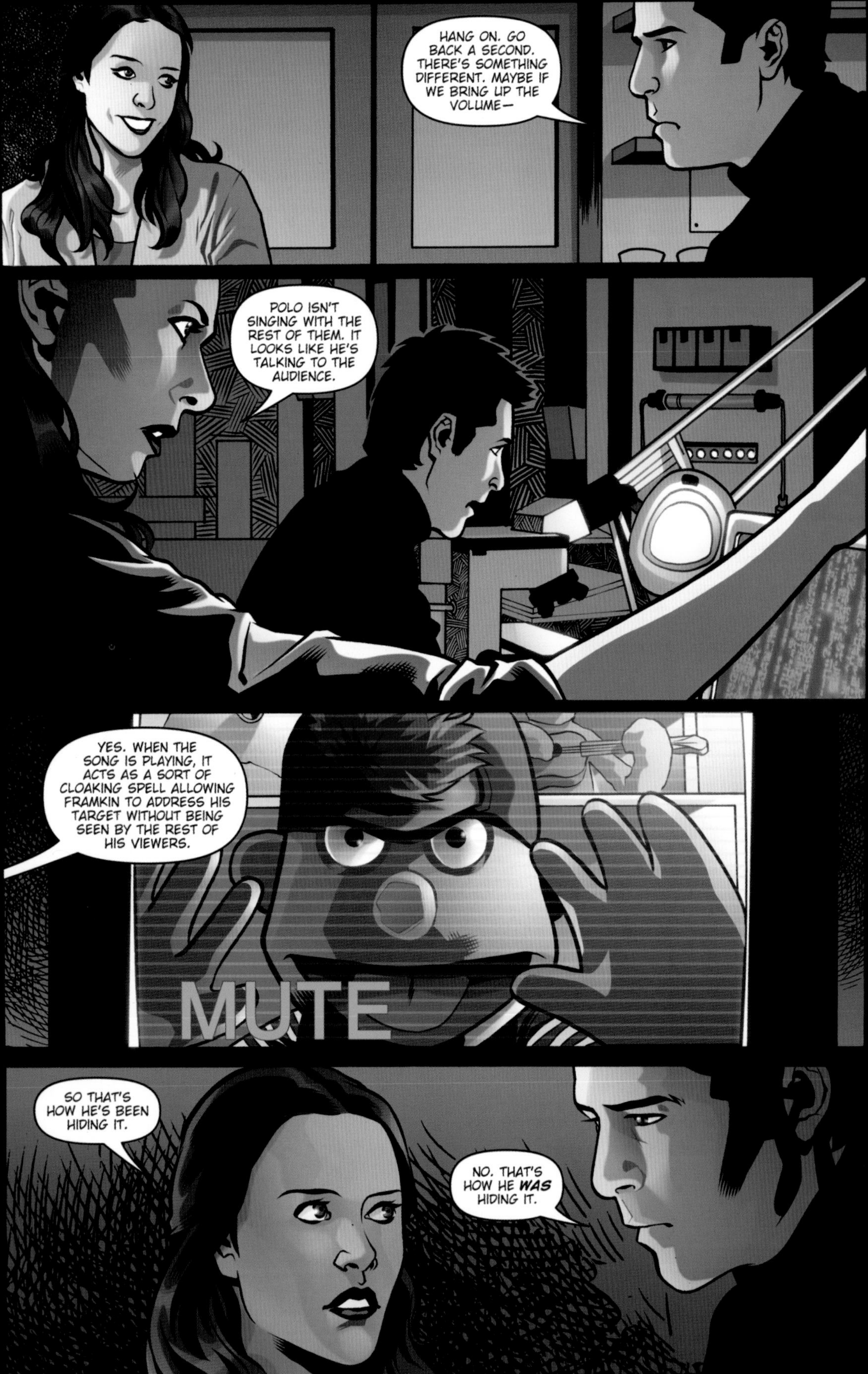
HANG ON. GO BACK A SECOND. THERE'S SOMETHING DIFFERENT. MAYBE IF WE BRING UP THE VOLUME—
POLO ISN'T SINGING WITH THE REST OF THEM. IT LOOKS LIKE HE'S TALKING TO THE AUDIENCE.
YES. WHEN THE SONG IS PLAYING, IT ACTS AS A SORT OF CLOAKING SPELL ALLOWING FRAMKIN TO ADDRESS HIS TARGET WITHOUT BEING SEEN BY THE REST OF HIS VIEWERS.
MUTE
SO THAT'S HOW HE'S BEEN HIDING IT.
NO. THAT'S HOW HE *WAS* HIDING IT.

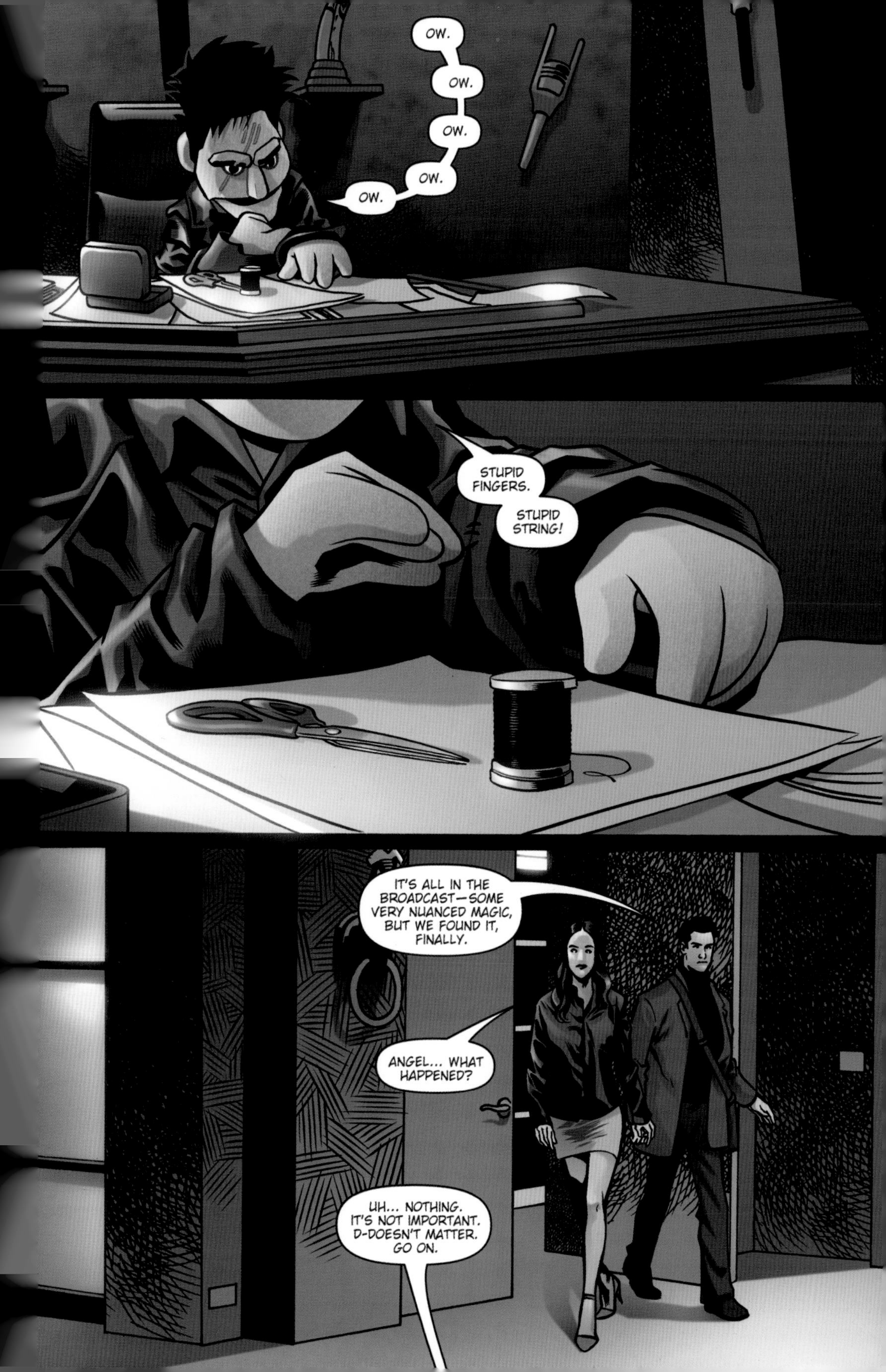
OW.
OW.
OW.
OW.
OW.
STUPID FINGERS.
STUPID STRING!
IT'S ALL IN THE BROADCAST—SOME VERY NUANCED MAGIC, BUT WE FOUND IT, FINALLY.
ANGEL... WHAT HAPPENED?
UH... NOTHING. IT'S NOT IMPORTANT. D-DOESN'T MATTER. GO ON.

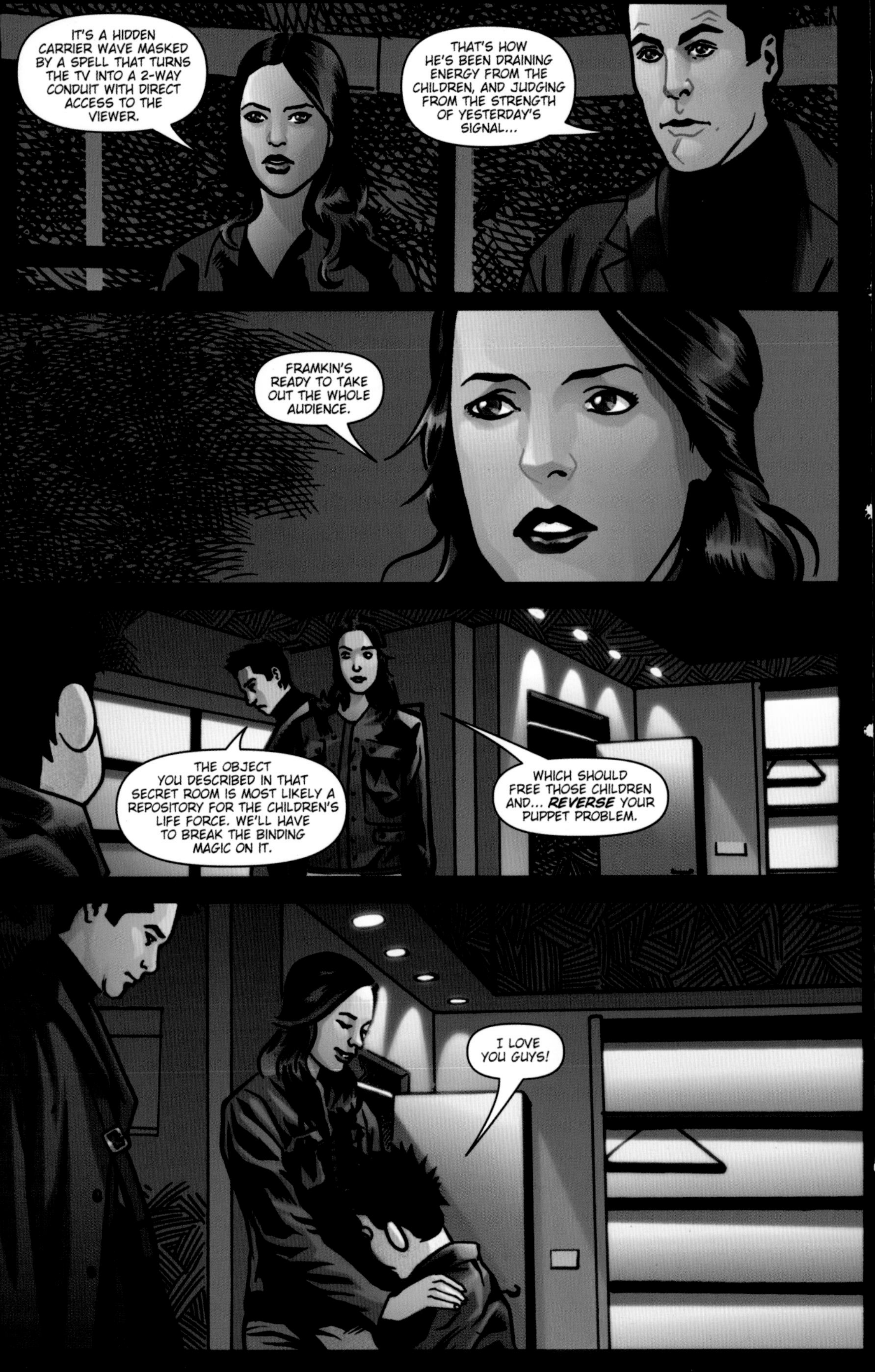
IT'S A HIDDEN CARRIER WAVE MASKED BY A SPELL THAT TURNS THE TV INTO A 2-WAY CONDUIT WITH DIRECT ACCESS TO THE VIEWER.
THAT'S HOW HE'S BEEN DRAINING ENERGY FROM THE CHILDREN, AND JUDGING FROM THE STRENGTH OF YESTERDAY'S SIGNAL...
FRAMKIN'S READY TO TAKE OUT THE WHOLE AUDIENCE.
THE OBJECT YOU DESCRIBED IN THAT SECRET ROOM IS MOST LIKELY A REPOSITORY FOR THE CHILDREN'S LIFE FORCE. WE'LL HAVE TO BREAK THE BINDING MAGIC ON IT.
WHICH SHOULD FREE THOSE CHILDREN AND... *REVERSE* YOUR PUPPET PROBLEM.
I LOVE YOU GUYS!

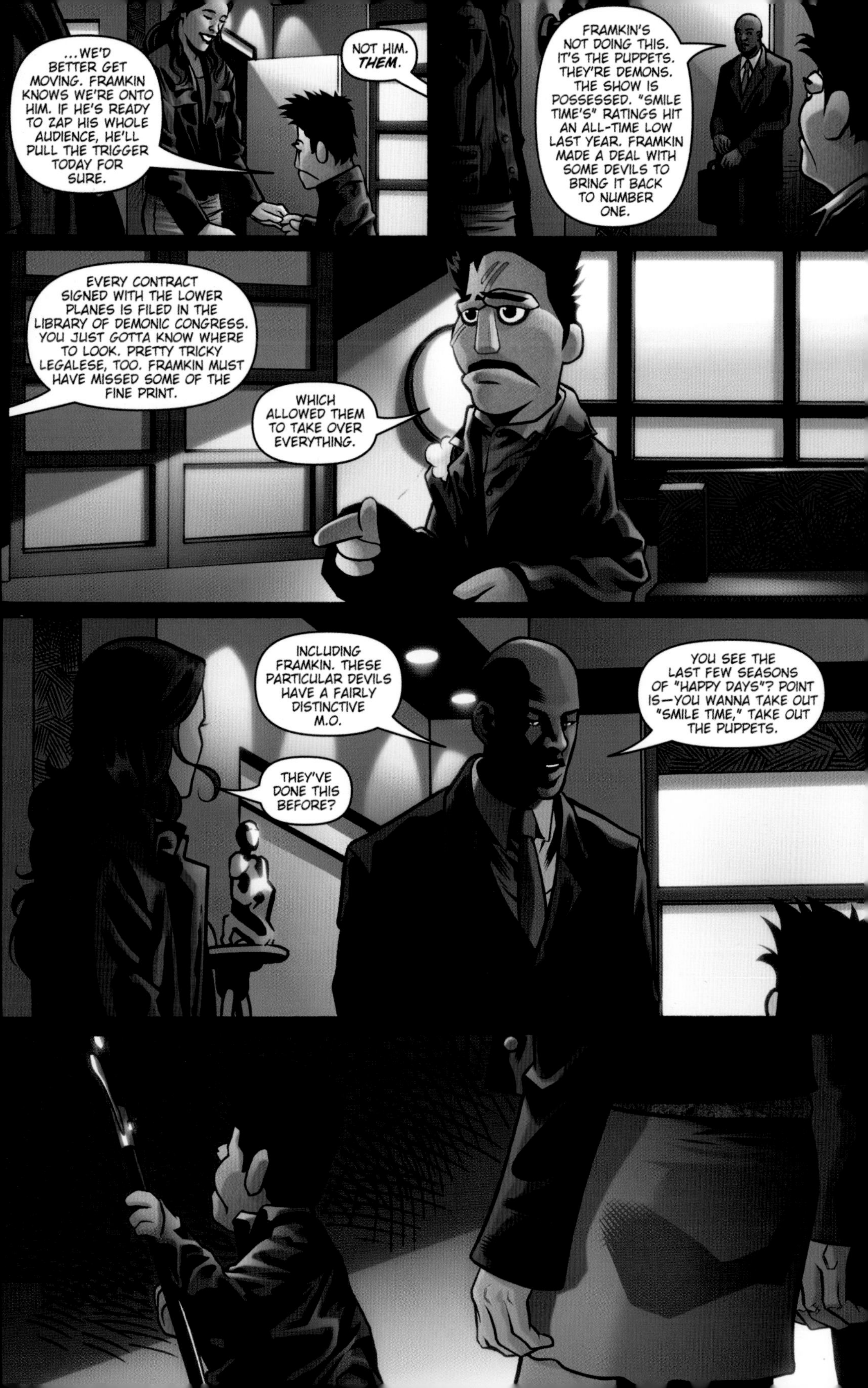
...WE'D BETTER GET MOVING. FRAMKIN KNOWS WE'RE ONTO HIM. IF HE'S READY TO ZAP HIS WHOLE AUDIENCE, HE'LL PULL THE TRIGGER TODAY FOR SURE.
NOT HIM. *THEM*.
FRAMKIN'S NOT DOING THIS. IT'S THE PUPPETS. THEY'RE DEMONS. THE SHOW IS POSSESSED. "SMILE TIME'S" RATINGS HIT AN ALL-TIME LOW LAST YEAR. FRAMKIN MADE A DEAL WITH SOME DEVILS TO BRING IT BACK TO NUMBER ONE.
EVERY CONTRACT SIGNED WITH THE LOWER PLANES IS FILED IN THE LIBRARY OF DEMONIC CONGRESS. YOU JUST GOTTA KNOW WHERE TO LOOK. PRETTY TRICKY LEGALESE, TOO. FRAMKIN MUST HAVE MISSED SOME OF THE FINE PRINT.
WHICH ALLOWED THEM TO TAKE OVER EVERYTHING.
INCLUDING FRAMKIN. THESE PARTICULAR DEVILS HAVE A FAIRLY DISTINCTIVE M.O.
THEY'VE DONE THIS BEFORE?
YOU SEE THE LAST FEW SEASONS OF "HAPPY DAYS"? POINT IS—YOU WANNA TAKE OUT "SMILE TIME," TAKE OUT THE PUPPETS.

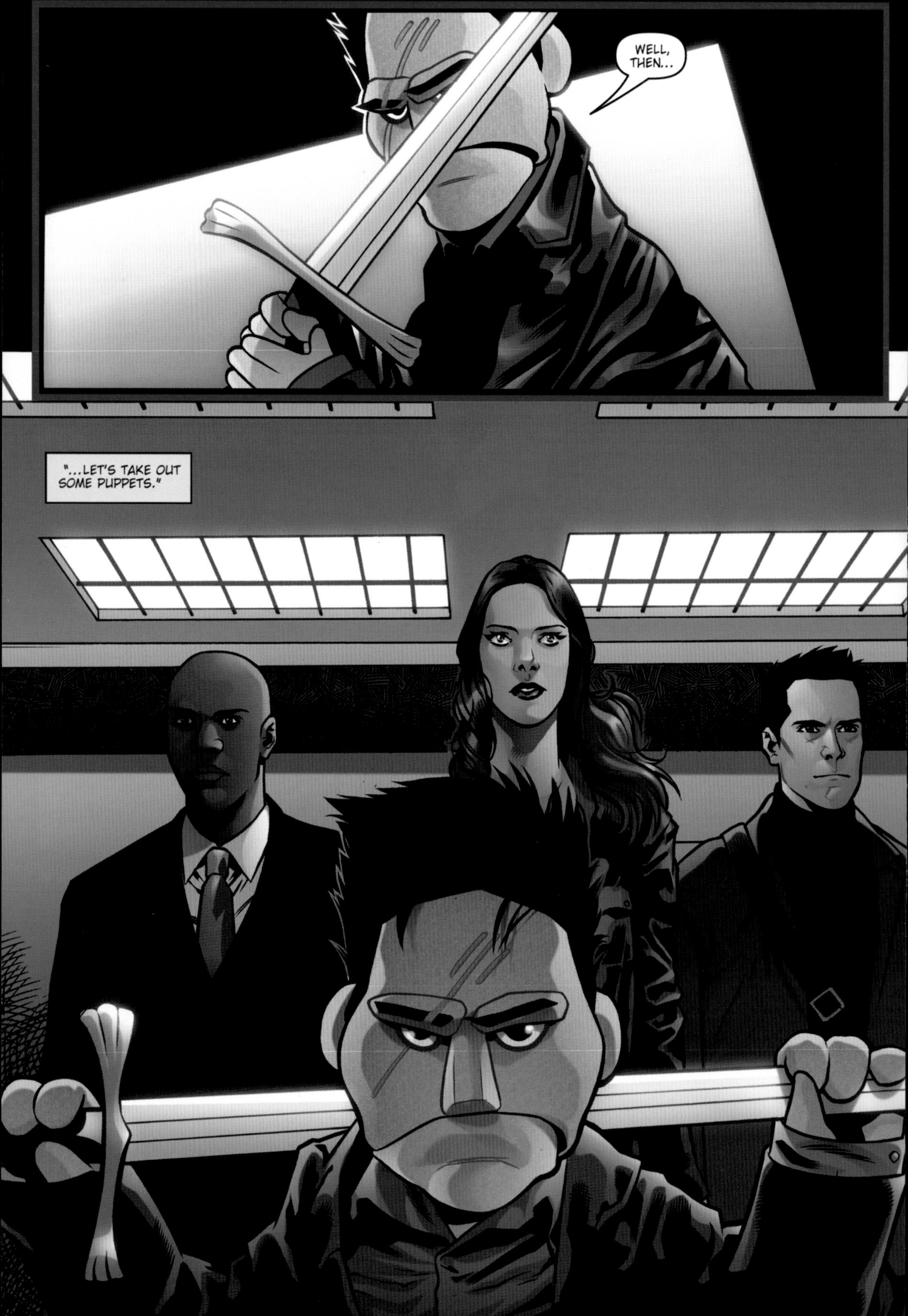
WELL, THEN...
"...LET'S TAKE OUT SOME PUPPETS."

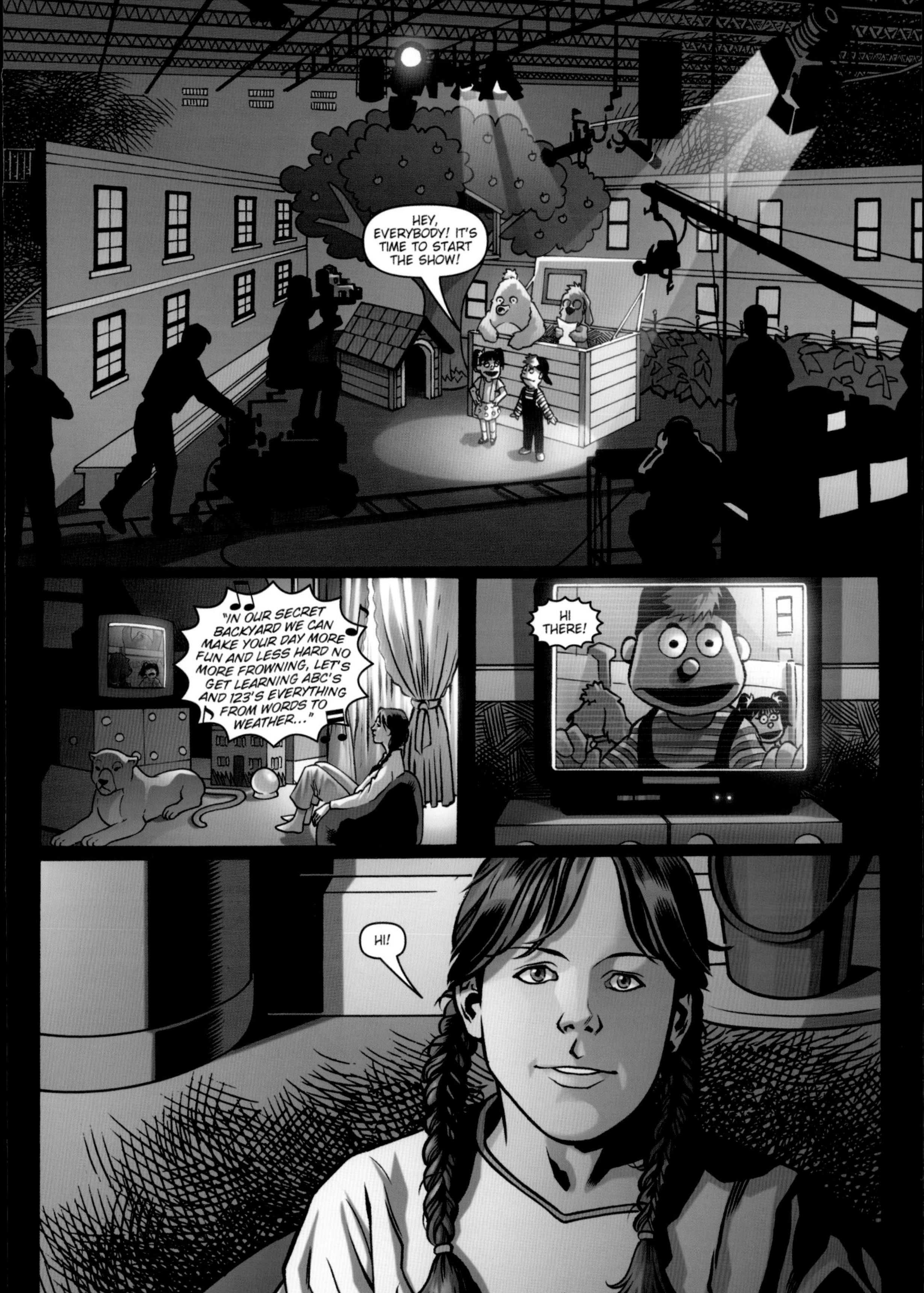
HEY, EVERYBODY! IT'S TIME TO START THE SHOW!
"IN OUR SECRET BACKYARD WE CAN MAKE YOUR DAY MORE FUN AND LESS HARD NO MORE FROWNING, LET'S GET LEARNING ABC'S AND 123'S EVERYTHING FROM WORDS TO WEATHER..."
HI THERE!
HI!

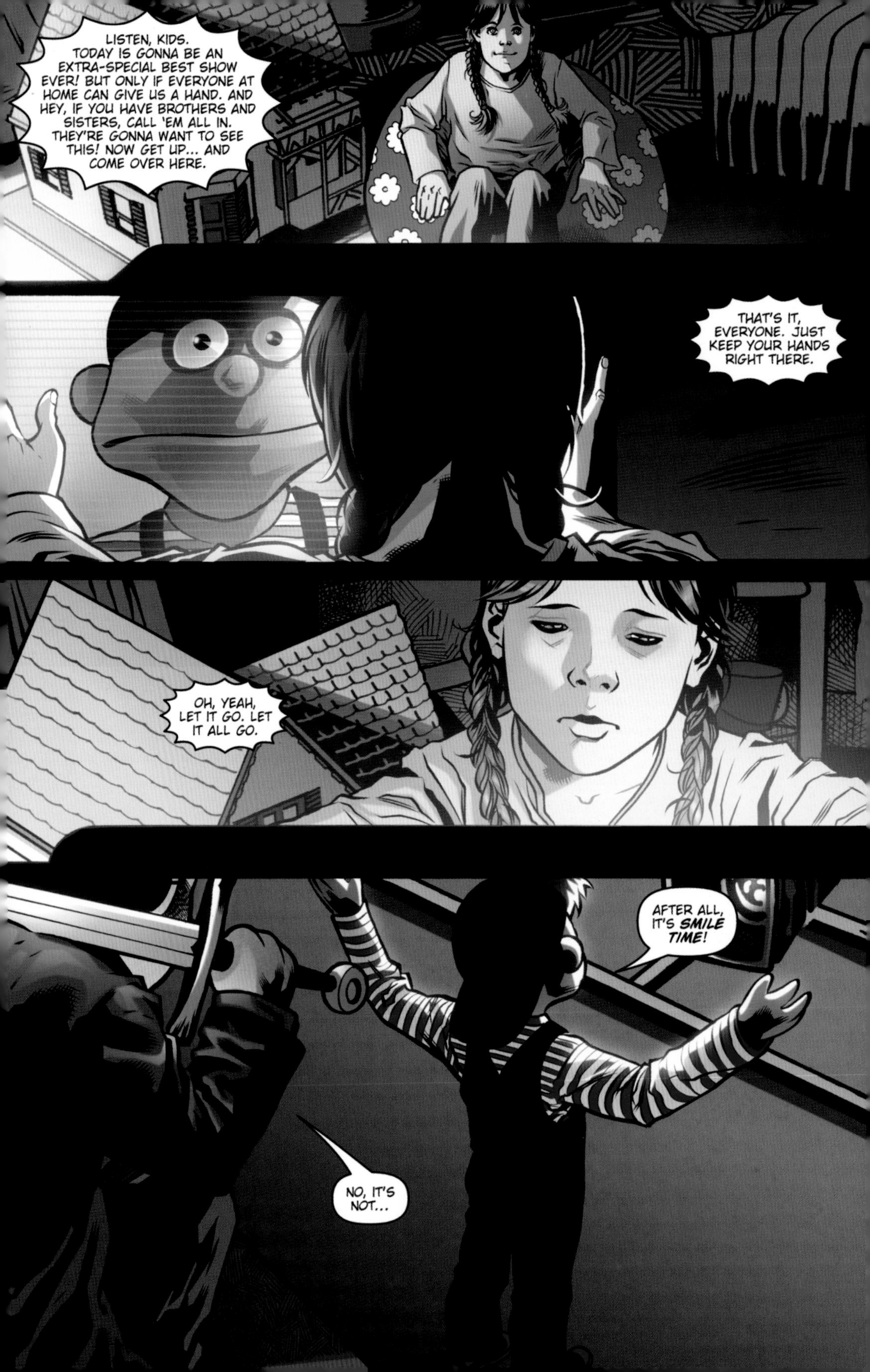
LISTEN, KIDS. TODAY IS GONNA BE AN EXTRA-SPECIAL BEST SHOW EVER! BUT ONLY IF EVERYONE AT HOME CAN GIVE US A HAND. AND HEY, IF YOU HAVE BROTHERS AND SISTERS, CALL 'EM ALL IN. THEY'RE GONNA WANT TO SEE THIS! NOW GET UP... AND COME OVER HERE.
THAT'S IT, EVERYONE. JUST KEEP YOUR HANDS RIGHT THERE.
OH, YEAH, LET IT GO. LET IT ALL GO.
AFTER ALL, IT'S SMILE TIME!
NO, IT'S NOT...

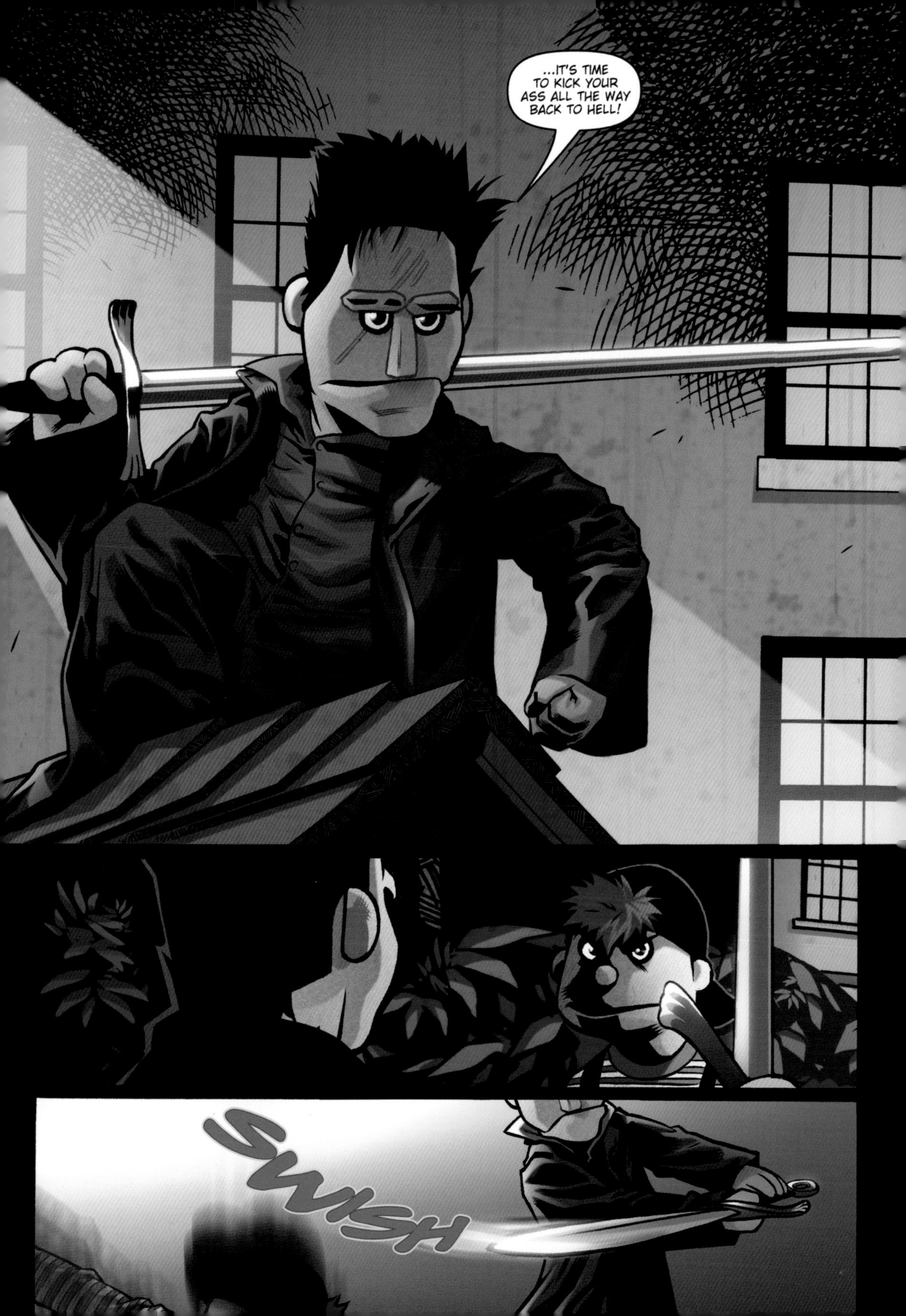
...IT'S TIME TO KICK YOUR ASS ALL THE WAY BACK TO HELL!
SWISH

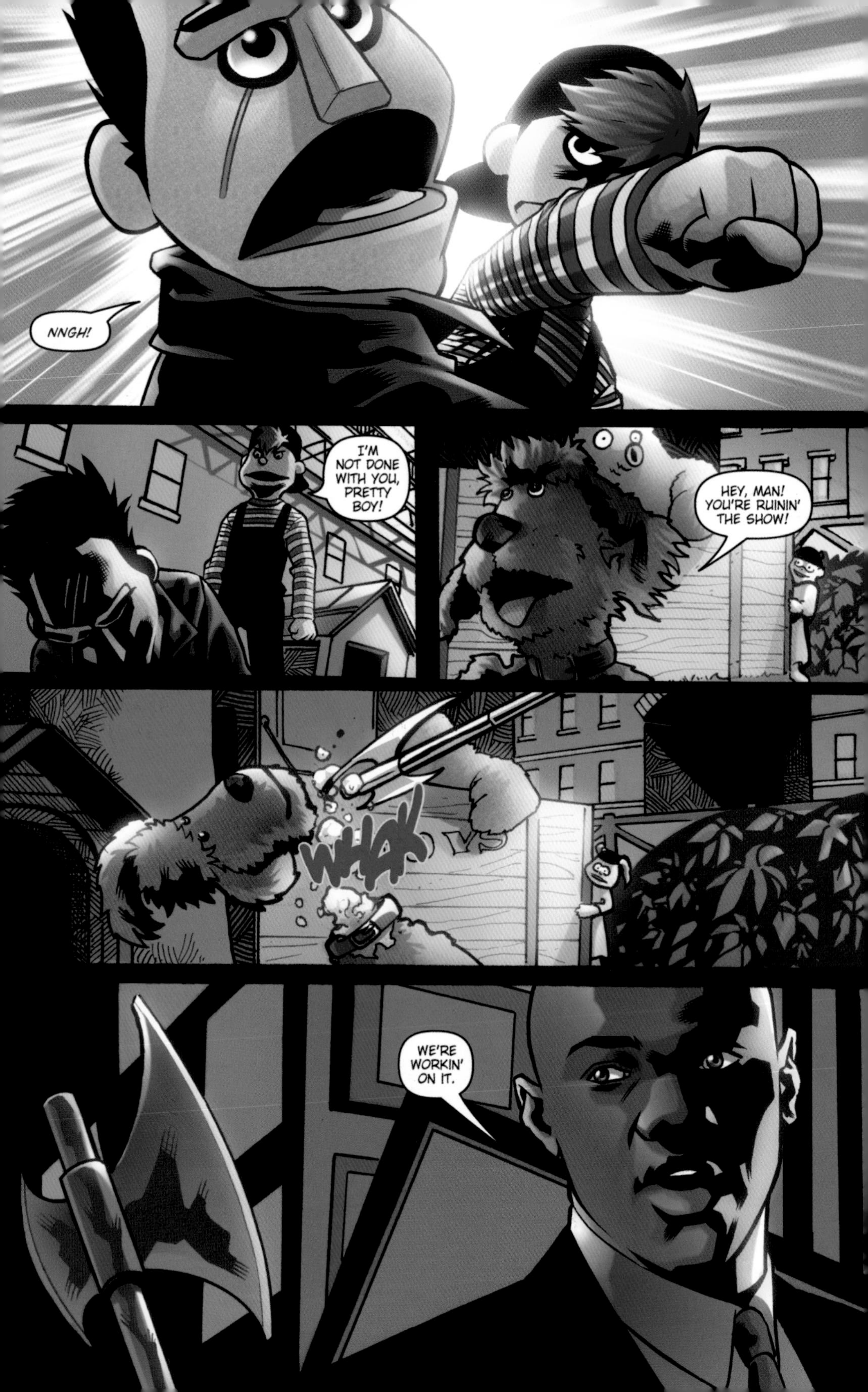
NNGH!
I'M NOT DONE WITH YOU, PRETTY BOY!
HEY, MAN! YOU'RE RUININ' THE SHOW!
WHAK
WE'RE WORKIN' ON IT.

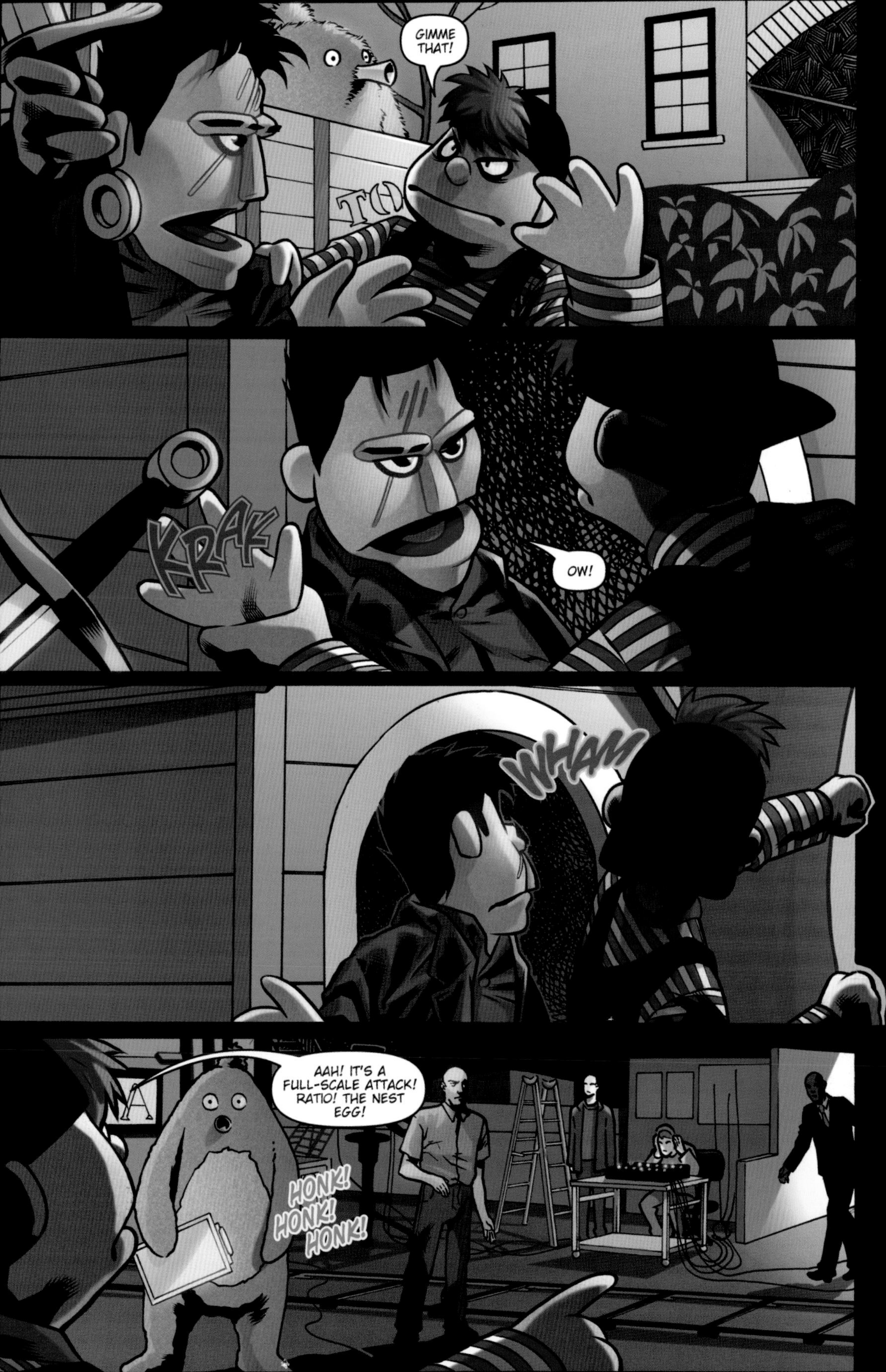
GIMME THAT!
KRAK
OW!
WHAM
AAH! IT'S A FULL-SCALE ATTACK! RATIO! THE NEST EGG!
HONK! HONK! HONK!

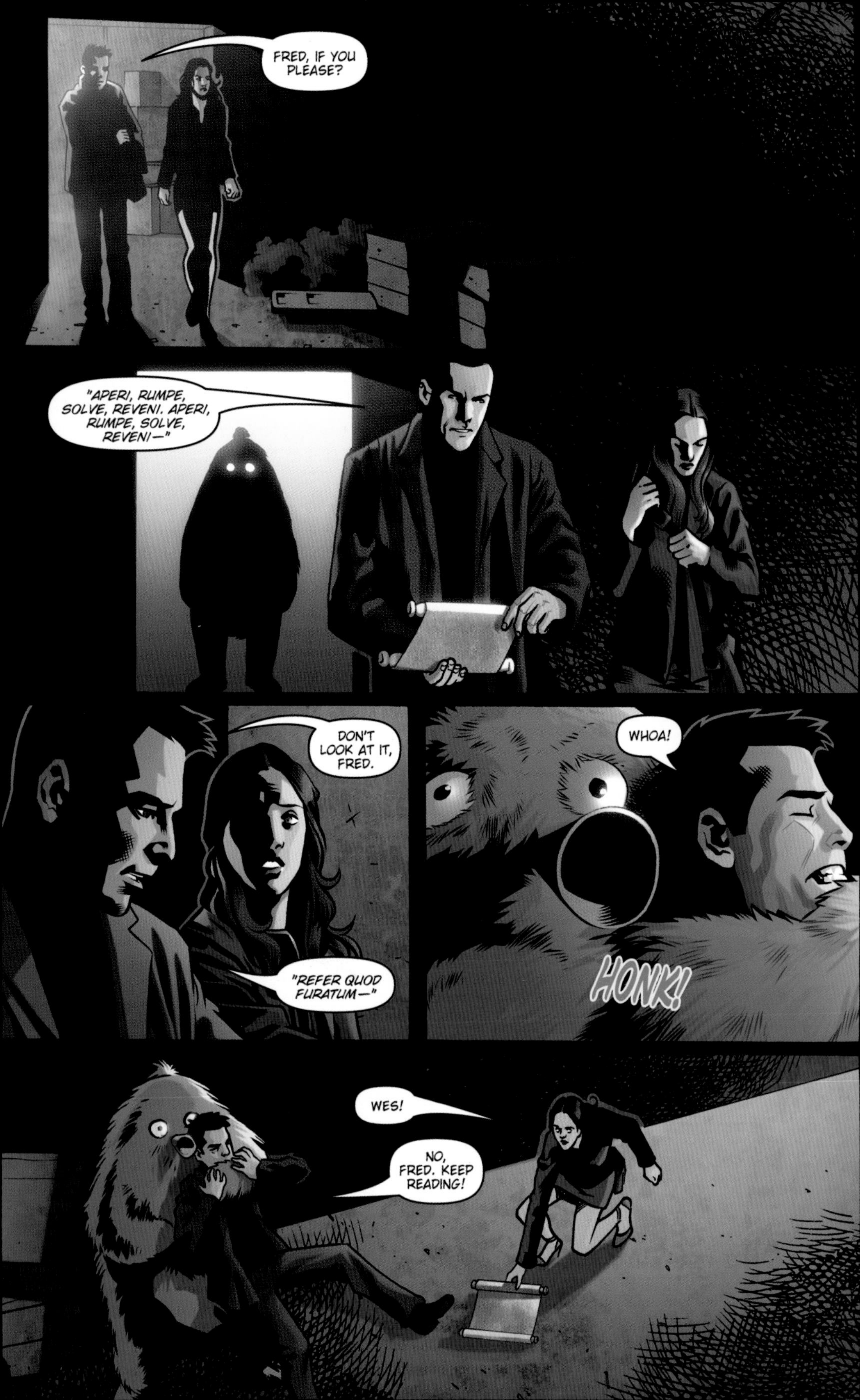
FRED, IF YOU PLEASE?
"APERI, RUMPE, SOLVE, REVENI. APERI, RUMPE, SOLVE, REVENI—"
DON'T LOOK AT IT, FRED.
"REFER QUOD FURATUM—"
WHOA!
HONK!
WES!
NO, FRED. KEEP READING!

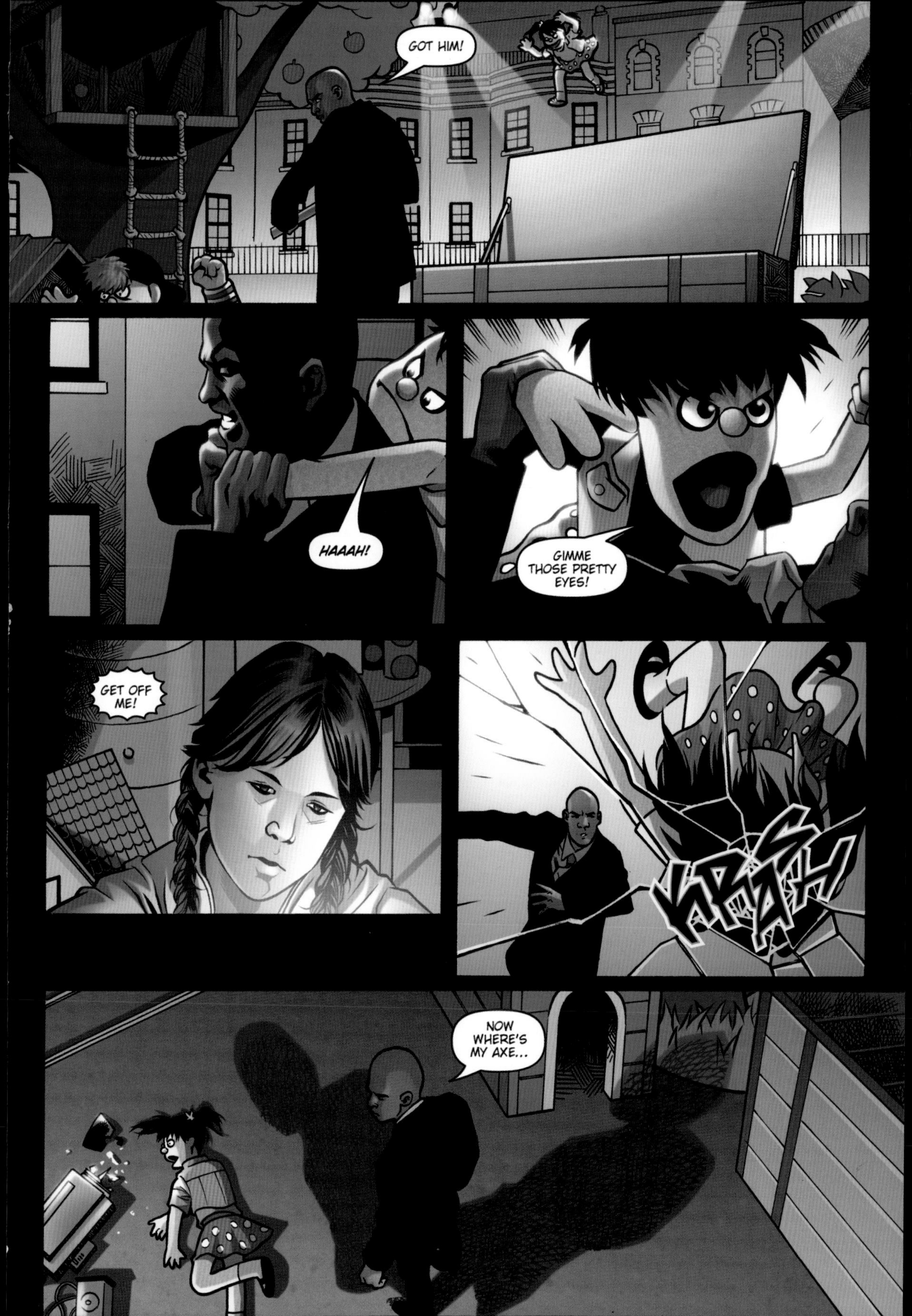
GOT HIM!
HAAAH!
GIMME THOSE PRETTY EYES!
GET OFF ME!
KRASH
NOW WHERE'S MY AXE...

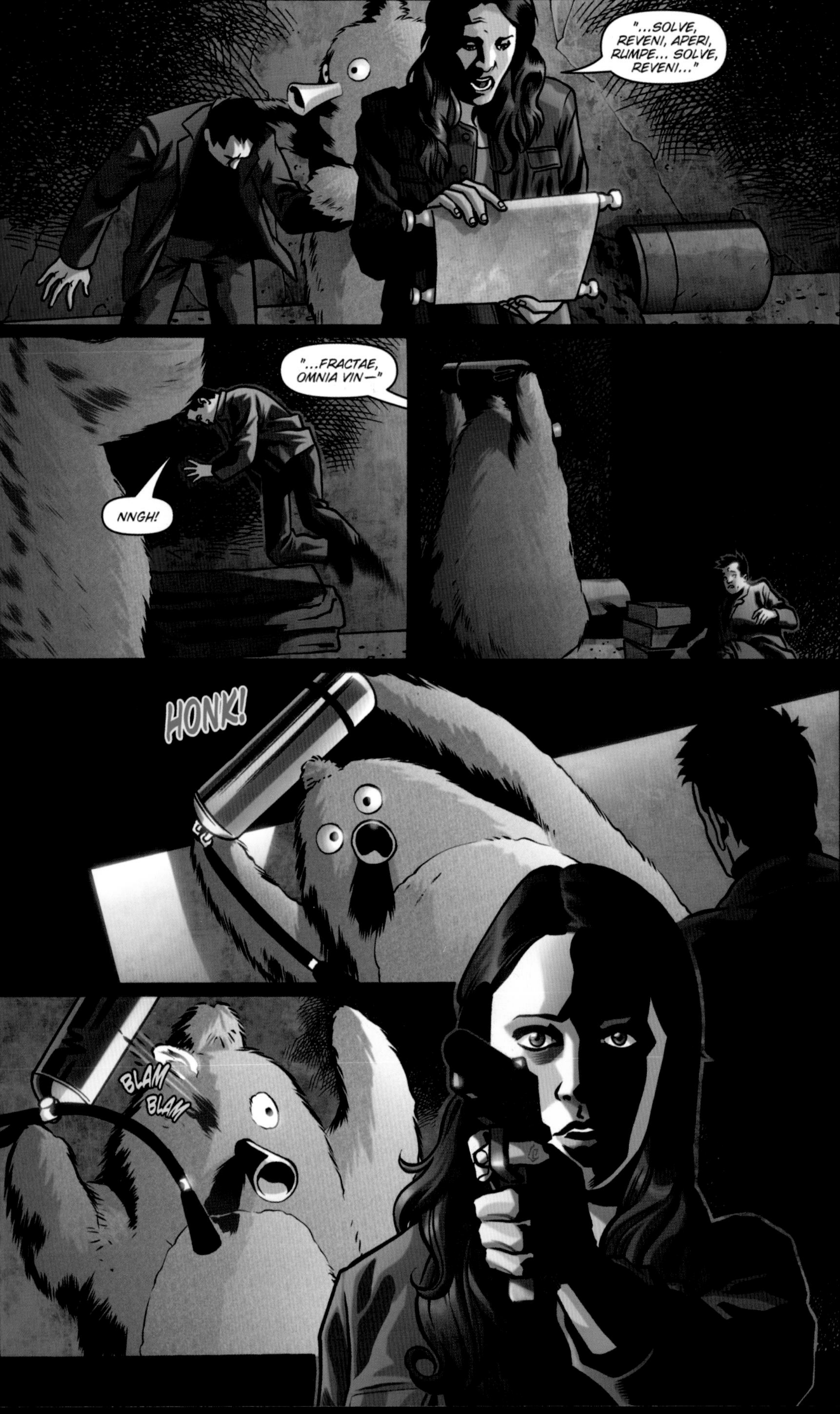
"...SOLVE, REVENI, APERI, RUMPE... SOLVE, REVENI..."
"...FRACTAE, OMNIA VIN—"
NNGH!
HONK!
BLAM
BLAM

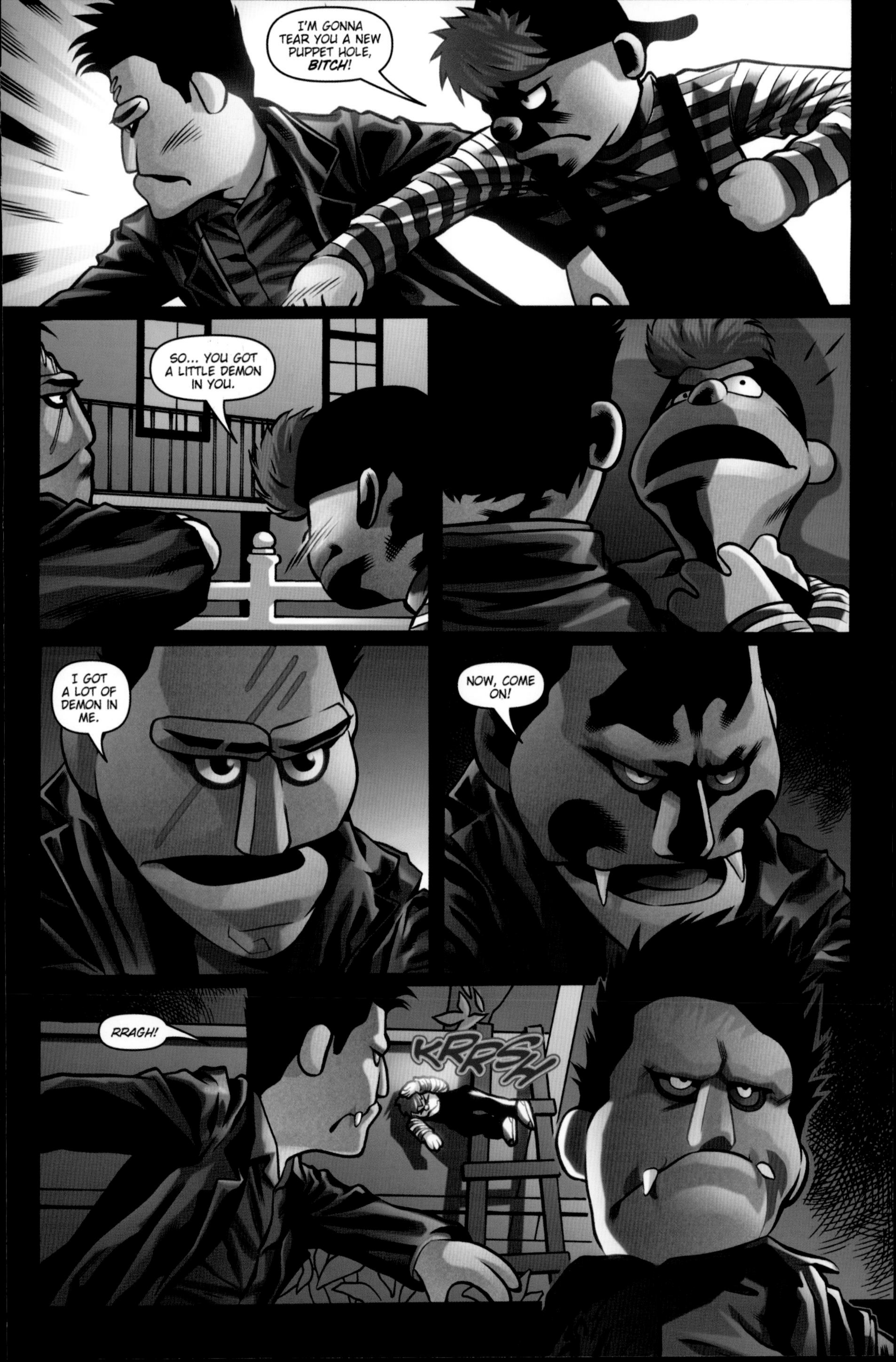
I'M GONNA TEAR YOU A NEW PUPPET HOLE, *BITCH*!
SO... YOU GOT A LITTLE DEMON IN YOU.
I GOT A LOT OF DEMON IN ME.
NOW, COME ON!
RRAGH!
KRRSH

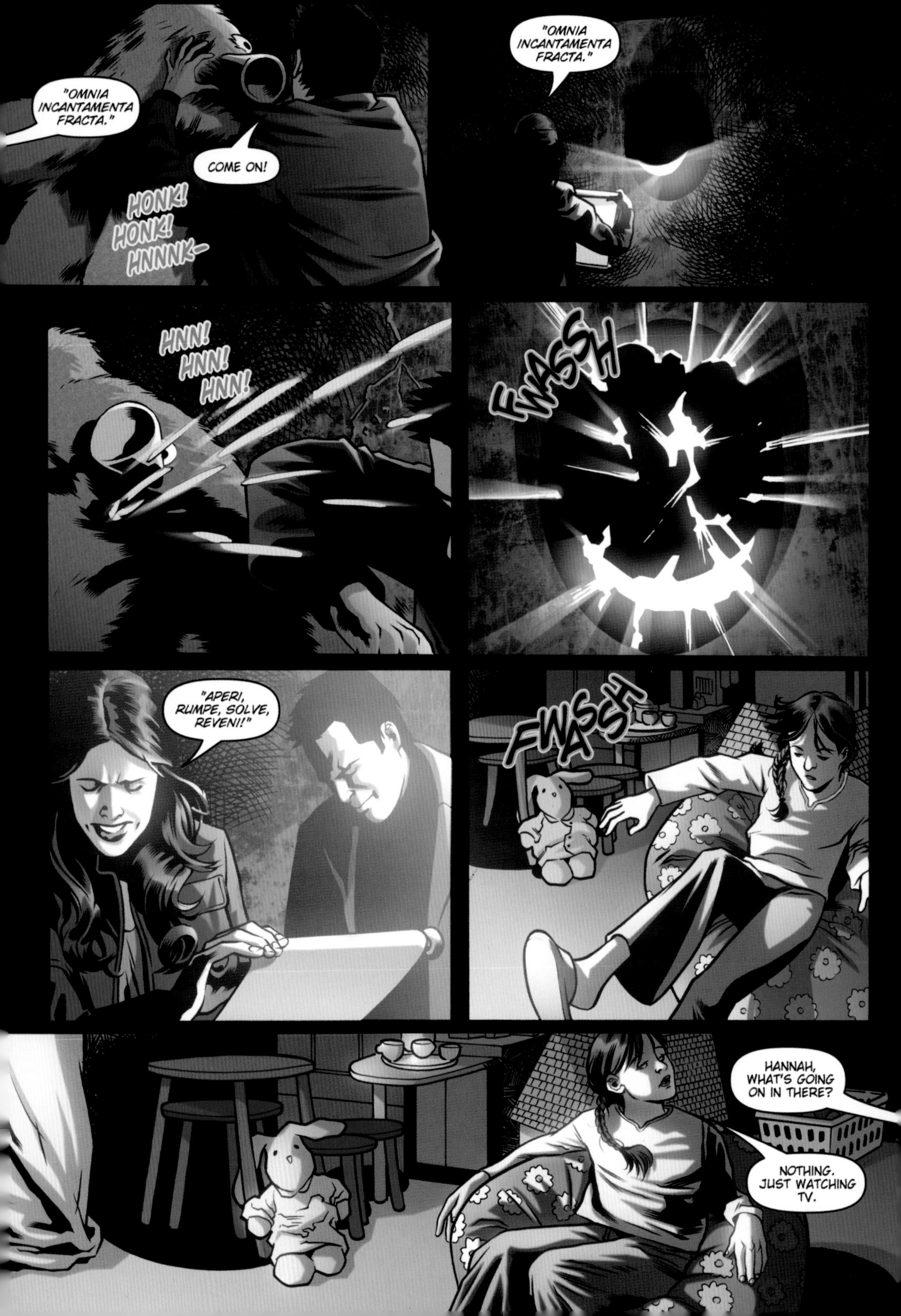
"OMNIA INCANTAMENTA FRACTA."
COME ON!
HONK! HONK! HNNNK-
"OMNIA INCANTAMENTA FRACTA."
HNN! HNN! HNN!
FWASH
"APERI, RUMPE, SOLVE, REVENI!"
FWASH
HANNAH, WHAT'S GOING ON IN THERE?
NOTHING. JUST WATCHING TV.

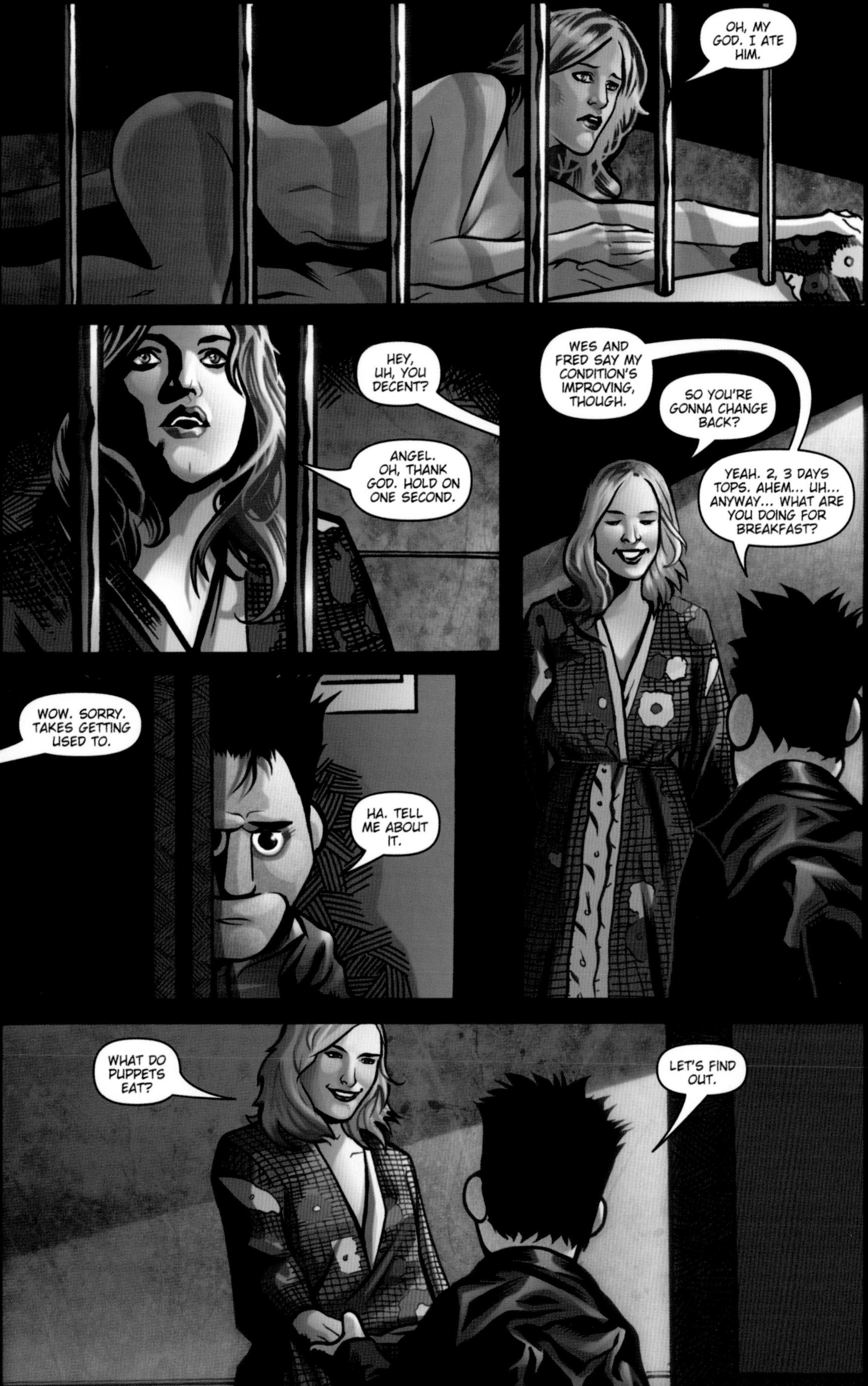
OH, MY GOD. I ATE HIM.
HEY, UH, YOU DECENT?
ANGEL. OH, THANK GOD. HOLD ON ONE SECOND.
WOW. SORRY. TAKES GETTING USED TO.
HA. TELL ME ABOUT IT.
WES AND FRED SAY MY CONDITION'S IMPROVING, THOUGH.
SO YOU'RE GONNA CHANGE BACK?
YEAH. 2, 3 DAYS TOPS. AHEM... UH... ANYWAY... WHAT ARE YOU DOING FOR BREAKFAST?
WHAT DO PUPPETS EAT?
LET'S FIND OUT.

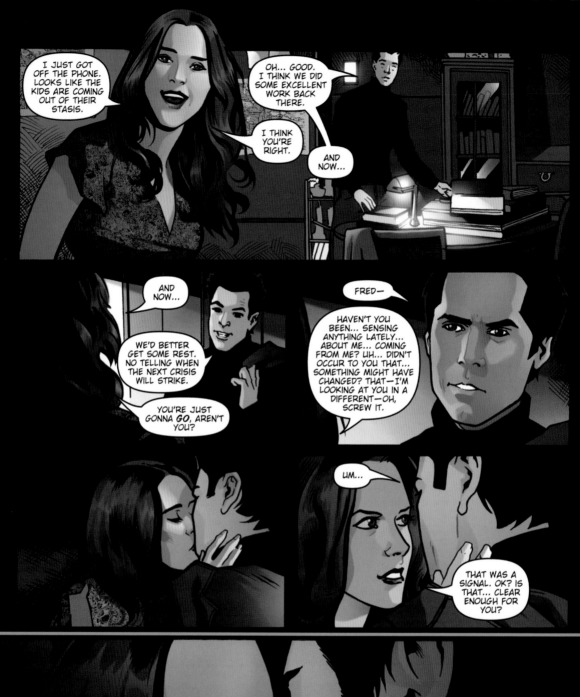

I JUST GOT OFF THE PHONE. LOOKS LIKE THE KIDS ARE COMING OUT OF THEIR STASIS.

OH... GOOD. I THINK WE DID SOME EXCELLENT WORK BACK THERE.

I THINK YOU'RE RIGHT.

AND NOW...

AND NOW...

WE'D BETTER GET SOME REST. NO TELLING WHEN THE NEXT CRISIS WILL STRIKE.

YOU'RE JUST GONNA *GO*, AREN'T YOU?

FRED—

HAVEN'T YOU BEEN... SENSING ANYTHING LATELY... ABOUT ME... COMING FROM ME? UH... DIDN'T OCCUR TO YOU THAT... SOMETHING MIGHT HAVE CHANGED? THAT—I'M LOOKING AT YOU IN A DIFFERENT—OH, SCREW IT.

UM...

THAT WAS A SIGNAL. OK? IS THAT... CLEAR ENOUGH FOR YOU?

NOT EVEN CLOSE.

THE END, FOR A BRIEF, BLISSFUL MOMENT...

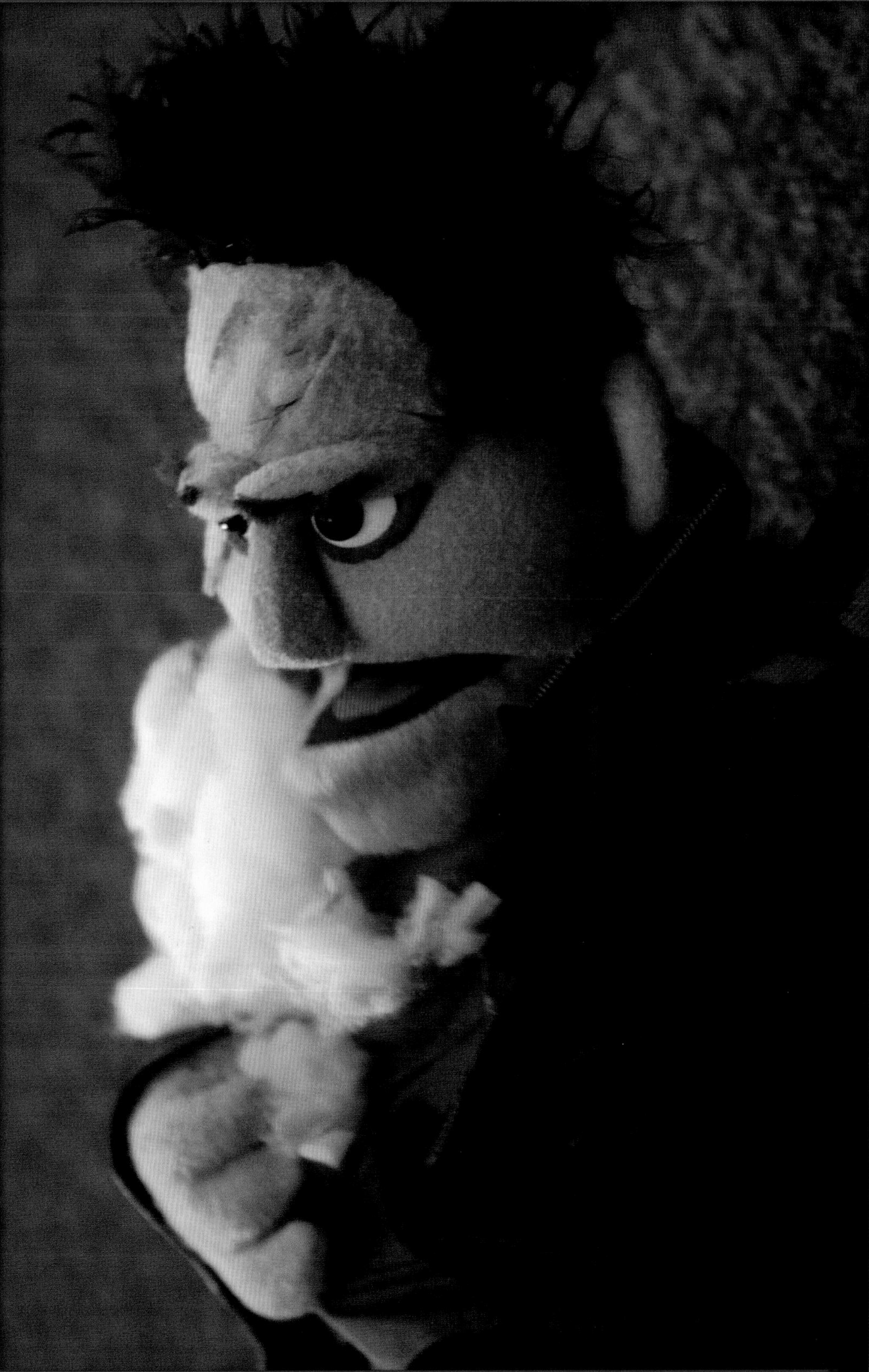

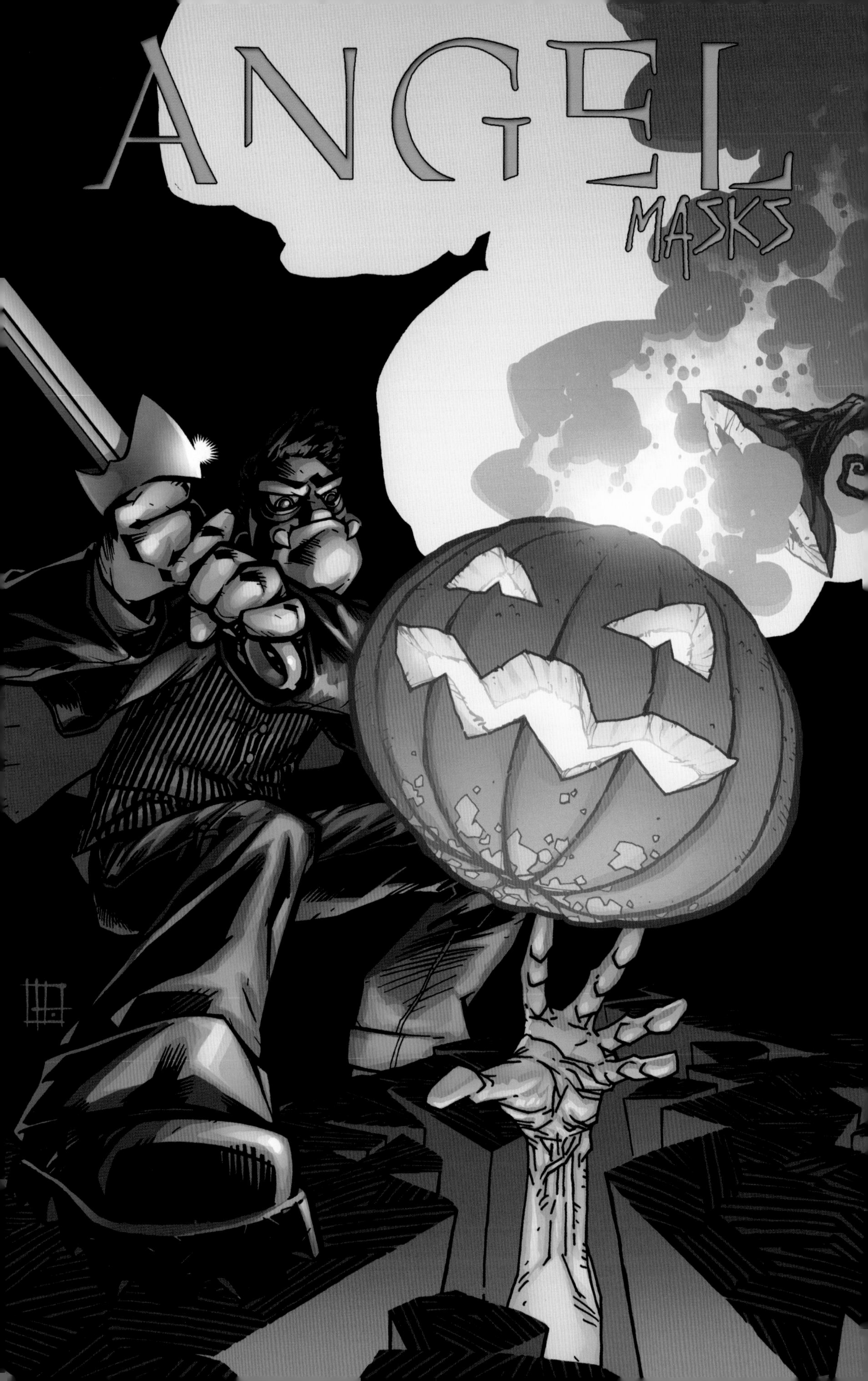
ANGEL™
MASKS

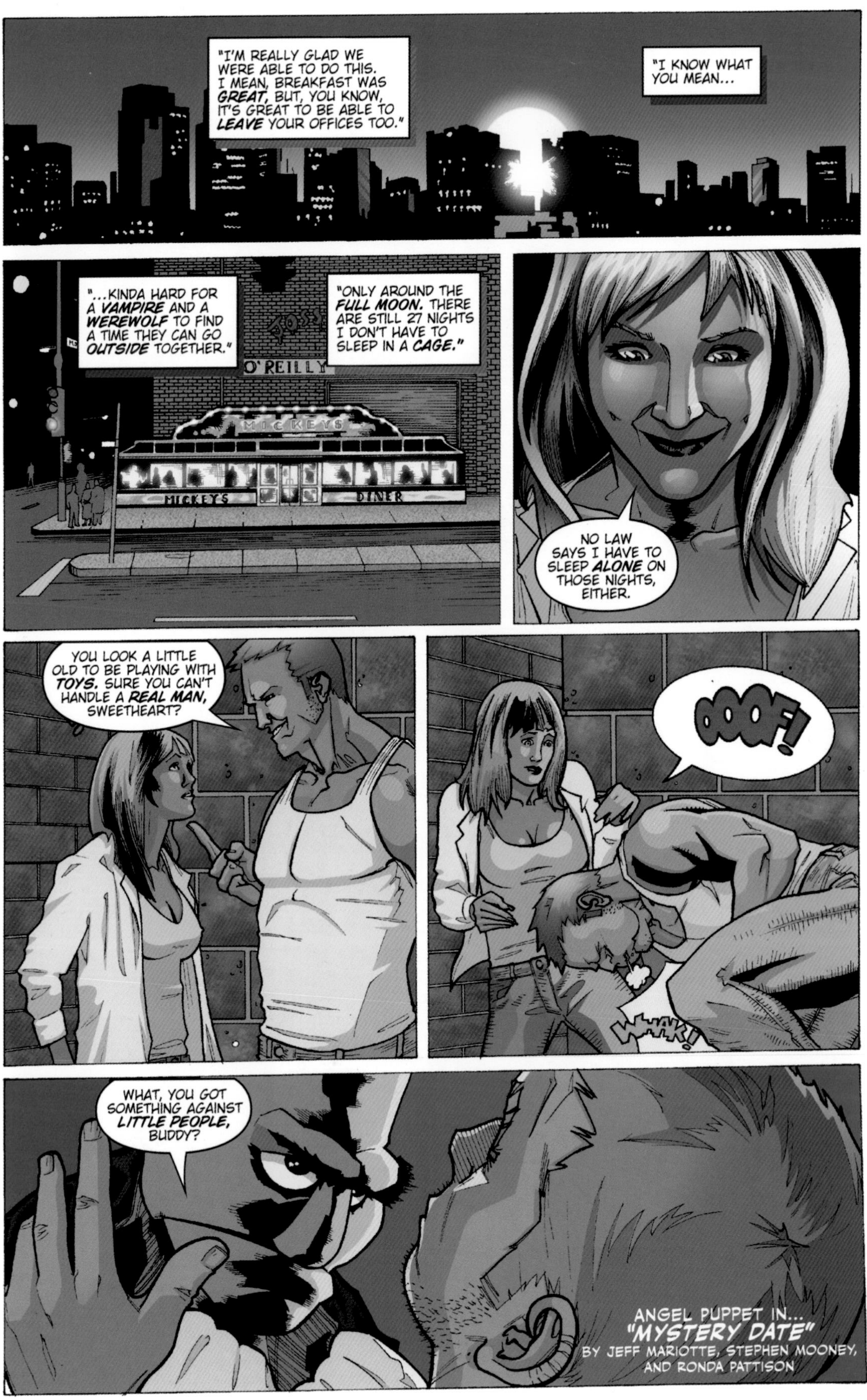
"I'M REALLY GLAD WE WERE ABLE TO DO THIS. I MEAN, BREAKFAST WAS GREAT, BUT, YOU KNOW, IT'S GREAT TO BE ABLE TO LEAVE YOUR OFFICES TOO."
"I KNOW WHAT YOU MEAN...
"...KINDA HARD FOR A VAMPIRE AND A WEREWOLF TO FIND A TIME THEY CAN GO OUTSIDE TOGETHER."
"ONLY AROUND THE FULL MOON. THERE ARE STILL 27 NIGHTS I DON'T HAVE TO SLEEP IN A CAGE."
O'REILLY
MICKEY'S
DINER
NO LAW SAYS I HAVE TO SLEEP ALONE ON THOSE NIGHTS, EITHER.
YOU LOOK A LITTLE OLD TO BE PLAYING WITH TOYS. SURE YOU CAN'T HANDLE A REAL MAN, SWEETHEART?
OOOF!
WHAK!
WHAT, YOU GOT SOMETHING AGAINST LITTLE PEOPLE, BUDDY?
ANGEL PUPPET IN... "MYSTERY DATE"
BY JEFF MARIOTTE, STEPHEN MOONEY, AND RONDA PATTISON

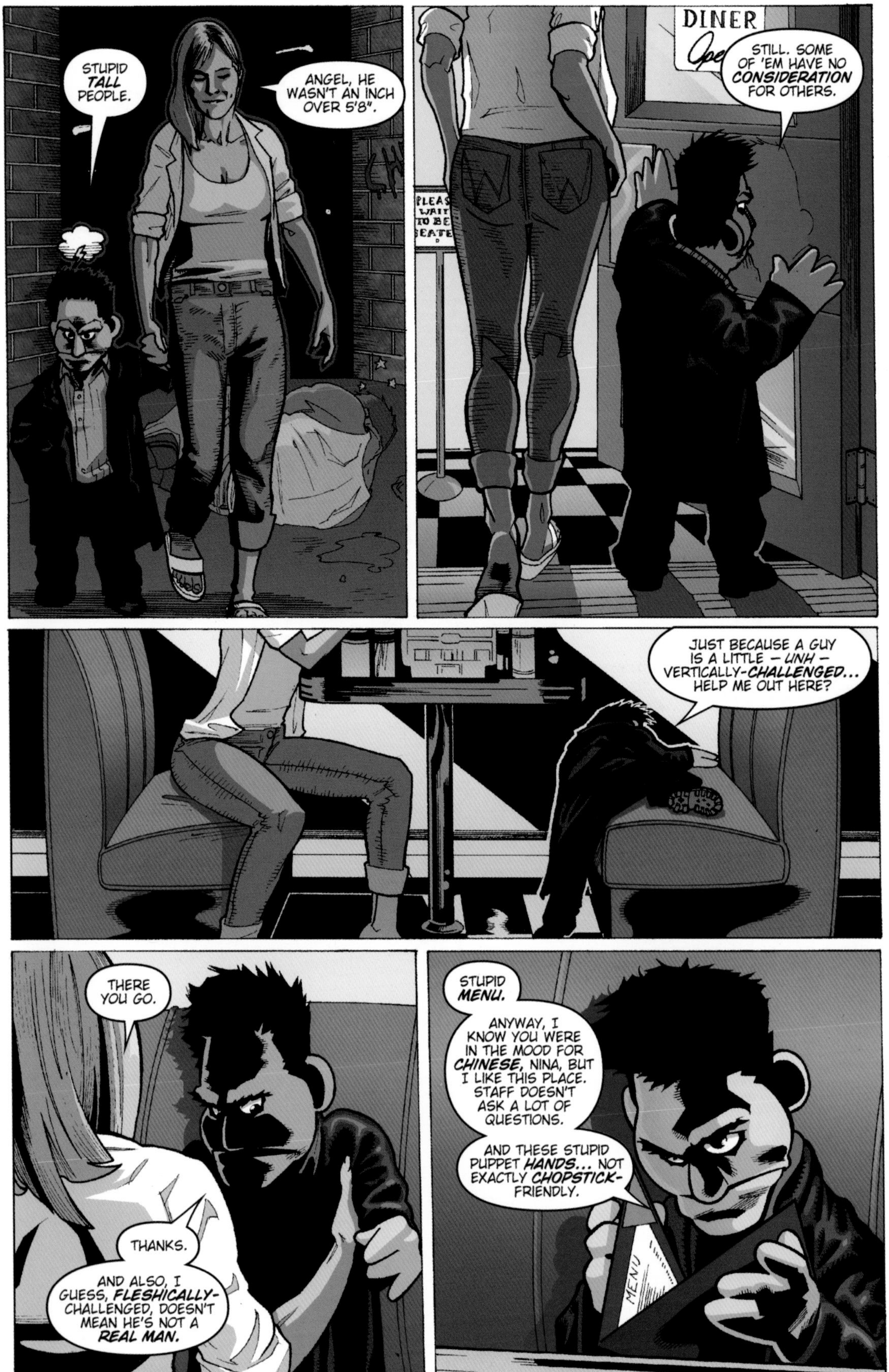
STUPID TALL PEOPLE.
ANGEL, HE WASN'T AN INCH OVER 5'8".
DINER
PLEASE WAIT TO BE SEATED
STILL. SOME OF 'EM HAVE NO CONSIDERATION FOR OTHERS.
JUST BECAUSE A GUY IS A LITTLE — UNH — VERTICALLY-CHALLENGED... HELP ME OUT HERE?
THERE YOU GO.
THANKS.
AND ALSO, I GUESS, FLESHICALLY-CHALLENGED, DOESN'T MEAN HE'S NOT A REAL MAN.
STUPID MENU.
ANYWAY, I KNOW YOU WERE IN THE MOOD FOR CHINESE, NINA, BUT I LIKE THIS PLACE. STAFF DOESN'T ASK A LOT OF QUESTIONS.
AND THESE STUPID PUPPET HANDS... NOT EXACTLY CHOPSTICK-FRIENDLY.
MENU

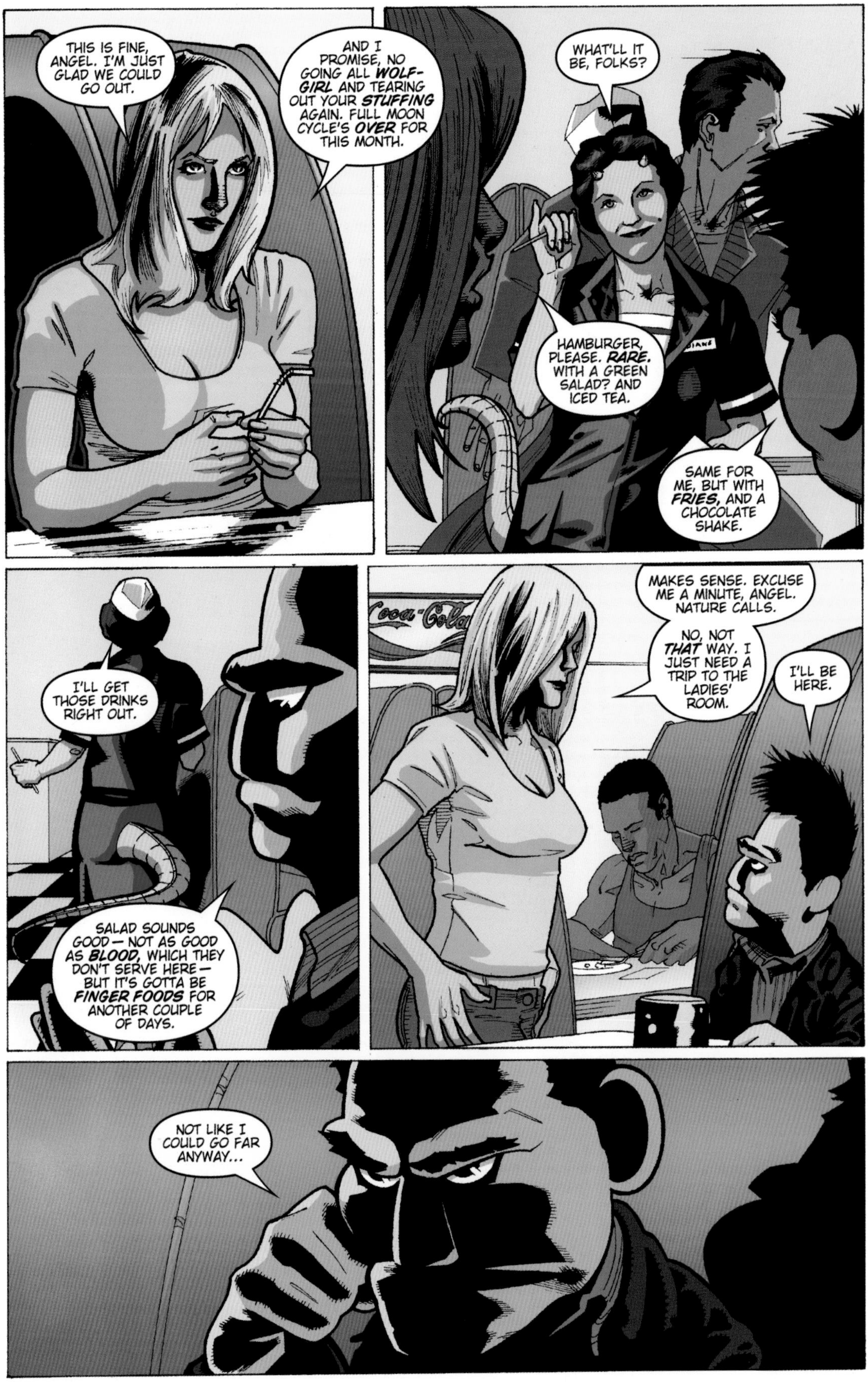
THIS IS FINE, ANGEL. I'M JUST GLAD WE COULD GO OUT.
AND I PROMISE, NO GOING ALL WOLF-GIRL AND TEARING OUT YOUR STUFFING AGAIN. FULL MOON CYCLE'S OVER FOR THIS MONTH.
WHAT'LL IT BE, FOLKS?
HAMBURGER, PLEASE. RARE. WITH A GREEN SALAD? AND ICED TEA.
SAME FOR ME, BUT WITH FRIES, AND A CHOCOLATE SHAKE.
I'LL GET THOSE DRINKS RIGHT OUT.
SALAD SOUNDS GOOD—NOT AS GOOD AS BLOOD, WHICH THEY DON'T SERVE HERE—BUT IT'S GOTTA BE FINGER FOODS FOR ANOTHER COUPLE OF DAYS.
MAKES SENSE. EXCUSE ME A MINUTE, ANGEL. NATURE CALLS.
NO, NOT THAT WAY. I JUST NEED A TRIP TO THE LADIES' ROOM.
I'LL BE HERE.
NOT LIKE I COULD GO FAR ANYWAY...

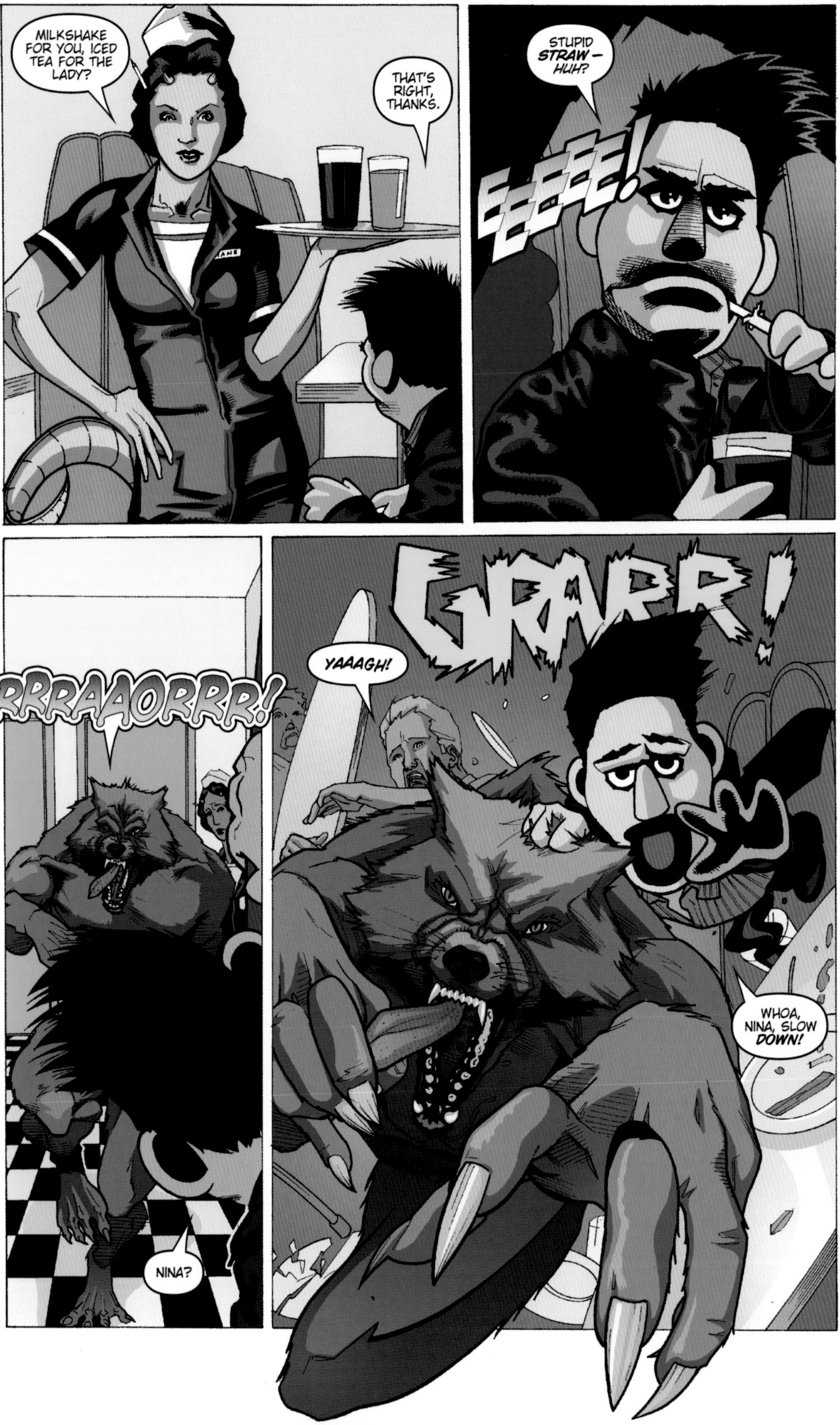
MILKSHAKE FOR YOU, ICED TEA FOR THE LADY?
THAT'S RIGHT, THANKS.
STUPID STRAW— HUH?
EEEEE!
RRRAAORRRR!
NINA?
GRARR!
YAAAGH!
WHOA, NINA, SLOW DOWN!

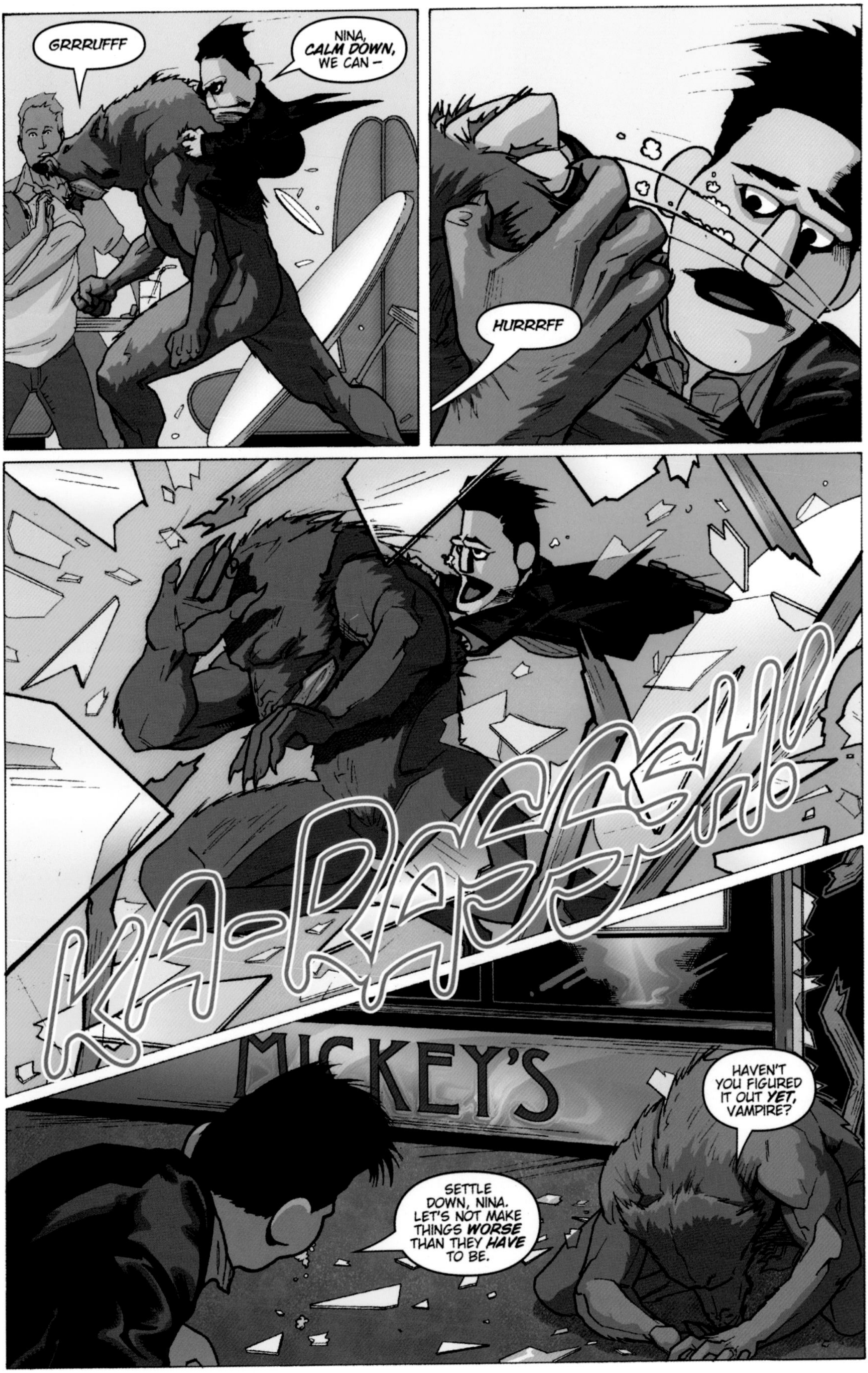
GRRRUFFF
NINA, CALM DOWN, WE CAN –
HURRRFF
KA-RASSSH!
MICKEY'S
HAVEN'T YOU FIGURED IT OUT YET, VAMPIRE?
SETTLE DOWN, NINA. LET'S NOT MAKE THINGS WORSE THAN THEY HAVE TO BE.

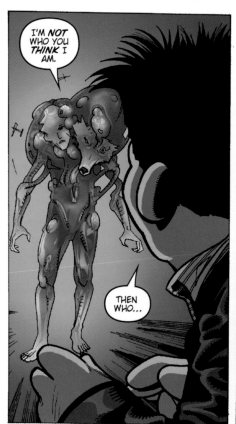

I'M *NOT* WHO YOU *THINK* I AM.

THEN WHO...

THAT BETTER?

NO.

YOU'RE NOT *ME!*

THOK

I MIGHT AS WELL BE YOU...

...ONLY *BETTER.*

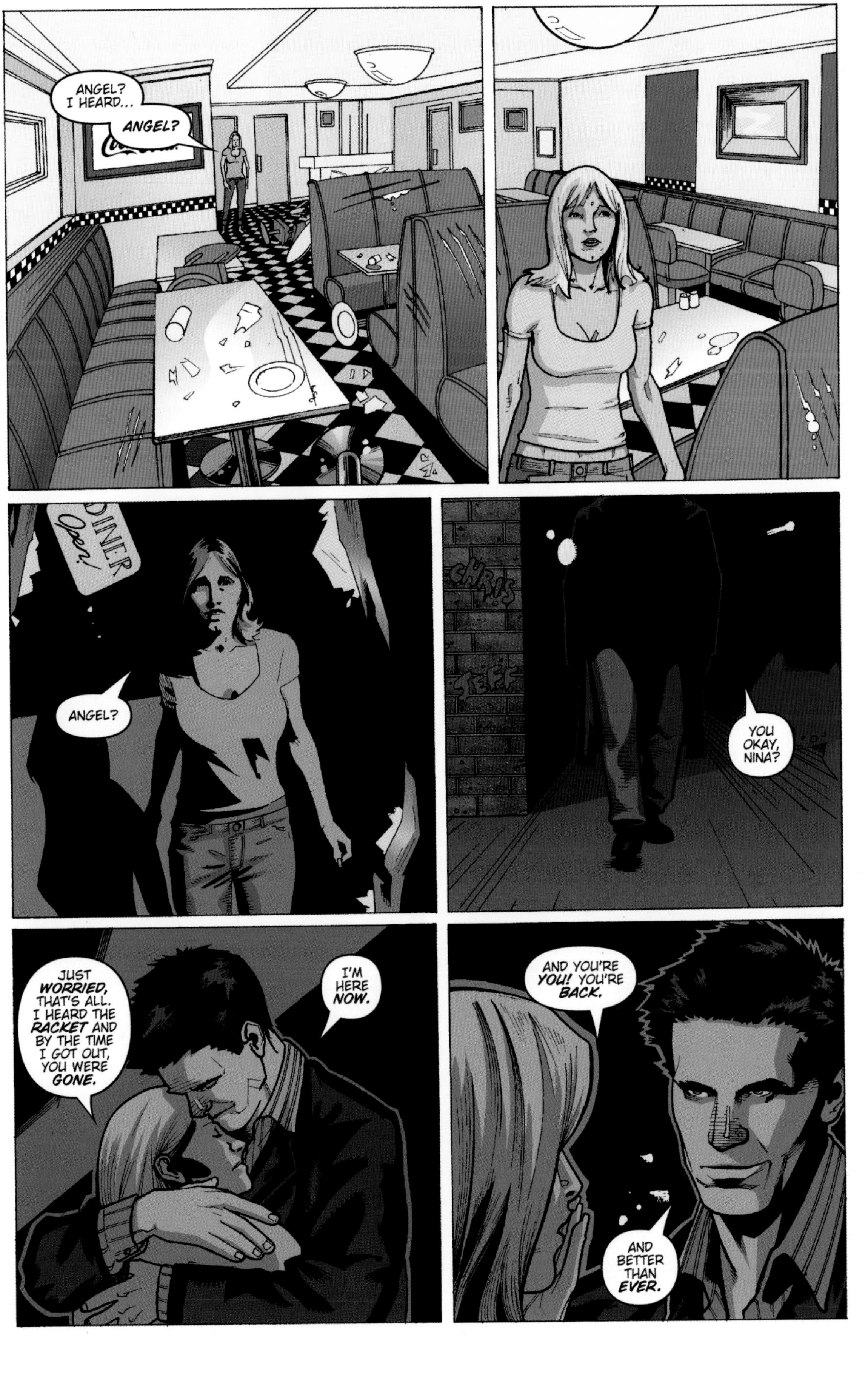
ANGEL? I HEARD...
ANGEL?
ANGEL?
YOU OKAY, NINA?
JUST WORRIED, THAT'S ALL. I HEARD THE RACKET AND BY THE TIME I GOT OUT, YOU WERE GONE.
I'M HERE NOW.
AND YOU'RE YOU! YOU'RE BACK.
AND BETTER THAN EVER.

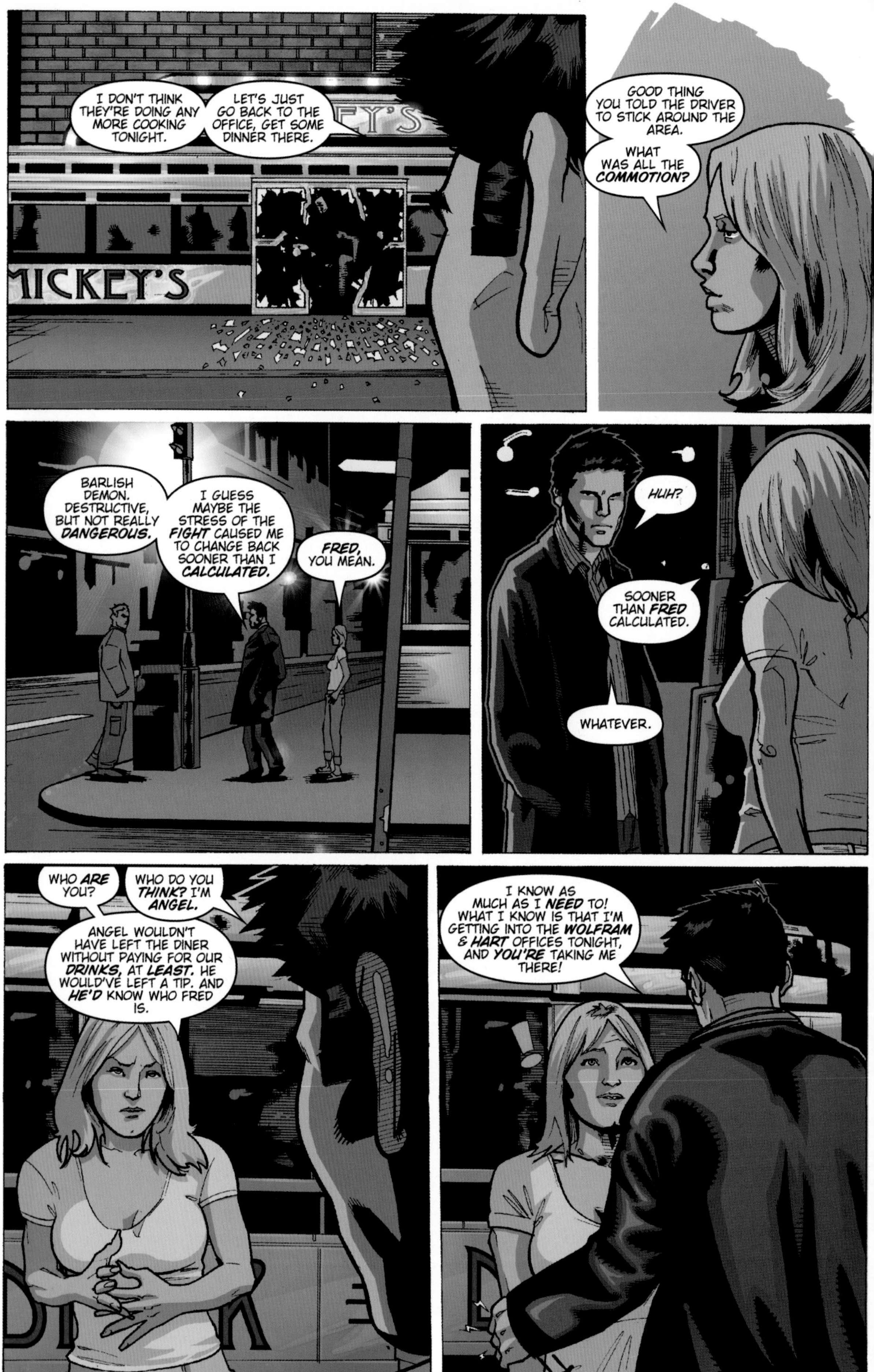
MICKEY'S
I DON'T THINK THEY'RE DOING ANY MORE COOKING TONIGHT.
LET'S JUST GO BACK TO THE OFFICE, GET SOME DINNER THERE.
GOOD THING YOU TOLD THE DRIVER TO STICK AROUND THE AREA.
WHAT WAS ALL THE **COMMOTION?**
BARLISH DEMON. DESTRUCTIVE, BUT NOT REALLY **DANGEROUS.**
I GUESS MAYBE THE STRESS OF THE **FIGHT** CAUSED ME TO CHANGE BACK SOONER THAN I **CALCULATED.**
FRED, YOU MEAN.
HUH?
SOONER THAN **FRED** CALCULATED.
WHATEVER.
WHO **ARE** YOU?
WHO DO YOU **THINK?** I'M **ANGEL.**
ANGEL WOULDN'T HAVE LEFT THE DINER WITHOUT PAYING FOR OUR **DRINKS,** AT **LEAST.** HE WOULD'VE LEFT A TIP. AND **HE'D** KNOW WHO FRED IS.
I KNOW AS MUCH AS I **NEED** TO! WHAT I KNOW IS THAT I'M GETTING INTO THE **WOLFRAM & HART** OFFICES TONIGHT, AND **YOU'RE** TAKING ME THERE!

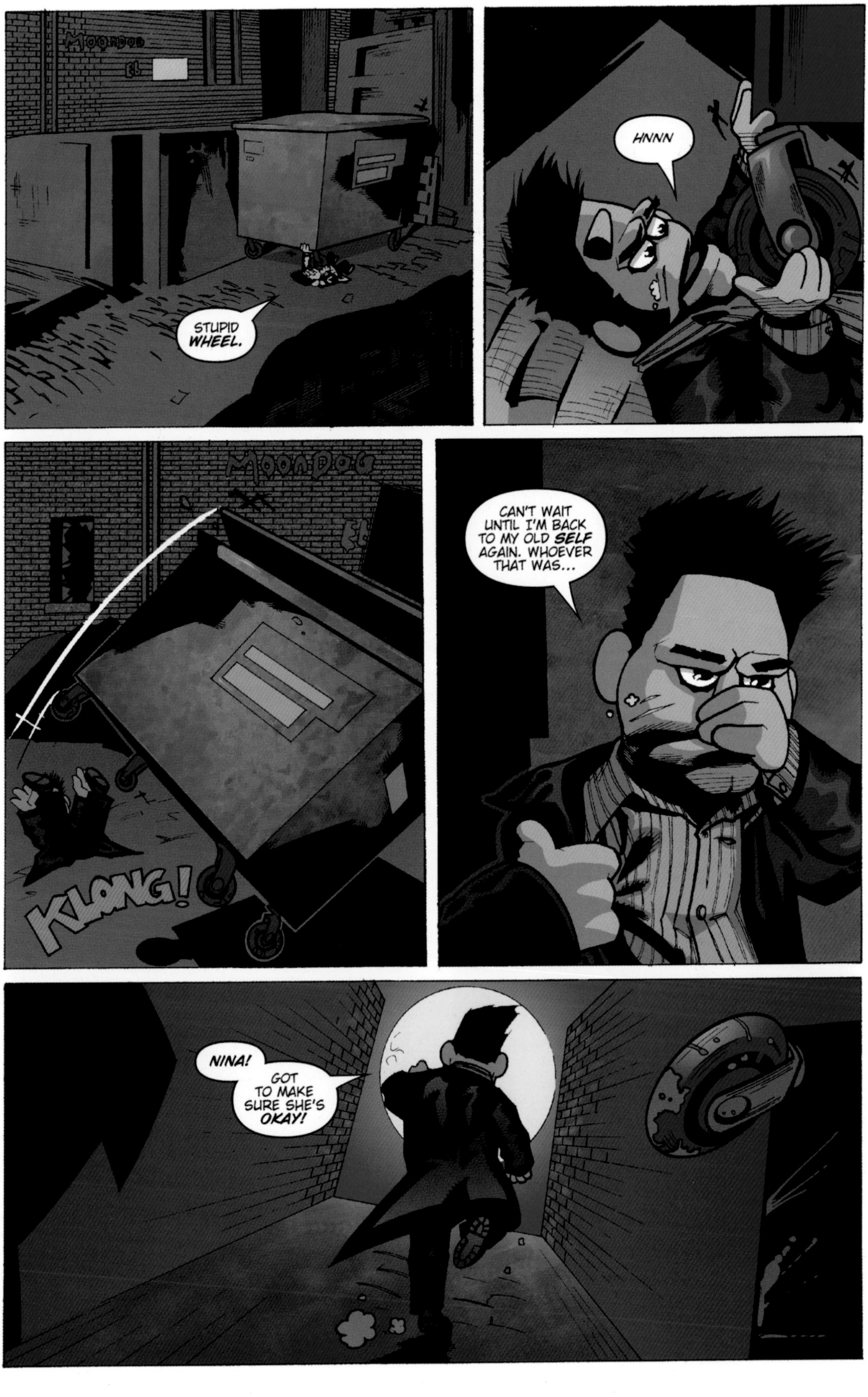
STUPID WHEEL.
HNNN
KLONG!
CAN'T WAIT UNTIL I'M BACK TO MY OLD SELF AGAIN. WHOEVER THAT WAS...
NINA!
GOT TO MAKE SURE SHE'S OKAY!

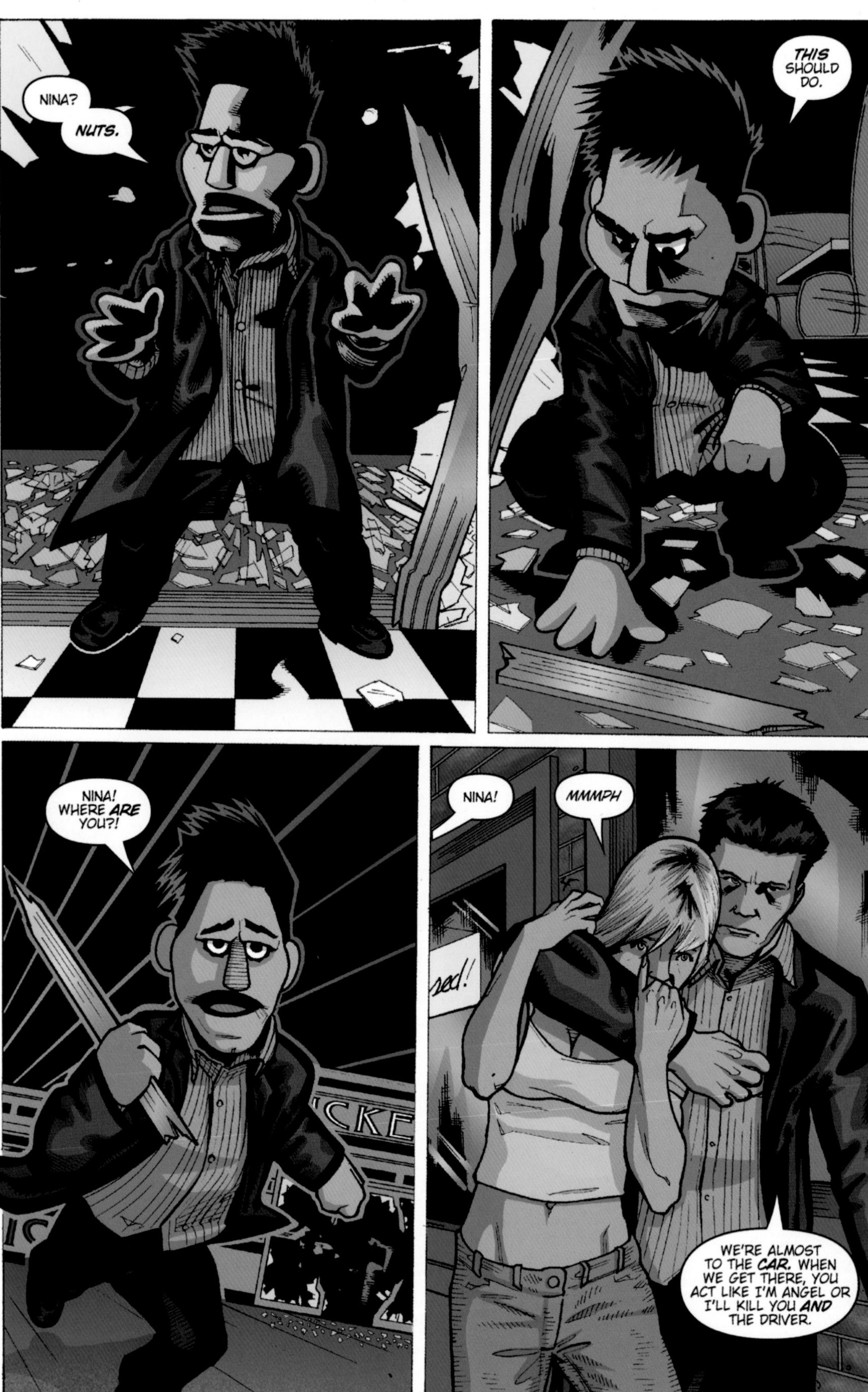
NINA?
NUTS.
THIS SHOULD DO.
NINA! WHERE ARE YOU?!
NINA!
MMMPH
WE'RE ALMOST TO THE CAR. WHEN WE GET THERE, YOU ACT LIKE I'M ANGEL OR I'LL KILL YOU AND THE DRIVER.

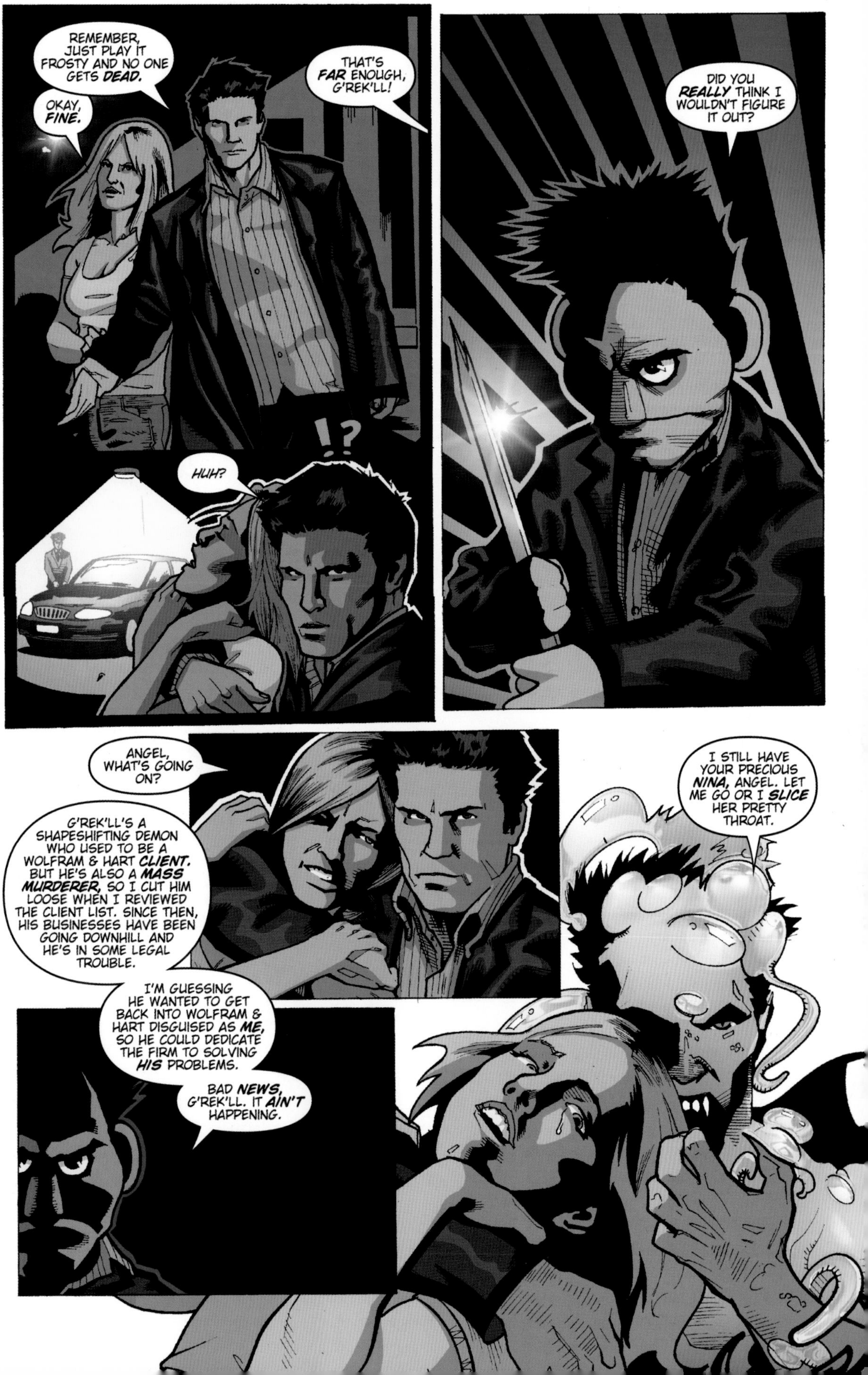
REMEMBER, JUST PLAY IT FROSTY AND NO ONE GETS **DEAD.**
OKAY, **FINE.**
THAT'S **FAR** ENOUGH, G'REK'LL!
DID YOU **REALLY** THINK I WOULDN'T FIGURE IT OUT?
!?
HUH?
ANGEL, WHAT'S GOING ON?
G'REK'LL'S A SHAPESHIFTING DEMON WHO USED TO BE A WOLFRAM & HART **CLIENT.** BUT HE'S ALSO A **MASS MURDERER,** SO I CUT HIM LOOSE WHEN I REVIEWED THE CLIENT LIST. SINCE THEN, HIS BUSINESSES HAVE BEEN GOING DOWNHILL AND HE'S IN SOME LEGAL TROUBLE.
I STILL HAVE YOUR PRECIOUS **NINA,** ANGEL. LET ME GO OR I **SLICE** HER PRETTY THROAT.
I'M GUESSING HE WANTED TO GET BACK INTO WOLFRAM & HART DISGUISED AS **ME,** SO HE COULD DEDICATE THE FIRM TO SOLVING **HIS** PROBLEMS.
BAD **NEWS,** G'REK'LL. IT **AIN'T** HAPPENING.

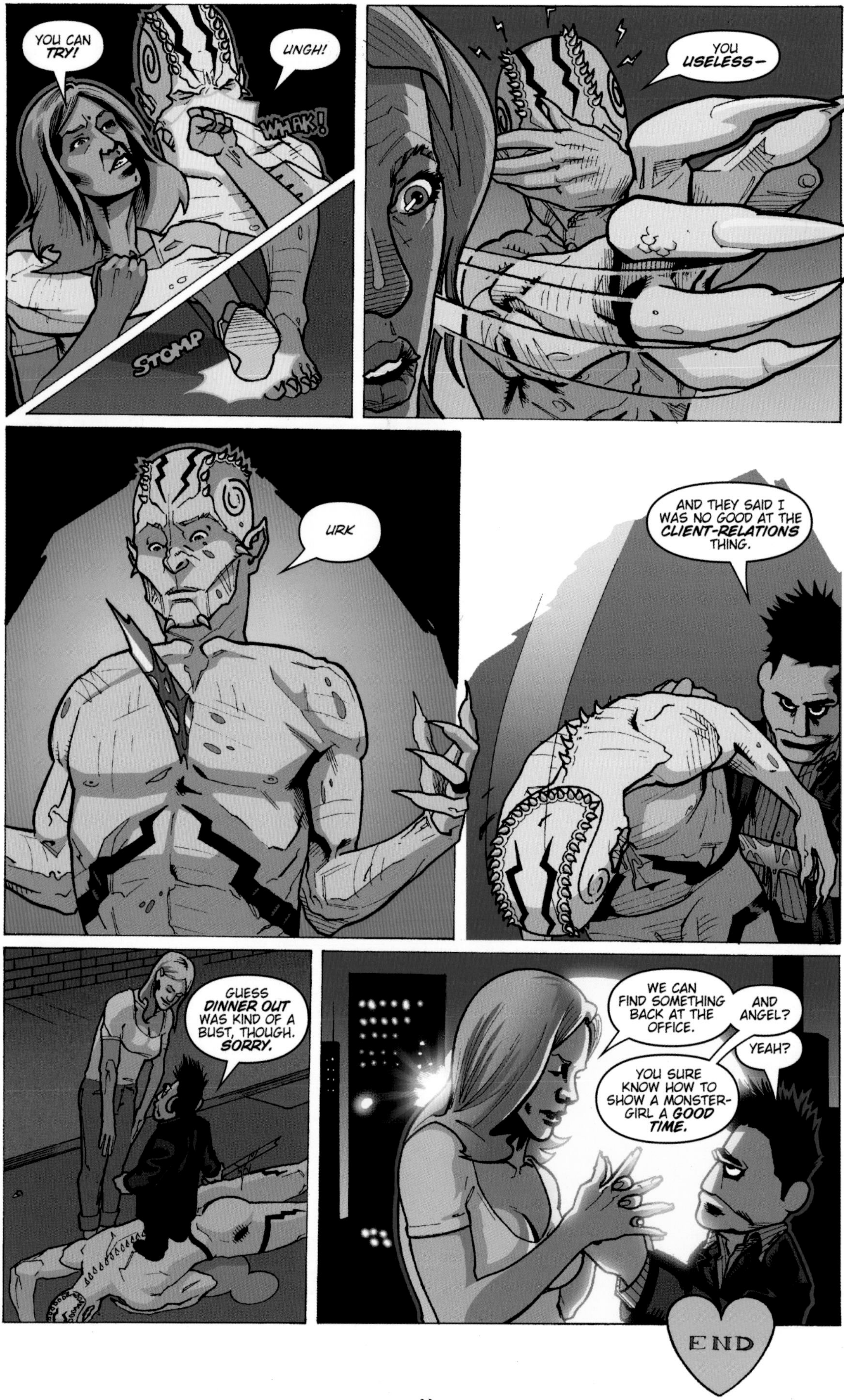
YOU CAN TRY!
UNGH!
WHAK!
STOMP
YOU USELESS–
URK
AND THEY SAID I WAS NO GOOD AT THE CLIENT-RELATIONS THING.
GUESS DINNER OUT WAS KIND OF A BUST, THOUGH. SORRY.
WE CAN FIND SOMETHING BACK AT THE OFFICE.
AND ANGEL?
YEAH?
YOU SURE KNOW HOW TO SHOW A MONSTER-GIRL A GOOD TIME.
END

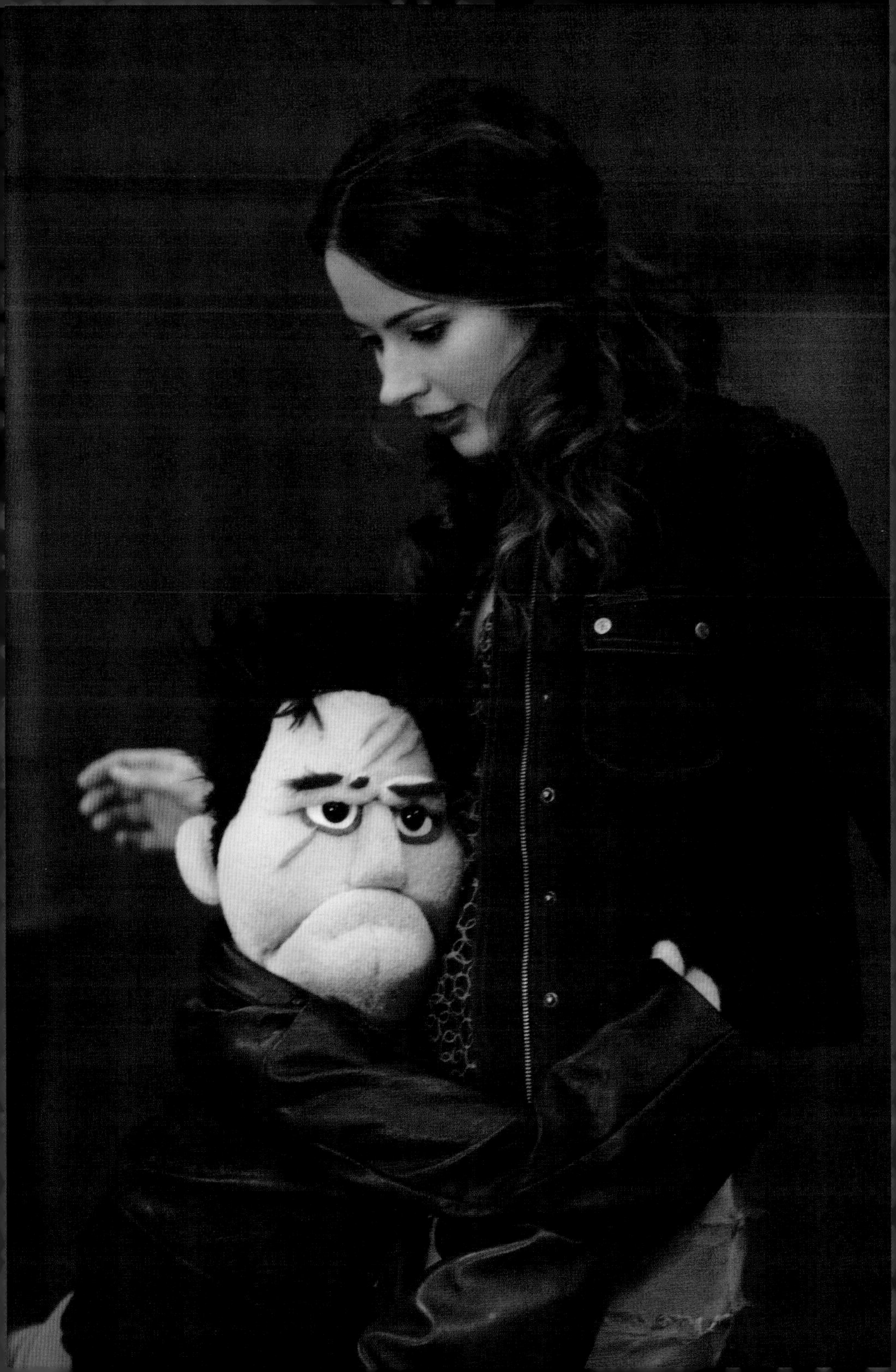

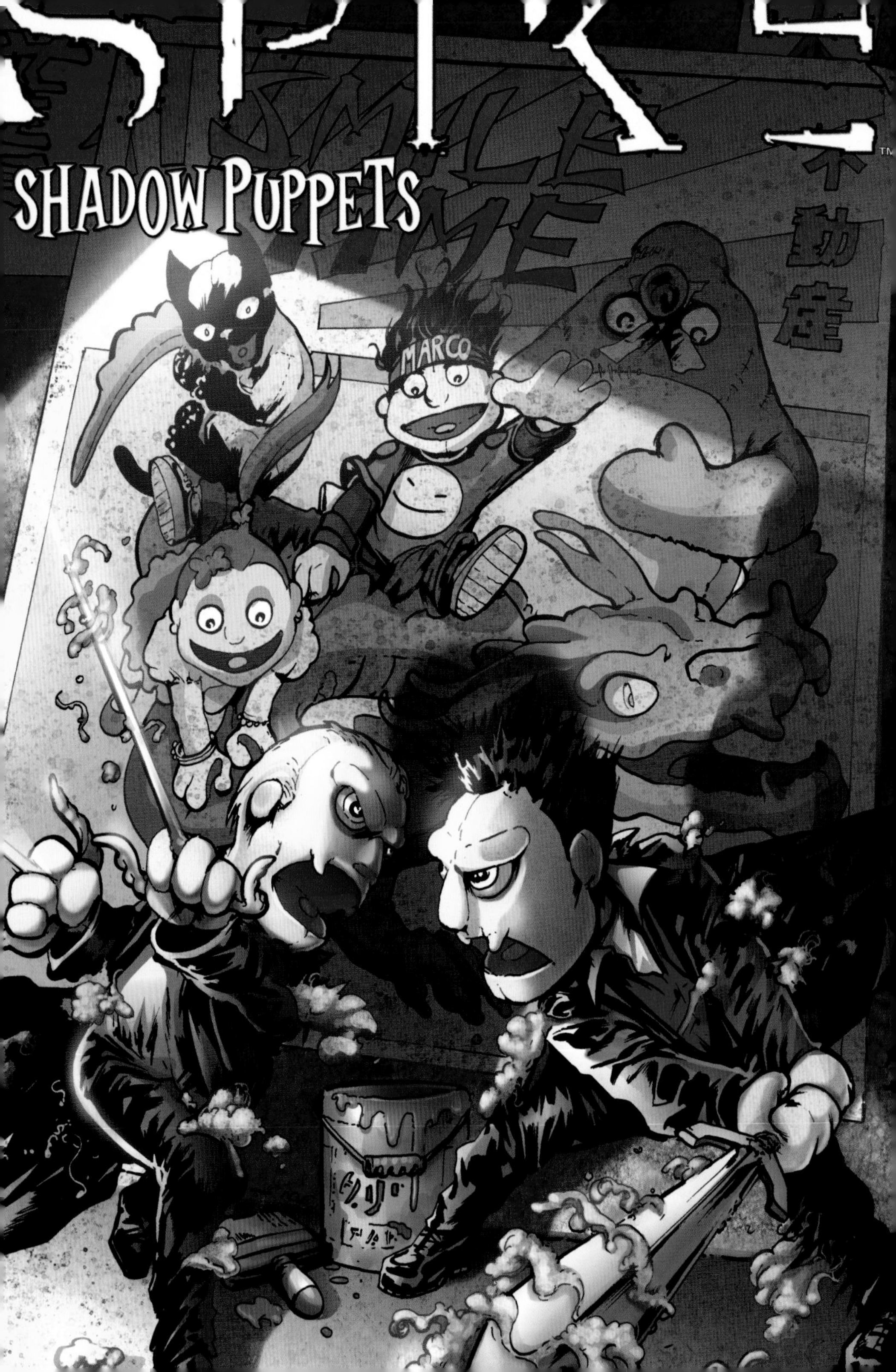
SHADOW PUPPETS
MARCO

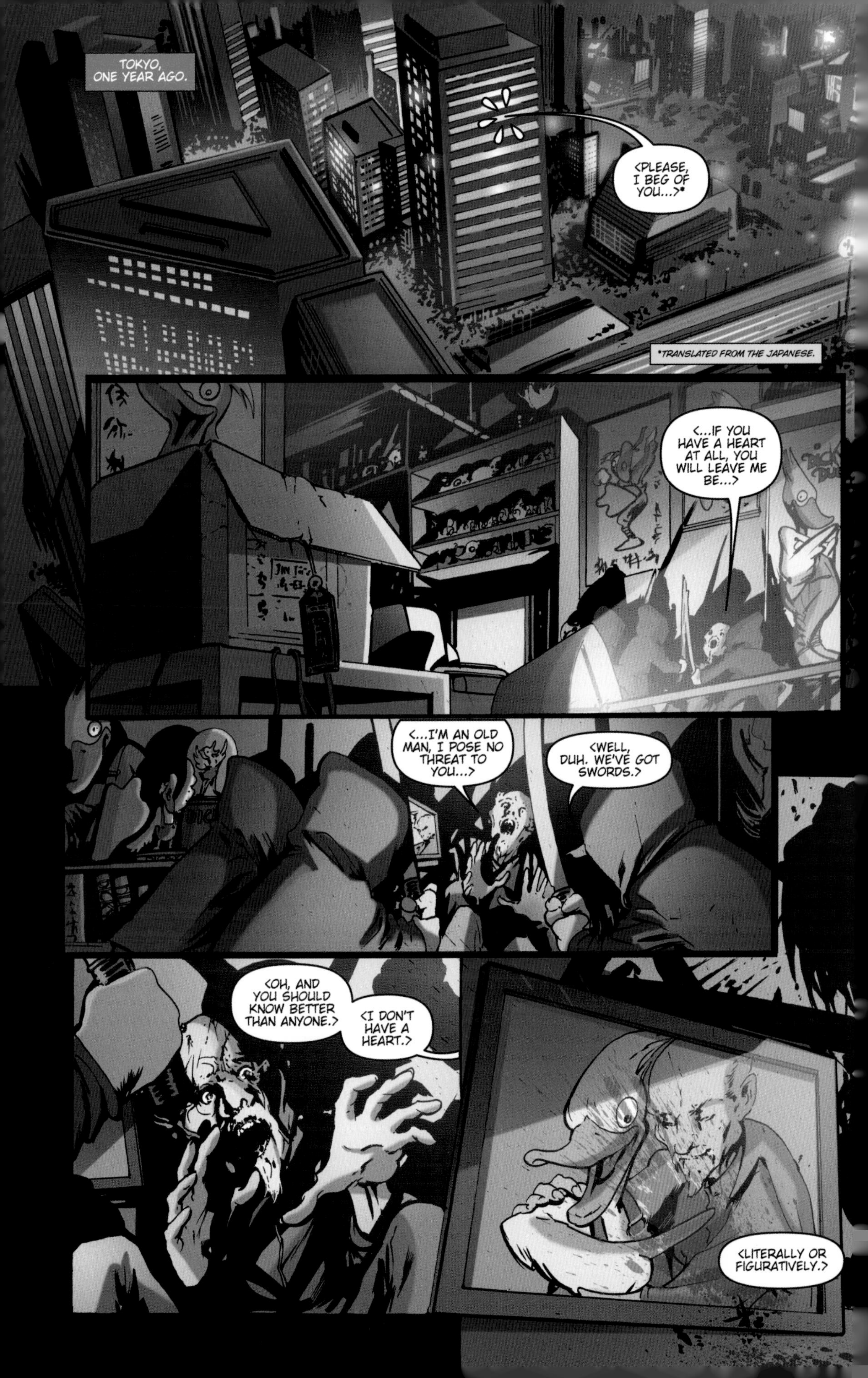
TOKYO, ONE YEAR AGO.
<PLEASE, I BEG OF YOU...>*
*TRANSLATED FROM THE JAPANESE.
<...IF YOU HAVE A HEART AT ALL, YOU WILL LEAVE ME BE...>
<...I'M AN OLD MAN, I POSE NO THREAT TO YOU...>
<WELL, DUH. WE'VE GOT SWORDS.>
<OH, AND YOU SHOULD KNOW BETTER THAN ANYONE.>
<I DON'T HAVE A HEART.>
<LITERALLY OR FIGURATIVELY.>

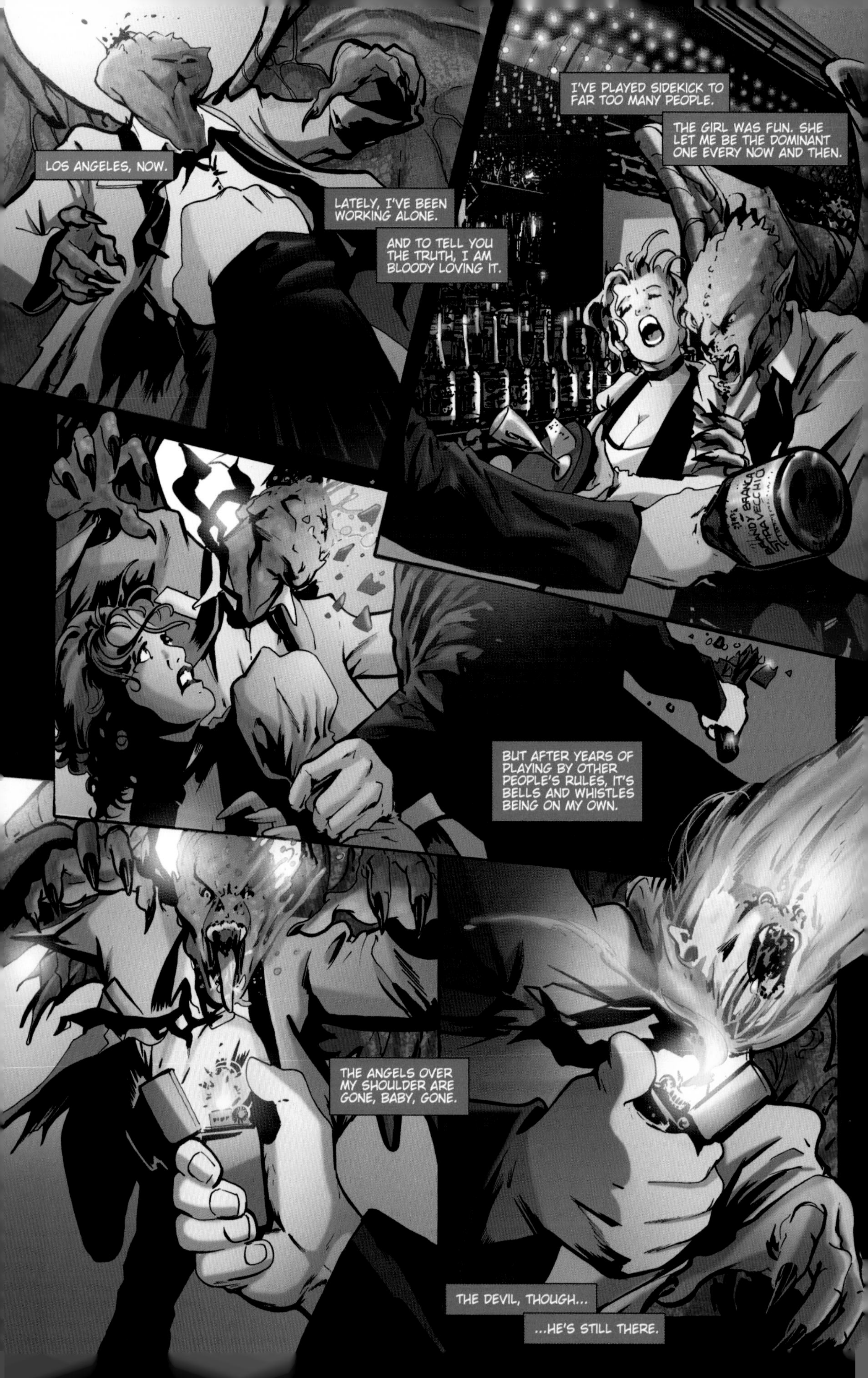
LOS ANGELES, NOW.
LATELY, I'VE BEEN WORKING ALONE.
AND TO TELL YOU THE TRUTH, I AM BLOODY LOVING IT.
I'VE PLAYED SIDEKICK TO FAR TOO MANY PEOPLE.
THE GIRL WAS FUN. SHE LET ME BE THE DOMINANT ONE EVERY NOW AND THEN.
BUT AFTER YEARS OF PLAYING BY OTHER PEOPLE'S RULES, IT'S BELLS AND WHISTLES BEING ON MY OWN.
THE ANGELS OVER MY SHOULDER ARE GONE, BABY, GONE.
THE DEVIL, THOUGH...
...HE'S STILL THERE.

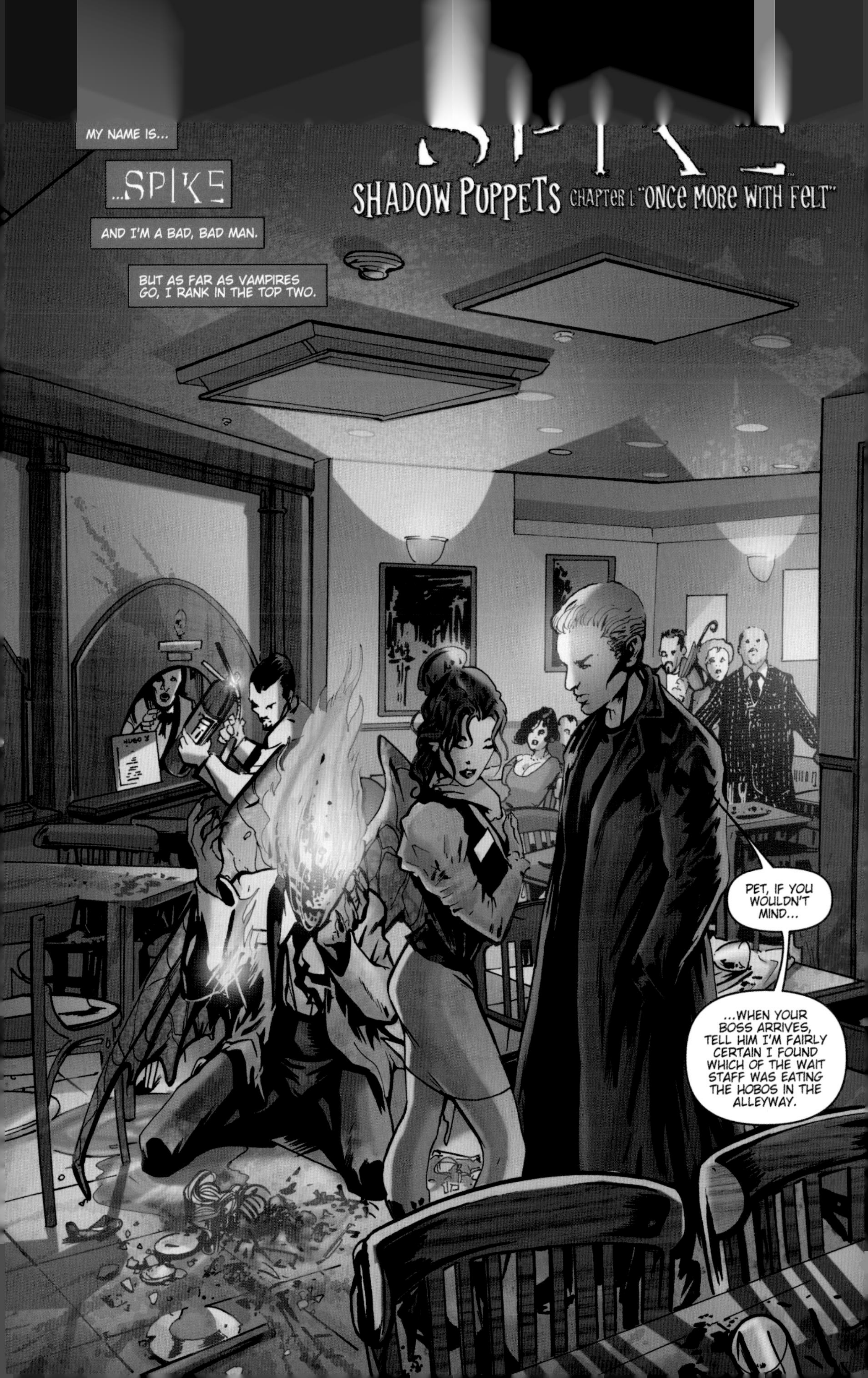

MY NAME IS...
...SPIKE
AND I'M A BAD, BAD MAN.
BUT AS FAR AS VAMPIRES GO, I RANK IN THE TOP TWO.
SPIKE
SHADOW PUPPETS CHAPTER 1: "ONCE MORE WITH FELT"
PET, IF YOU WOULDN'T MIND...
...WHEN YOUR BOSS ARRIVES, TELL HIM I'M FAIRLY CERTAIN I FOUND WHICH OF THE WAIT STAFF WAS EATING THE HOBOS IN THE ALLEYWAY.

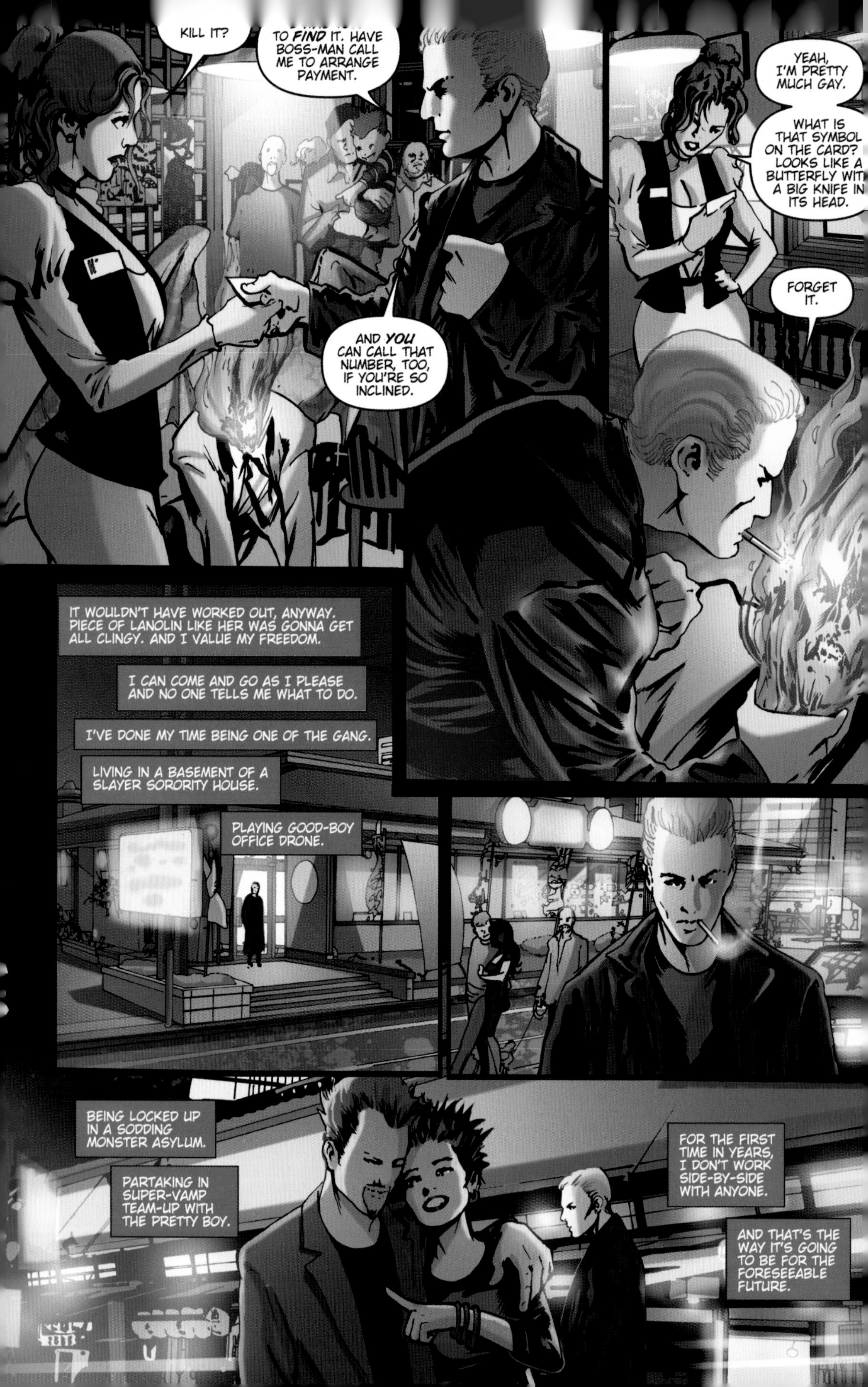
KILL IT?
TO FIND IT. HAVE BOSS-MAN CALL ME TO ARRANGE PAYMENT.
AND YOU CAN CALL THAT NUMBER, TOO, IF YOU'RE SO INCLINED.
YEAH, I'M PRETTY MUCH GAY.
WHAT IS THAT SYMBOL ON THE CARD? LOOKS LIKE A BUTTERFLY WITH A BIG KNIFE IN ITS HEAD.
FORGET IT.
IT WOULDN'T HAVE WORKED OUT, ANYWAY. PIECE OF LANOLIN LIKE HER WAS GONNA GET ALL CLINGY. AND I VALUE MY FREEDOM.
I CAN COME AND GO AS I PLEASE AND NO ONE TELLS ME WHAT TO DO.
I'VE DONE MY TIME BEING ONE OF THE GANG.
LIVING IN A BASEMENT OF A SLAYER SORORITY HOUSE.
PLAYING GOOD-BOY OFFICE DRONE.
BEING LOCKED UP IN A SODDING MONSTER ASYLUM.
PARTAKING IN SUPER-VAMP TEAM-UP WITH THE PRETTY BOY.
FOR THE FIRST TIME IN YEARS, I DON'T WORK SIDE-BY-SIDE WITH ANYONE.
AND THAT'S THE WAY IT'S GOING TO BE FOR THE FORESEEABLE FUTURE.

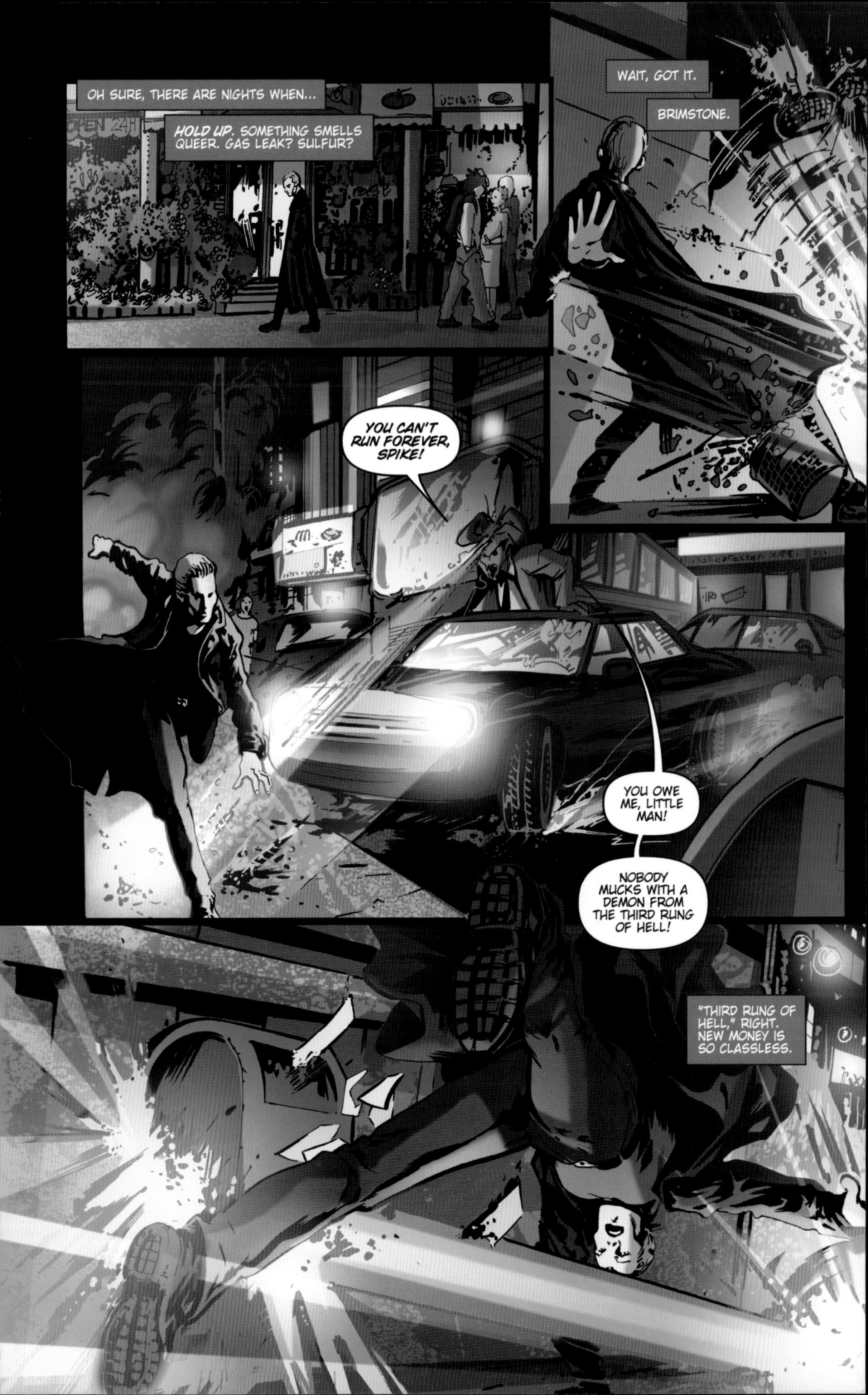
OH SURE, THERE ARE NIGHTS WHEN...
HOLD UP. SOMETHING SMELLS QUEER. GAS LEAK? SULFUR?
WAIT, GOT IT.
BRIMSTONE.
YOU CAN'T RUN FOREVER, SPIKE!
YOU OWE ME, LITTLE MAN!
NOBODY MUCKS WITH A DEMON FROM THE THIRD RUNG OF HELL!
"THIRD RUNG OF HELL," RIGHT. NEW MONEY IS SO CLASSLESS.

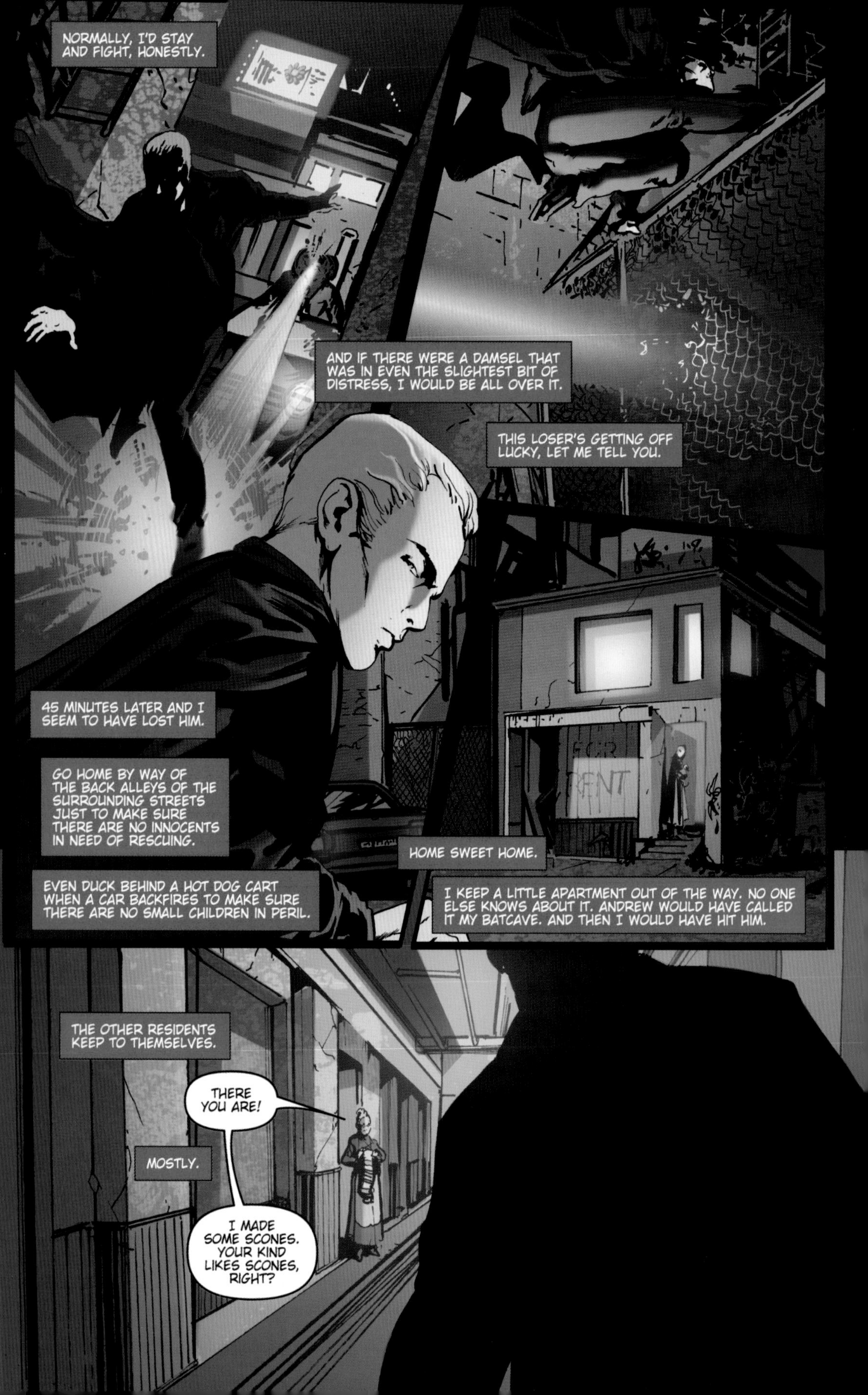
NORMALLY, I'D STAY AND FIGHT, HONESTLY.
AND IF THERE WERE A DAMSEL THAT WAS IN EVEN THE SLIGHTEST BIT OF DISTRESS, I WOULD BE ALL OVER IT.
THIS LOSER'S GETTING OFF LUCKY, LET ME TELL YOU.
45 MINUTES LATER AND I SEEM TO HAVE LOST HIM.
GO HOME BY WAY OF THE BACK ALLEYS OF THE SURROUNDING STREETS JUST TO MAKE SURE THERE ARE NO INNOCENTS IN NEED OF RESCUING.
EVEN DUCK BEHIND A HOT DOG CART WHEN A CAR BACKFIRES TO MAKE SURE THERE ARE NO SMALL CHILDREN IN PERIL.
FOR RENT
HOME SWEET HOME.
I KEEP A LITTLE APARTMENT OUT OF THE WAY. NO ONE ELSE KNOWS ABOUT IT. ANDREW WOULD HAVE CALLED IT MY BATCAVE. AND THEN I WOULD HAVE HIT HIM.
THE OTHER RESIDENTS KEEP TO THEMSELVES.
THERE YOU ARE!
MOSTLY.
I MADE SOME SCONES. YOUR KIND LIKES SCONES, RIGHT?

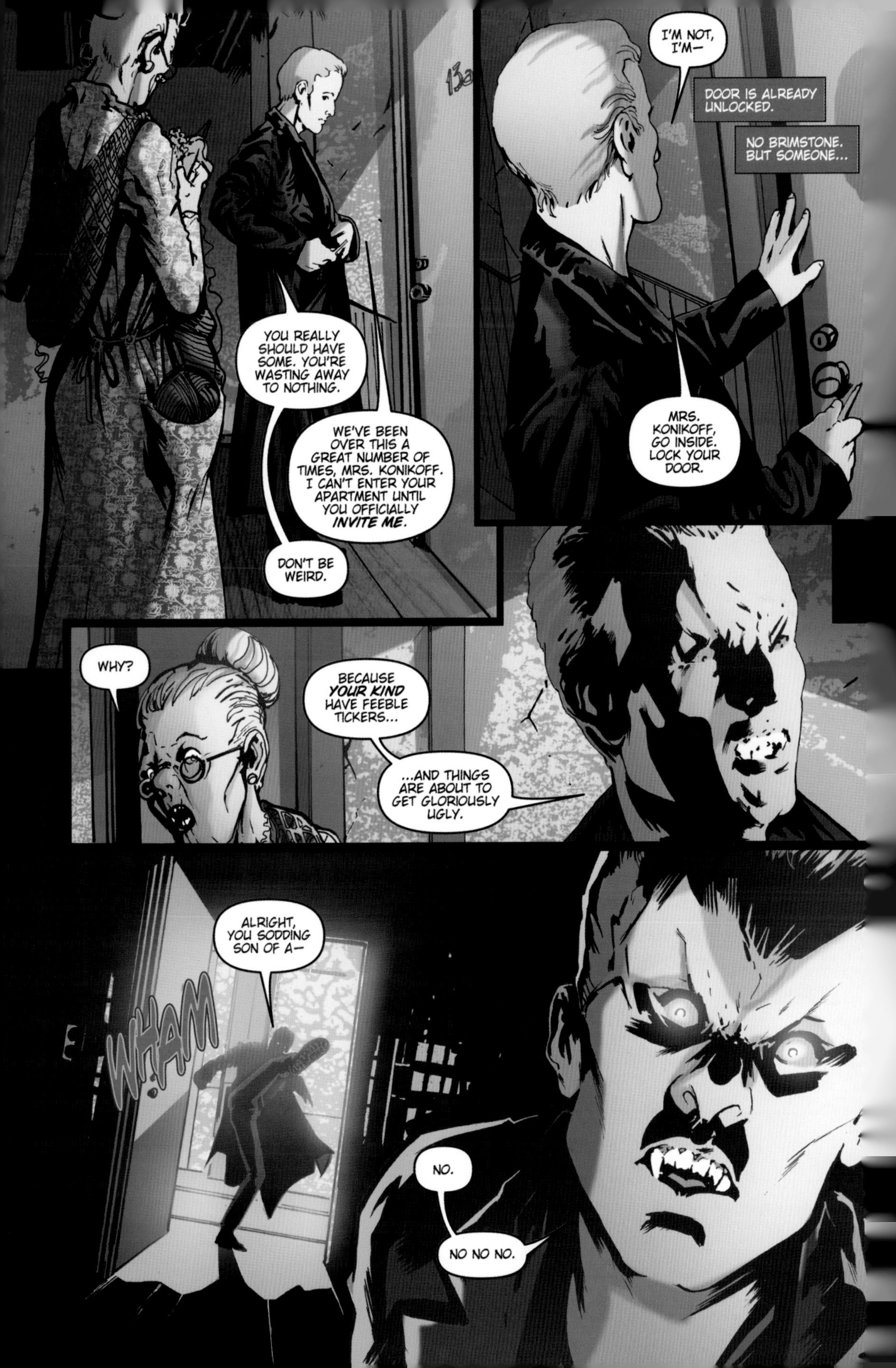
YOU REALLY SHOULD HAVE SOME. YOU'RE WASTING AWAY TO NOTHING.
WE'VE BEEN OVER THIS A GREAT NUMBER OF TIMES, MRS. KONIKOFF. I CAN'T ENTER YOUR APARTMENT UNTIL YOU OFFICIALLY INVITE ME.
DON'T BE WEIRD.
13a
I'M NOT, I'M—
DOOR IS ALREADY UNLOCKED.
NO BRIMSTONE. BUT SOMEONE...
MRS. KONIKOFF, GO INSIDE. LOCK YOUR DOOR.
WHY?
BECAUSE YOUR KIND HAVE FEEBLE TICKERS...
...AND THINGS ARE ABOUT TO GET GLORIOUSLY UGLY.
ALRIGHT, YOU SODDING SON OF A—
WHAM
NO.
NO NO NO.

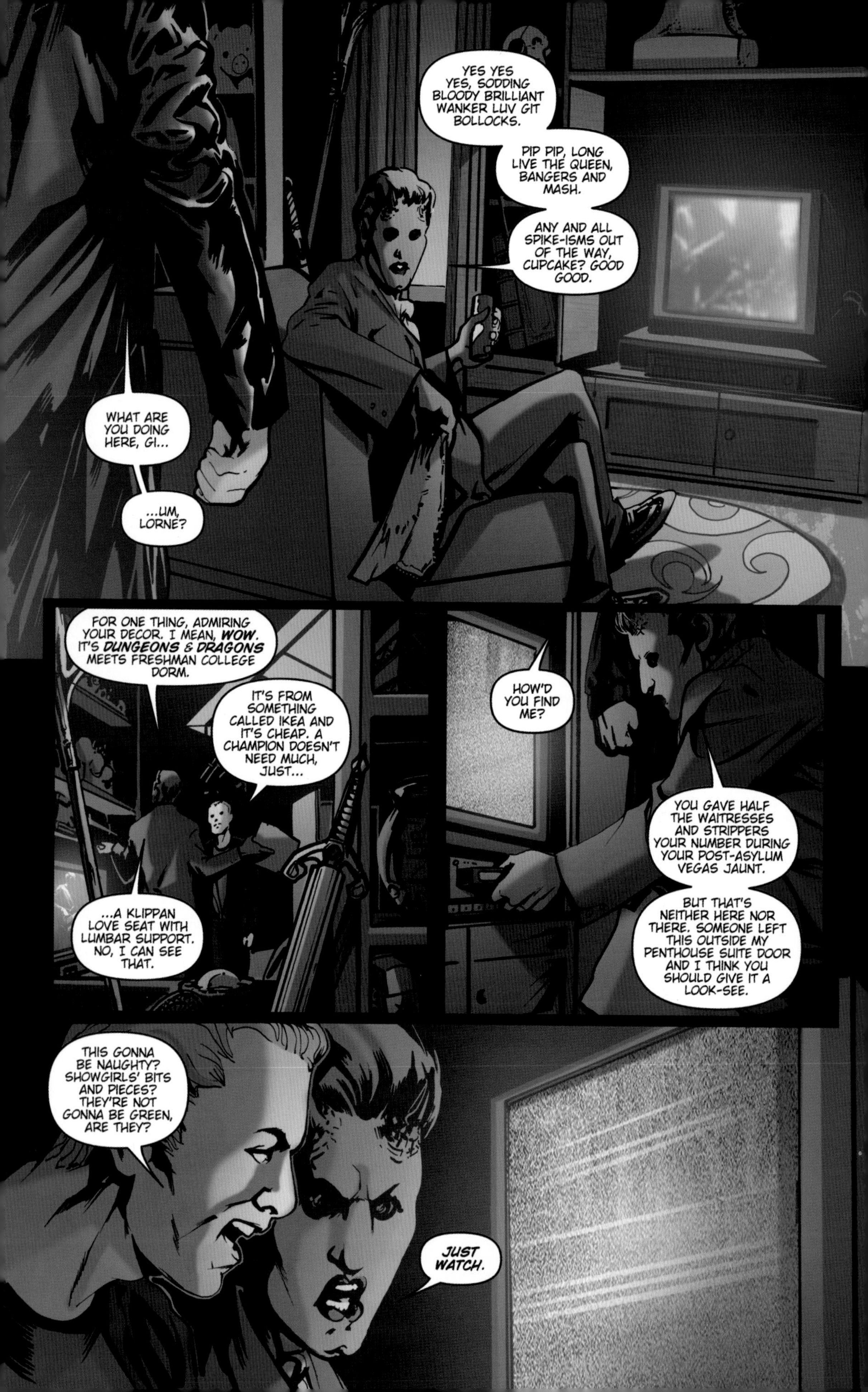
YES YES YES, SODDING BLOODY BRILLIANT WANKER LUV GIT BOLLOCKS.
PIP PIP, LONG LIVE THE QUEEN, BANGERS AND MASH.
ANY AND ALL SPIKE-ISMS OUT OF THE WAY, CUPCAKE? GOOD GOOD.
WHAT ARE YOU DOING HERE, GI...
...UM, LORNE?
FOR ONE THING, ADMIRING YOUR DECOR. I MEAN, WOW. IT'S DUNGEONS & DRAGONS MEETS FRESHMAN COLLEGE DORM.
IT'S FROM SOMETHING CALLED IKEA AND IT'S CHEAP. A CHAMPION DOESN'T NEED MUCH, JUST...
...A KLIPPAN LOVE SEAT WITH LUMBAR SUPPORT. NO, I CAN SEE THAT.
HOW'D YOU FIND ME?
YOU GAVE HALF THE WAITRESSES AND STRIPPERS YOUR NUMBER DURING YOUR POST-ASYLUM VEGAS JAUNT.
BUT THAT'S NEITHER HERE NOR THERE. SOMEONE LEFT THIS OUTSIDE MY PENTHOUSE SUITE DOOR AND I THINK YOU SHOULD GIVE IT A LOOK-SEE.
THIS GONNA BE NAUGHTY? SHOWGIRLS' BITS AND PIECES? THEY'RE NOT GONNA BE GREEN, ARE THEY?
JUST WATCH.

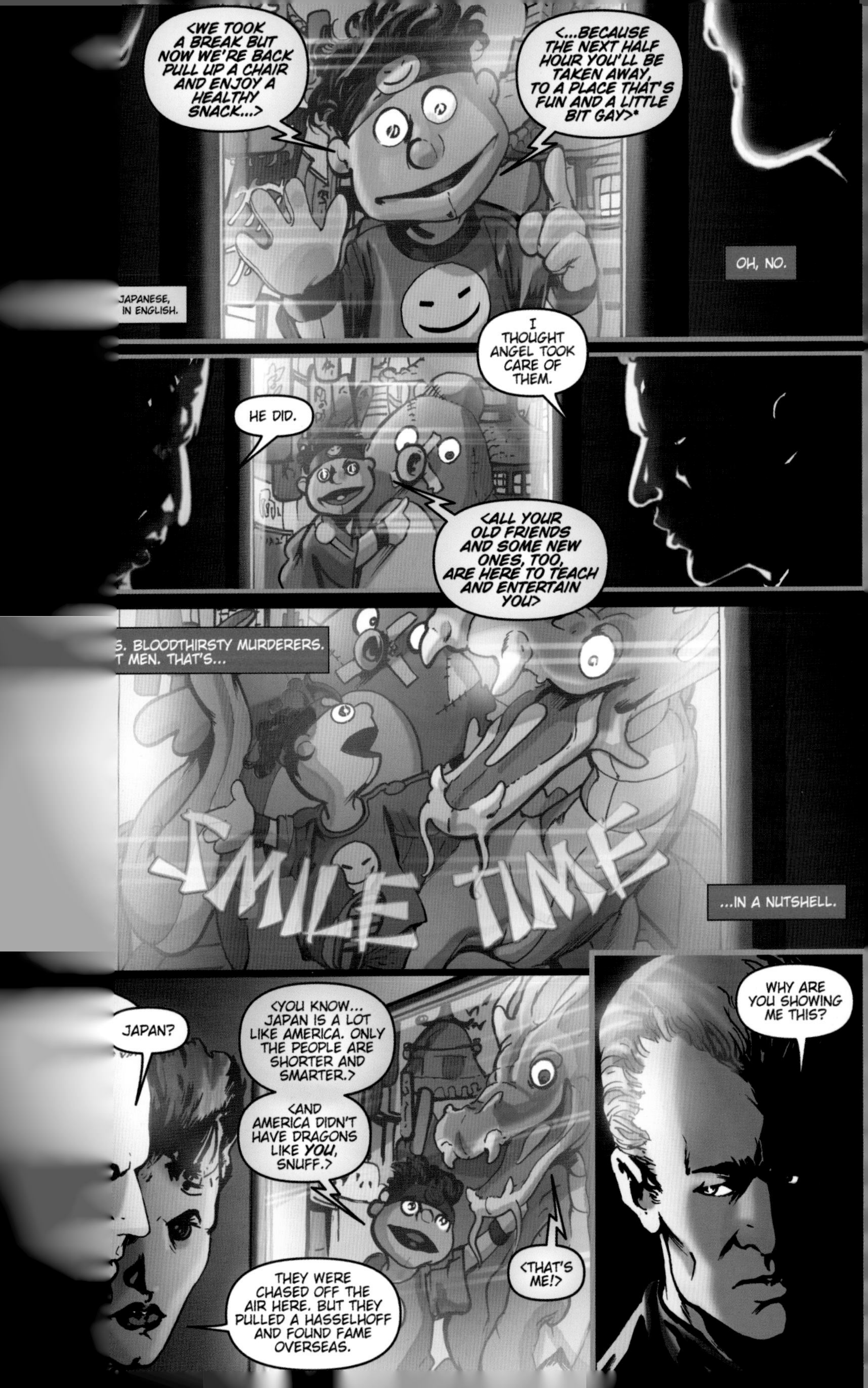

<WE TOOK A BREAK BUT NOW WE'RE BACK PULL UP A CHAIR AND ENJOY A HEALTHY SNACK...>
<...BECAUSE THE NEXT HALF HOUR YOU'LL BE TAKEN AWAY, TO A PLACE THAT'S FUN AND A LITTLE BIT GAY>*
OH, NO.
JAPANESE, IN ENGLISH.
I THOUGHT ANGEL TOOK CARE OF THEM.
HE DID.
<ALL YOUR OLD FRIENDS AND SOME NEW ONES, TOO, ARE HERE TO TEACH AND ENTERTAIN YOU>
S. BLOODTHIRSTY MURDERERS. T MEN. THAT'S...
SMILE TIME
...IN A NUTSHELL.
JAPAN?
<YOU KNOW... JAPAN IS A LOT LIKE AMERICA. ONLY THE PEOPLE ARE SHORTER AND SMARTER.>
<AND AMERICA DIDN'T HAVE DRAGONS LIKE *YOU*, SNUFF.>
WHY ARE YOU SHOWING ME THIS?
<THAT'S ME!>
THEY WERE CHASED OFF THE AIR HERE. BUT THEY PULLED A HASSELHOFF AND FOUND FAME OVERSEAS.

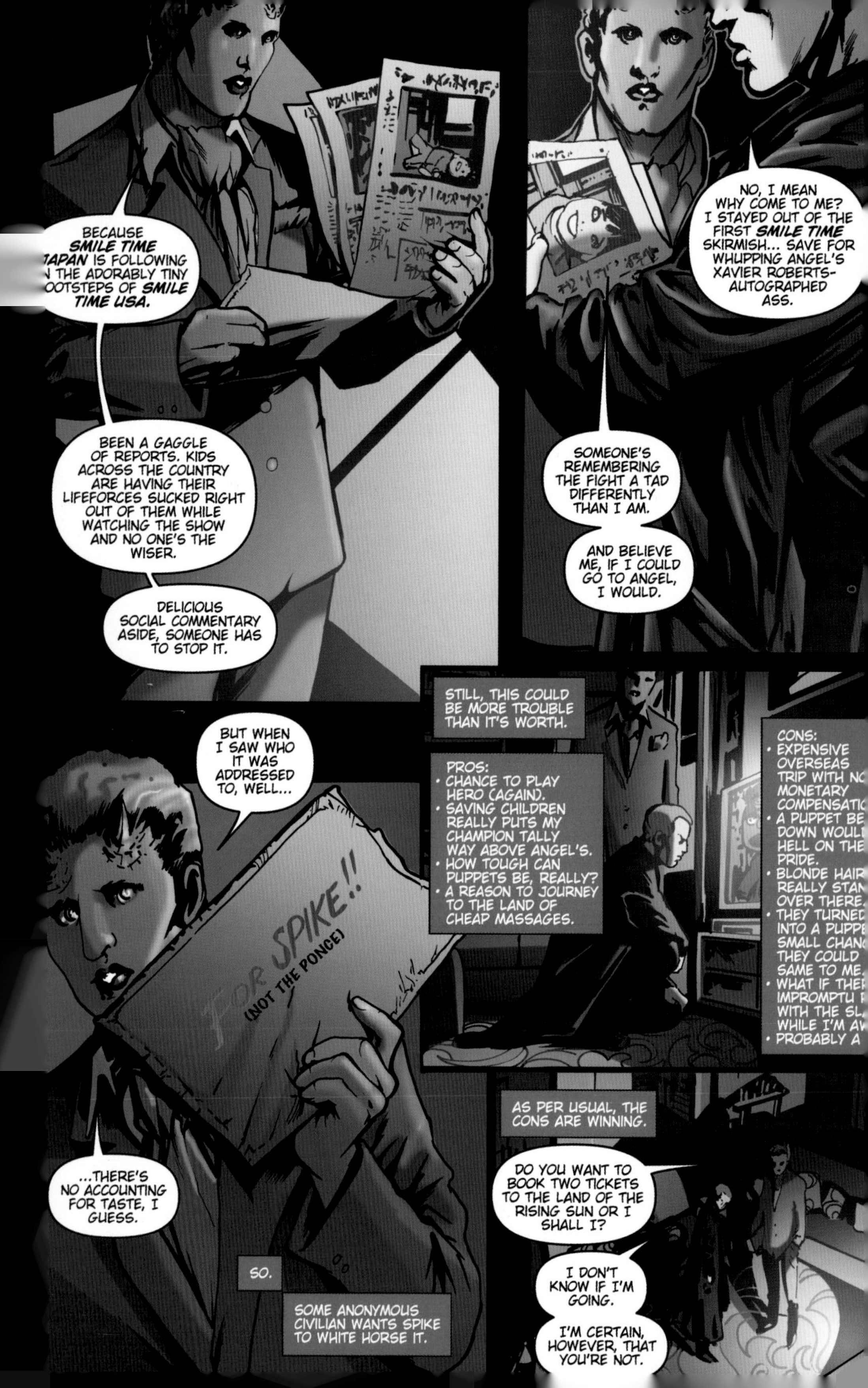
BECAUSE SMILE TIME JAPAN IS FOLLOWING IN THE ADORABLY TINY FOOTSTEPS OF SMILE TIME USA.
BEEN A GAGGLE OF REPORTS. KIDS ACROSS THE COUNTRY ARE HAVING THEIR LIFEFORCES SUCKED RIGHT OUT OF THEM WHILE WATCHING THE SHOW AND NO ONE'S THE WISER.
DELICIOUS SOCIAL COMMENTARY ASIDE, SOMEONE HAS TO STOP IT.
NO, I MEAN WHY COME TO ME? I STAYED OUT OF THE FIRST SMILE TIME SKIRMISH... SAVE FOR WHUPPING ANGEL'S XAVIER ROBERTS-AUTOGRAPHED ASS.
SOMEONE'S REMEMBERING THE FIGHT A TAD DIFFERENTLY THAN I AM.
AND BELIEVE ME, IF I COULD GO TO ANGEL, I WOULD.
BUT WHEN I SAW WHO IT WAS ADDRESSED TO, WELL...
FOR SPIKE!! (NOT THE PONCE)
...THERE'S NO ACCOUNTING FOR TASTE, I GUESS.
SO.
SOME ANONYMOUS CIVILIAN WANTS SPIKE TO WHITE HORSE IT.
STILL, THIS COULD BE MORE TROUBLE THAN IT'S WORTH.
PROS:
• CHANCE TO PLAY HERO (AGAIN).
• SAVING CHILDREN REALLY PUTS MY CHAMPION TALLY WAY ABOVE ANGEL'S.
• HOW TOUGH CAN PUPPETS BE, REALLY?
• A REASON TO JOURNEY TO THE LAND OF CHEAP MASSAGES.
CONS:
• EXPENSIVE OVERSEAS TRIP WITH NO MONETARY COMPENSATIO
• A PUPPET BE DOWN WOULD HELL ON THE PRIDE.
• BLONDE HAIR REALLY STAN OVER THERE
• THEY TURNED INTO A PUPPE SMALL CHANC THEY COULD SAME TO ME
• WHAT IF THE IMPROMPTU WITH THE SL WHILE I'M AW
• PROBABLY A
AS PER USUAL, THE CONS ARE WINNING.
DO YOU WANT TO BOOK TWO TICKETS TO THE LAND OF THE RISING SUN OR I SHALL I?
I DON'T KNOW IF I'M GOING.
I'M CERTAIN, HOWEVER, THAT YOU'RE NOT.

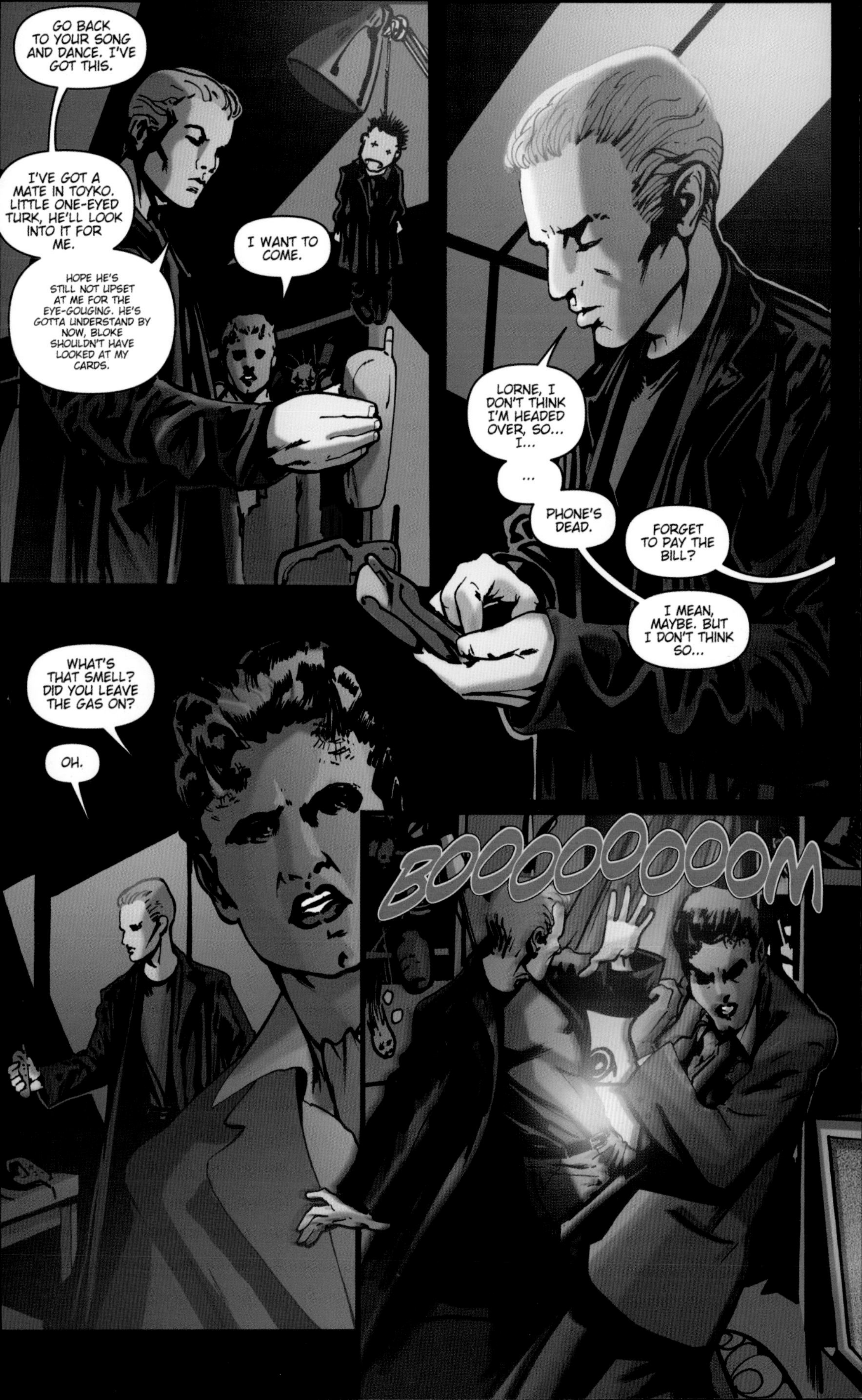
GO BACK TO YOUR SONG AND DANCE. I'VE GOT THIS.
I'VE GOT A MATE IN TOYKO. LITTLE ONE-EYED TURK, HE'LL LOOK INTO IT FOR ME.
HOPE HE'S STILL NOT UPSET AT ME FOR THE EYE-GOUGING. HE'S GOTTA UNDERSTAND BY NOW, BLOKE SHOULDN'T HAVE LOOKED AT MY CARDS.
I WANT TO COME.
LORNE, I DON'T THINK I'M HEADED OVER, SO... I...
...
PHONE'S DEAD.
FORGET TO PAY THE BILL?
I MEAN, MAYBE. BUT I DON'T THINK SO...
WHAT'S THAT SMELL? DID YOU LEAVE THE GAS ON?
OH.
BOOOOOOOOOM

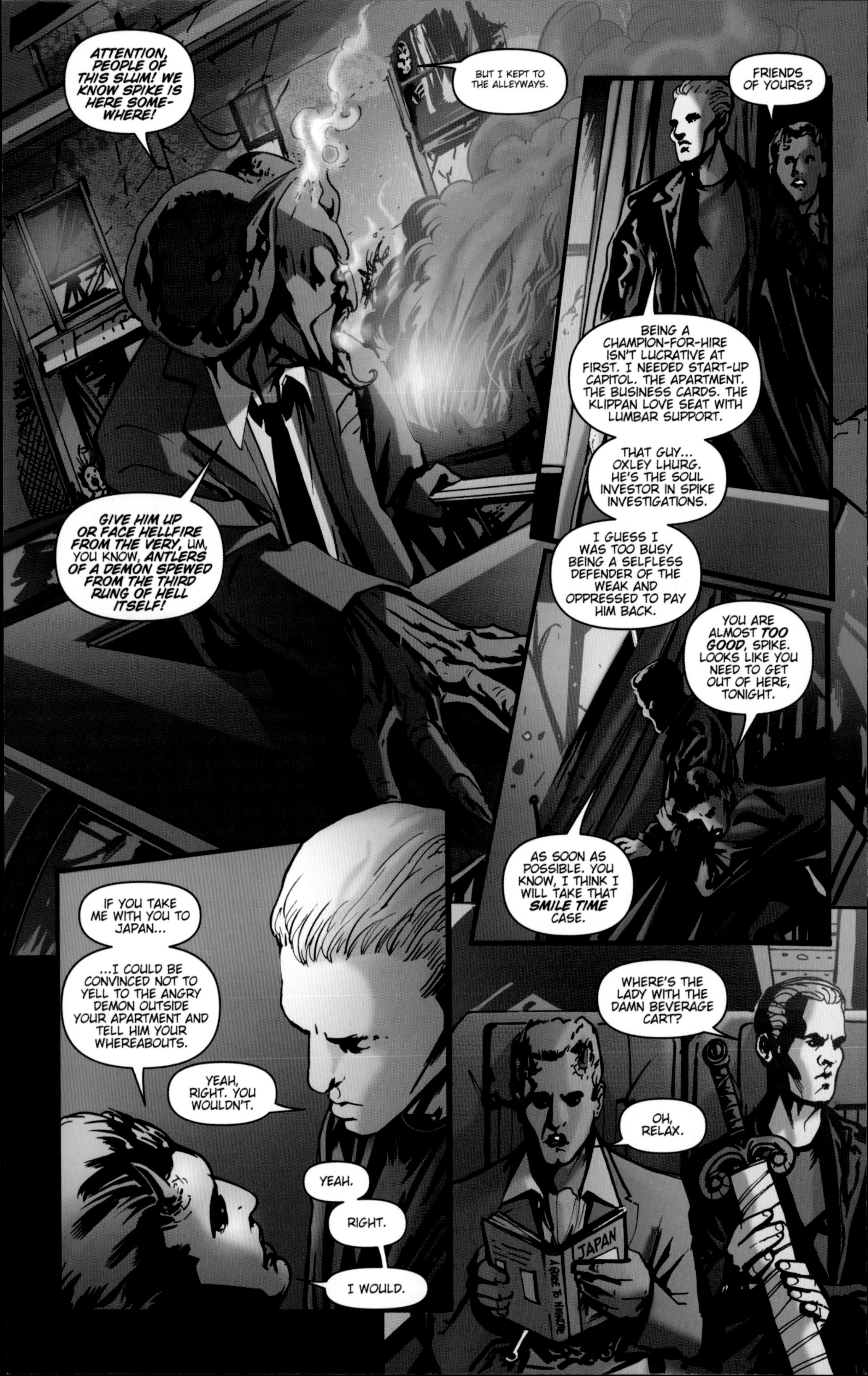
ATTENTION, PEOPLE OF THIS SLUM! WE KNOW SPIKE IS HERE SOMEWHERE!
BUT I KEPT TO THE ALLEYWAYS.
GIVE HIM UP OR FACE HELLFIRE FROM THE VERY, UM, YOU KNOW, ANTLERS OF A DEMON SPEWED FROM THE THIRD RUNG OF HELL ITSELF!
FRIENDS OF YOURS?
BEING A CHAMPION-FOR-HIRE ISN'T LUCRATIVE AT FIRST. I NEEDED START-UP CAPITOL. THE APARTMENT. THE BUSINESS CARDS. THE KLIPPAN LOVE SEAT WITH LUMBAR SUPPORT.
THAT GUY... OXLEY LHURG. HE'S THE SOUL INVESTOR IN SPIKE INVESTIGATIONS.
I GUESS I WAS TOO BUSY BEING A SELFLESS DEFENDER OF THE WEAK AND OPPRESSED TO PAY HIM BACK.
YOU ARE ALMOST TOO GOOD, SPIKE. LOOKS LIKE YOU NEED TO GET OUT OF HERE, TONIGHT.
AS SOON AS POSSIBLE. YOU KNOW, I THINK I WILL TAKE THAT SMILE TIME CASE.
IF YOU TAKE ME WITH YOU TO JAPAN...
...I COULD BE CONVINCED NOT TO YELL TO THE ANGRY DEMON OUTSIDE YOUR APARTMENT AND TELL HIM YOUR WHEREABOUTS.
YEAH, RIGHT. YOU WOULDN'T.
YEAH.
RIGHT.
I WOULD.
WHERE'S THE LADY WITH THE DAMN BEVERAGE CART?
OH, RELAX.
JAPAN
A GUIDE TO NIHONGO

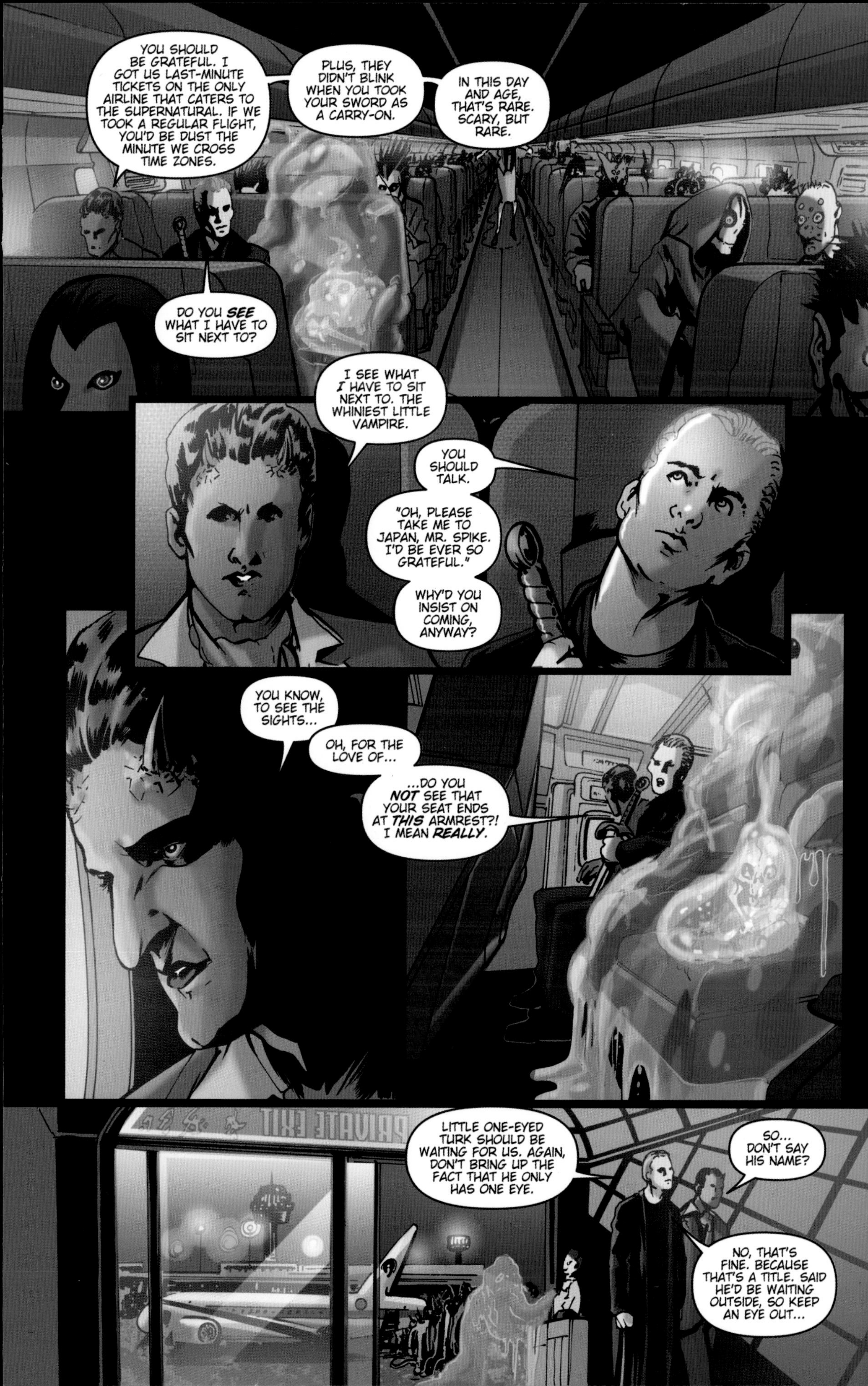
YOU SHOULD BE GRATEFUL. I GOT US LAST-MINUTE TICKETS ON THE ONLY AIRLINE THAT CATERS TO THE SUPERNATURAL. IF WE TOOK A REGULAR FLIGHT, YOU'D BE DUST THE MINUTE WE CROSS TIME ZONES.
PLUS, THEY DIDN'T BLINK WHEN YOU TOOK YOUR SWORD AS A CARRY-ON.
IN THIS DAY AND AGE, THAT'S RARE. SCARY, BUT RARE.
DO YOU *SEE* WHAT I HAVE TO SIT NEXT TO?
I SEE WHAT *I* HAVE TO SIT NEXT TO. THE WHINIEST LITTLE VAMPIRE.
YOU SHOULD TALK.
"OH, PLEASE TAKE ME TO JAPAN, MR. SPIKE. I'D BE EVER SO GRATEFUL."
WHY'D YOU INSIST ON COMING, ANYWAY?
YOU KNOW, TO SEE THE SIGHTS...
OH, FOR THE LOVE OF...
...DO YOU *NOT* SEE THAT YOUR SEAT ENDS AT *THIS* ARMREST?! I MEAN *REALLY*.
PRIVATE EXIT
LITTLE ONE-EYED TURK SHOULD BE WAITING FOR US. AGAIN, DON'T BRING UP THE FACT THAT HE ONLY HAS ONE EYE.
SO... DON'T SAY HIS NAME?
NO, THAT'S FINE. BECAUSE THAT'S A TITLE. SAID HE'D BE WAITING OUTSIDE, SO KEEP AN EYE OUT...

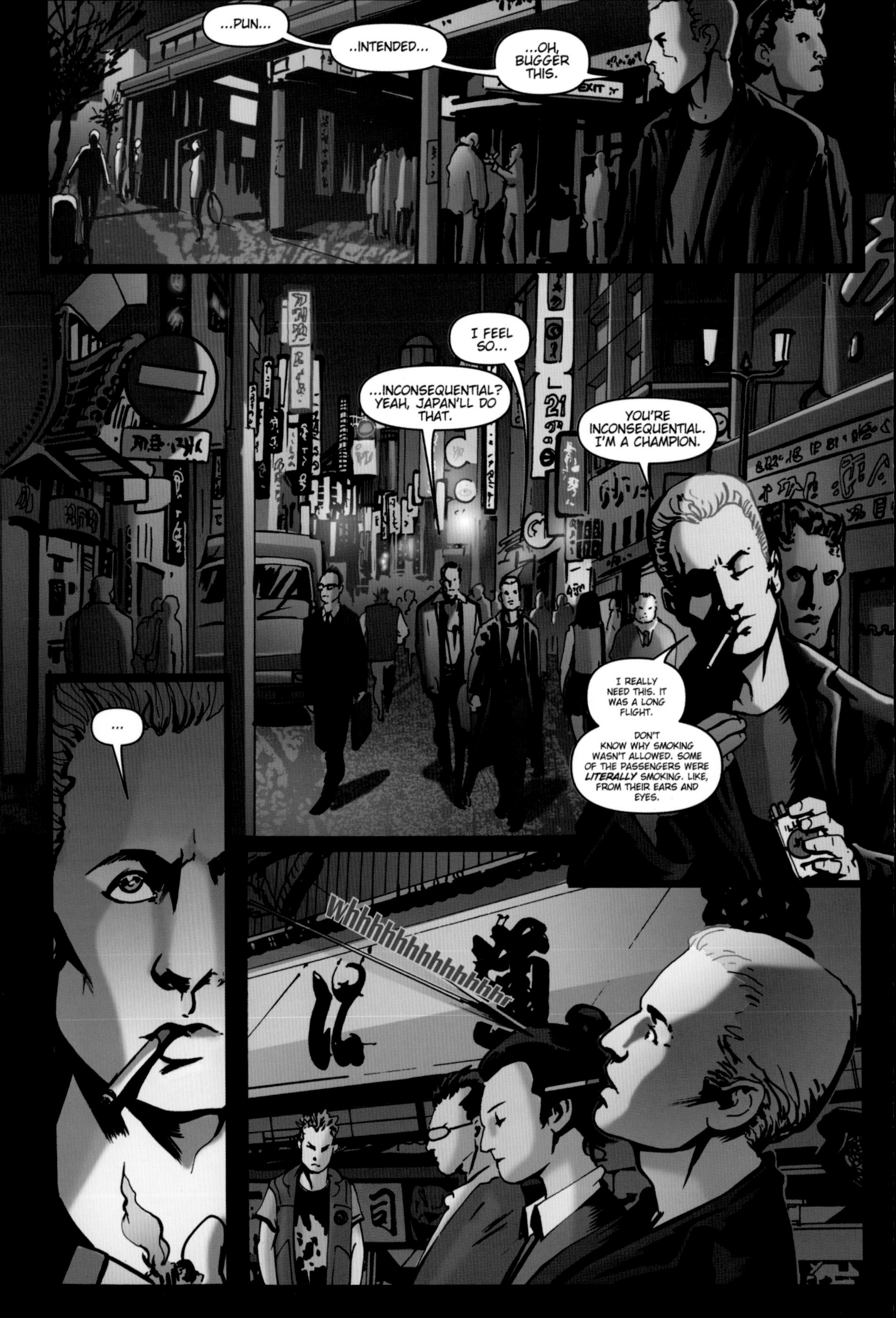
...PUN...
..INTENDED...
...OH, BUGGER THIS.
I FEEL SO...
...INCONSEQUENTIAL? YEAH, JAPAN'LL DO THAT.
YOU'RE INCONSEQUENTIAL. I'M A CHAMPION.
I REALLY NEED THIS. IT WAS A LONG FLIGHT.
DON'T KNOW WHY SMOKING WASN'T ALLOWED. SOME OF THE PASSENGERS WERE ***LITERALLY*** SMOKING. LIKE, FROM THEIR EARS AND EYES.
...
whhhhhhhhhhhhhhhr

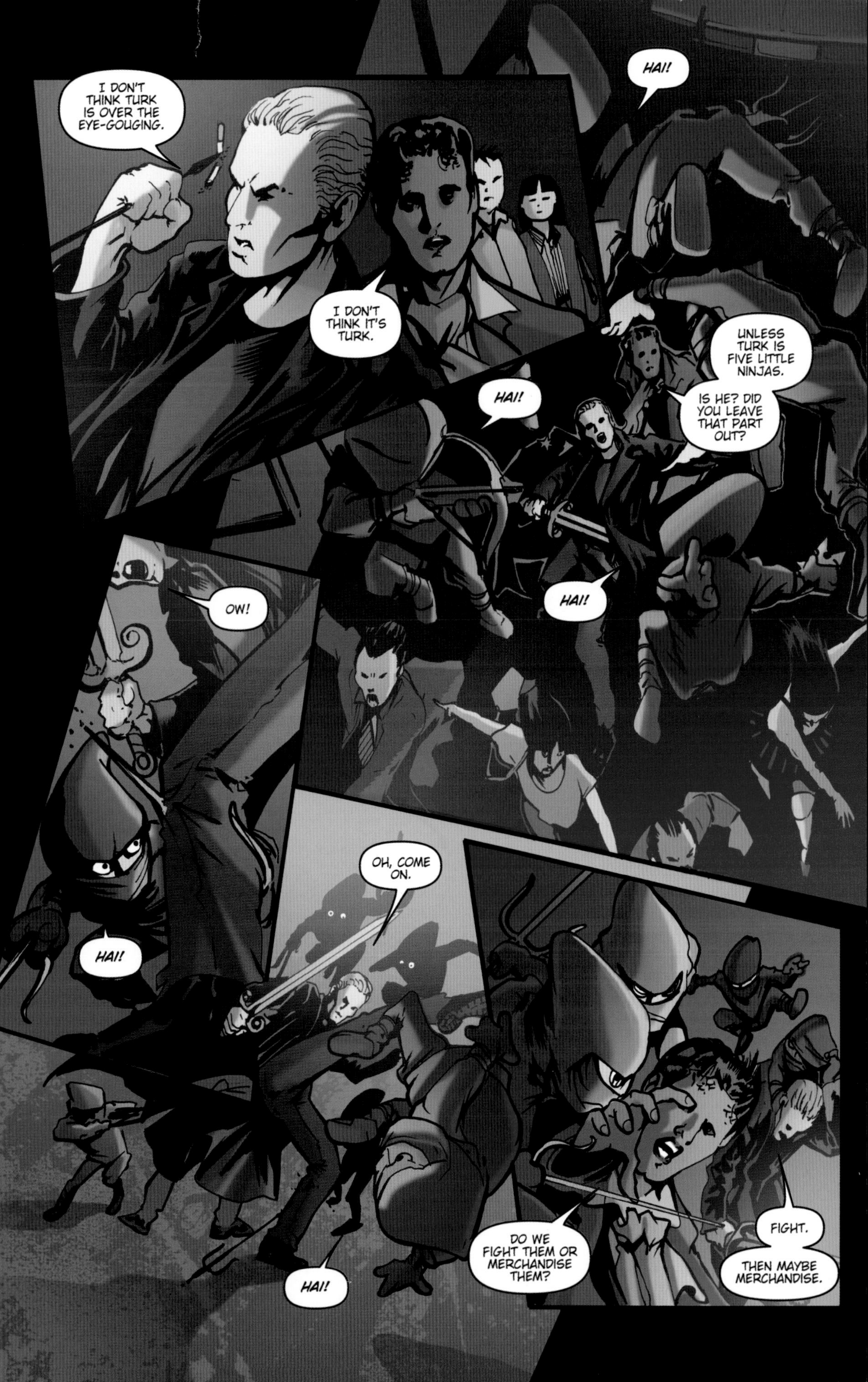
I DON'T THINK TURK IS OVER THE EYE-GOUGING.
I DON'T THINK IT'S TURK.
HAI!
UNLESS TURK IS FIVE LITTLE NINJAS.
IS HE? DID YOU LEAVE THAT PART OUT?
HAI!
HAI!
OW!
HAI!
OH, COME ON.
HAI!
DO WE FIGHT THEM OR MERCHANDISE THEM?
FIGHT.
THEN MAYBE MERCHANDISE.

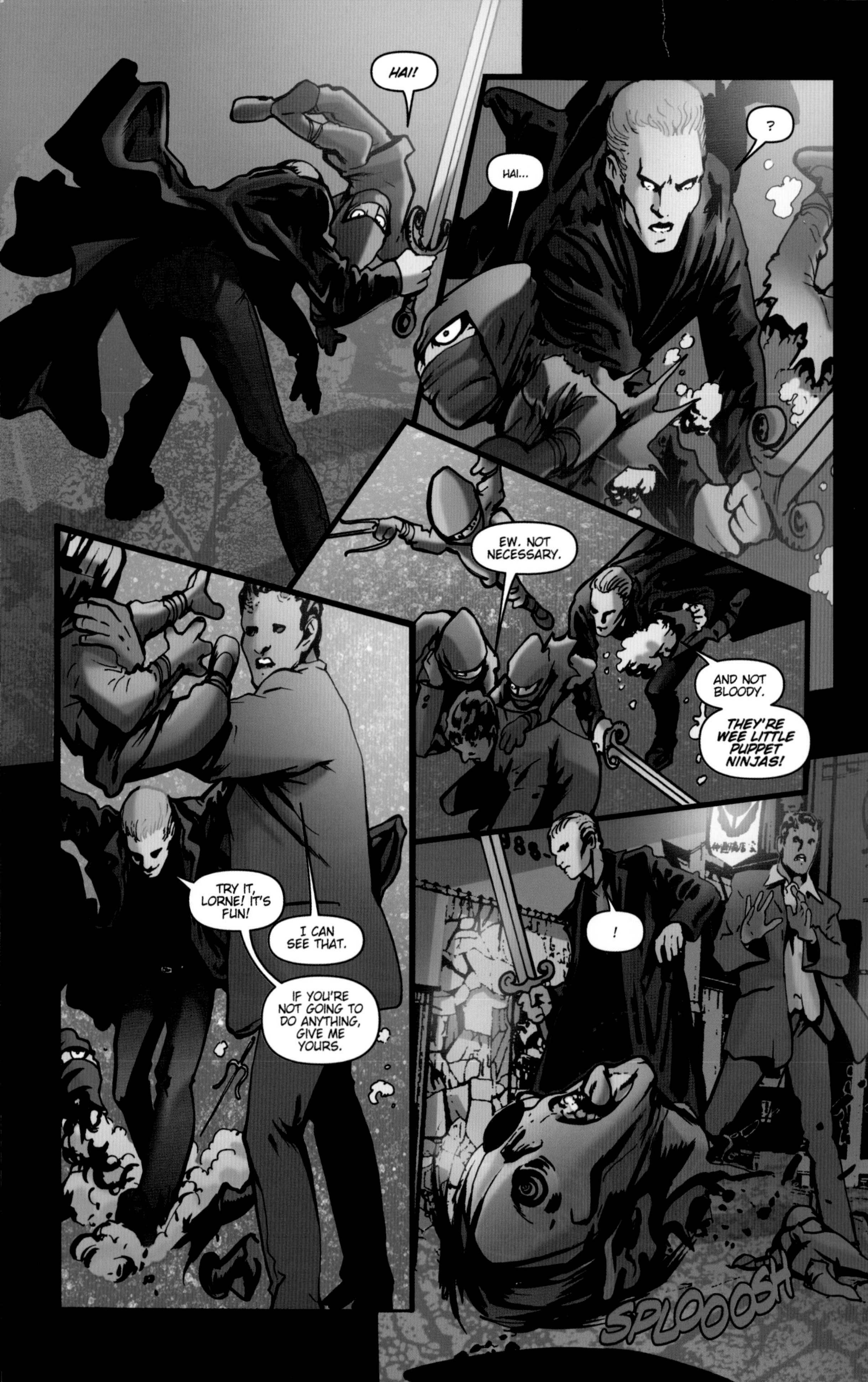
HAI!
HAI...
?
EW. NOT NECESSARY.
AND NOT BLOODY.
THEY'RE WEE LITTLE PUPPET NINJAS!
TRY IT, LORNE! IT'S FUN!
I CAN SEE THAT.
IF YOU'RE NOT GOING TO DO ANYTHING, GIVE ME YOURS.
!
SPLOOOSH

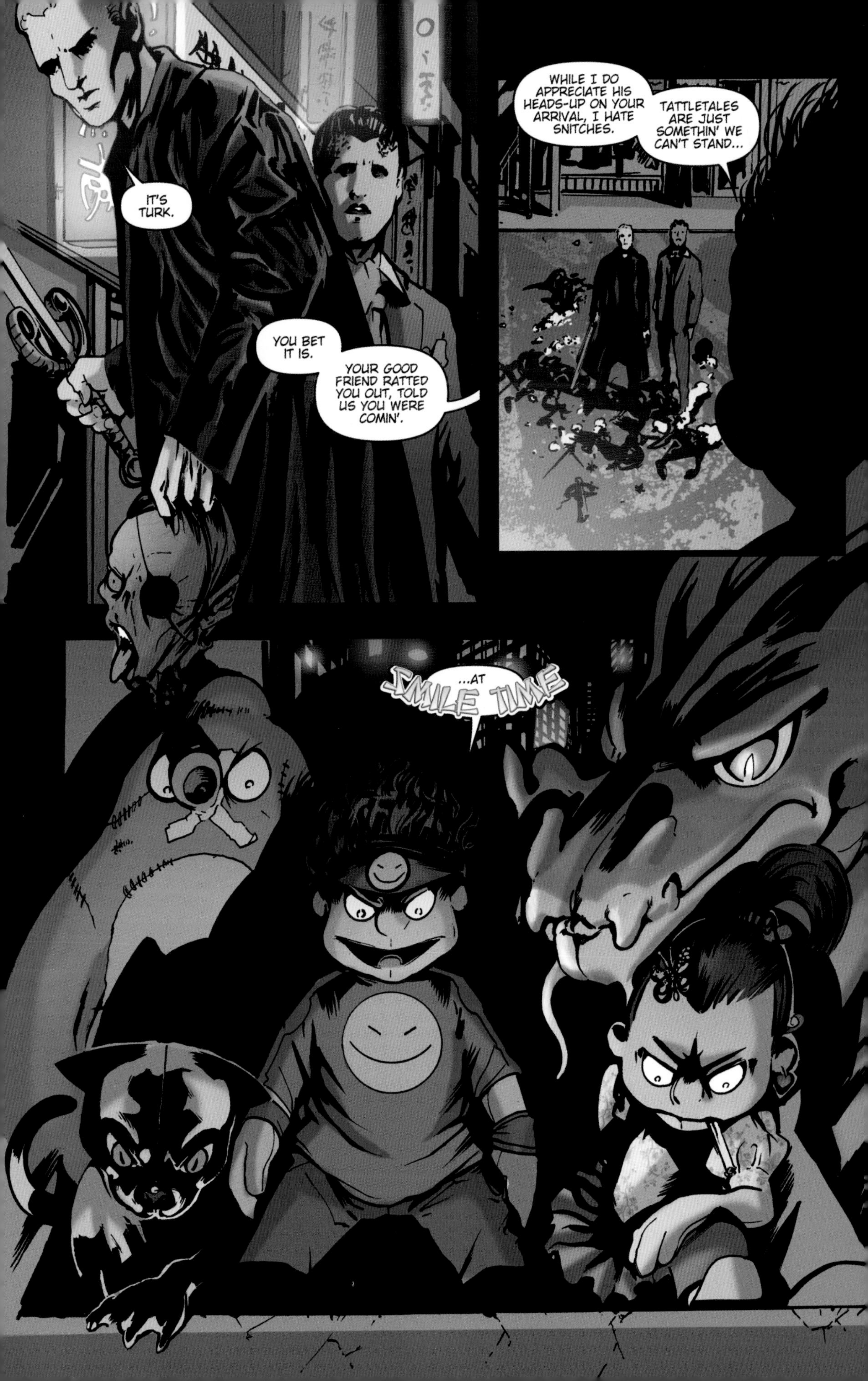
IT'S TURK.
YOU BET IT IS.
YOUR GOOD FRIEND RATTED YOU OUT, TOLD US YOU WERE COMIN'.
WHILE I DO APPRECIATE HIS HEADS-UP ON YOUR ARRIVAL, I HATE SNITCHES.
TATTLETALES ARE JUST SOMETHIN' WE CAN'T STAND...
...AT
SMILE TIME

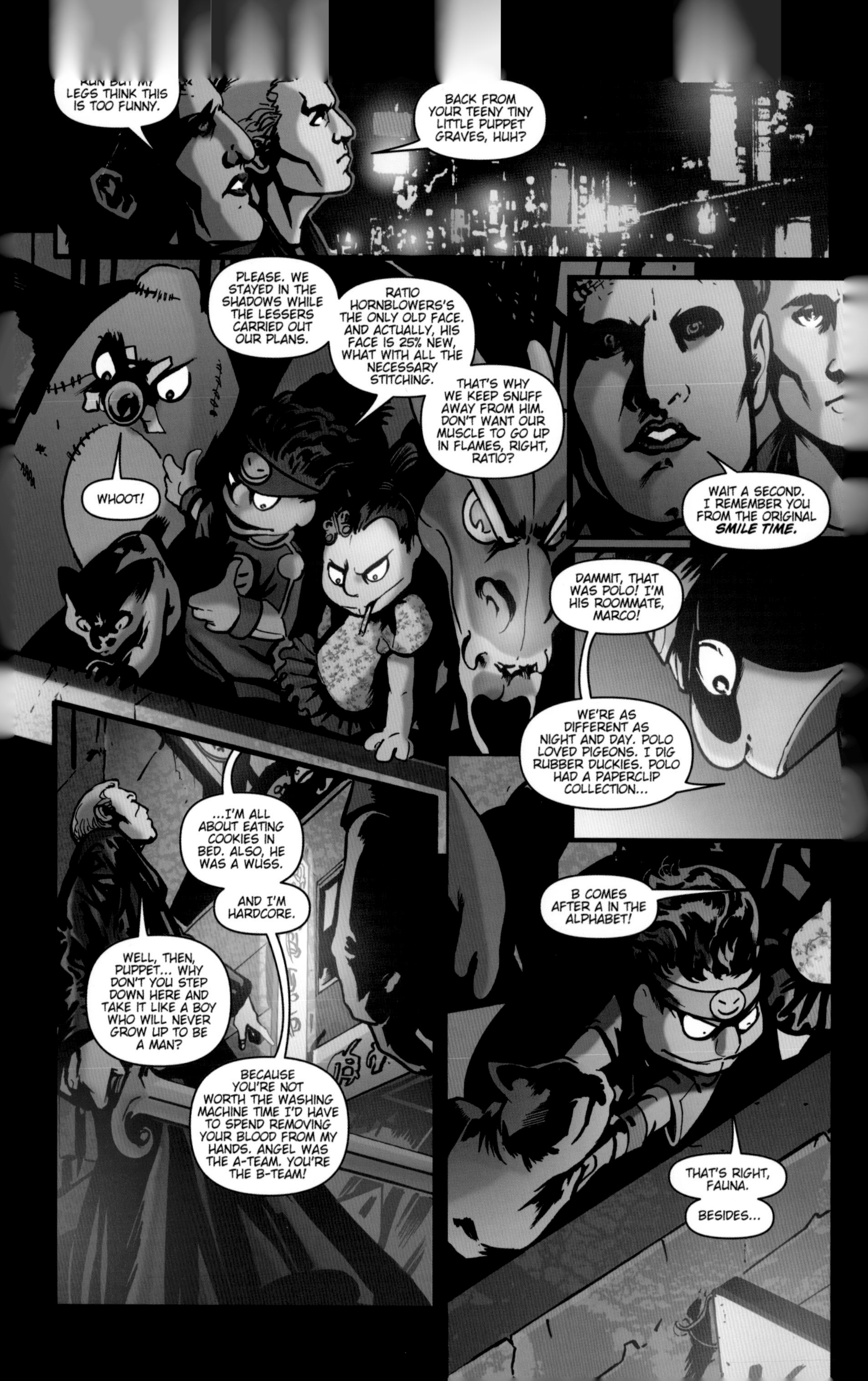
LEGS THINK THIS IS TOO FUNNY.
BACK FROM YOUR TEENY TINY LITTLE PUPPET GRAVES, HUH?
PLEASE. WE STAYED IN THE SHADOWS WHILE THE LESSERS CARRIED OUT OUR PLANS.
RATIO HORNBLOWERS'S THE ONLY OLD FACE. AND ACTUALLY, HIS FACE IS 25% NEW, WHAT WITH ALL THE NECESSARY STITCHING.
THAT'S WHY WE KEEP SNUFF AWAY FROM HIM. DON'T WANT OUR MUSCLE TO GO UP IN FLAMES, RIGHT, RATIO?
WHOOT!
WAIT A SECOND. I REMEMBER YOU FROM THE ORIGINAL *SMILE TIME.*
DAMMIT, THAT WAS POLO! I'M HIS ROOMMATE, MARCO!
WE'RE AS DIFFERENT AS NIGHT AND DAY. POLO LOVED PIGEONS. I DIG RUBBER DUCKIES. POLO HAD A PAPERCLIP COLLECTION...
...I'M ALL ABOUT EATING COOKIES IN BED. ALSO, HE WAS A WUSS.
AND I'M HARDCORE.
WELL, THEN, PUPPET... WHY DON'T YOU STEP DOWN HERE AND TAKE IT LIKE A BOY WHO WILL NEVER GROW UP TO BE A MAN?
BECAUSE YOU'RE NOT WORTH THE WASHING MACHINE TIME I'D HAVE TO SPEND REMOVING YOUR BLOOD FROM MY HANDS. ANGEL WAS THE A-TEAM. YOU'RE THE B-TEAM!
B COMES AFTER A IN THE ALPHABET!
THAT'S RIGHT, FAUNA.
BESIDES...

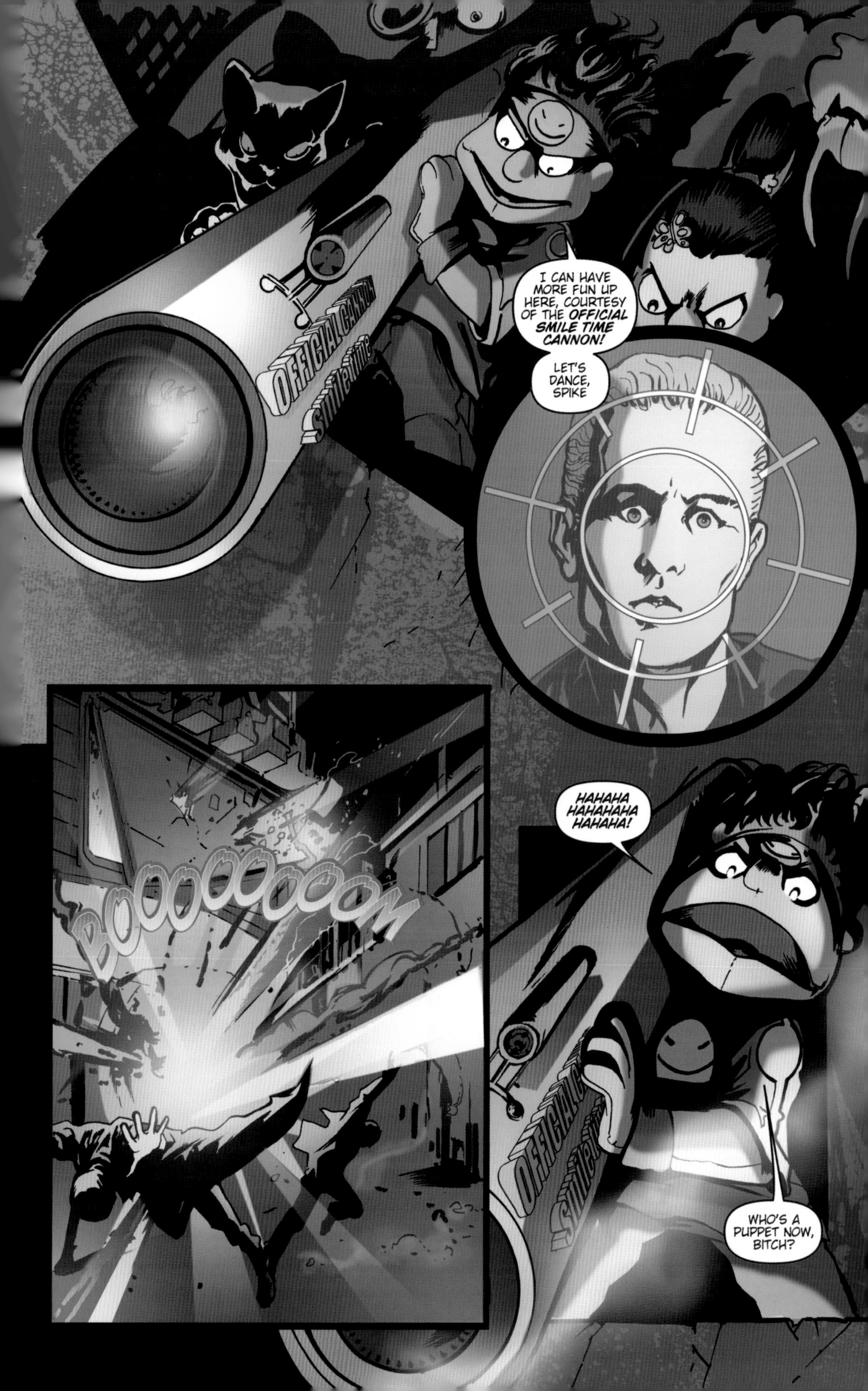
I CAN HAVE MORE FUN UP HERE, COURTESY OF THE *OFFICIAL SMILE TIME CANNON!*
LET'S DANCE, SPIKE
OFFICIAL CANNON
BOOOOOOOOM
HAHAHA HAHAHAHA HAHAHA!
WHO'S A PUPPET NOW, BITCH?

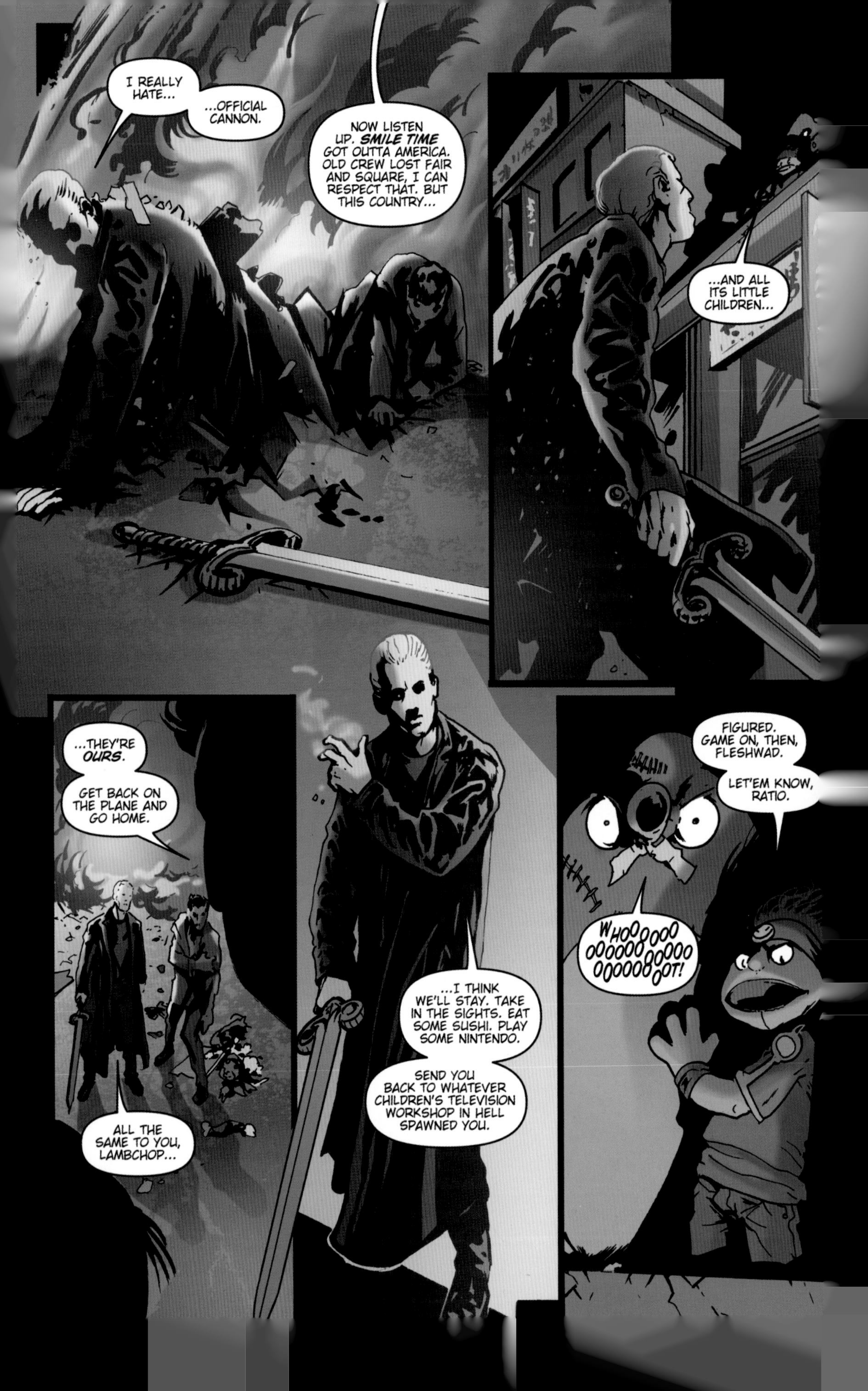
I REALLY HATE...
...OFFICIAL CANNON.
NOW LISTEN UP. SMILE TIME GOT OUTTA AMERICA. OLD CREW LOST FAIR AND SQUARE, I CAN RESPECT THAT. BUT THIS COUNTRY...
...AND ALL ITS LITTLE CHILDREN...
...THEY'RE OURS.
GET BACK ON THE PLANE AND GO HOME.
ALL THE SAME TO YOU, LAMBCHOP...
...I THINK WE'LL STAY. TAKE IN THE SIGHTS. EAT SOME SUSHI. PLAY SOME NINTENDO.
SEND YOU BACK TO WHATEVER CHILDREN'S TELEVISION WORKSHOP IN HELL SPAWNED YOU.
FIGURED. GAME ON, THEN, FLESHWAD.
LET'EM KNOW, RATIO.
WHOOOOOOOOOOOOOOOOOOOOOOOOT!

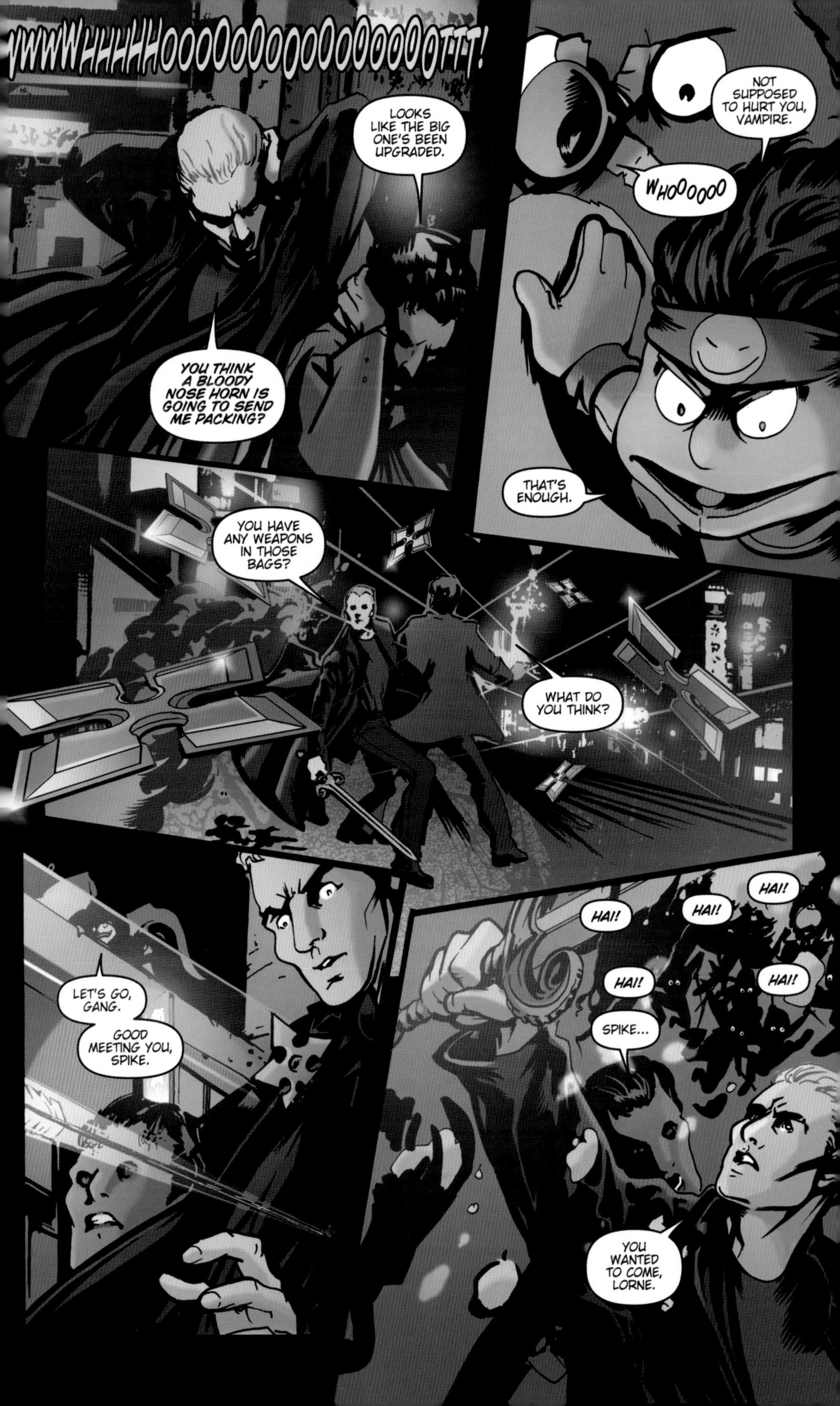
WWWWHHHHOOOOOOOOOOOOOOOOTTT!
YOU THINK A BLOODY NOSE HORN IS GOING TO SEND ME PACKING?
LOOKS LIKE THE BIG ONE'S BEEN UPGRADED.
NOT SUPPOSED TO HURT YOU, VAMPIRE.
WHOOOOOO
THAT'S ENOUGH.
YOU HAVE ANY WEAPONS IN THOSE BAGS?
WHAT DO YOU THINK?
LET'S GO, GANG.
GOOD MEETING YOU, SPIKE.
HAI!
HAI!
HAI!
HAI!
HAI!
SPIKE...
YOU WANTED TO COME, LORNE.

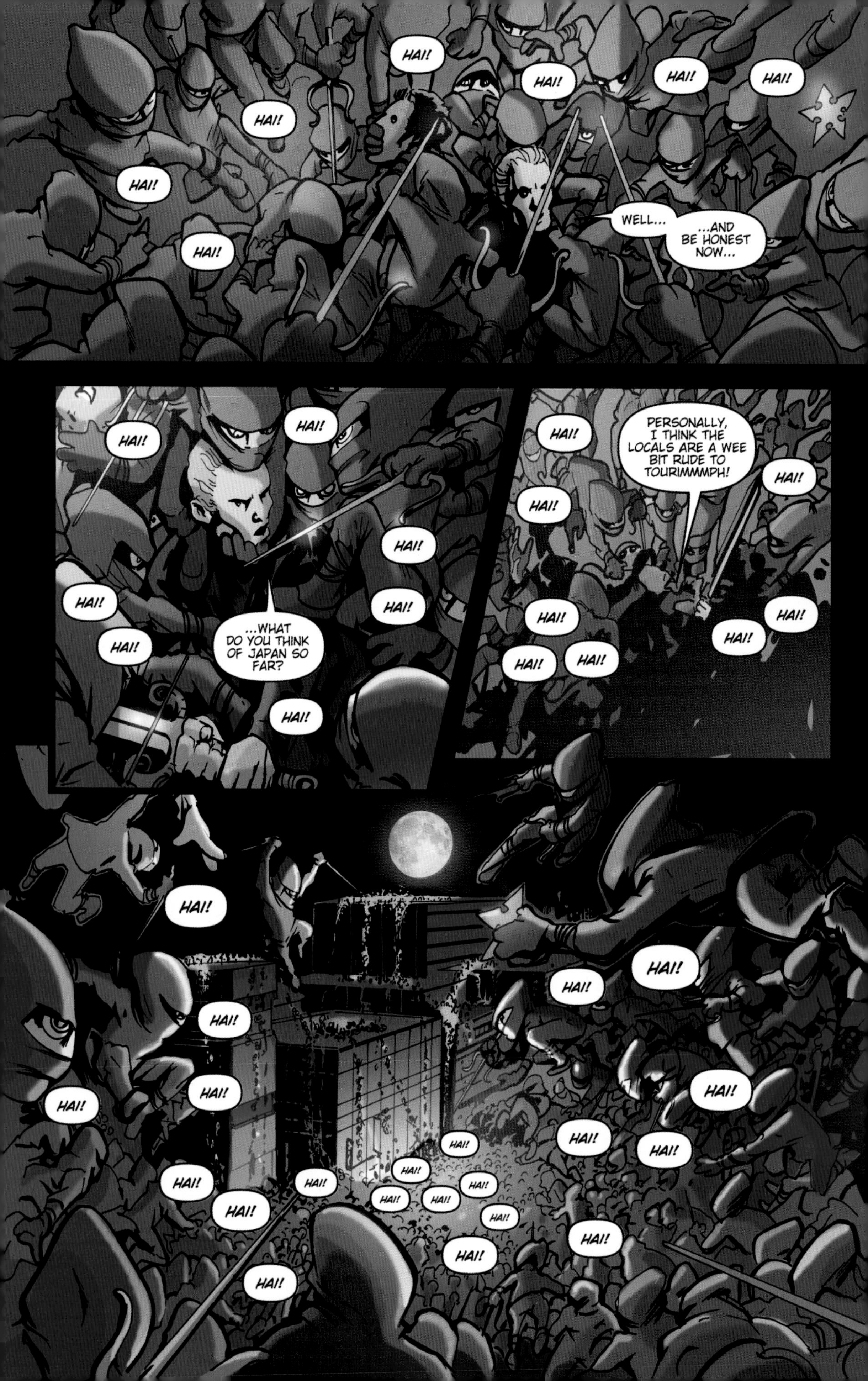
HAI!
HAI!
HAI!
HAI!
HAI!
HAI!
HAI!
WELL...
...AND BE HONEST NOW...
HAI!
HAI!
HAI!
HAI!
HAI!
HAI!
...WHAT DO YOU THINK OF JAPAN SO FAR?
HAI!
HAI!
PERSONALLY, I THINK THE LOCALS ARE A WEE BIT RUDE TO TOURIMMMPH!
HAI!
HAI!
HAI!
HAI!
HAI!
HAI!
HAI!
HAI!
HAI!
HAI!
HAI!
HAI!
HAI!
HAI!
HAI!
HAI!
HAI!
HAI!
HAI!
HAI!
HAI!
HAI!
HAI!
HAI!
HAI!
HAI!
HAI!
HAI!
HAI!

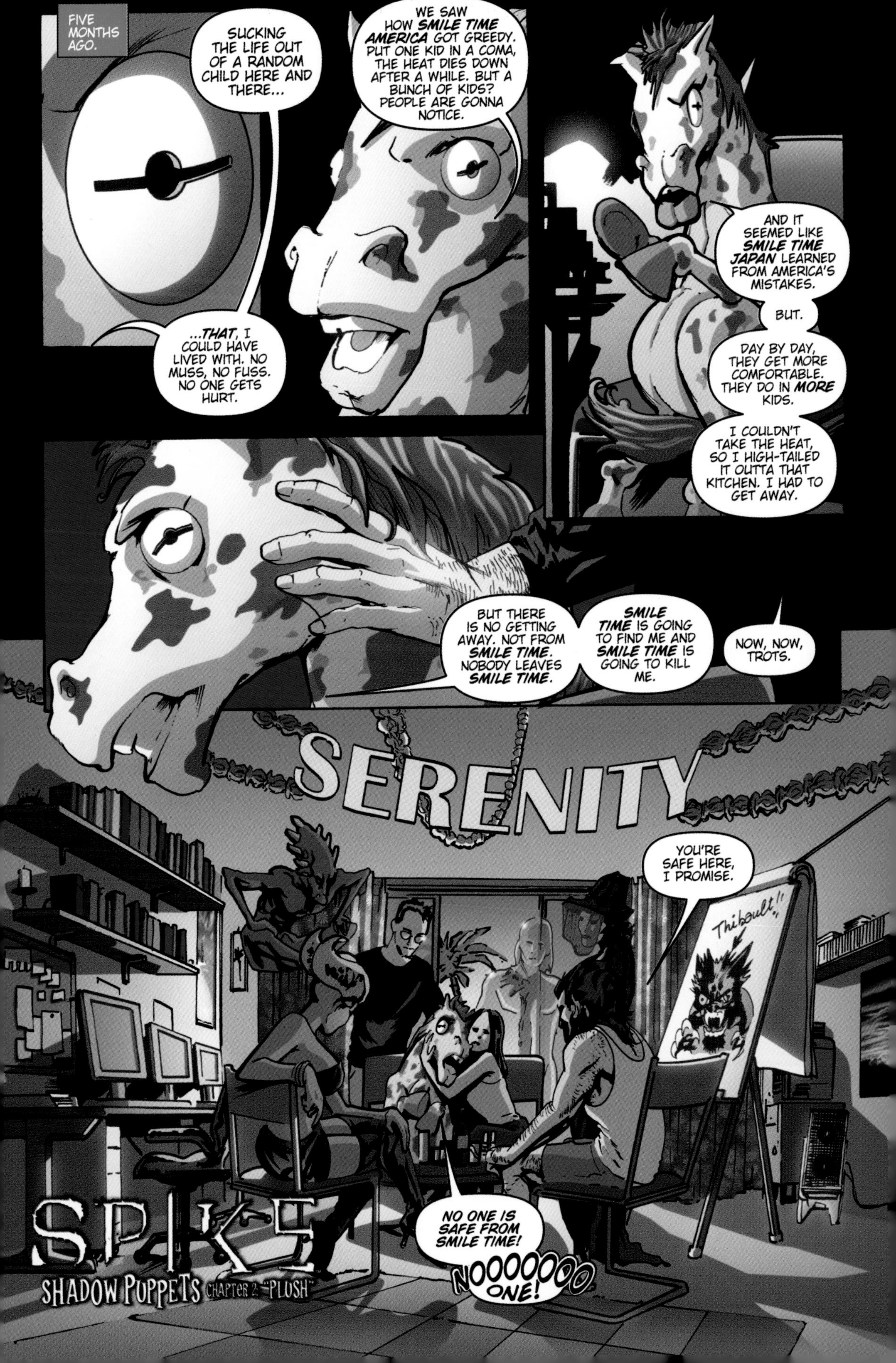
FIVE MONTHS AGO.
SUCKING THE LIFE OUT OF A RANDOM CHILD HERE AND THERE...
...THAT, I COULD HAVE LIVED WITH. NO MUSS, NO FUSS. NO ONE GETS HURT.
WE SAW HOW SMILE TIME AMERICA GOT GREEDY. PUT ONE KID IN A COMA, THE HEAT DIES DOWN AFTER A WHILE. BUT A BUNCH OF KIDS? PEOPLE ARE GONNA NOTICE.
AND IT SEEMED LIKE SMILE TIME JAPAN LEARNED FROM AMERICA'S MISTAKES.
BUT.
DAY BY DAY, THEY GET MORE COMFORTABLE. THEY DO IN MORE KIDS.
I COULDN'T TAKE THE HEAT, SO I HIGH-TAILED IT OUTTA THAT KITCHEN. I HAD TO GET AWAY.
BUT THERE IS NO GETTING AWAY. NOT FROM SMILE TIME. NOBODY LEAVES SMILE TIME.
SMILE TIME IS GOING TO FIND ME AND SMILE TIME IS GOING TO KILL ME.
NOW, NOW, TROTS.
SERENITY
YOU'RE SAFE HERE, I PROMISE.
Thibault!!
NO ONE IS SAFE FROM SMILE TIME!
NOOOOOOO ONE!
SPIKE
SHADOW PUPPETS CHAPTER 2: "PLUSH"

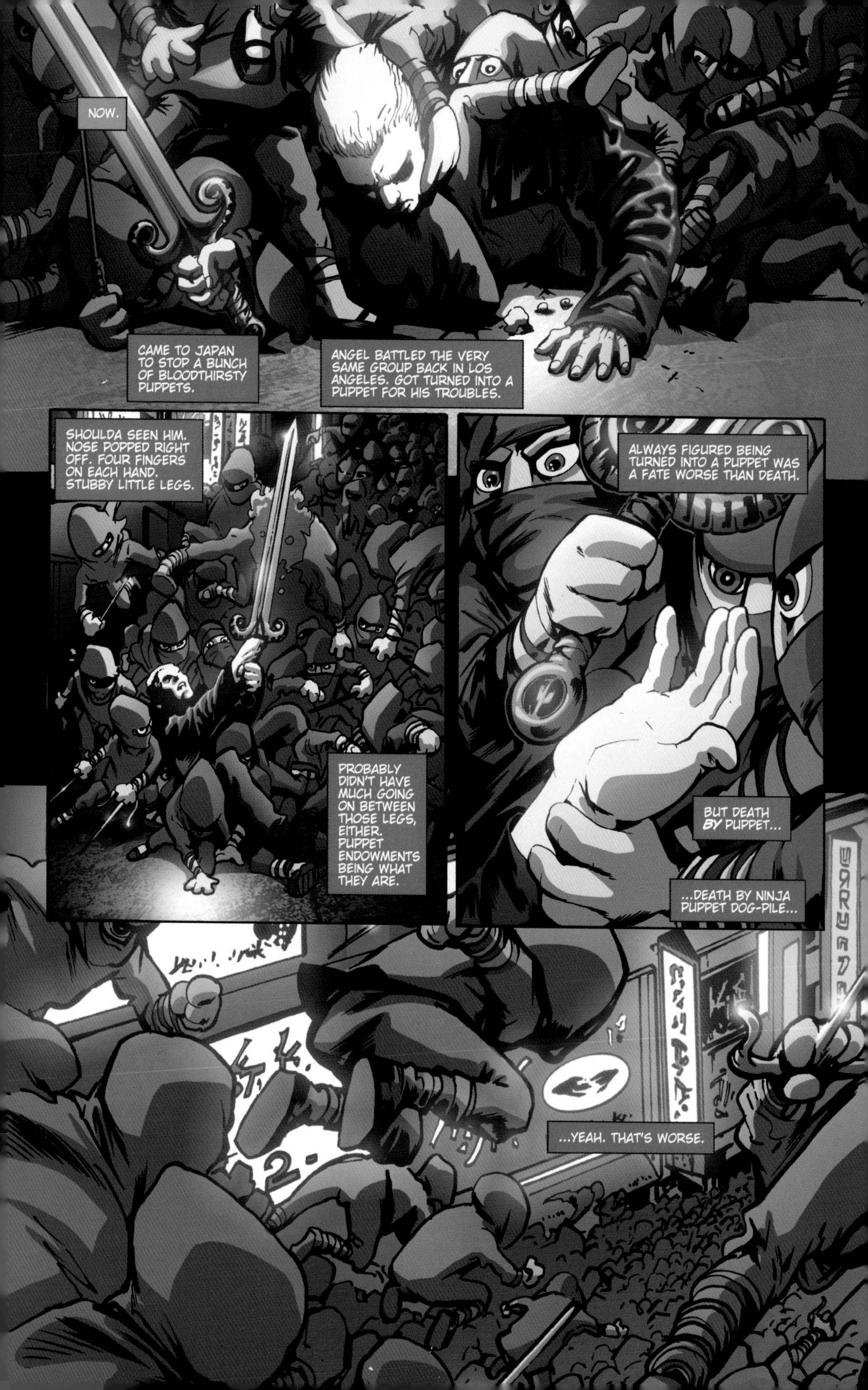
NOW.
CAME TO JAPAN TO STOP A BUNCH OF BLOODTHIRSTY PUPPETS.
ANGEL BATTLED THE VERY SAME GROUP BACK IN LOS ANGELES. GOT TURNED INTO A PUPPET FOR HIS TROUBLES.
SHOULDA SEEN HIM. NOSE POPPED RIGHT OFF. FOUR FINGERS ON EACH HAND. STUBBY LITTLE LEGS.
PROBABLY DIDN'T HAVE MUCH GOING ON BETWEEN THOSE LEGS, EITHER. PUPPET ENDOWMENTS BEING WHAT THEY ARE.
ALWAYS FIGURED BEING TURNED INTO A PUPPET WAS A FATE WORSE THAN DEATH.
BUT DEATH *BY* PUPPET...
...DEATH BY NINJA PUPPET DOG-PILE...
...YEAH. THAT'S WORSE.

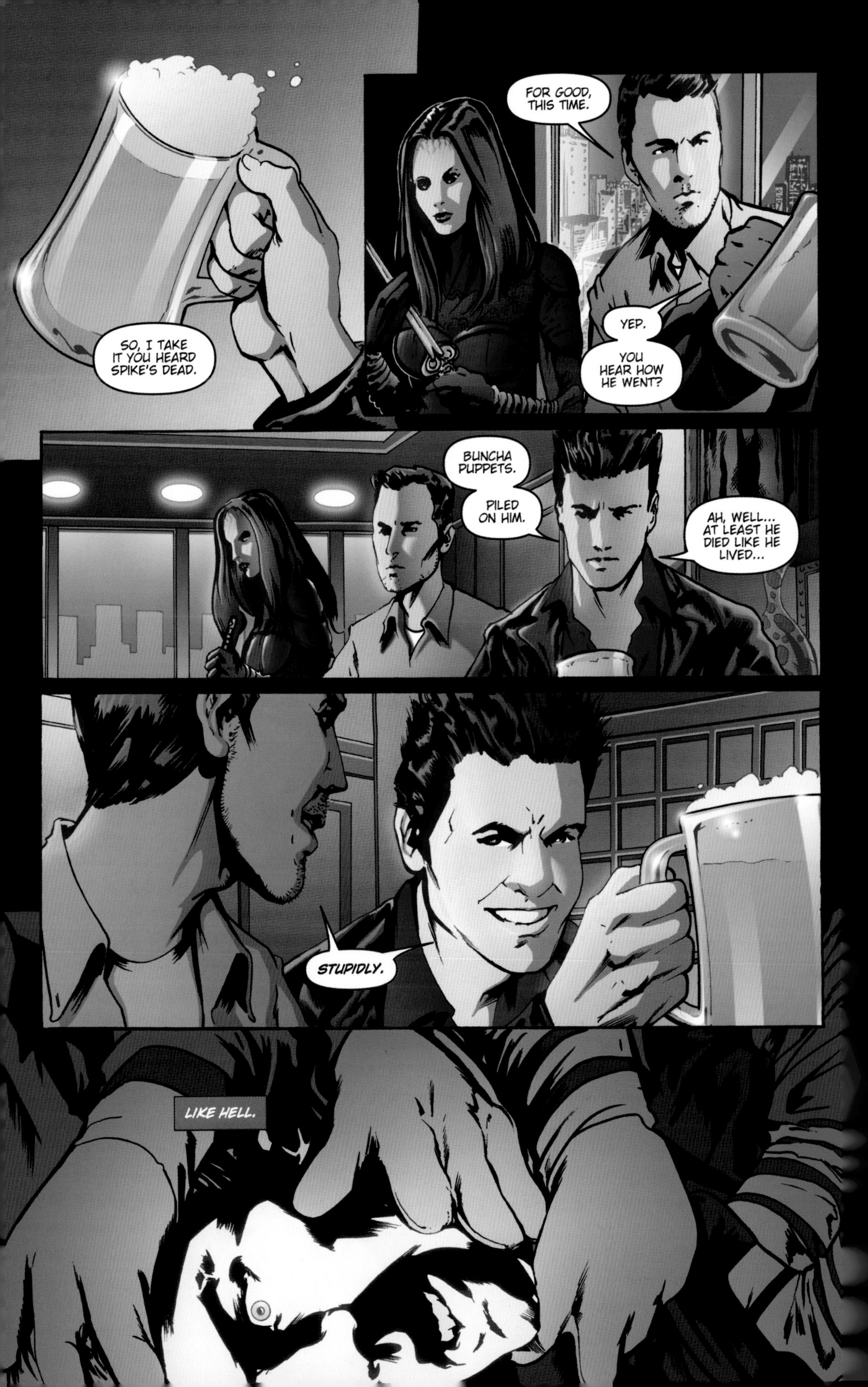
SO, I TAKE IT YOU HEARD SPIKE'S DEAD.
FOR GOOD, THIS TIME.
YEP.
YOU HEAR HOW HE WENT?
BUNCHA PUPPETS.
PILED ON HIM.
AH, WELL... AT LEAST HE DIED LIKE HE LIVED...
STUPIDLY.
LIKE HELL.

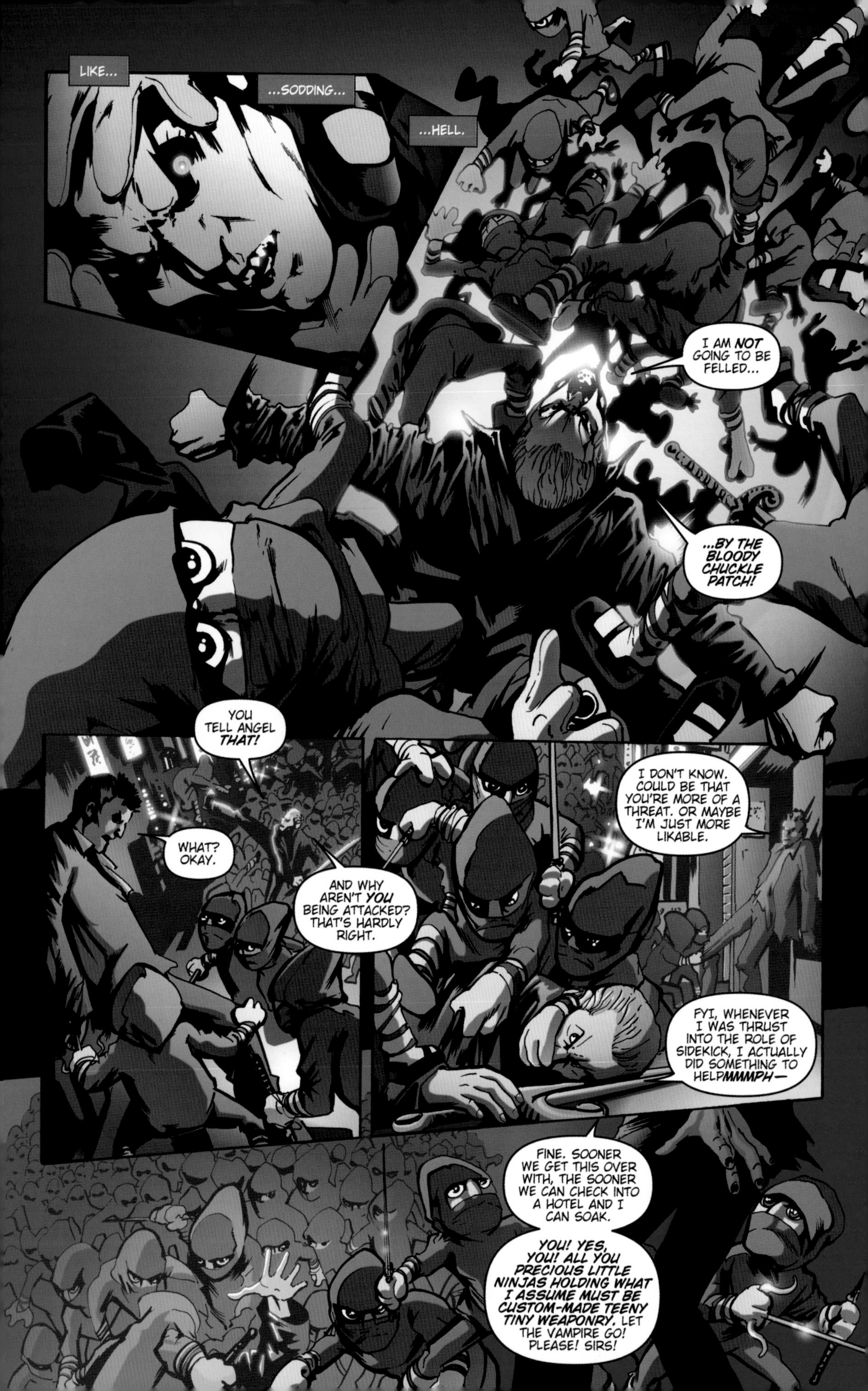
LIKE...
...SODDING...
...HELL.
I AM NOT GOING TO BE FELLED...
...BY THE BLOODY CHUCKLE PATCH!
YOU TELL ANGEL THAT!
WHAT? OKAY.
AND WHY AREN'T YOU BEING ATTACKED? THAT'S HARDLY RIGHT.
I DON'T KNOW. COULD BE THAT YOU'RE MORE OF A THREAT. OR MAYBE I'M JUST MORE LIKABLE.
FYI, WHENEVER I WAS THRUST INTO THE ROLE OF SIDEKICK, I ACTUALLY DID SOMETHING TO HELPMMMPH—
FINE. SOONER WE GET THIS OVER WITH, THE SOONER WE CAN CHECK INTO A HOTEL AND I CAN SOAK.
YOU! YES, YOU! ALL YOU PRECIOUS LITTLE NINJAS HOLDING WHAT I ASSUME MUST BE CUSTOM-MADE TEENY TINY WEAPONRY. LET THE VAMPIRE GO! PLEASE! SIRS!

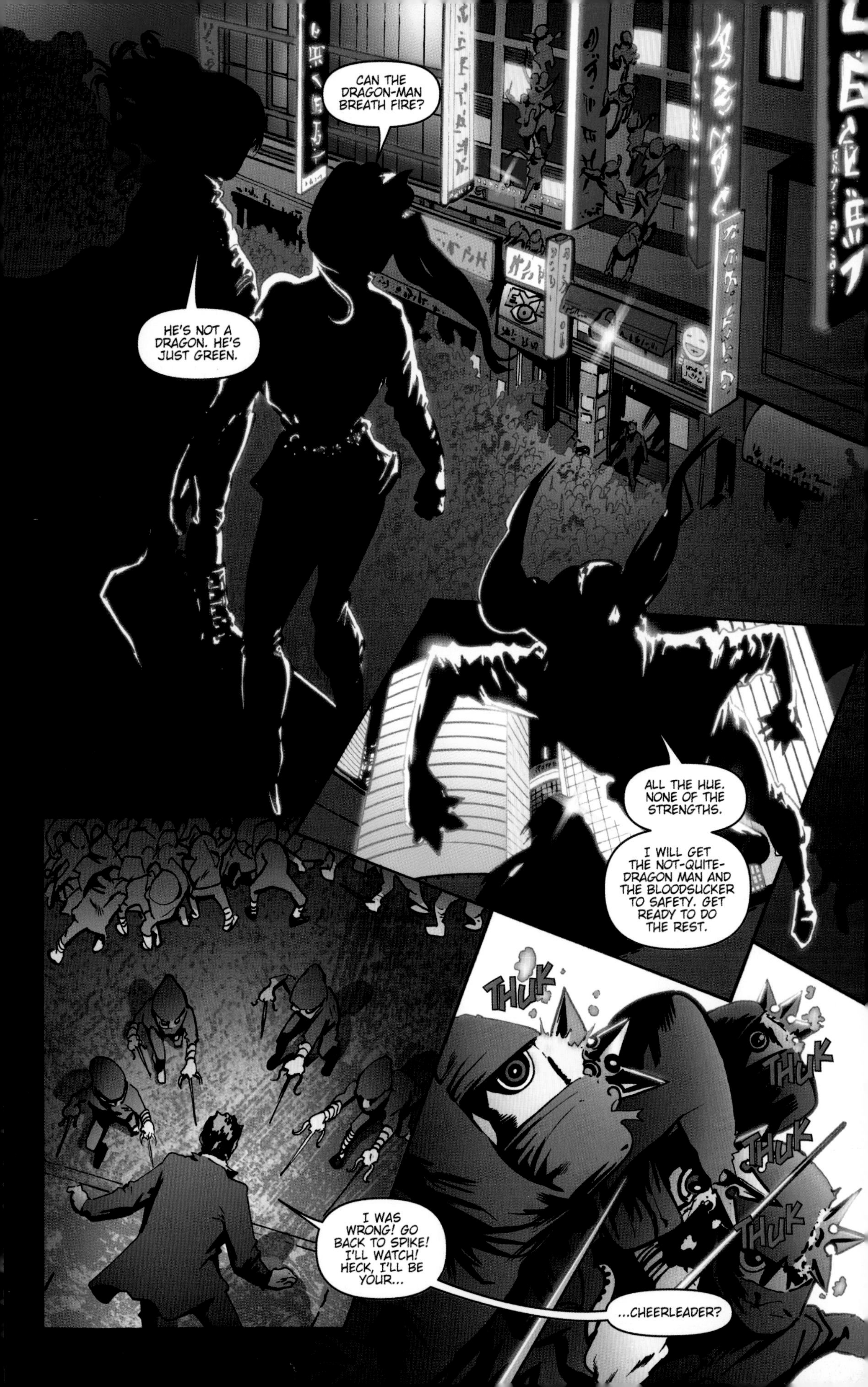
CAN THE DRAGON-MAN BREATH FIRE?
HE'S NOT A DRAGON. HE'S JUST GREEN.
ALL THE HUE. NONE OF THE STRENGTHS.
I WILL GET THE NOT-QUITE-DRAGON MAN AND THE BLOODSUCKER TO SAFETY. GET READY TO DO THE REST.
THUK
THUK
THUK
THUK
I WAS WRONG! GO BACK TO SPIKE! I'LL WATCH! HECK, I'LL BE YOUR...
...CHEERLEADER?

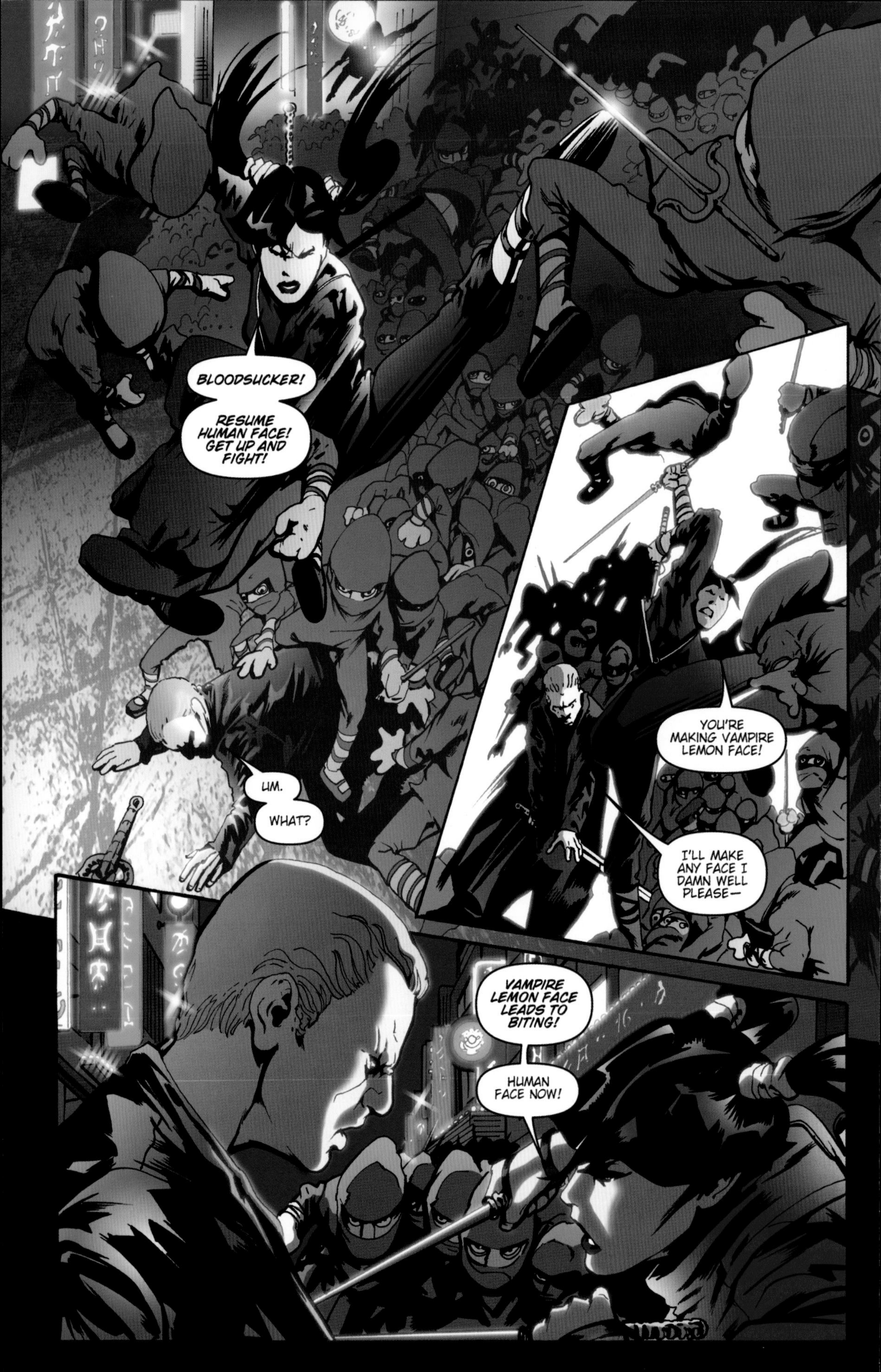
BLOODSUCKER!
RESUME HUMAN FACE! GET UP AND FIGHT!
UM.
WHAT?
YOU'RE MAKING VAMPIRE LEMON FACE!
I'LL MAKE ANY FACE I DAMN WELL PLEASE—
VAMPIRE LEMON FACE LEADS TO BITING!
HUMAN FACE NOW!

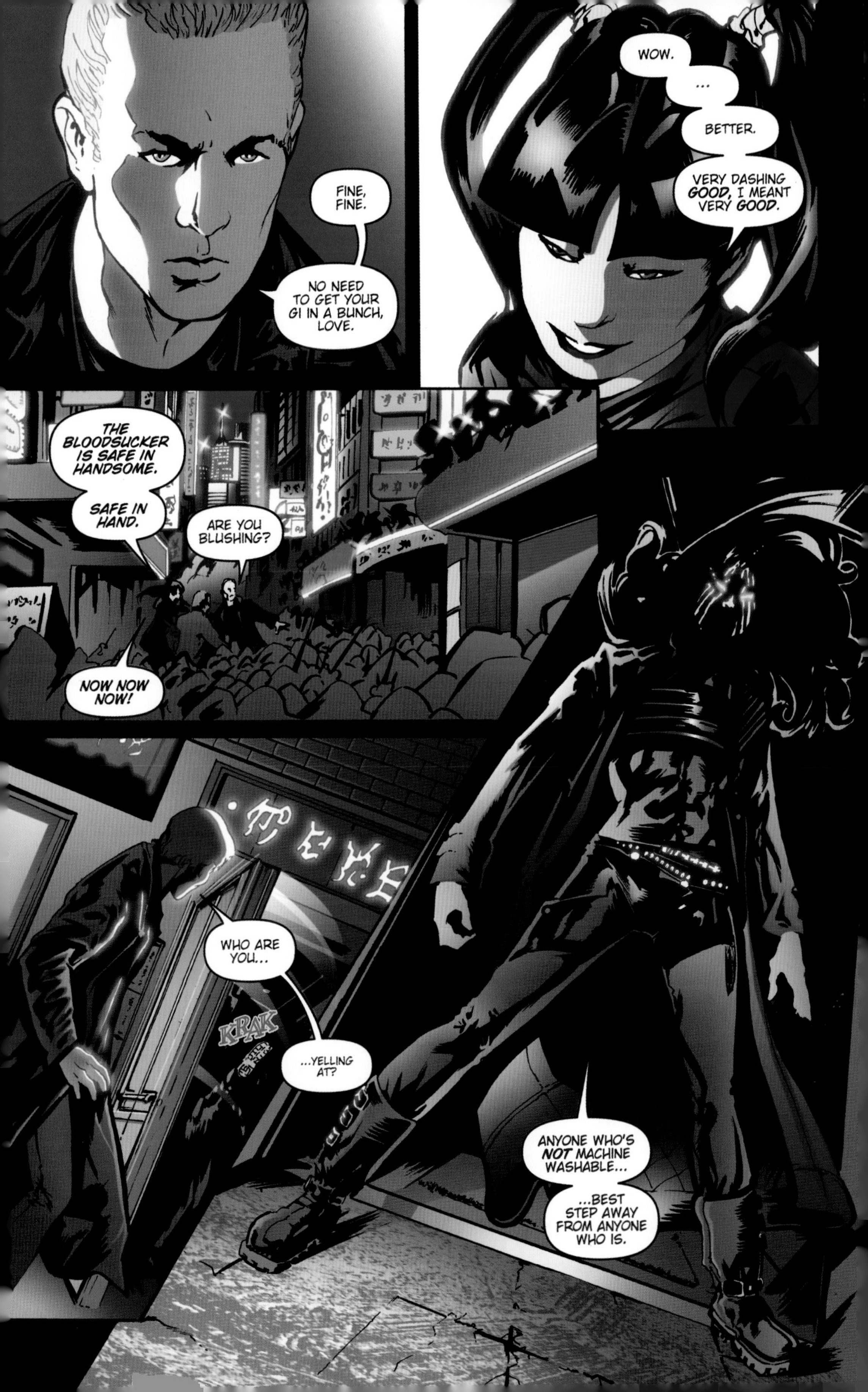
FINE, FINE.
NO NEED TO GET YOUR GI IN A BUNCH, LOVE.
WOW.
...
BETTER.
VERY DASHING **GOOD,** I MEANT VERY **GOOD.**
THE BLOODSUCKER IS SAFE IN HANDSOME.
SAFE IN HAND.
ARE YOU BLUSHING?
NOW NOW NOW!
KRAK
WHO ARE YOU...
...YELLING AT?
ANYONE WHO'S **NOT** MACHINE WASHABLE...
...BEST STEP AWAY FROM ANYONE WHO IS.

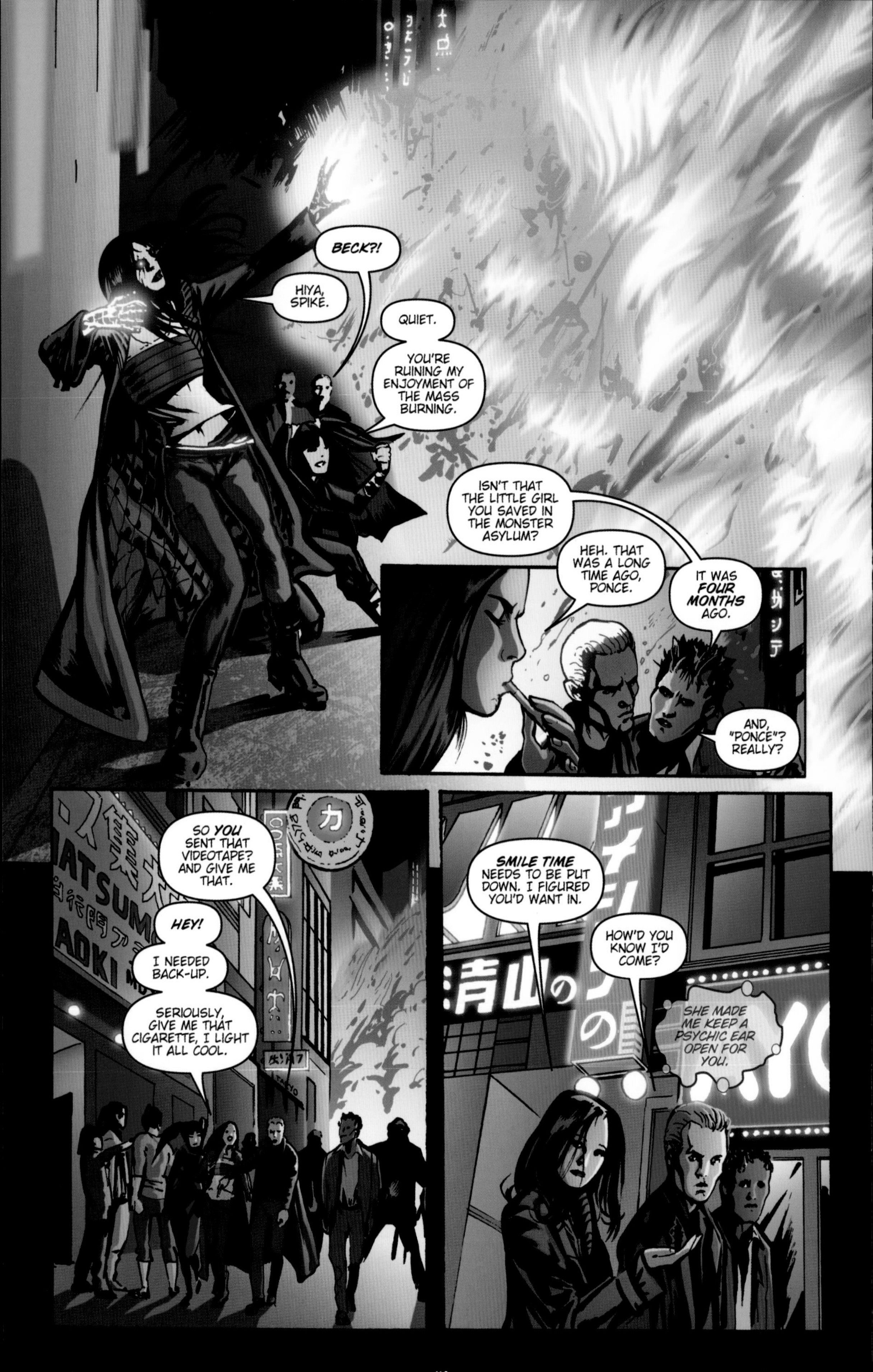
BECK?!
HIYA, SPIKE.
QUIET.
YOU'RE RUINING MY ENJOYMENT OF THE MASS BURNING.
ISN'T THAT THE LITTLE GIRL YOU SAVED IN THE MONSTER ASYLUM?
HEH. THAT WAS A LONG TIME AGO, PONCE.
IT WAS FOUR MONTHS AGO.
AND, "PONCE"? REALLY?
SO YOU SENT THAT VIDEOTAPE? AND GIVE ME THAT.
HEY!
I NEEDED BACK-UP.
SERIOUSLY, GIVE ME THAT CIGARETTE, I LIGHT IT ALL COOL.
SMILE TIME NEEDS TO BE PUT DOWN. I FIGURED YOU'D WANT IN.
HOW'D YOU KNOW I'D COME?
SHE MADE ME KEEP A PSYCHIC EAR OPEN FOR YOU.

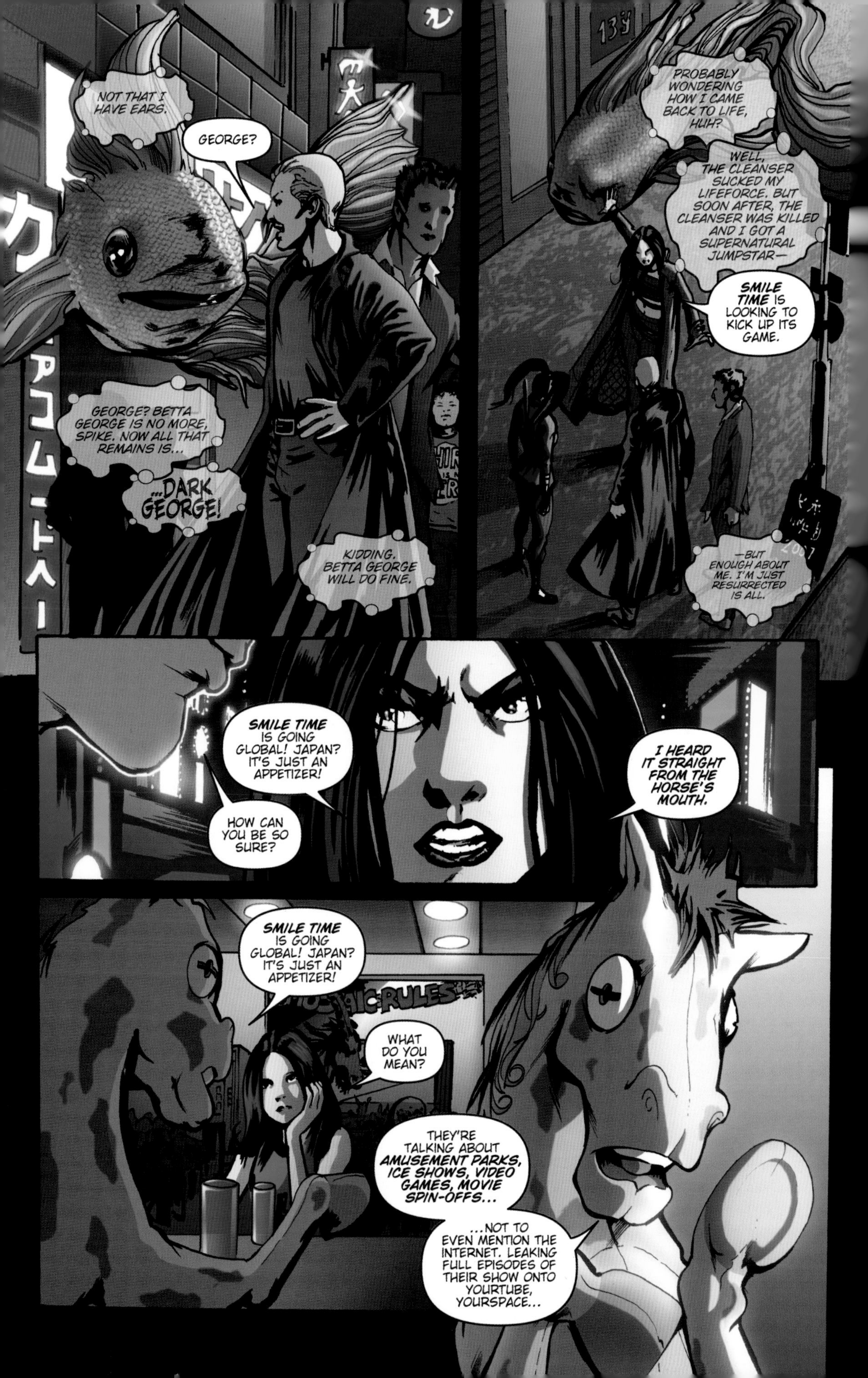
NOT THAT I HAVE EARS.
GEORGE?
GEORGE? BETTA GEORGE IS NO MORE, SPIKE. NOW ALL THAT REMAINS IS...
...DARK GEORGE!
KIDDING. BETTA GEORGE WILL DO FINE.
PROBABLY WONDERING HOW I CAME BACK TO LIFE, HUH?
WELL, THE CLEANSER SUCKED MY LIFEFORCE. BUT SOON AFTER, THE CLEANSER WAS KILLED AND I GOT A SUPERNATURAL JUMPSTAR—
SMILE TIME IS LOOKING TO KICK UP ITS GAME.
—BUT ENOUGH ABOUT ME. I'M JUST RESURRECTED IS ALL.
SMILE TIME IS GOING GLOBAL! JAPAN? IT'S JUST AN APPETIZER!
HOW CAN YOU BE SO SURE?
I HEARD IT STRAIGHT FROM THE HORSE'S MOUTH.
SMILE TIME IS GOING GLOBAL! JAPAN? IT'S JUST AN APPETIZER!
WHAT DO YOU MEAN?
THEY'RE TALKING ABOUT AMUSEMENT PARKS, ICE SHOWS, VIDEO GAMES, MOVIE SPIN-OFFS...
...NOT TO EVEN MENTION THE INTERNET. LEAKING FULL EPISODES OF THEIR SHOW ONTO YOURTUBE, YOURSPACE...

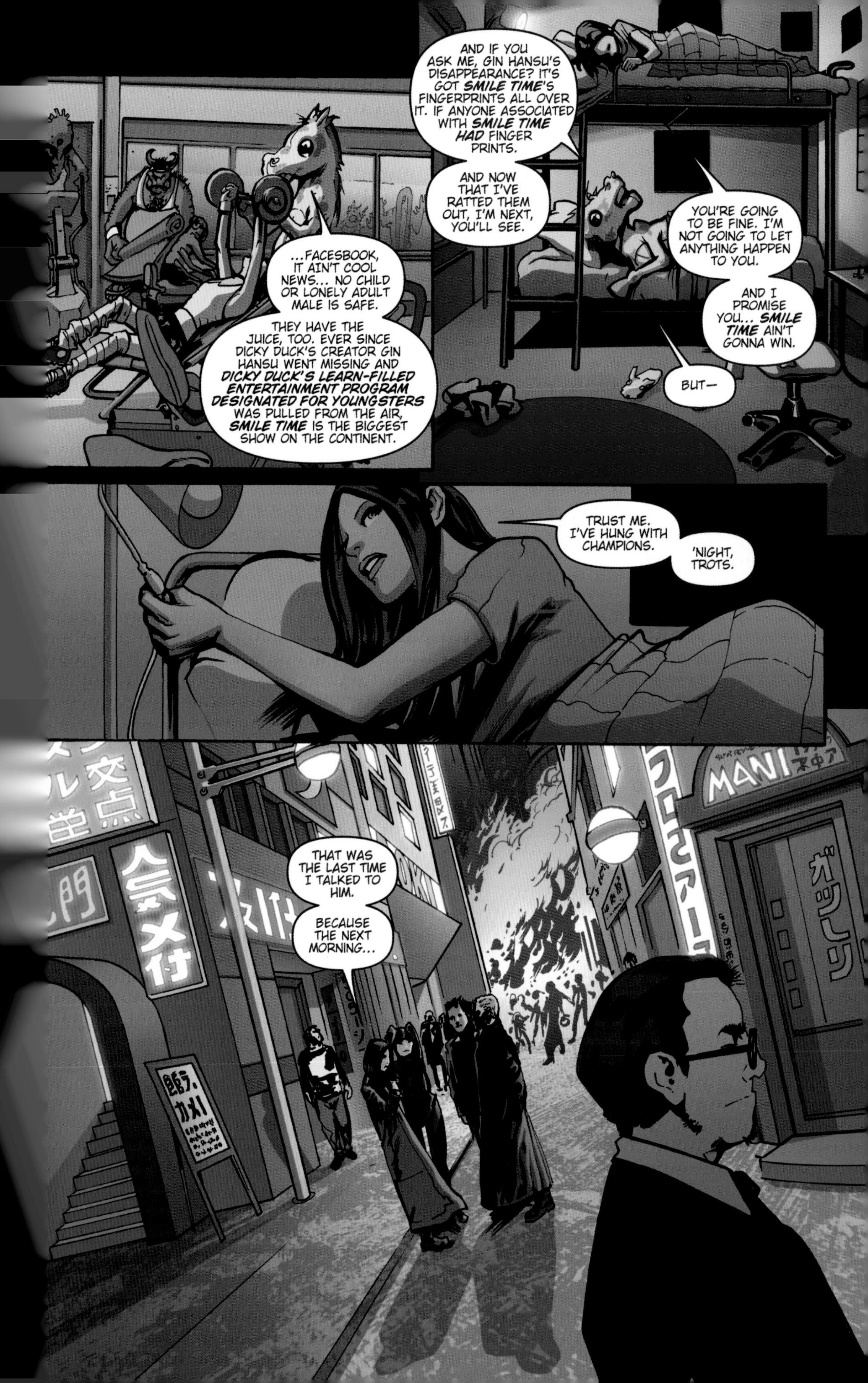
...FACESBOOK, IT AIN'T COOL NEWS... NO CHILD OR LONELY ADULT MALE IS SAFE.
THEY HAVE THE JUICE, TOO. EVER SINCE DICKY DUCK'S CREATOR GIN HANSU WENT MISSING AND DICKY DUCK'S LEARN-FILLED ENTERTAINMENT PROGRAM DESIGNATED FOR YOUNGSTERS WAS PULLED FROM THE AIR, SMILE TIME IS THE BIGGEST SHOW ON THE CONTINENT.
AND IF YOU ASK ME, GIN HANSU'S DISAPPEARANCE? IT'S GOT SMILE TIME'S FINGERPRINTS ALL OVER IT. IF ANYONE ASSOCIATED WITH SMILE TIME HAD FINGER PRINTS.
AND NOW THAT I'VE RATTED THEM OUT, I'M NEXT, YOU'LL SEE.
YOU'RE GOING TO BE FINE. I'M NOT GOING TO LET ANYTHING HAPPEN TO YOU.
AND I PROMISE YOU... SMILE TIME AIN'T GONNA WIN.
BUT—
TRUST ME. I'VE HUNG WITH CHAMPIONS.
'NIGHT, TROTS.
THAT WAS THE LAST TIME I TALKED TO HIM.
BECAUSE THE NEXT MORNING...
MANI

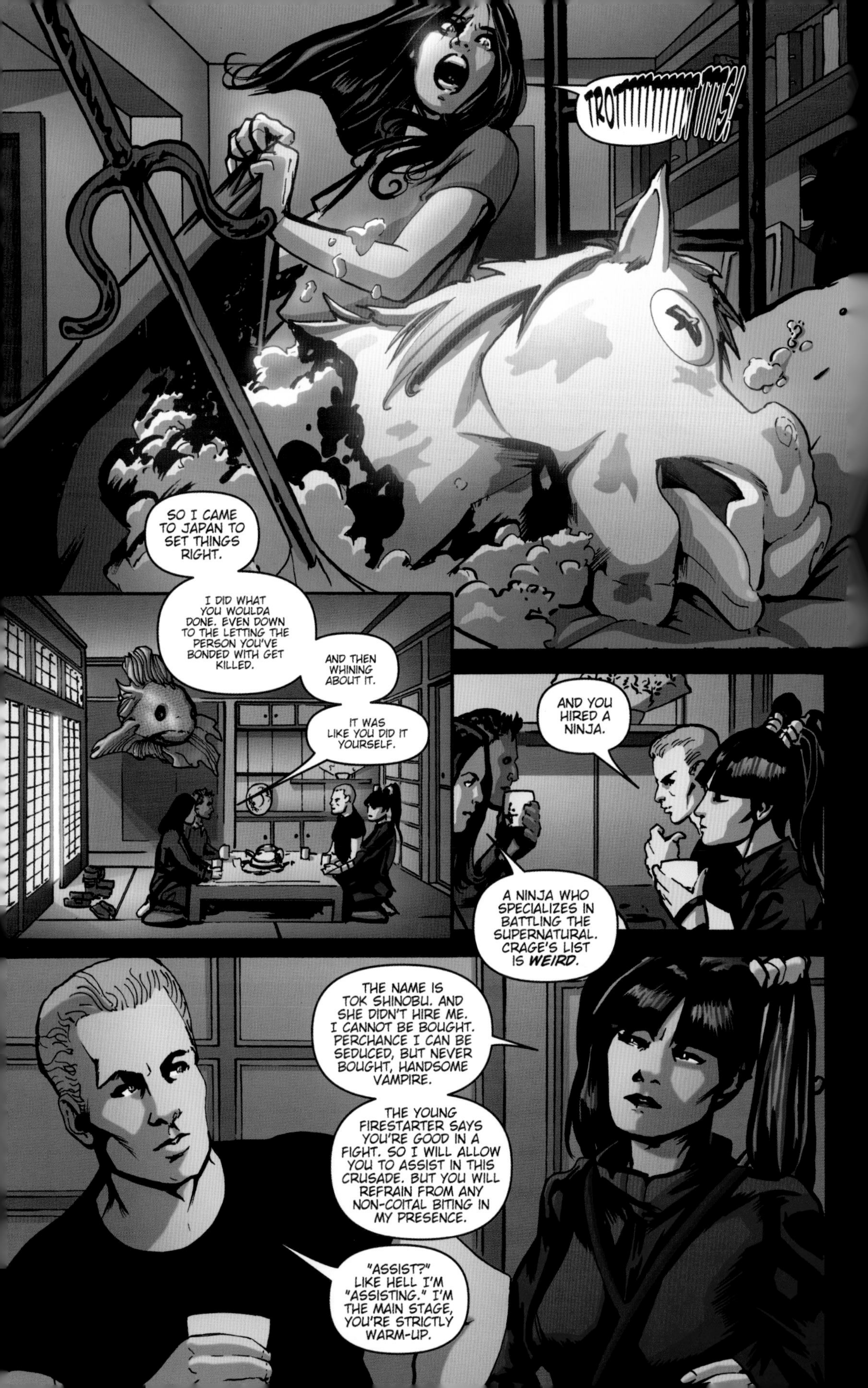
TROTTTTTTTTTTTTTTTTTS!
SO I CAME TO JAPAN TO SET THINGS RIGHT.
I DID WHAT YOU WOULDA DONE. EVEN DOWN TO THE LETTING THE PERSON YOU'VE BONDED WITH GET KILLED.
AND THEN WHINING ABOUT IT.
IT WAS LIKE YOU DID IT YOURSELF.
AND YOU HIRED A NINJA.
A NINJA WHO SPECIALIZES IN BATTLING THE SUPERNATURAL. CRAGE'S LIST IS *WEIRD*.
THE NAME IS TOK SHINOBU. AND SHE DIDN'T HIRE ME. I CANNOT BE BOUGHT. PERCHANCE I CAN BE SEDUCED, BUT NEVER BOUGHT, HANDSOME VAMPIRE.
THE YOUNG FIRESTARTER SAYS YOU'RE GOOD IN A FIGHT. SO I WILL ALLOW YOU TO ASSIST IN THIS CRUSADE. BUT YOU WILL REFRAIN FROM ANY NON-COITAL BITING IN MY PRESENCE.
"ASSIST?" LIKE HELL I'M "ASSISTING." I'M THE MAIN STAGE, YOU'RE STRICTLY WARM-UP.

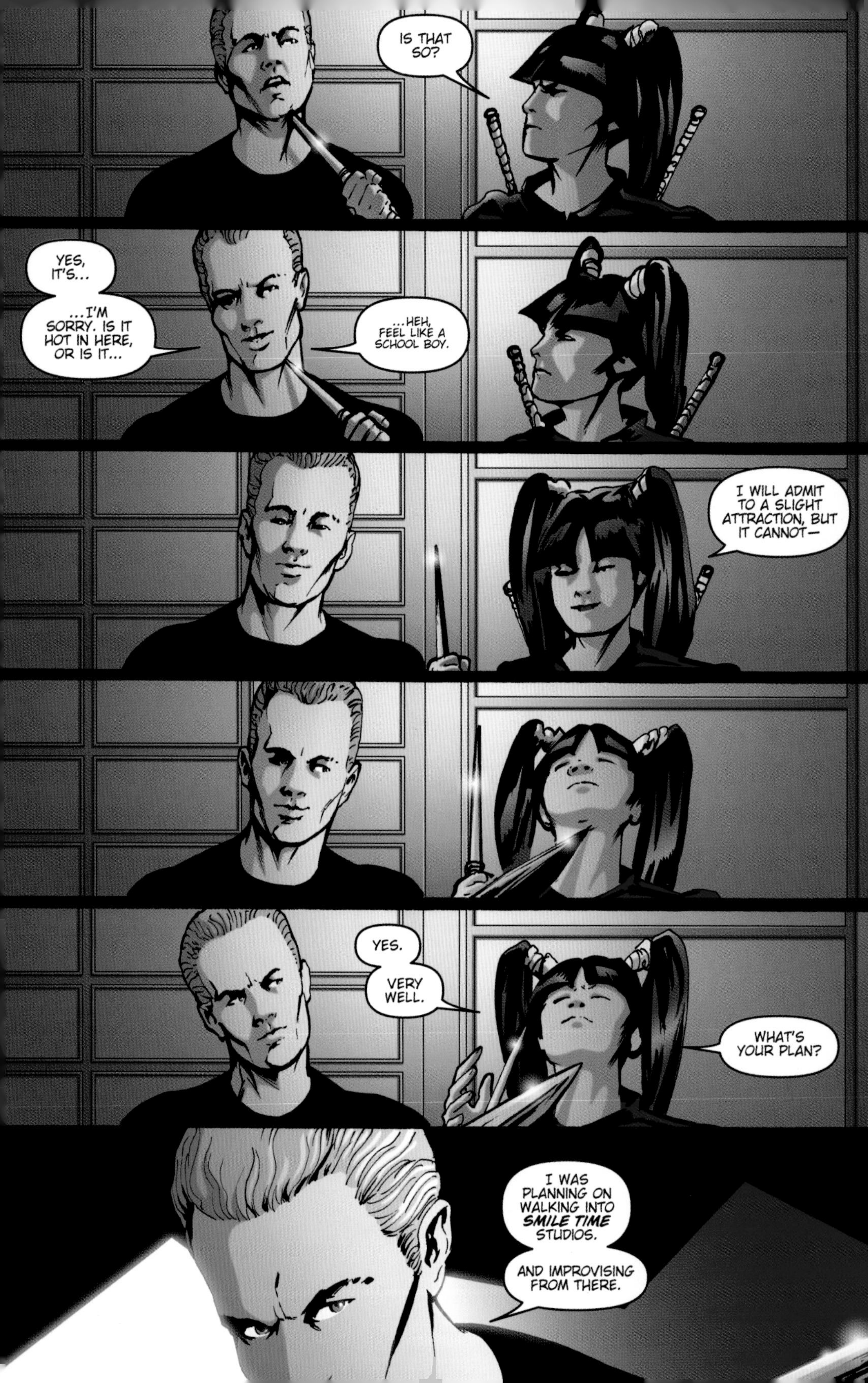
IS THAT SO?
YES, IT'S...
...I'M SORRY. IS IT HOT IN HERE, OR IS IT...
...HEH, FEEL LIKE A SCHOOL BOY.
I WILL ADMIT TO A SLIGHT ATTRACTION, BUT IT CANNOT—
YES.
VERY WELL.
WHAT'S YOUR PLAN?
I WAS PLANNING ON WALKING INTO **SMILE TIME** STUDIOS.
AND IMPROVISING FROM THERE.

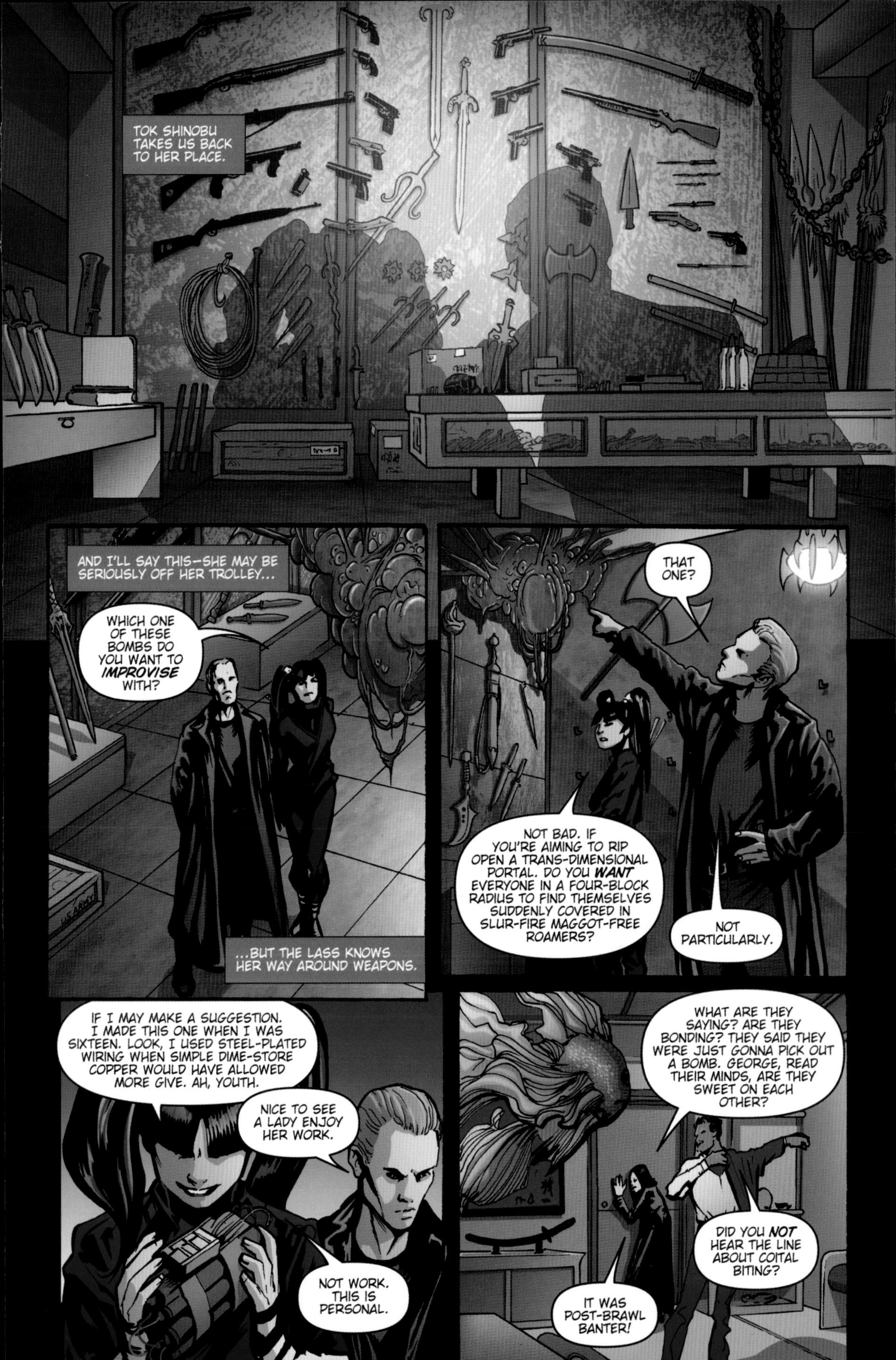

TOK SHINOBU TAKES US BACK TO HER PLACE.
AND I'LL SAY THIS—SHE MAY BE SERIOUSLY OFF HER TROLLEY...
WHICH ONE OF THESE BOMBS DO YOU WANT TO *IMPROVISE* WITH?
...BUT THE LASS KNOWS HER WAY AROUND WEAPONS.
THAT ONE?
NOT BAD. IF YOU'RE AIMING TO RIP OPEN A TRANS-DIMENSIONAL PORTAL. DO YOU *WANT* EVERYONE IN A FOUR-BLOCK RADIUS TO FIND THEMSELVES SUDDENLY COVERED IN SLUR-FIRE MAGGOT-FREE ROAMERS?
NOT PARTICULARLY.
IF I MAY MAKE A SUGGESTION. I MADE THIS ONE WHEN I WAS SIXTEEN. LOOK, I USED STEEL-PLATED WIRING WHEN SIMPLE DIME-STORE COPPER WOULD HAVE ALLOWED MORE GIVE. AH, YOUTH.
NICE TO SEE A LADY ENJOY HER WORK.
NOT WORK. THIS IS PERSONAL.
WHAT ARE THEY SAYING? ARE THEY BONDING? THEY SAID THEY WERE JUST GONNA PICK OUT A BOMB. GEORGE, READ THEIR MINDS, ARE THEY SWEET ON EACH OTHER?
DID YOU *NOT* HEAR THE LINE ABOUT COITAL BITING?
IT WAS POST-BRAWL BANTER!

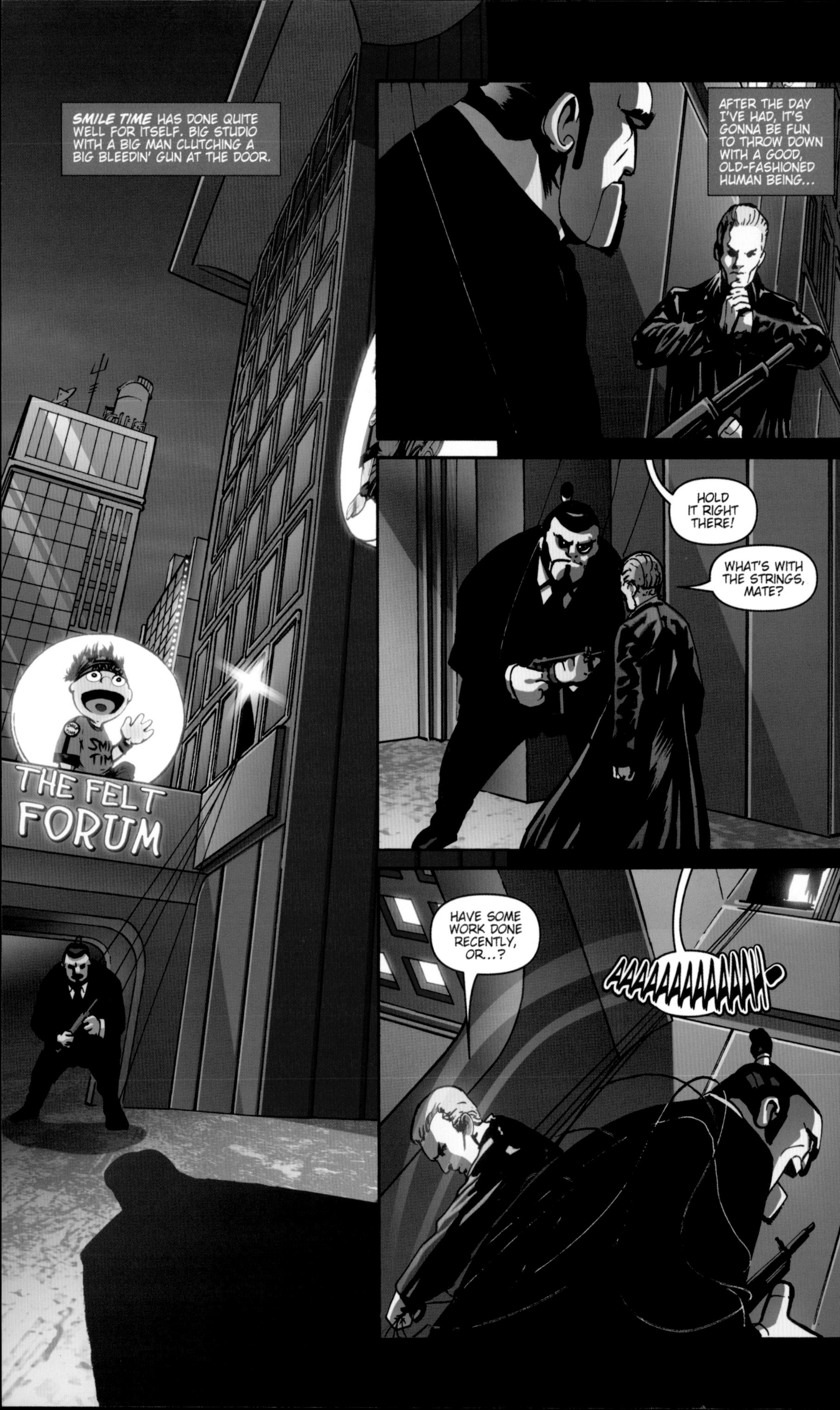
SMILE TIME HAS DONE QUITE WELL FOR ITSELF. BIG STUDIO WITH A BIG MAN CLUTCHING A BIG BLEEDIN' GUN AT THE DOOR.
THE FELT FORUM
AFTER THE DAY I'VE HAD, IT'S GONNA BE FUN TO THROW DOWN WITH A GOOD, OLD-FASHIONED HUMAN BEING...
HOLD IT RIGHT THERE!
WHAT'S WITH THE STRINGS, MATE?
HAVE SOME WORK DONE RECENTLY, OR...?
AAAAAAAAAAAAH-

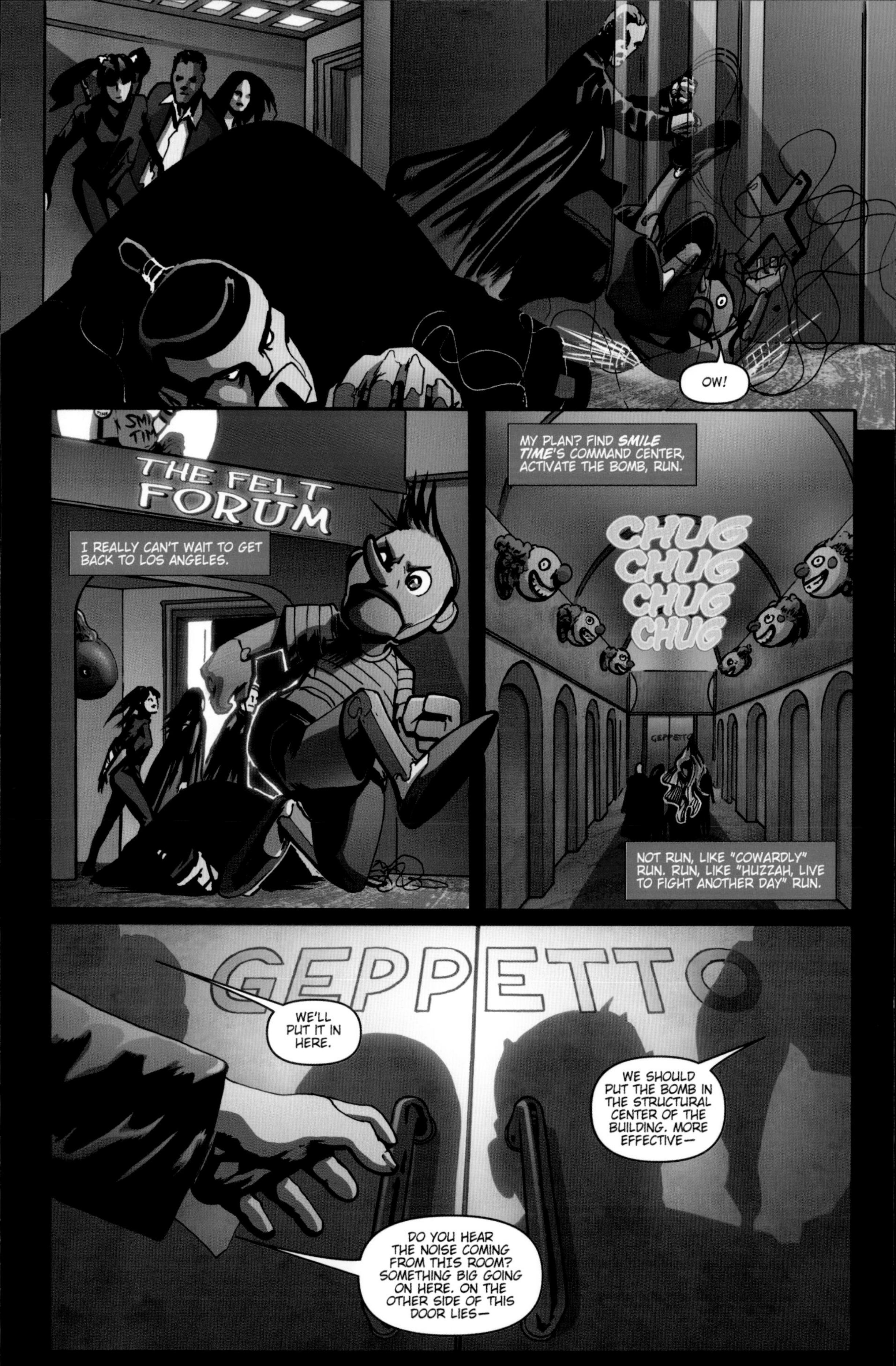
OW!
THE FELT FORUM
I REALLY CAN'T WAIT TO GET BACK TO LOS ANGELES.
MY PLAN? FIND SMILE TIME'S COMMAND CENTER, ACTIVATE THE BOMB, RUN.
CHUG CHUG CHUG CHUG
NOT RUN, LIKE "COWARDLY" RUN. RUN, LIKE "HUZZAH, LIVE TO FIGHT ANOTHER DAY" RUN.
GEPPETTO
WE'LL PUT IT IN HERE.
WE SHOULD PUT THE BOMB IN THE STRUCTURAL CENTER OF THE BUILDING. MORE EFFECTIVE—
DO YOU HEAR THE NOISE COMING FROM THIS ROOM? SOMETHING BIG GOING ON HERE. ON THE OTHER SIDE OF THIS DOOR LIES—

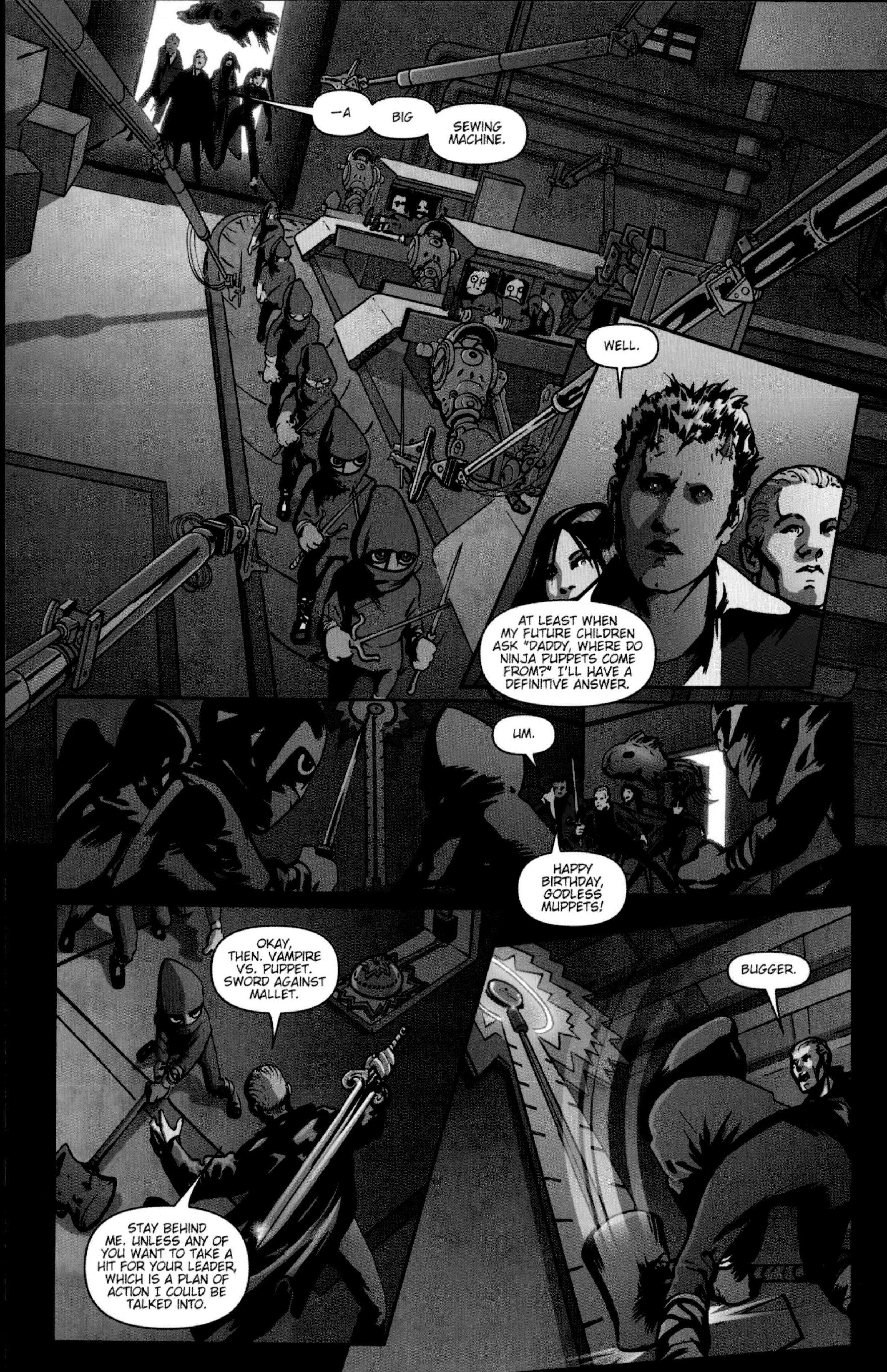
—A
BIG
SEWING MACHINE.
WELL.
AT LEAST WHEN MY FUTURE CHILDREN ASK "DADDY, WHERE DO NINJA PUPPETS COME FROM?" I'LL HAVE A DEFINITIVE ANSWER.
UM.
HAPPY BIRTHDAY, GODLESS MUPPETS!
OKAY, THEN. VAMPIRE VS. PUPPET. SWORD AGAINST MALLET.
STAY BEHIND ME. UNLESS ANY OF YOU WANT TO TAKE A HIT FOR YOUR LEADER, WHICH IS A PLAN OF ACTION I COULD BE TALKED INTO.
BUGGER.

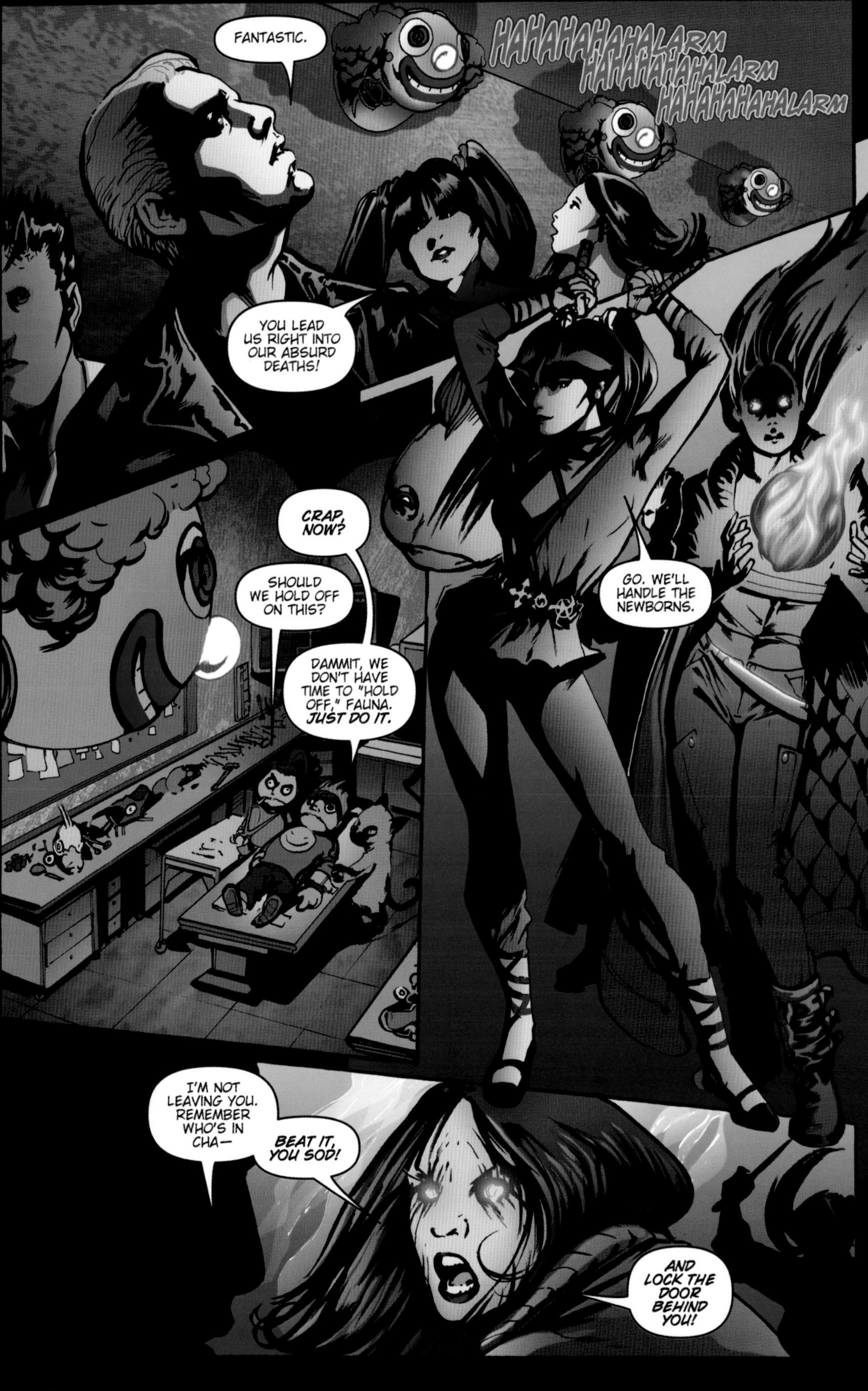
FANTASTIC.
HAHAHAHAHALARM
HAHAHAHAHALARM
HAHAHAHAHALARM
YOU LEAD US RIGHT INTO OUR ABSURD DEATHS!
CRAP, NOW?
SHOULD WE HOLD OFF ON THIS?
DAMMIT, WE DON'T HAVE TIME TO "HOLD OFF," FAUNA. JUST DO IT.
GO. WE'LL HANDLE THE NEWBORNS.
I'M NOT LEAVING YOU. REMEMBER WHO'S IN CHA—
BEAT IT, YOU SOD!
AND LOCK THE DOOR BEHIND YOU!

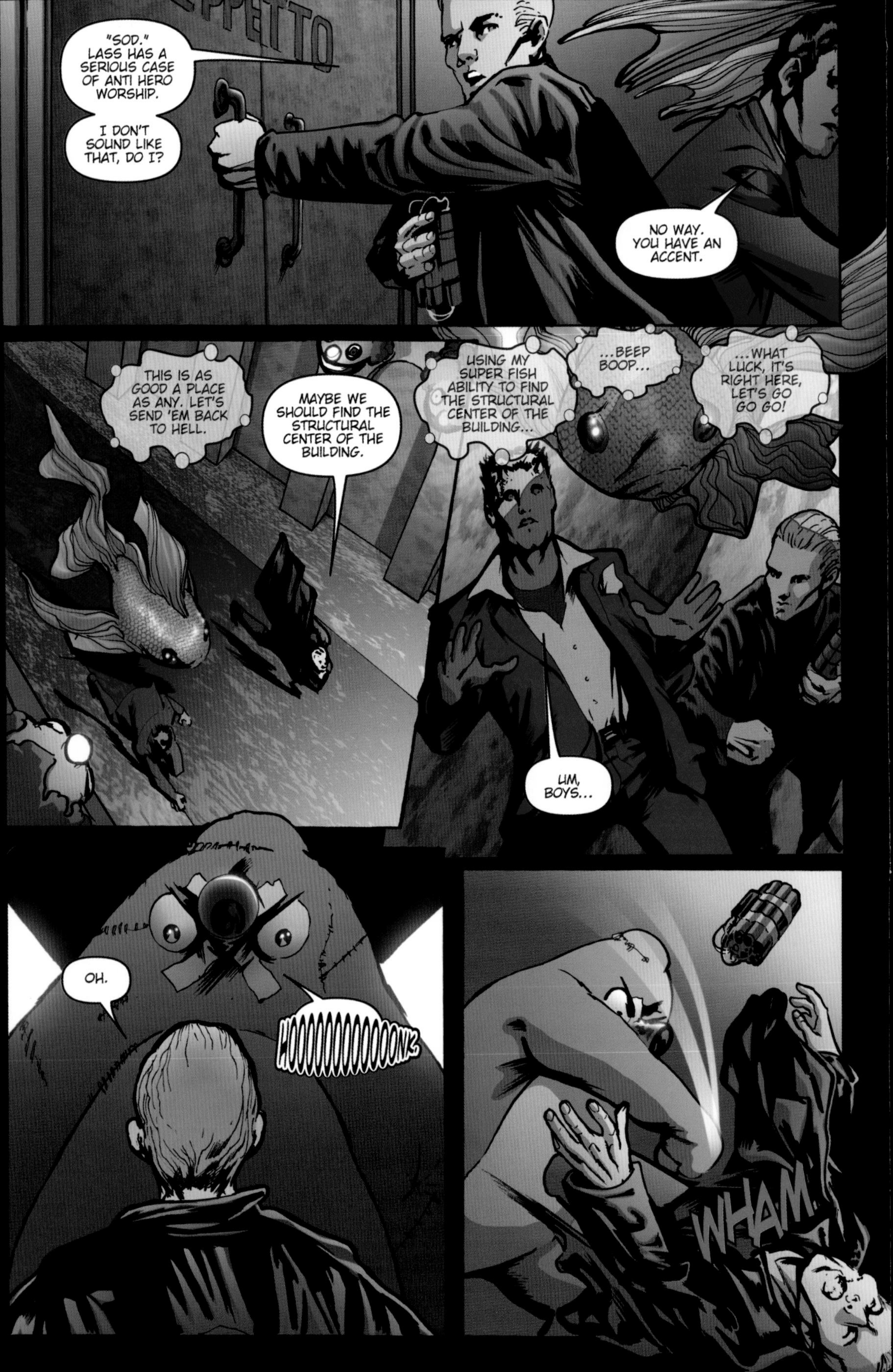
"SOD." LASS HAS A SERIOUS CASE OF ANTI HERO WORSHIP.
I DON'T SOUND LIKE THAT, DO I?
NO WAY. YOU HAVE AN ACCENT.
THIS IS AS GOOD A PLACE AS ANY. LET'S SEND 'EM BACK TO HELL.
MAYBE WE SHOULD FIND THE STRUCTURAL CENTER OF THE BUILDING.
USING MY SUPER FISH ABILITY TO FIND THE STRUCTURAL CENTER OF THE BUILDING...
...BEEP BOOP...
...WHAT LUCK, IT'S RIGHT HERE, LET'S GO GO GO!
UM, BOYS...
OH.
HOOOOOOOOOOONK
WHAM

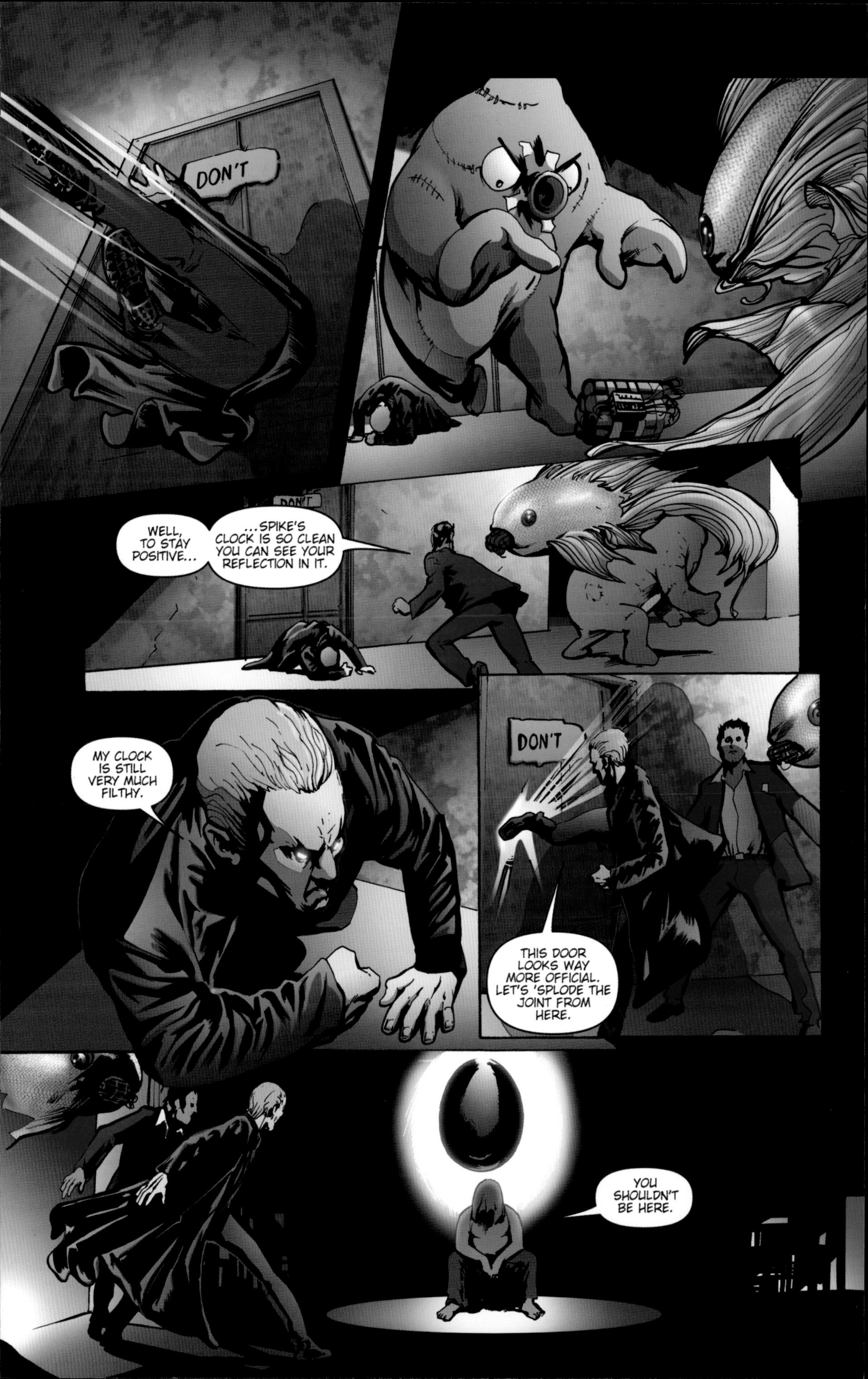
DON'T
WELL, TO STAY POSITIVE...
...SPIKE'S CLOCK IS SO CLEAN YOU CAN SEE YOUR REFLECTION IN IT.
MY CLOCK IS STILL VERY MUCH FILTHY.
DON'T
THIS DOOR LOOKS WAY MORE OFFICIAL. LET'S 'SPLODE THE JOINT FROM HERE.
YOU SHOULDN'T BE HERE.

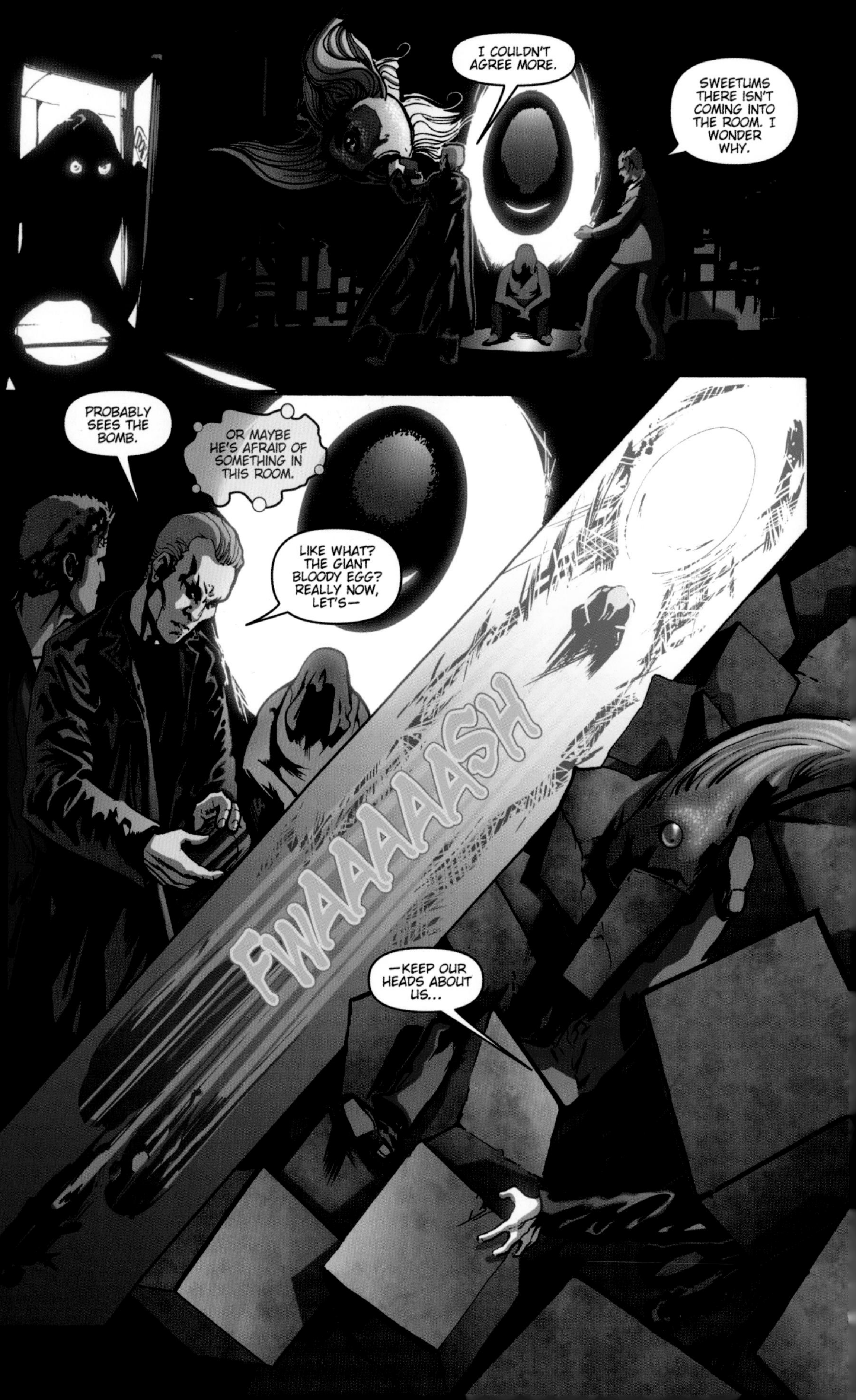
I COULDN'T AGREE MORE.
SWEETUMS THERE ISN'T COMING INTO THE ROOM. I WONDER WHY.
PROBABLY SEES THE BOMB.
OR MAYBE HE'S AFRAID OF SOMETHING IN THIS ROOM.
LIKE WHAT? THE GIANT BLOODY EGG? REALLY NOW, LET'S—
FWAAAAASH
—KEEP OUR HEADS ABOUT US...

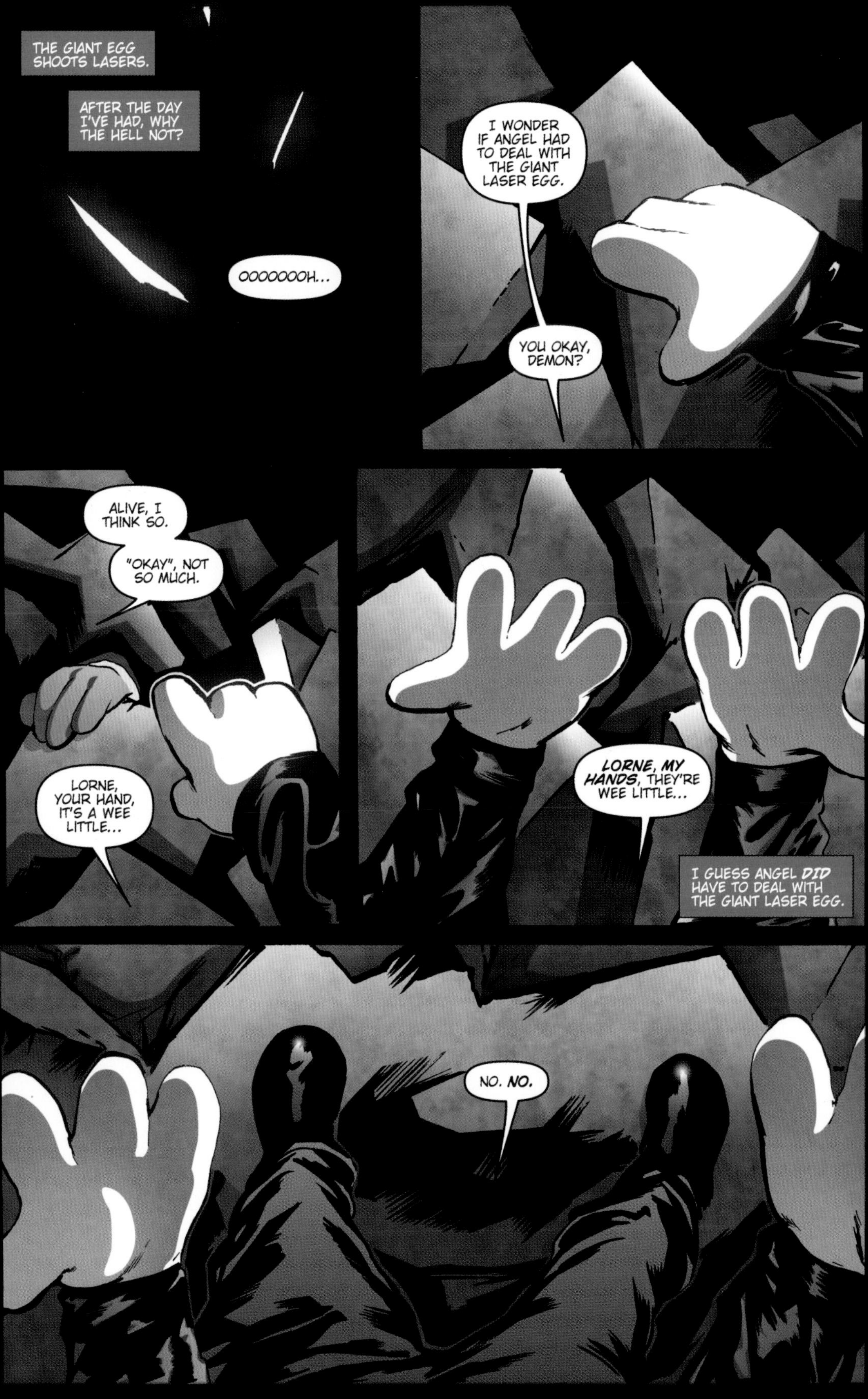
THE GIANT EGG SHOOTS LASERS.
AFTER THE DAY I'VE HAD, WHY THE HELL NOT?
OOOOOOOH...
I WONDER IF ANGEL HAD TO DEAL WITH THE GIANT LASER EGG.
YOU OKAY, DEMON?
ALIVE, I THINK SO.
"OKAY", NOT SO MUCH.
LORNE, YOUR HAND, IT'S A WEE LITTLE...
LORNE, MY HANDS, THEY'RE WEE LITTLE...
I GUESS ANGEL DID HAVE TO DEAL WITH THE GIANT LASER EGG.
NO. NO.

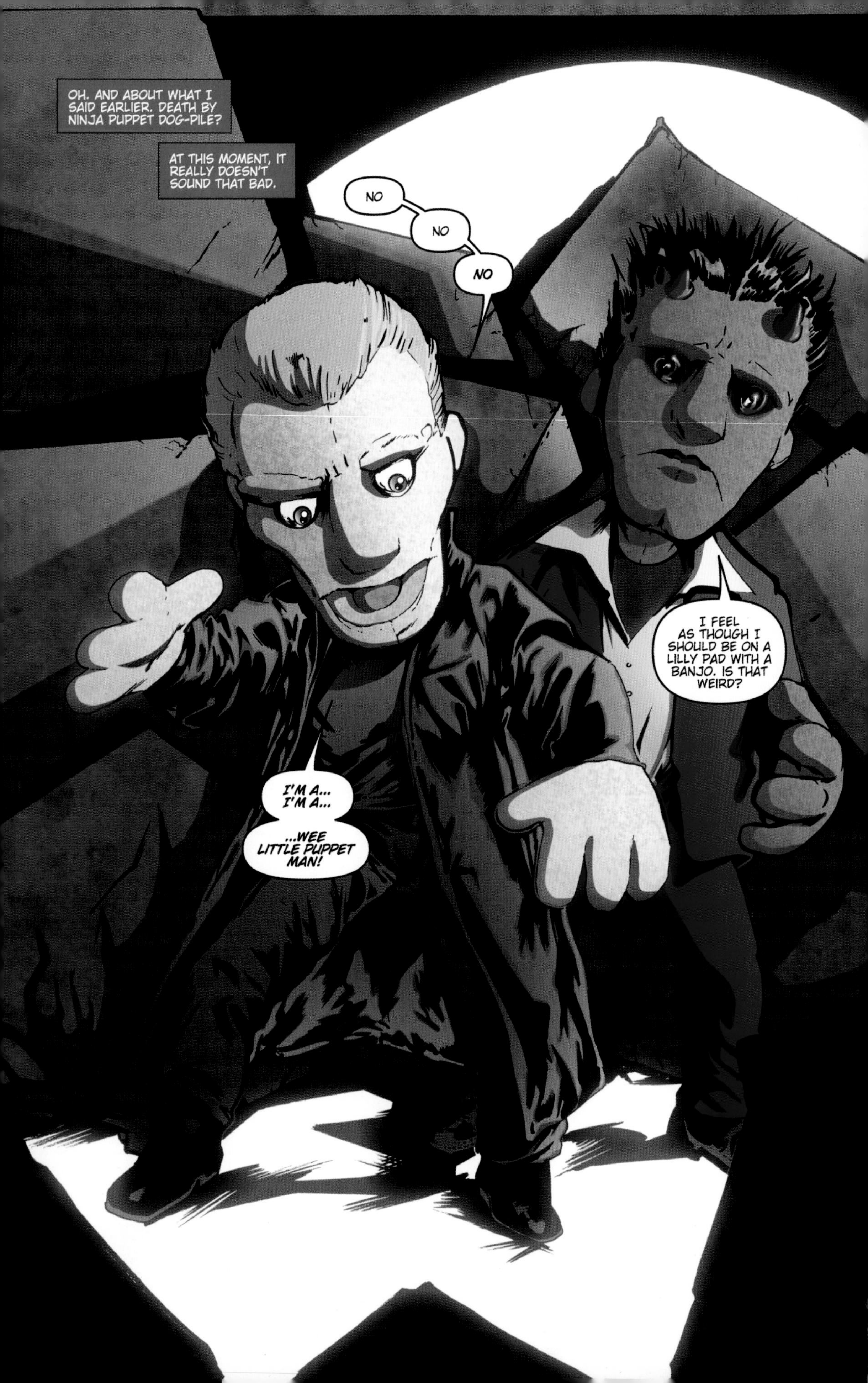
OH. AND ABOUT WHAT I SAID EARLIER. DEATH BY NINJA PUPPET DOG-PILE?
AT THIS MOMENT, IT REALLY DOESN'T SOUND THAT BAD.
NO
NO
NO
I FEEL AS THOUGH I SHOULD BE ON A LILLY PAD WITH A BANJO. IS THAT WEIRD?
I'M A... I'M A...
...WEE LITTLE PUPPET MAN!

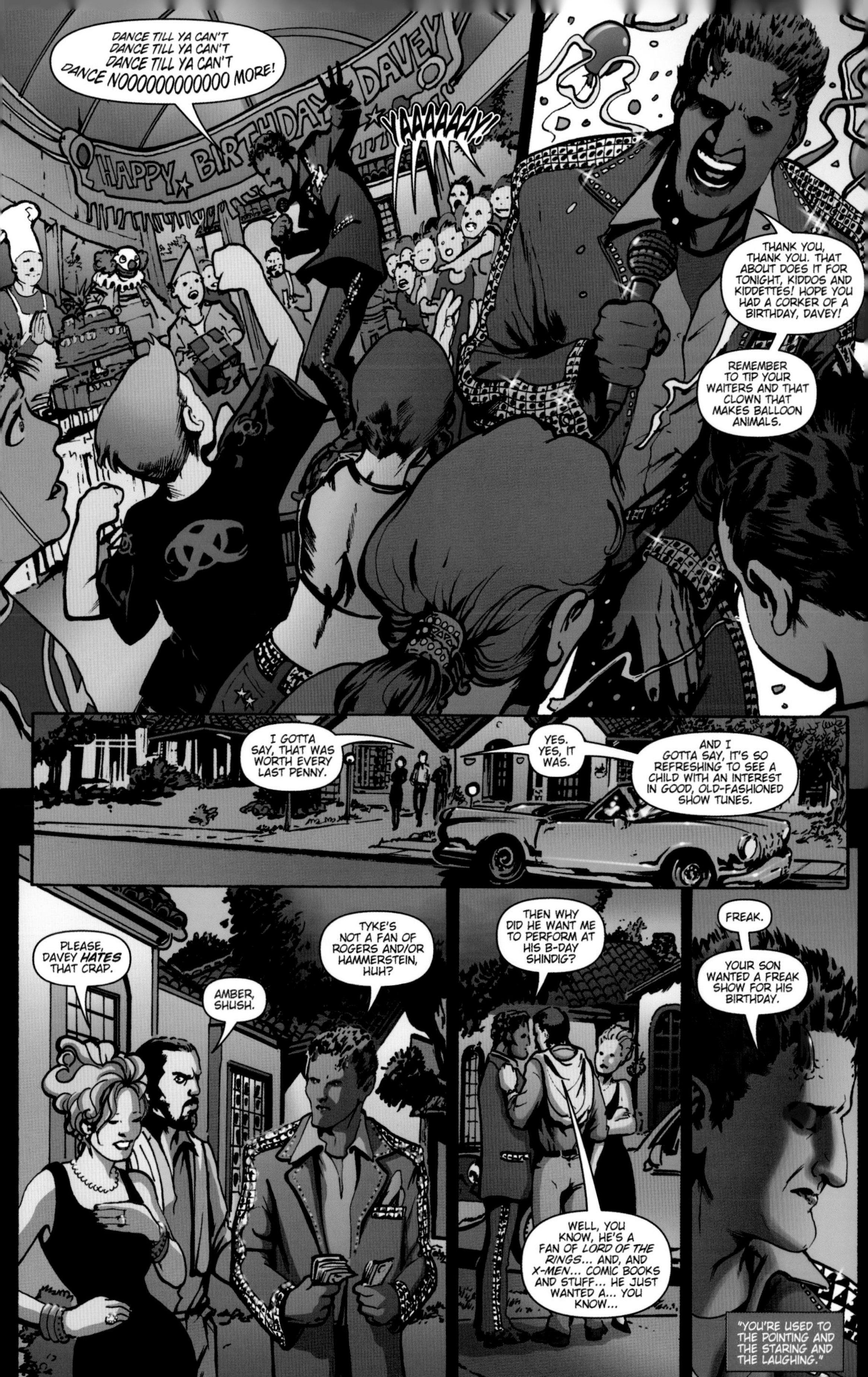

DANCE TILL YA CAN'T
DANCE TILL YA CAN'T
DANCE TILL YA CAN'T
DANCE NOOOOOOOOOOOO MORE!
HAPPY BIRTHDAY DAVEY
YAAAAAAY!
THANK YOU, THANK YOU. THAT ABOUT DOES IT FOR TONIGHT, KIDDOS AND KIDDETTES! HOPE YOU HAD A CORKER OF A BIRTHDAY, DAVEY!
REMEMBER TO TIP YOUR WAITERS AND THAT CLOWN THAT MAKES BALLOON ANIMALS.
I GOTTA SAY, THAT WAS WORTH EVERY LAST PENNY.
YES. YES, IT WAS.
AND I GOTTA SAY, IT'S SO REFRESHING TO SEE A CHILD WITH AN INTEREST IN GOOD, OLD-FASHIONED SHOW TUNES.
PLEASE, DAVEY ***HATES*** THAT CRAP.
AMBER, SHUSH.
TYKE'S NOT A FAN OF ROGERS AND/OR HAMMERSTEIN, HUH?
THEN WHY DID HE WANT ME TO PERFORM AT HIS B-DAY SHINDIG?
WELL, YOU KNOW, HE'S A FAN OF *LORD OF THE RINGS*... AND, AND *X-MEN*... COMIC BOOKS AND STUFF... HE JUST WANTED A... YOU KNOW...
FREAK.
YOUR SON WANTED A FREAK SHOW FOR HIS BIRTHDAY.
"YOU'RE USED TO THE POINTING AND THE STARING AND THE LAUGHING."

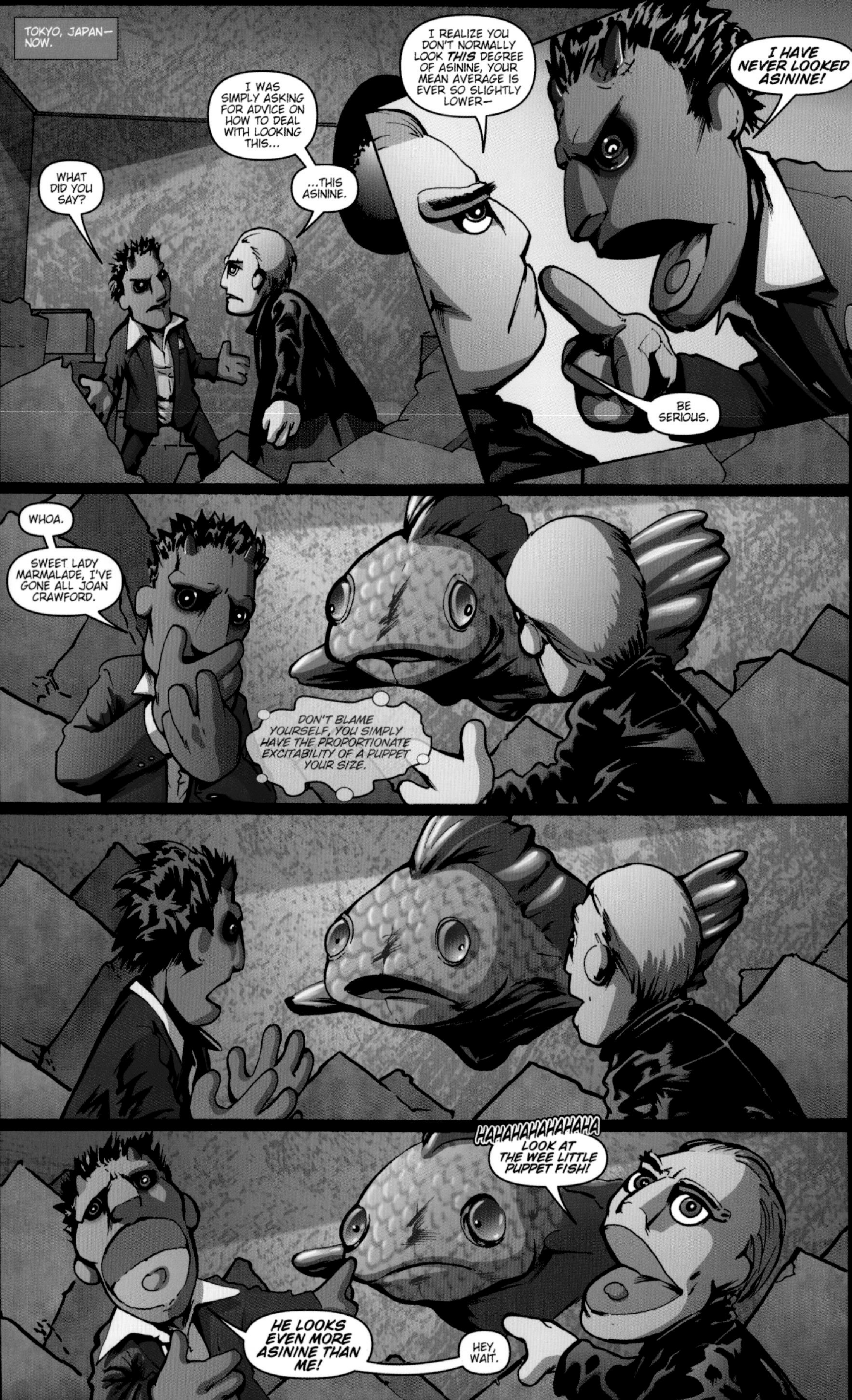
TOKYO, JAPAN—
NOW.
WHAT DID YOU SAY?
I WAS SIMPLY ASKING FOR ADVICE ON HOW TO DEAL WITH LOOKING THIS...
...THIS ASININE.
I REALIZE YOU DON'T NORMALLY LOOK THIS DEGREE OF ASININE, YOUR MEAN AVERAGE IS EVER SO SLIGHTLY LOWER—
I HAVE NEVER LOOKED ASININE!
BE SERIOUS.
WHOA.
SWEET LADY MARMALADE, I'VE GONE ALL JOAN CRAWFORD.
DON'T BLAME YOURSELF, YOU SIMPLY HAVE THE PROPORTIONATE EXCITABILITY OF A PUPPET YOUR SIZE.
HAHAHAHAHAHAHA
LOOK AT THE WEE LITTLE PUPPET FISH!
HE LOOKS EVEN MORE ASININE THAN ME!
HEY, WAIT.

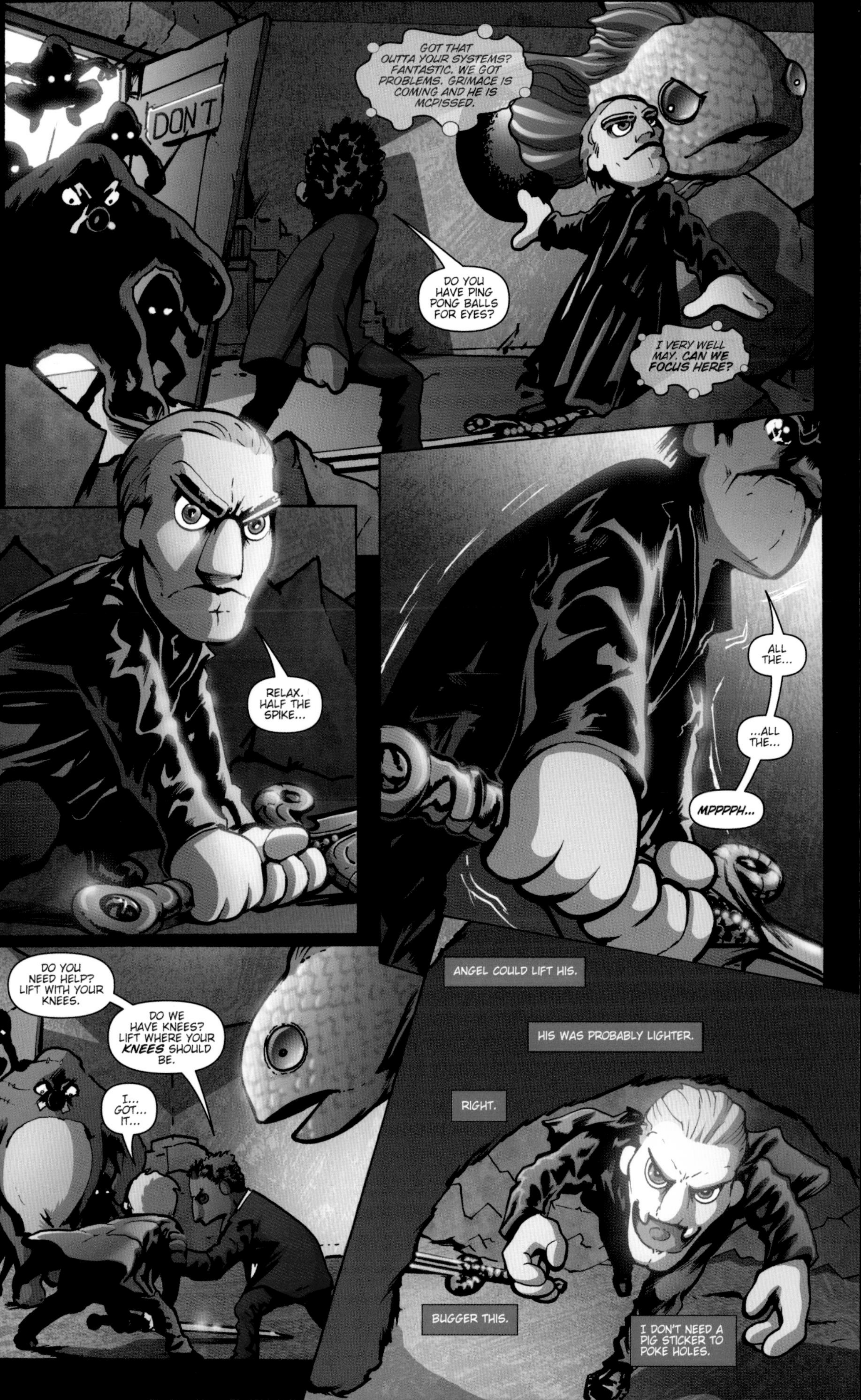
GOT THAT OUTTA YOUR SYSTEMS? FANTASTIC. WE GOT PROBLEMS. GRIMACE IS COMING AND HE IS MCPISSED.
DON'T
DO YOU HAVE PING PONG BALLS FOR EYES?
I VERY WELL MAY. CAN WE FOCUS HERE?
RELAX. HALF THE SPIKE...
ALL THE...
...ALL THE...
MPPPPH...
DO YOU NEED HELP? LIFT WITH YOUR KNEES.
DO WE HAVE KNEES? LIFT WHERE YOUR KNEES SHOULD BE.
I... GOT... IT...
ANGEL COULD LIFT HIS.
HIS WAS PROBABLY LIGHTER.
RIGHT.
BUGGER THIS.
I DON'T NEED A PIG STICKER TO POKE HOLES.

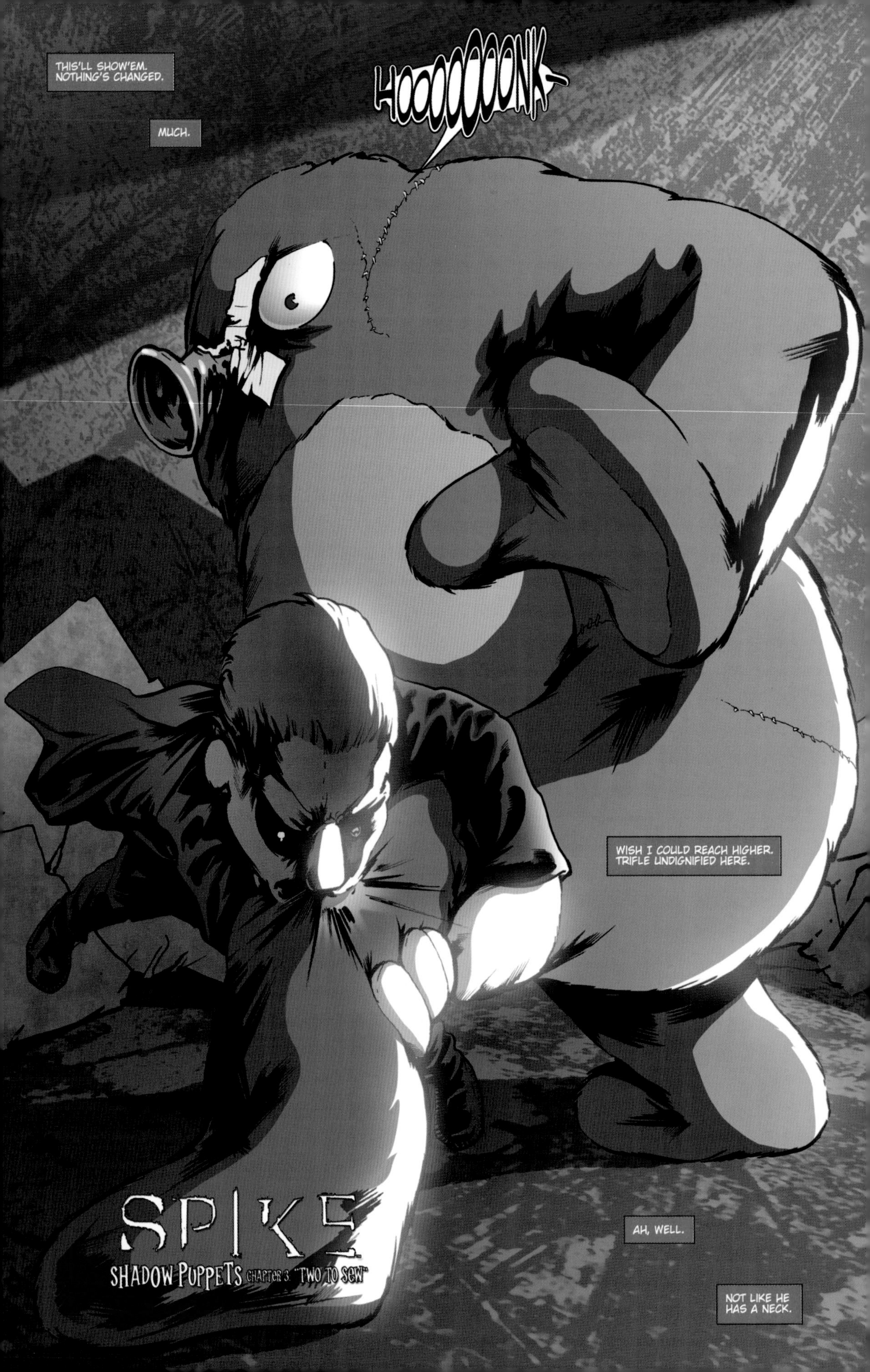
THIS'LL SHOW'EM. NOTHING'S CHANGED.
MUCH.
HOOOOOOOONK
WISH I COULD REACH HIGHER. TRIFLE UNDIGNIFIED HERE.
SPIKE
SHADOW PUPPETS CHAPTER 3: "TWO TO SEW"
AH, WELL.
NOT LIKE HE HAS A NECK.

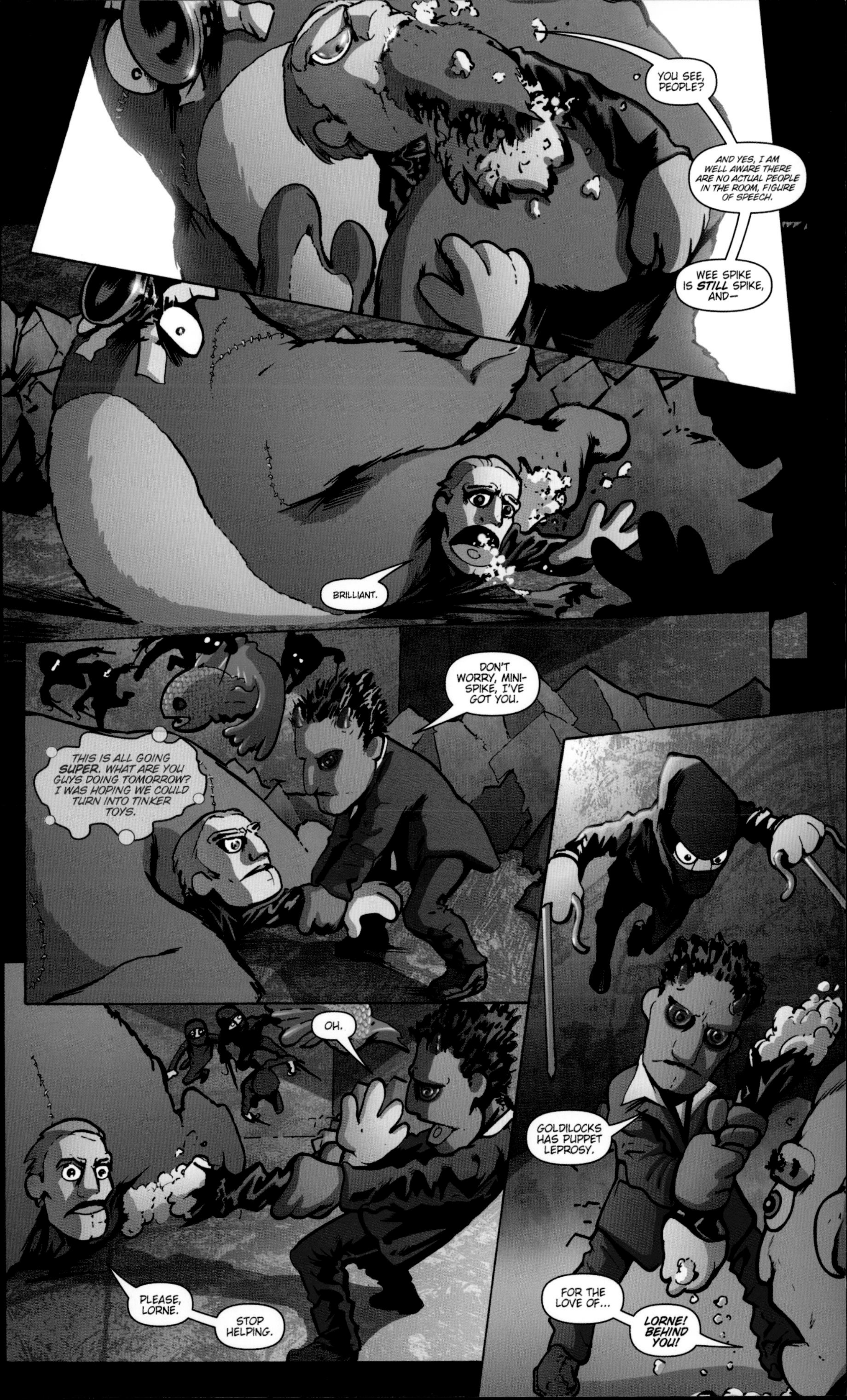

YOU SEE, PEOPLE?
AND YES, I AM WELL AWARE THERE ARE NO ACTUAL PEOPLE IN THE ROOM, FIGURE OF SPEECH.
WEE SPIKE IS STILL SPIKE, AND—
BRILLIANT.
DON'T WORRY, MINI-SPIKE, I'VE GOT YOU.
THIS IS ALL GOING SUPER. WHAT ARE YOU GUYS DOING TOMORROW? I WAS HOPING WE COULD TURN INTO TINKER TOYS.
OH.
PLEASE, LORNE.
STOP HELPING.
GOLDILOCKS HAS PUPPET LEPROSY.
FOR THE LOVE OF...
LORNE! BEHIND YOU!

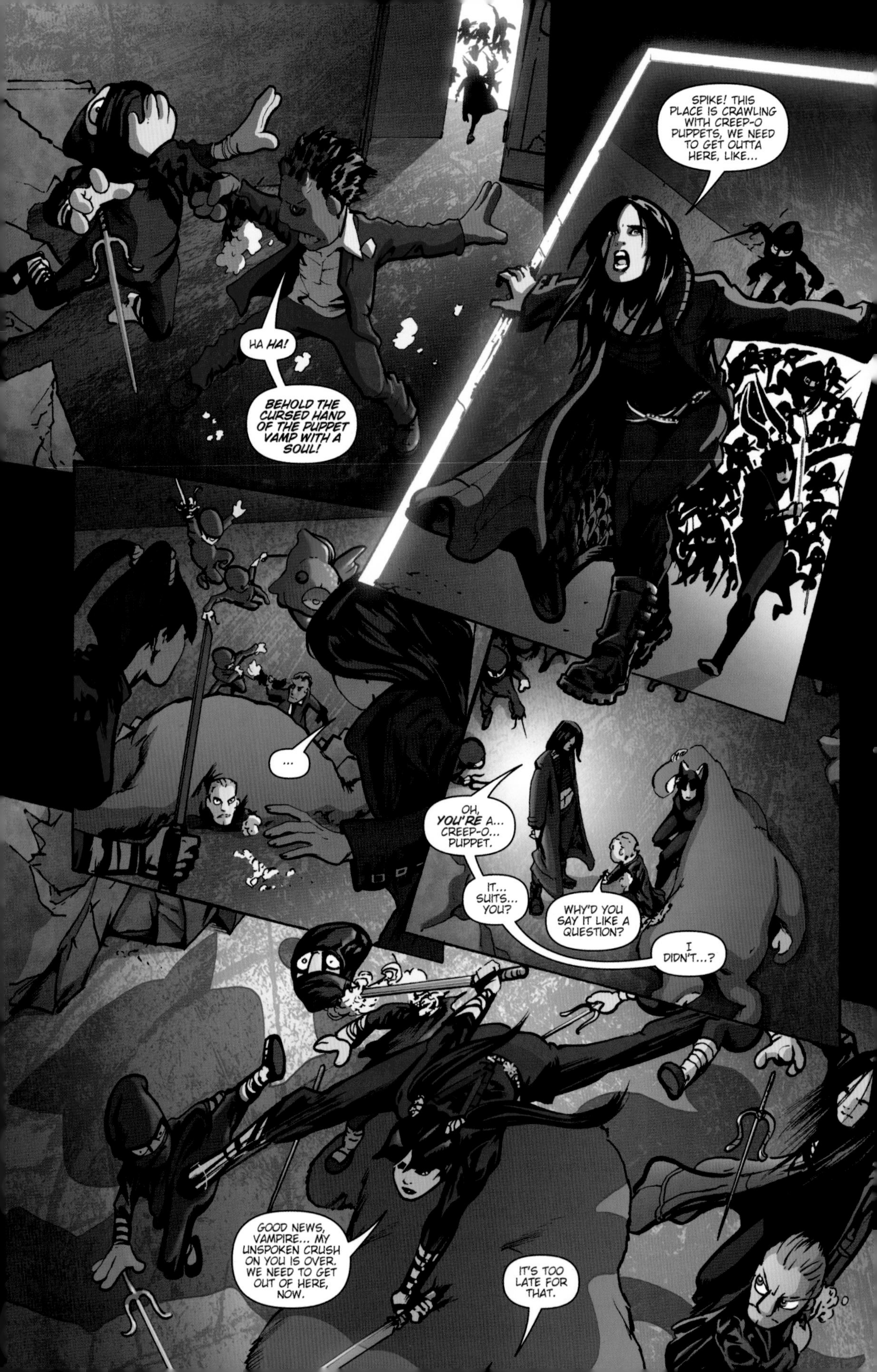
SPIKE! THIS PLACE IS CRAWLING WITH CREEP-O PUPPETS, WE NEED TO GET OUTTA HERE, LIKE...
HA HA!
BEHOLD THE CURSED HAND OF THE PUPPET VAMP WITH A SOUL!
...
OH, YOU'RE A... CREEP-O... PUPPET.
IT... SUITS... YOU?
WHY'D YOU SAY IT LIKE A QUESTION?
I DIDN'T...?
GOOD NEWS, VAMPIRE... MY UNSPOKEN CRUSH ON YOU IS OVER. WE NEED TO GET OUT OF HERE, NOW.
IT'S TOO LATE FOR THAT.

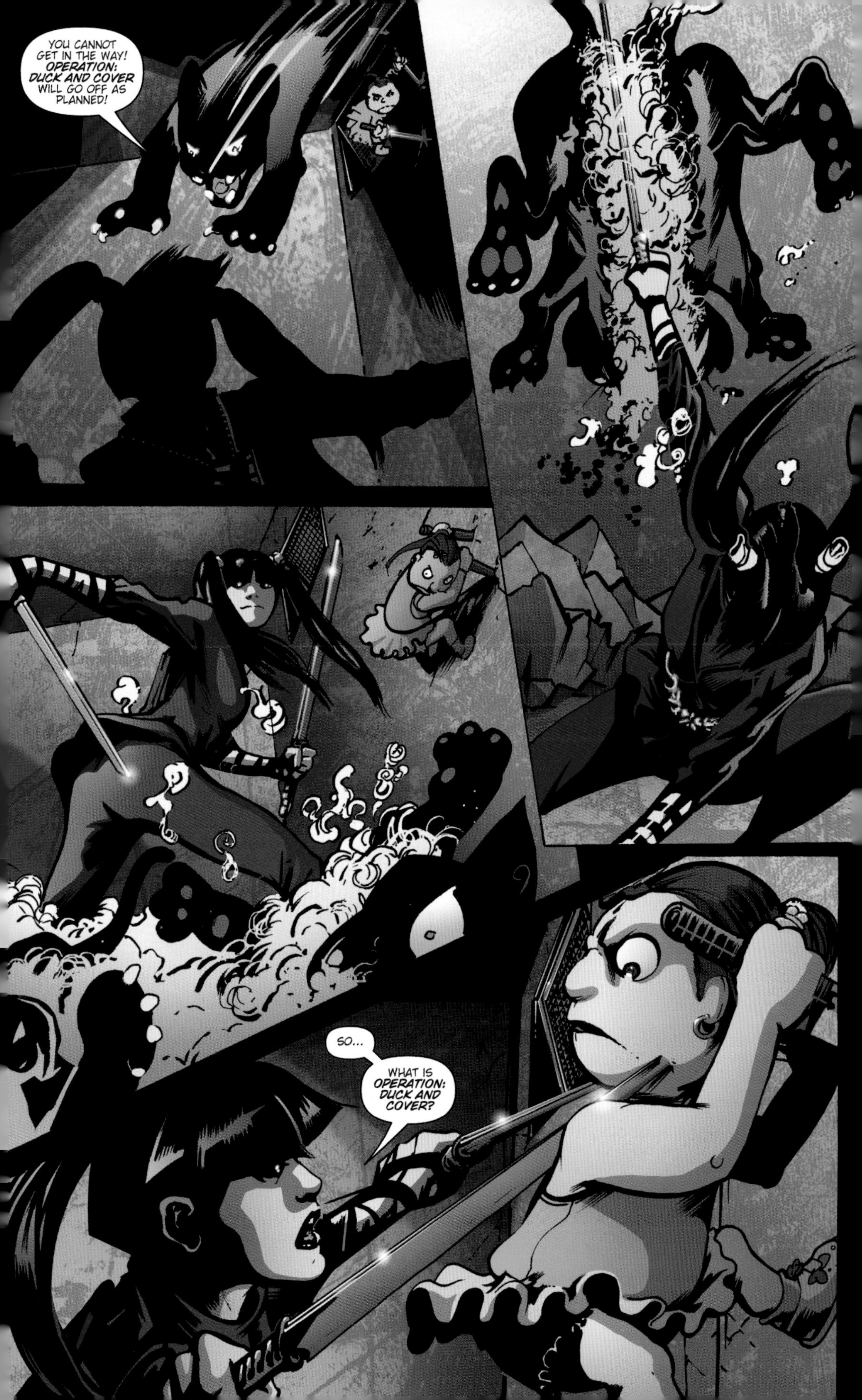
YOU CANNOT GET IN THE WAY! OPERATION: DUCK AND COVER WILL GO OFF AS PLANNED!
SO...
WHAT IS OPERATION: DUCK AND COVER?

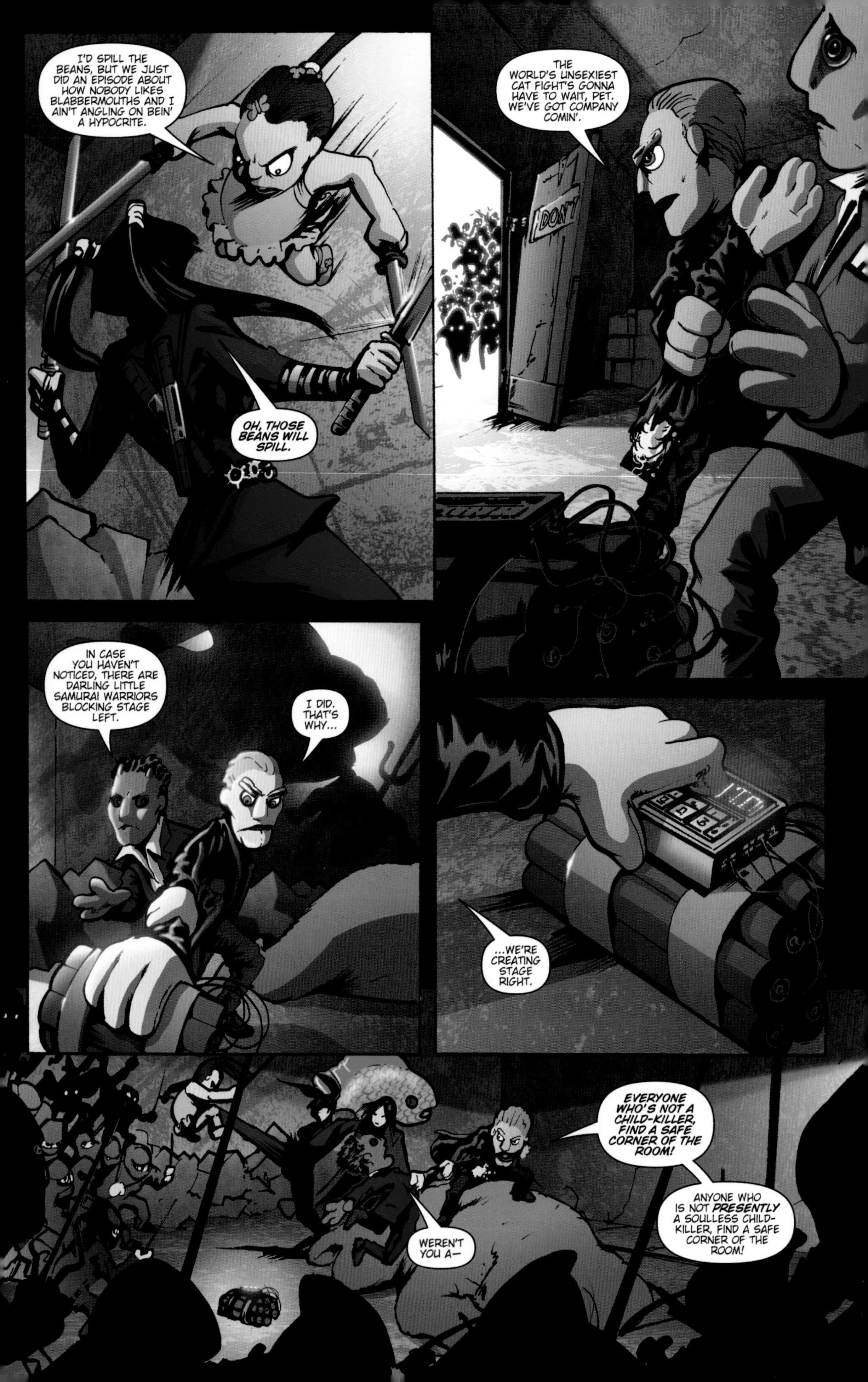
I'D SPILL THE BEANS, BUT WE JUST DID AN EPISODE ABOUT HOW NOBODY LIKES BLABBERMOUTHS AND I AIN'T ANGLING ON BEIN' A HYPOCRITE.
OH, THOSE BEANS WILL SPILL.
THE WORLD'S UNSEXIEST CAT FIGHT'S GONNA HAVE TO WAIT, PET. WE'VE GOT COMPANY COMIN'.
DON'T
IN CASE YOU HAVEN'T NOTICED, THERE ARE DARLING LITTLE SAMURAI WARRIORS BLOCKING STAGE LEFT.
I DID. THAT'S WHY...
...WE'RE CREATING STAGE RIGHT.
EVERYONE WHO'S NOT A CHILD-KILLER, FIND A SAFE CORNER OF THE ROOM!
ANYONE WHO IS NOT PRESENTLY A SOULLESS CHILD-KILLER, FIND A SAFE CORNER OF THE ROOM!
WEREN'T YOU A—

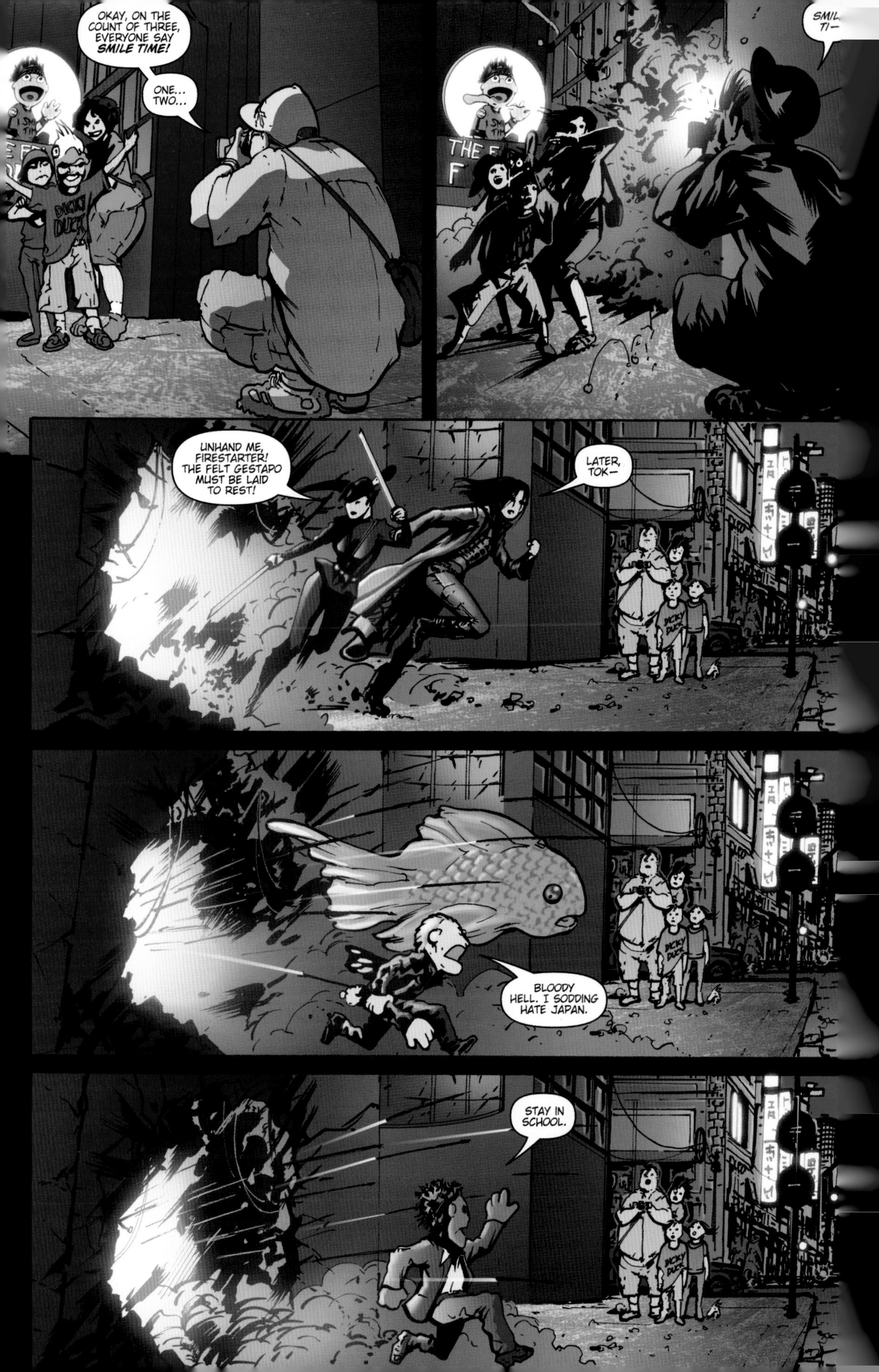
OKAY, ON THE COUNT OF THREE, EVERYONE SAY SMILE TIME!
ONE... TWO...
SMILE TI—
UNHAND ME, FIRESTARTER! THE FELT GESTAPO MUST BE LAID TO REST!
LATER, TOK—
BLOODY HELL. I SODDING HATE JAPAN.
STAY IN SCHOOL.

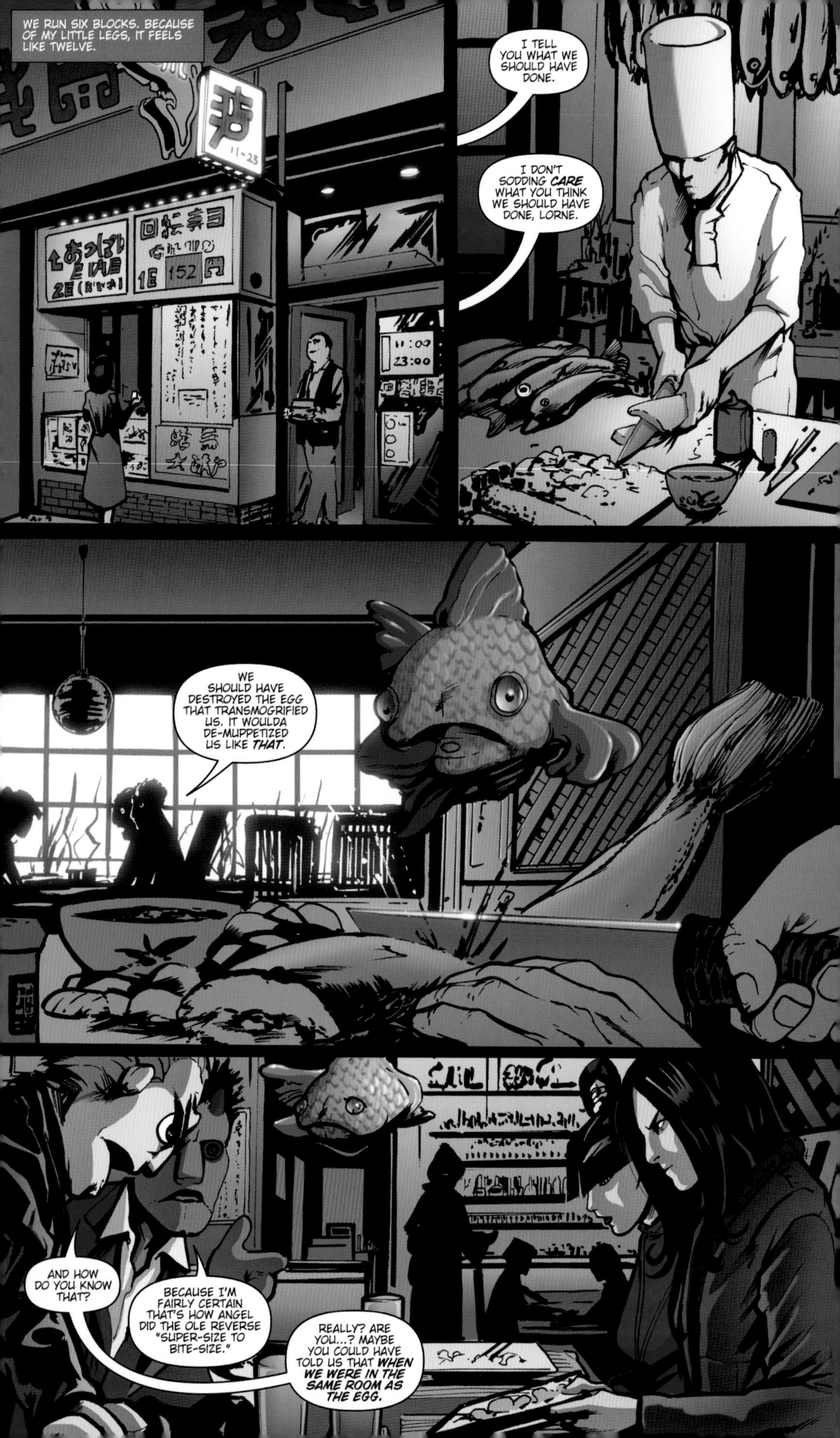
WE RUN SIX BLOCKS. BECAUSE OF MY LITTLE LEGS, IT FEELS LIKE TWELVE.
I TELL YOU WHAT WE SHOULD HAVE DONE.
I DON'T SODDING CARE WHAT YOU THINK WE SHOULD HAVE DONE, LORNE.
WE SHOULD HAVE DESTROYED THE EGG THAT TRANSMOGRIFIED US. IT WOULDA DE-MUPPETIZED US LIKE THAT.
AND HOW DO YOU KNOW THAT?
BECAUSE I'M FAIRLY CERTAIN THAT'S HOW ANGEL DID THE OLE REVERSE "SUPER-SIZE TO BITE-SIZE."
REALLY? ARE YOU...? MAYBE YOU COULD HAVE TOLD US THAT WHEN WE WERE IN THE SAME ROOM AS THE EGG.

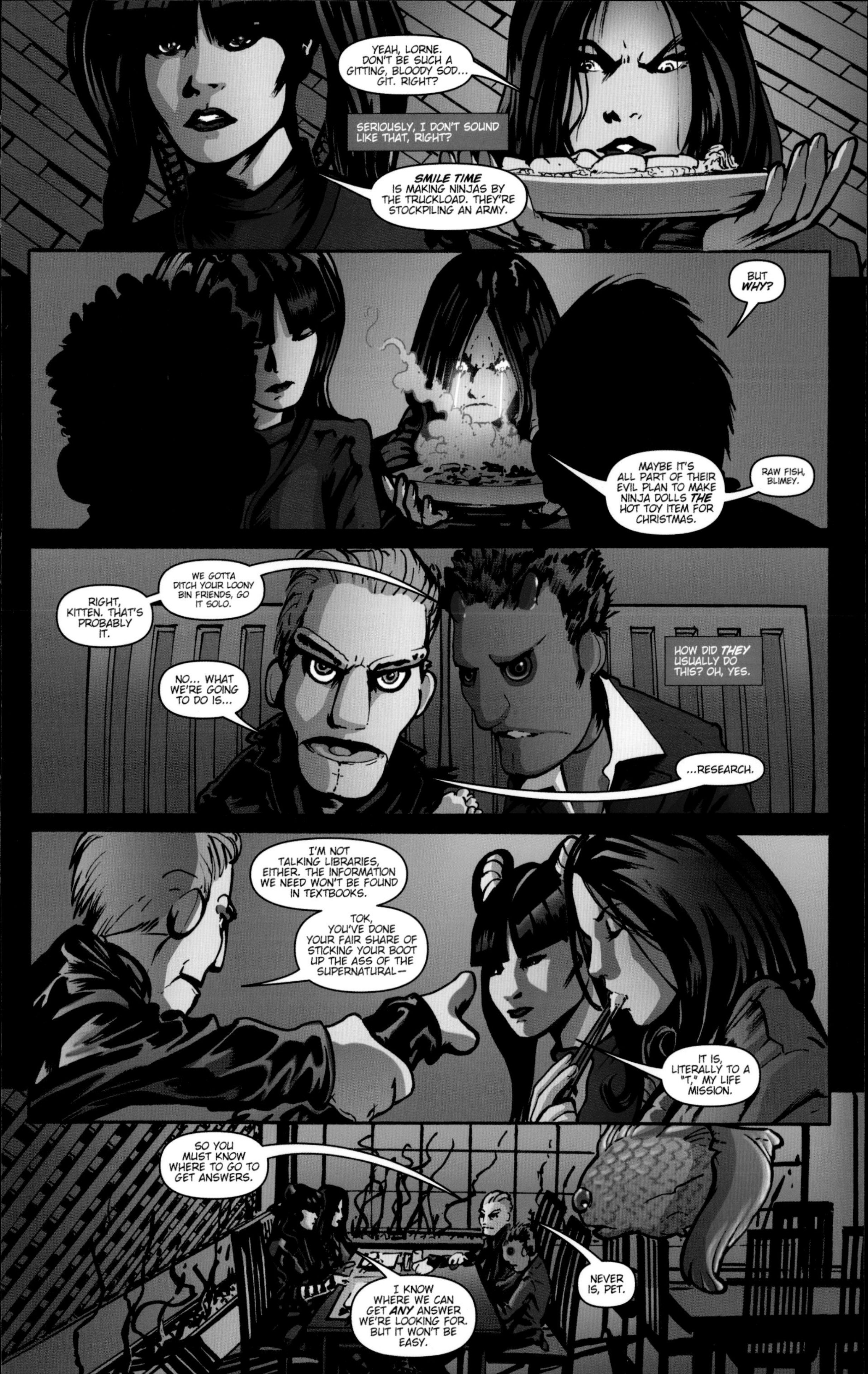
YEAH, LORNE. DON'T BE SUCH A GITTING, BLOODY SOD... GIT. RIGHT?
SERIOUSLY, I DON'T SOUND LIKE THAT, RIGHT?
SMILE TIME IS MAKING NINJAS BY THE TRUCKLOAD. THEY'RE STOCKPILING AN ARMY.
BUT WHY?
MAYBE IT'S ALL PART OF THEIR EVIL PLAN TO MAKE NINJA DOLLS THE HOT TOY ITEM FOR CHRISTMAS.
RAW FISH, BLIMEY.
RIGHT, KITTEN. THAT'S PROBABLY IT.
WE GOTTA DITCH YOUR LOONY BIN FRIENDS, GO IT SOLO.
NO... WHAT WE'RE GOING TO DO IS...
HOW DID THEY USUALLY DO THIS? OH, YES.
...RESEARCH.
I'M NOT TALKING LIBRARIES, EITHER. THE INFORMATION WE NEED WON'T BE FOUND IN TEXTBOOKS.
TOK, YOU'VE DONE YOUR FAIR SHARE OF STICKING YOUR BOOT UP THE ASS OF THE SUPERNATURAL—
IT IS, LITERALLY TO A "T," MY LIFE MISSION.
SO YOU MUST KNOW WHERE TO GO TO GET ANSWERS.
NEVER IS, PET.
I KNOW WHERE WE CAN GET ANY ANSWER WE'RE LOOKING FOR. BUT IT WON'T BE EASY.

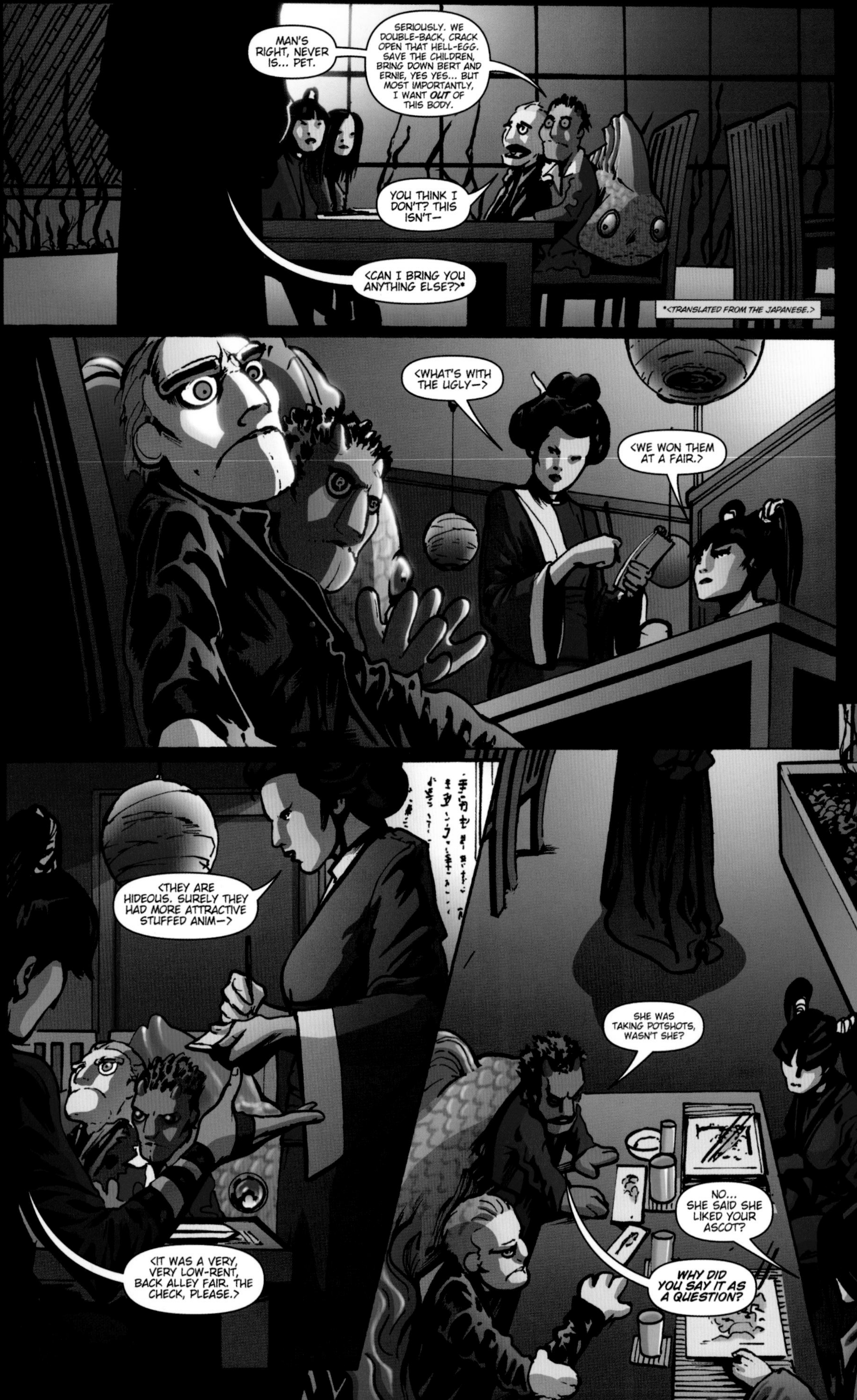
MAN'S RIGHT, NEVER IS... PET.
SERIOUSLY. WE DOUBLE-BACK, CRACK OPEN THAT HELL-EGG. SAVE THE CHILDREN, BRING DOWN BERT AND ERNIE, YES YES... BUT MOST IMPORTANTLY, I WANT OUT OF THIS BODY.
YOU THINK I DON'T? THIS ISN'T—
<CAN I BRING YOU ANYTHING ELSE?>*
*<TRANSLATED FROM THE JAPANESE.>
<WHAT'S WITH THE UGLY—>
<WE WON THEM AT A FAIR.>
<THEY ARE HIDEOUS. SURELY THEY HAD MORE ATTRACTIVE STUFFED ANIM—>
<IT WAS A VERY, VERY LOW-RENT, BACK ALLEY FAIR. THE CHECK, PLEASE.>
SHE WAS TAKING POTSHOTS, WASN'T SHE?
NO... SHE SAID SHE LIKED YOUR ASCOT?
WHY DID YOU SAY IT AS A QUESTION?

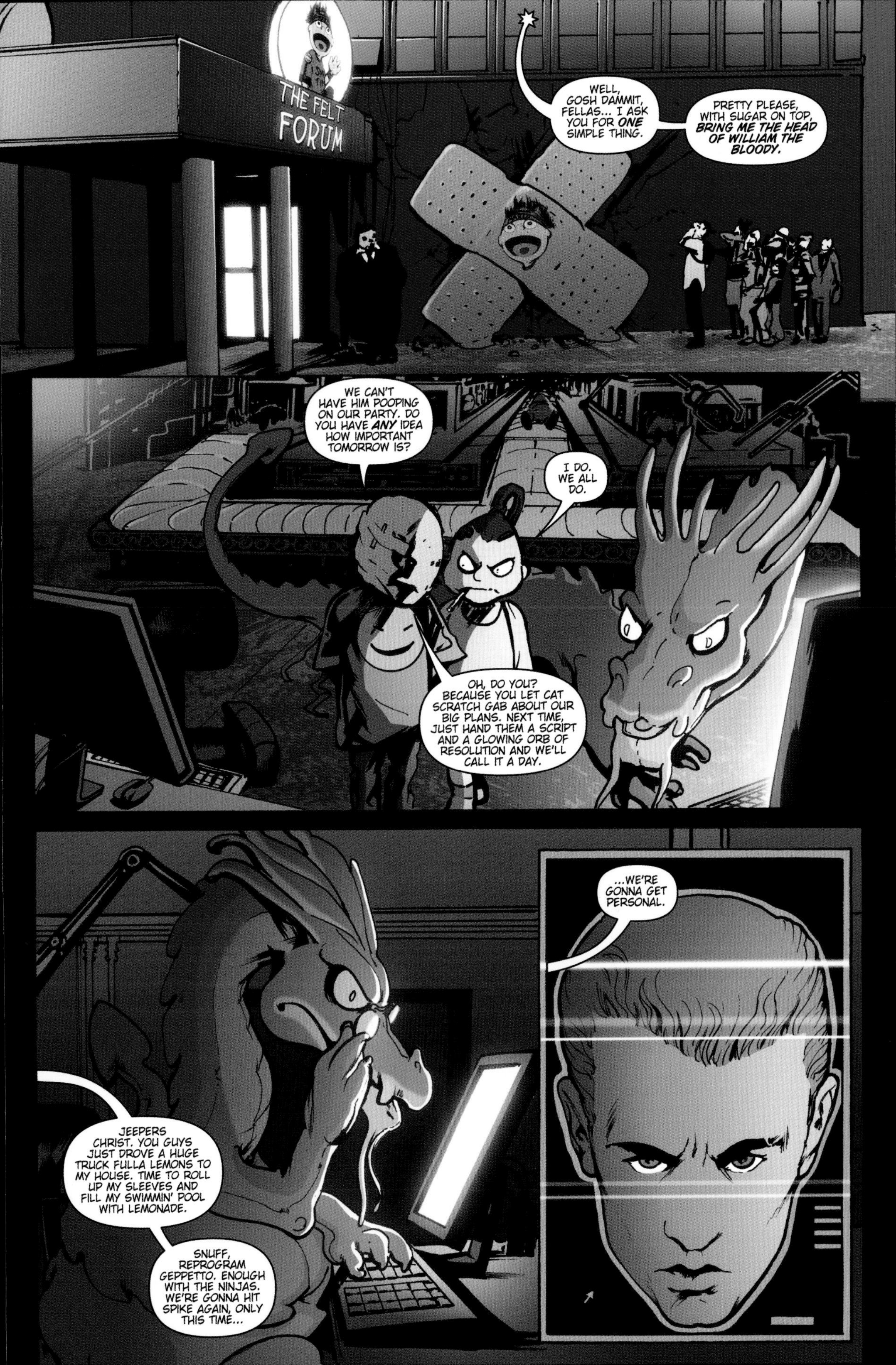
THE FELT FORUM
WELL, GOSH DAMMIT, FELLAS... I ASK YOU FOR ONE SIMPLE THING.
PRETTY PLEASE, WITH SUGAR ON TOP, BRING ME THE HEAD OF WILLIAM THE BLOODY.
WE CAN'T HAVE HIM POOPING ON OUR PARTY. DO YOU HAVE ANY IDEA HOW IMPORTANT TOMORROW IS?
I DO. WE ALL DO.
OH, DO YOU? BECAUSE YOU LET CAT SCRATCH GAB ABOUT OUR BIG PLANS. NEXT TIME, JUST HAND THEM A SCRIPT AND A GLOWING ORB OF RESOLUTION AND WE'LL CALL IT A DAY.
JEEPERS CHRIST. YOU GUYS JUST DROVE A HUGE TRUCK FULLA LEMONS TO MY HOUSE. TIME TO ROLL UP MY SLEEVES AND FILL MY SWIMMIN' POOL WITH LEMONADE.
SNUFF, REPROGRAM GEPPETTO. ENOUGH WITH THE NINJAS. WE'RE GONNA HIT SPIKE AGAIN, ONLY THIS TIME...
...WE'RE GONNA GET PERSONAL.

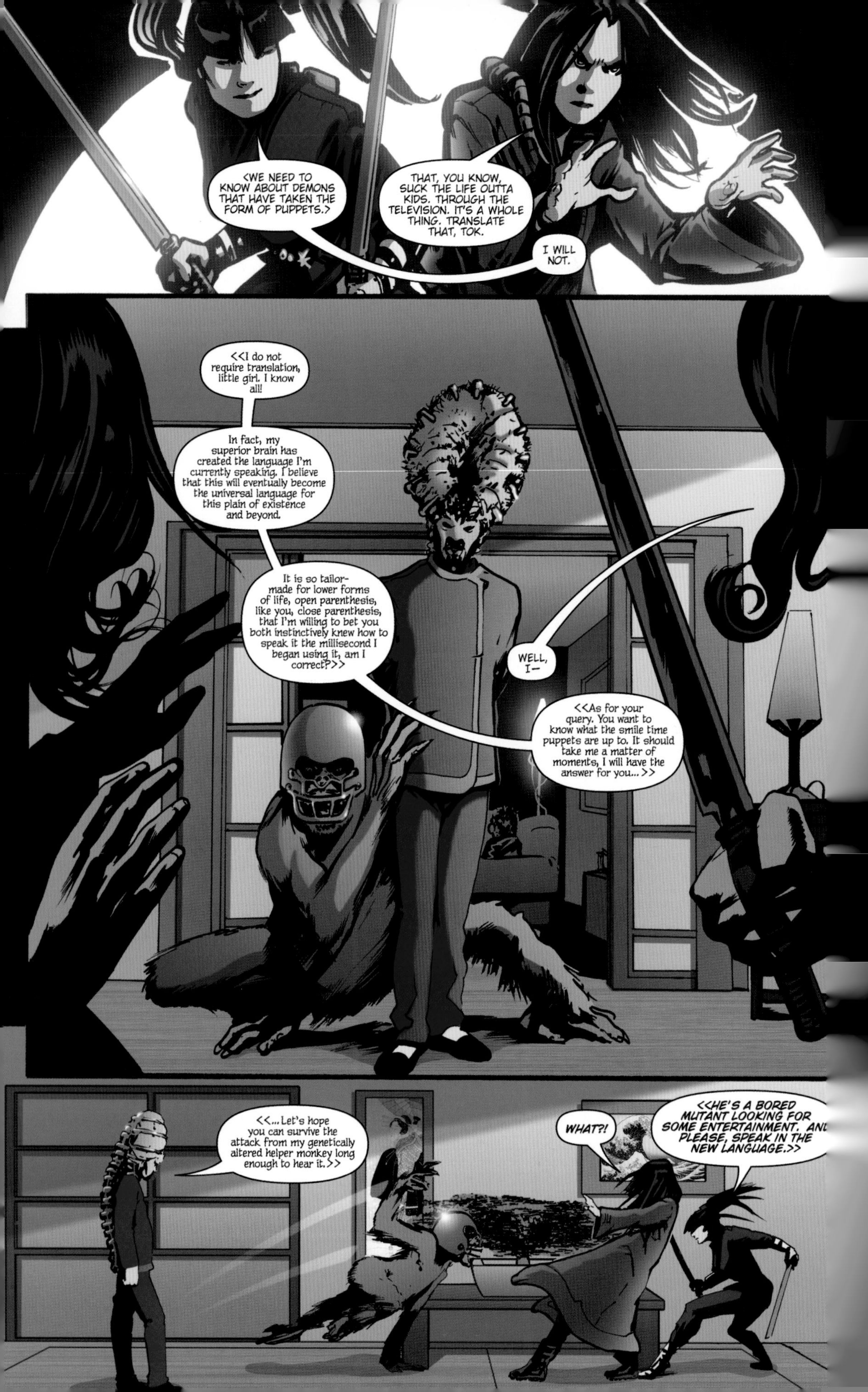

<WE NEED TO KNOW ABOUT DEMONS THAT HAVE TAKEN THE FORM OF PUPPETS.>
THAT, YOU KNOW, SUCK THE LIFE OUTTA KIDS. THROUGH THE TELEVISION. IT'S A WHOLE THING. TRANSLATE THAT, TOK.
I WILL NOT.
<<I do not require translation, little girl. I know all!
In fact, my superior brain has created the language I'm currently speaking. I believe that this will eventually become the universal language for this plain of existence and beyond.
It is so tailor-made for lower forms of life, open parenthesis, like you, close parenthesis, that I'm willing to bet you both instinctively knew how to speak it the millisecond I began using it, am I correct?>>
WELL, I—
<<As for your query. You want to know what the smile time puppets are up to. It should take me a matter of moments, I will have the answer for you...>>
<<...Let's hope you can survive the attack from my genetically altered helper monkey long enough to hear it.>>
WHAT?!
<<HE'S A BORED MUTANT LOOKING FOR SOME ENTERTAINMENT. AND PLEASE, SPEAK IN THE NEW LANGUAGE.>>

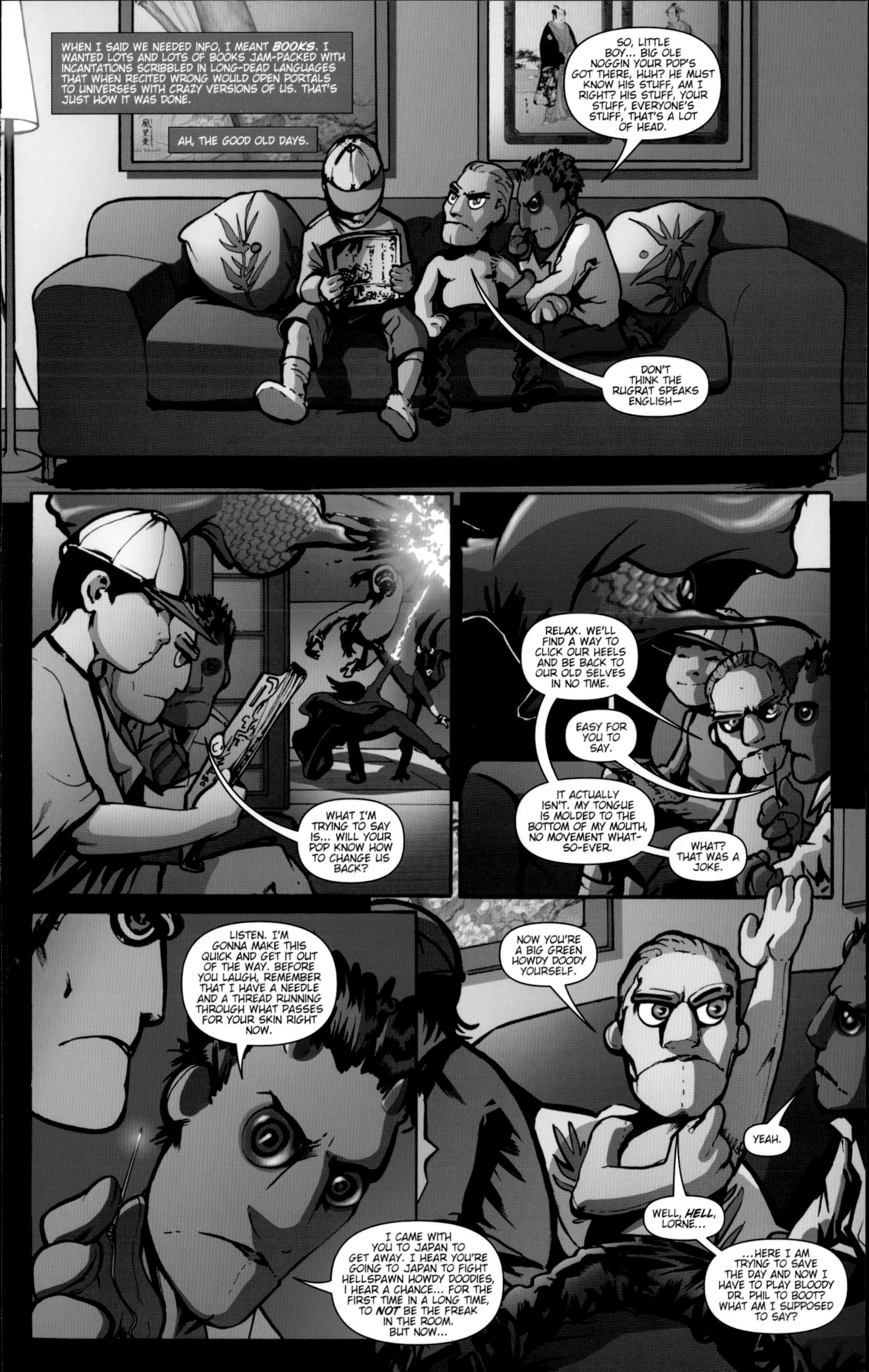

WHEN I SAID WE NEEDED INFO, I MEANT **BOOKS**. I WANTED LOTS AND LOTS OF BOOKS JAM-PACKED WITH INCANTATIONS SCRIBBLED IN LONG-DEAD LANGUAGES THAT WHEN RECITED WRONG WOULD OPEN PORTALS TO UNIVERSES WITH CRAZY VERSIONS OF US. THAT'S JUST HOW IT WAS DONE.
AH, THE GOOD OLD DAYS.
SO, LITTLE BOY... BIG OLE NOGGIN YOUR POP'S GOT THERE, HUH? HE MUST KNOW HIS STUFF, AM I RIGHT? HIS STUFF, YOUR STUFF, EVERYONE'S STUFF, THAT'S A LOT OF HEAD.
DON'T THINK THE RUGRAT SPEAKS ENGLISH—
WHAT I'M TRYING TO SAY IS... WILL YOUR POP KNOW HOW TO CHANGE US BACK?
RELAX. WE'LL FIND A WAY TO CLICK OUR HEELS AND BE BACK TO OUR OLD SELVES IN NO TIME.
EASY FOR YOU TO SAY.
IT ACTUALLY ISN'T. MY TONGUE IS MOLDED TO THE BOTTOM OF MY MOUTH, NO MOVEMENT WHAT-SO-EVER.
WHAT? THAT WAS A JOKE.
LISTEN. I'M GONNA MAKE THIS QUICK AND GET IT OUT OF THE WAY. BEFORE YOU LAUGH, REMEMBER THAT I HAVE A NEEDLE AND A THREAD RUNNING THROUGH WHAT PASSES FOR YOUR SKIN RIGHT NOW.
I CAME WITH YOU TO JAPAN TO GET AWAY. I HEAR YOU'RE GOING TO JAPAN TO FIGHT HELLSPAWN HOWDY DOODIES, I HEAR A CHANCE... FOR THE FIRST TIME IN A LONG TIME, TO **NOT** BE THE FREAK IN THE ROOM. BUT NOW...
NOW YOU'RE A BIG GREEN HOWDY DOODY YOURSELF.
YEAH.
WELL, **HELL**, LORNE...
...HERE I AM TRYING TO SAVE THE DAY AND NOW I HAVE TO PLAY BLOODY DR. PHIL TO BOOT? WHAT AM I SUPPOSED TO SAY?

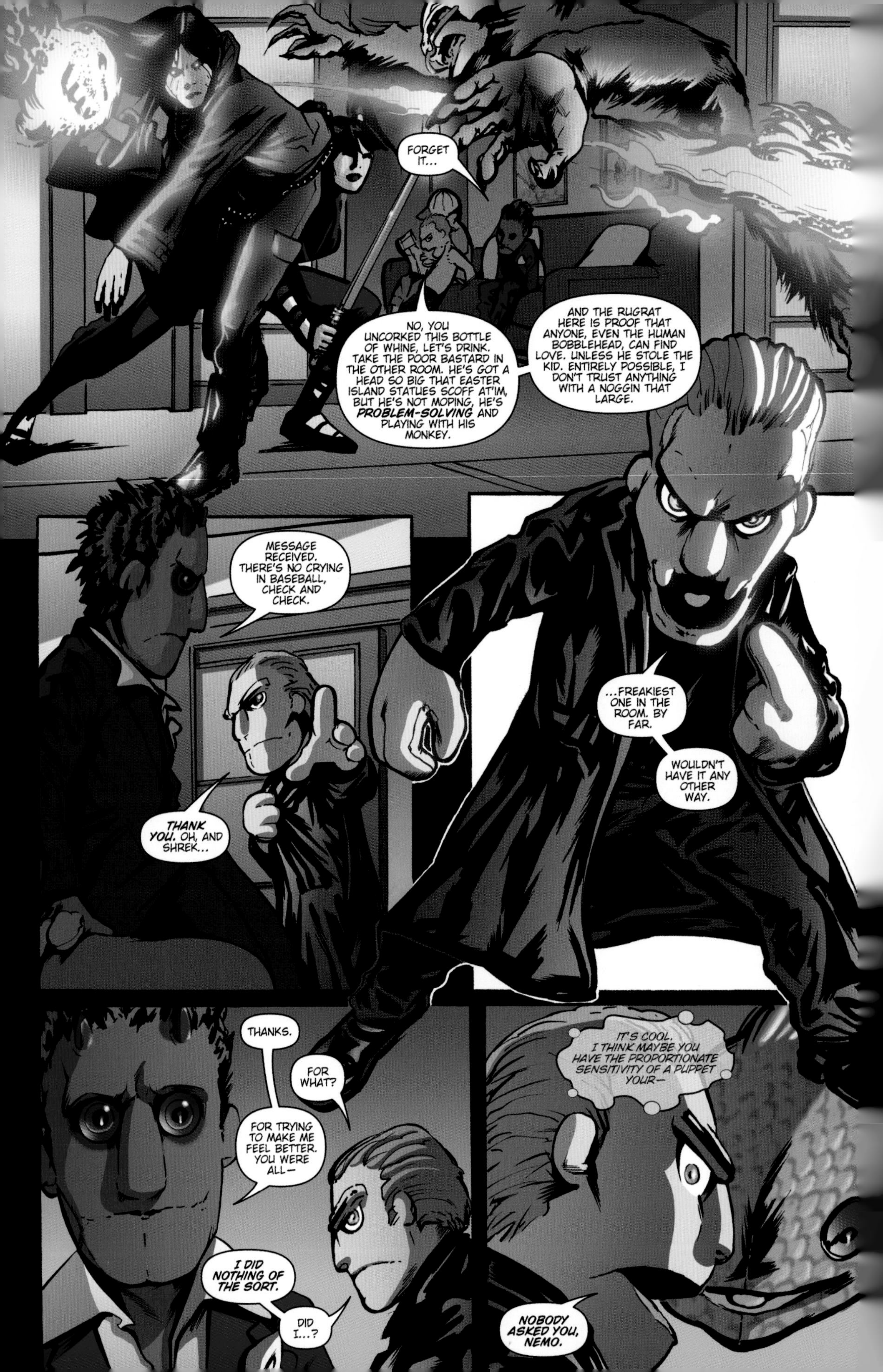

FORGET IT...
NO, YOU UNCORKED THIS BOTTLE OF WHINE, LET'S DRINK. TAKE THE POOR BASTARD IN THE OTHER ROOM. HE'S GOT A HEAD SO BIG THAT EASTER ISLAND STATUES SCOFF AT'IM, BUT HE'S NOT MOPING, HE'S PROBLEM-SOLVING AND PLAYING WITH HIS MONKEY.
AND THE RUGRAT HERE IS PROOF THAT ANYONE, EVEN THE HUMAN BOBBLEHEAD, CAN FIND LOVE. UNLESS HE STOLE THE KID. ENTIRELY POSSIBLE, I DON'T TRUST ANYTHING WITH A NOGGIN THAT LARGE.
MESSAGE RECEIVED. THERE'S NO CRYING IN BASEBALL, CHECK AND CHECK.
THANK YOU. OH, AND SHREK...
...FREAKIEST ONE IN THE ROOM. BY FAR.
WOULDN'T HAVE IT ANY OTHER WAY.
THANKS.
FOR WHAT?
FOR TRYING TO MAKE ME FEEL BETTER. YOU WERE ALL—
I DID NOTHING OF THE SORT.
DID I...?
IT'S COOL. I THINK MAYBE YOU HAVE THE PROPORTIONATE SENSITIVITY OF A PUPPET YOUR—
NOBODY ASKED YOU, NEMO.

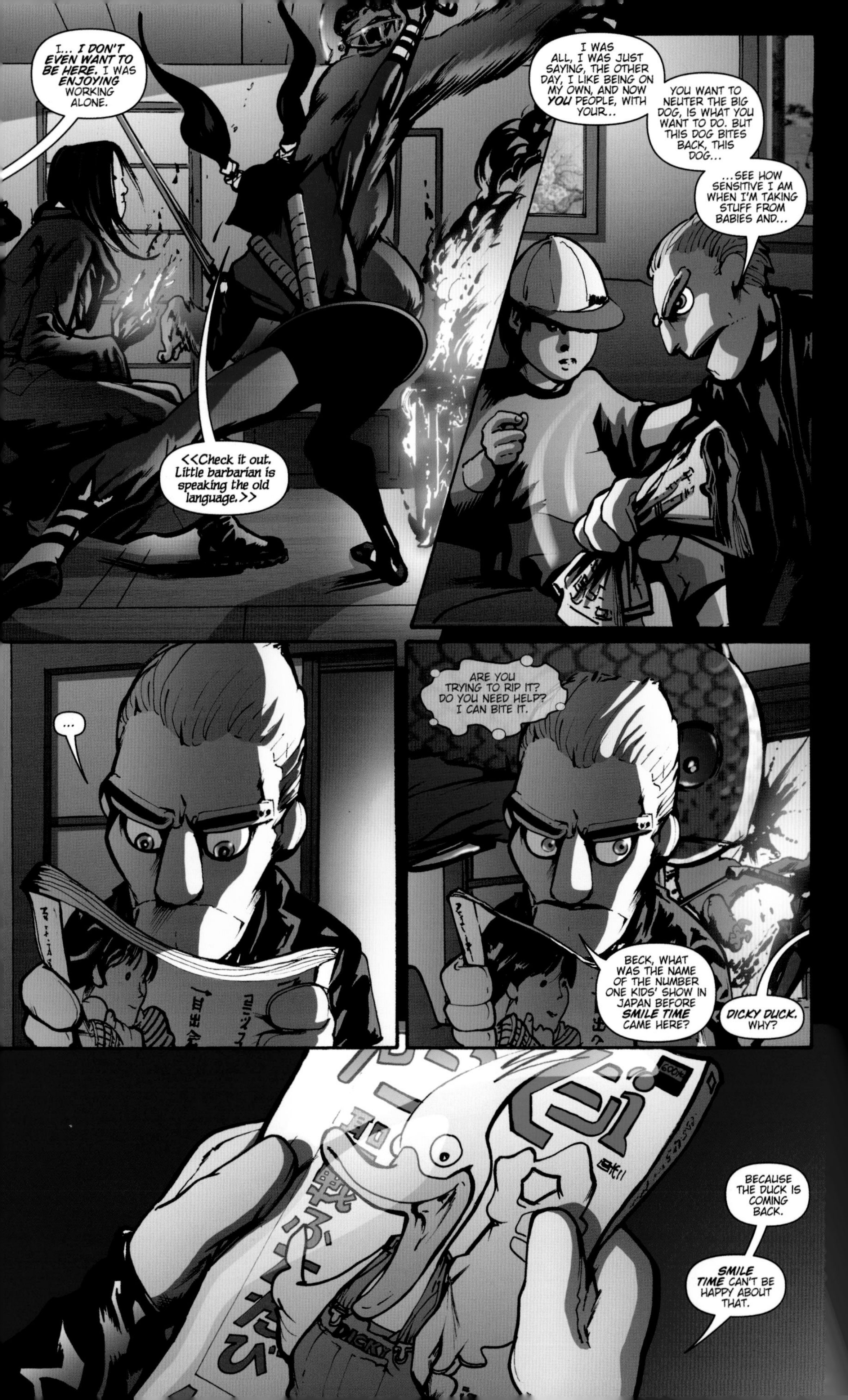
I... I DON'T EVEN WANT TO BE HERE. I WAS ENJOYING WORKING ALONE.
<<Check it out. Little barbarian is speaking the old language.>>
I WAS ALL, I WAS JUST SAYING, THE OTHER DAY, I LIKE BEING ON MY OWN, AND NOW YOU PEOPLE, WITH YOUR...
YOU WANT TO NEUTER THE BIG DOG, IS WHAT YOU WANT TO DO. BUT THIS DOG BITES BACK, THIS DOG...
...SEE HOW SENSITIVE I AM WHEN I'M TAKING STUFF FROM BABIES AND...
...
ARE YOU TRYING TO RIP IT? DO YOU NEED HELP? I CAN BITE IT.
BECK, WHAT WAS THE NAME OF THE NUMBER ONE KIDS' SHOW IN JAPAN BEFORE SMILE TIME CAME HERE?
DICKY DUCK. WHY?
BECAUSE THE DUCK IS COMING BACK.
SMILE TIME CAN'T BE HAPPY ABOUT THAT.

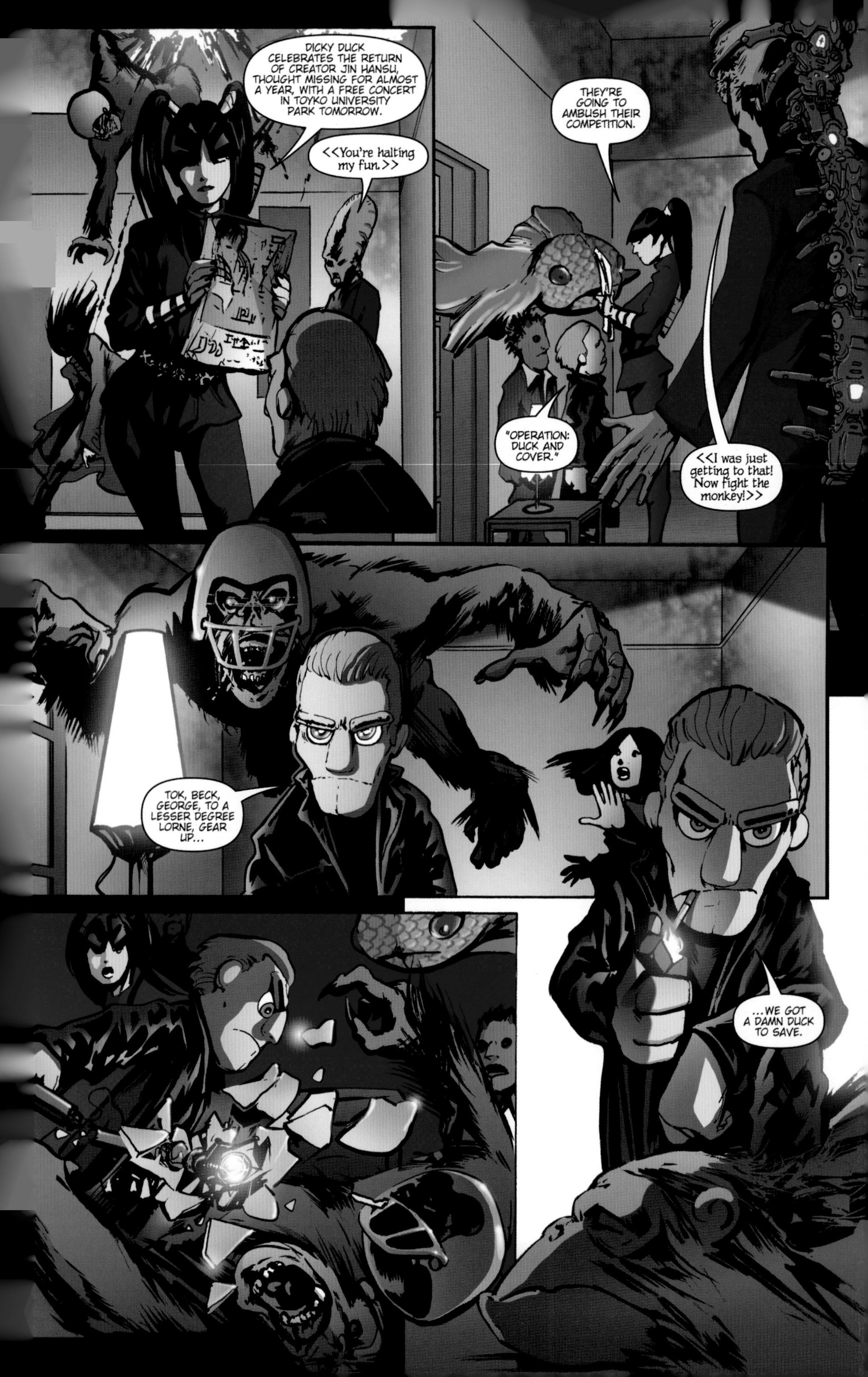
DICKY DUCK CELEBRATES THE RETURN OF CREATOR JIN HANSU, THOUGHT MISSING FOR ALMOST A YEAR, WITH A FREE CONCERT IN TOYKO UNIVERSITY PARK TOMORROW.
<<You're halting my fun.>>
THEY'RE GOING TO AMBUSH THEIR COMPETITION.
"OPERATION: DUCK AND COVER."
<<I was just getting to that! Now fight the monkey!>>
TOK, BECK, GEORGE, TO A LESSER DEGREE LORNE, GEAR UP...
...WE GOT A DAMN DUCK TO SAVE.

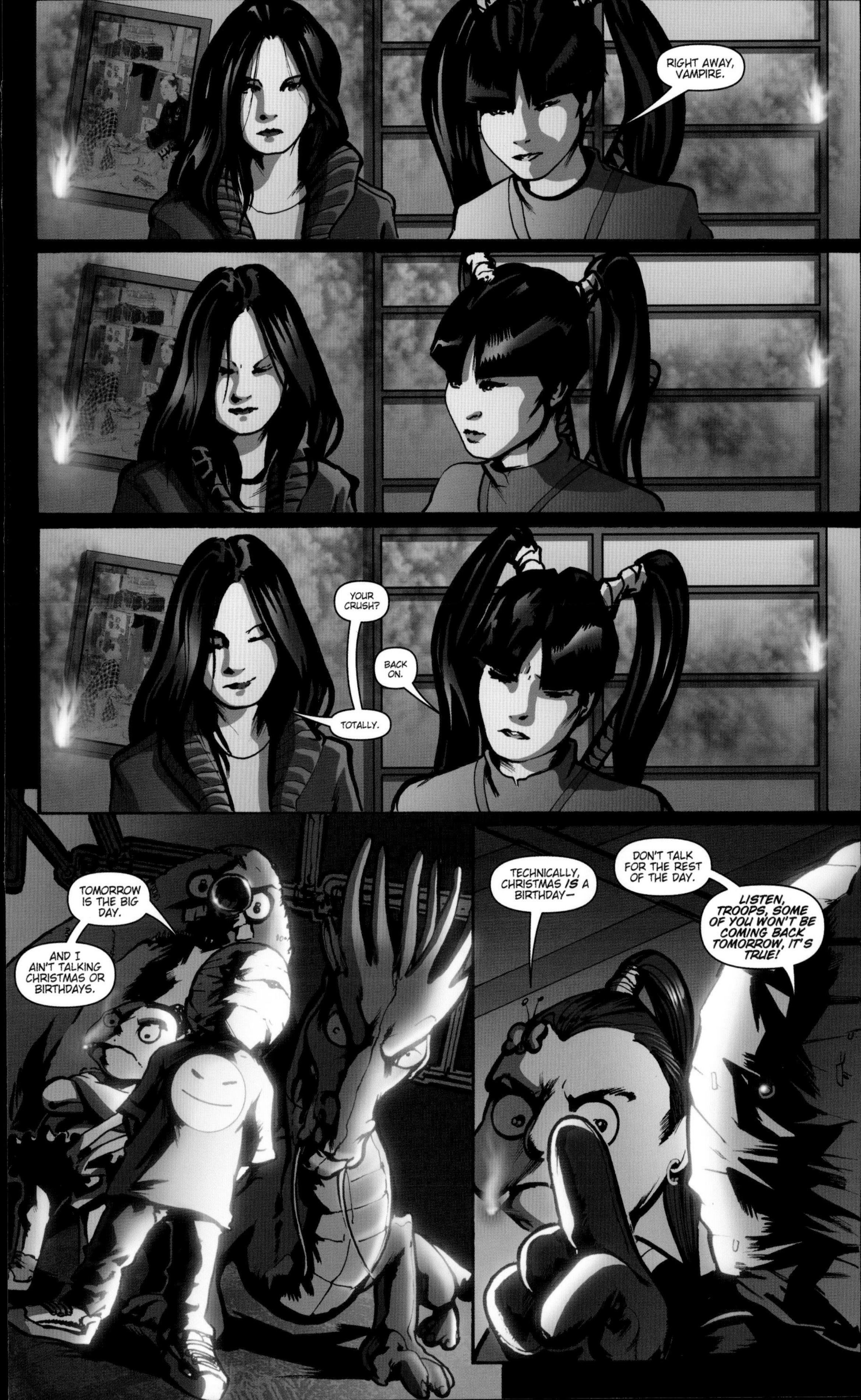
RIGHT AWAY, VAMPIRE.
YOUR CRUSH?
BACK ON.
TOTALLY.
TOMORROW IS THE BIG DAY.
AND I AIN'T TALKING CHRISTMAS OR BIRTHDAYS.
TECHNICALLY, CHRISTMAS *IS* A BIRTHDAY—
DON'T TALK FOR THE REST OF THE DAY.
LISTEN, TROOPS, SOME OF YOU WON'T BE COMING BACK TOMORROW, IT'S TRUE!

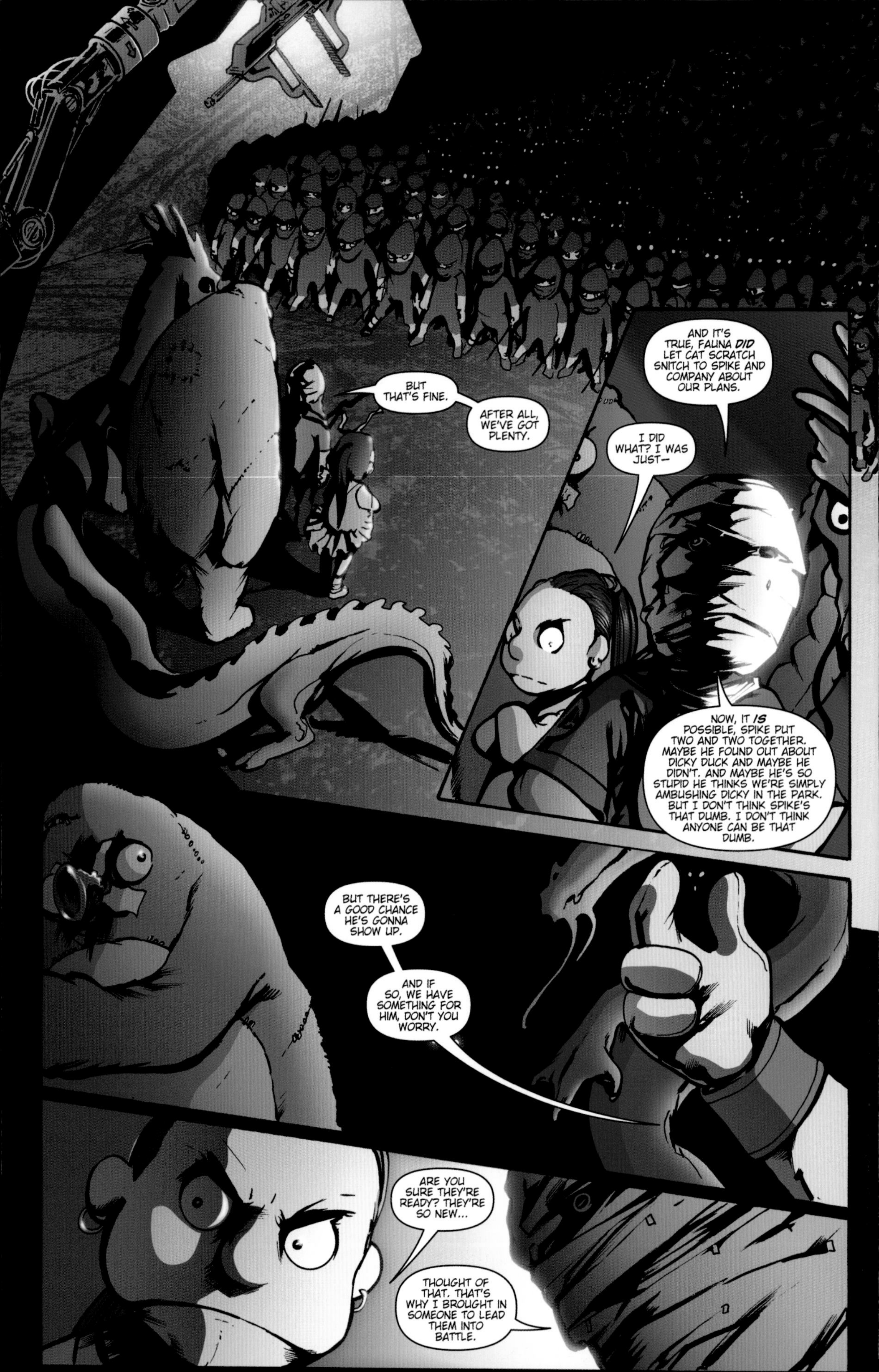
BUT THAT'S FINE.
AFTER ALL, WE'VE GOT PLENTY.
AND IT'S TRUE, FAUNA DID LET CAT SCRATCH SNITCH TO SPIKE AND COMPANY ABOUT OUR PLANS.
I DID WHAT? I WAS JUST—
NOW, IT IS POSSIBLE, SPIKE PUT TWO AND TWO TOGETHER. MAYBE HE FOUND OUT ABOUT DICKY DUCK AND MAYBE HE DIDN'T. AND MAYBE HE'S SO STUPID HE THINKS WE'RE SIMPLY AMBUSHING DICKY IN THE PARK. BUT I DON'T THINK SPIKE'S THAT DUMB. I DON'T THINK ANYONE CAN BE THAT DUMB.
BUT THERE'S A GOOD CHANCE HE'S GONNA SHOW UP.
AND IF SO, WE HAVE SOMETHING FOR HIM, DON'T YOU WORRY.
ARE YOU SURE THEY'RE READY? THEY'RE SO NEW...
THOUGHT OF THAT. THAT'S WHY I BROUGHT IN SOMEONE TO LEAD THEM INTO BATTLE.

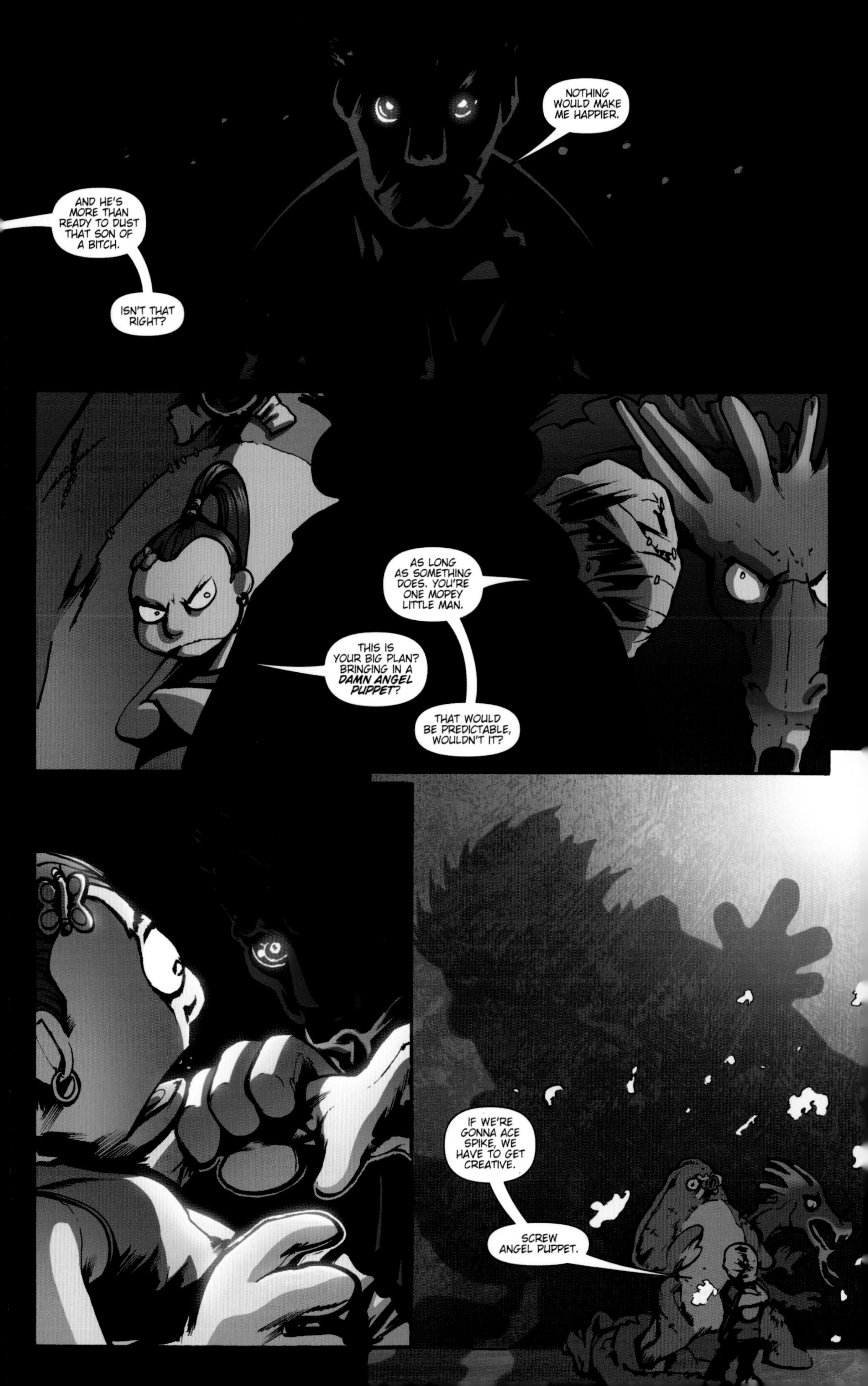

NOTHING WOULD MAKE ME HAPPIER.
AND HE'S MORE THAN READY TO DUST THAT SON OF A BITCH.
ISN'T THAT RIGHT?
THIS IS YOUR BIG PLAN? BRINGING IN A DAMN ANGEL PUPPET?
AS LONG AS SOMETHING DOES. YOU'RE ONE MOPEY LITTLE MAN.
THAT WOULD BE PREDICTABLE, WOULDN'T IT?
IF WE'RE GONNA ACE SPIKE, WE HAVE TO GET CREATIVE.
SCREW ANGEL PUPPET.

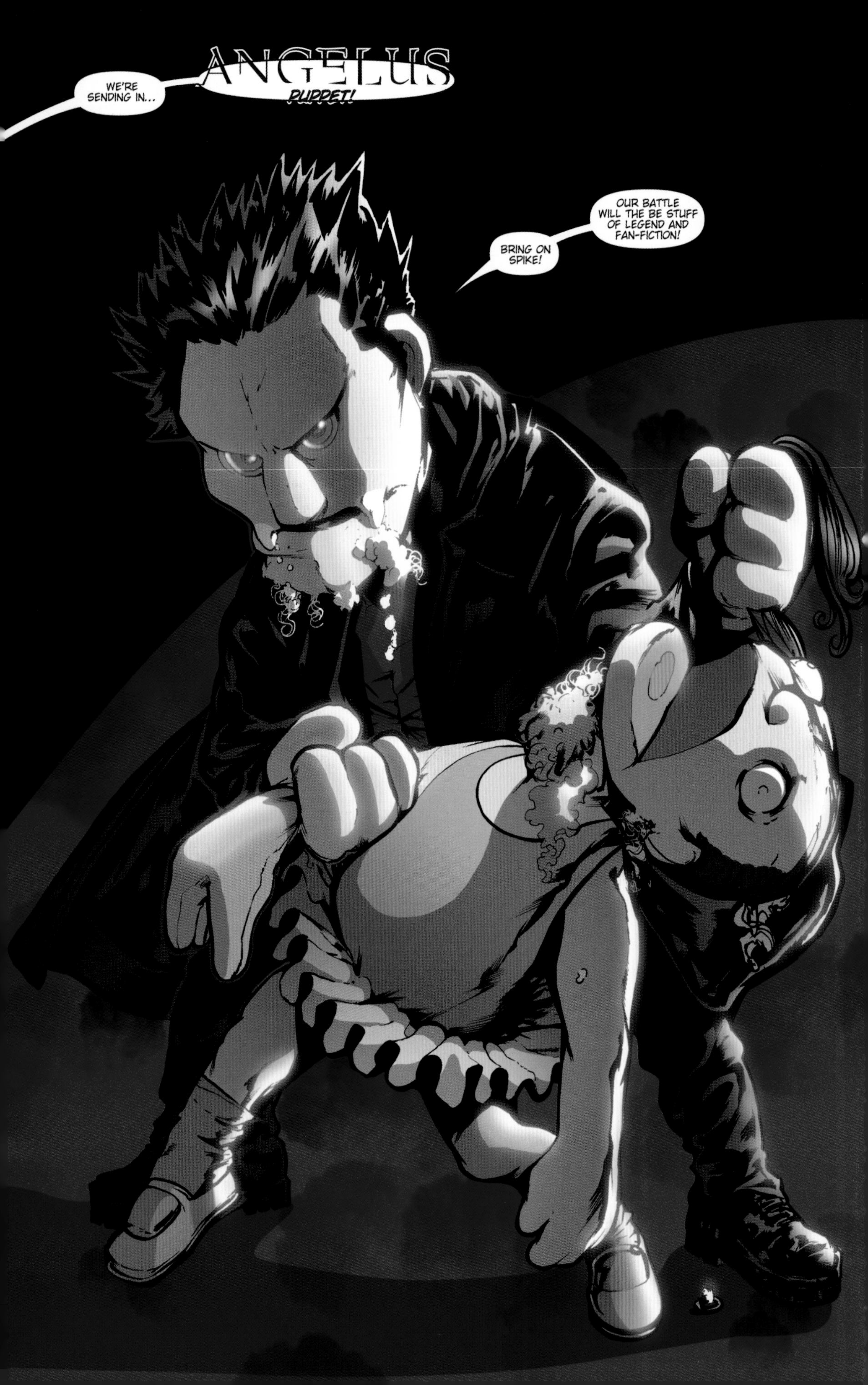
WE'RE SENDING IN...
ANGELUS
PUPPET!
BRING ON SPIKE!
OUR BATTLE WILL THE BE STUFF OF LEGEND AND FAN-FICTION!

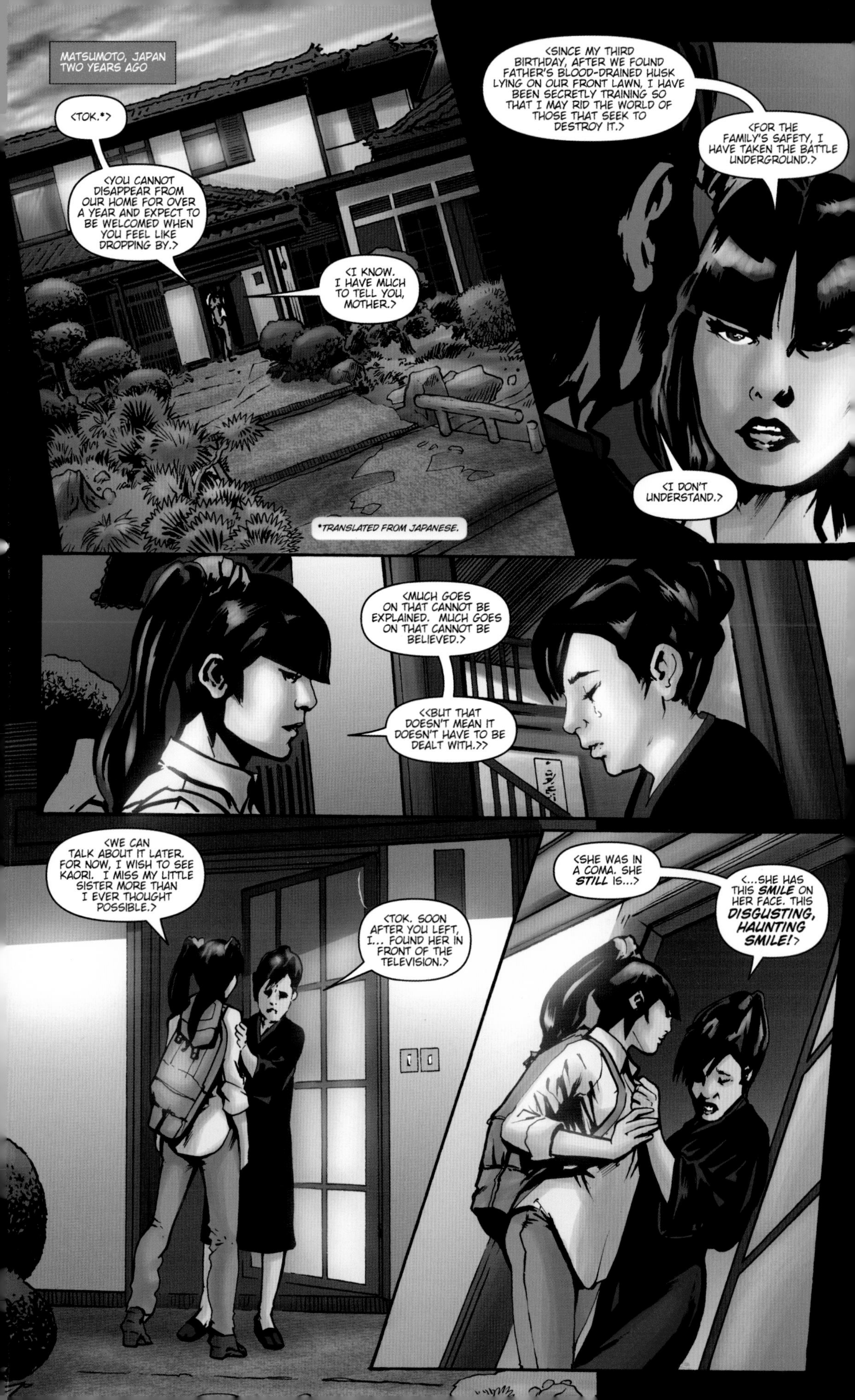
MATSUMOTO, JAPAN
TWO YEARS AGO
<TOK.*>
<YOU CANNOT DISAPPEAR FROM OUR HOME FOR OVER A YEAR AND EXPECT TO BE WELCOMED WHEN YOU FEEL LIKE DROPPING BY.>
<I KNOW. I HAVE MUCH TO TELL YOU, MOTHER.>
*TRANSLATED FROM JAPANESE.
<SINCE MY THIRD BIRTHDAY, AFTER WE FOUND FATHER'S BLOOD-DRAINED HUSK LYING ON OUR FRONT LAWN, I HAVE BEEN SECRETLY TRAINING SO THAT I MAY RID THE WORLD OF THOSE THAT SEEK TO DESTROY IT.>
<FOR THE FAMILY'S SAFETY, I HAVE TAKEN THE BATTLE UNDERGROUND.>
<I DON'T UNDERSTAND.>
<MUCH GOES ON THAT CANNOT BE EXPLAINED. MUCH GOES ON THAT CANNOT BE BELIEVED.>
<<BUT THAT DOESN'T MEAN IT DOESN'T HAVE TO BE DEALT WITH.>>
<WE CAN TALK ABOUT IT LATER. FOR NOW, I WISH TO SEE KAORI. I MISS MY LITTLE SISTER MORE THAN I EVER THOUGHT POSSIBLE.>
<TOK. SOON AFTER YOU LEFT, I... FOUND HER IN FRONT OF THE TELEVISION.>
<SHE WAS IN A COMA. SHE STILL IS...>
<...SHE HAS THIS SMILE ON HER FACE. THIS DISGUSTING, HAUNTING SMILE!>

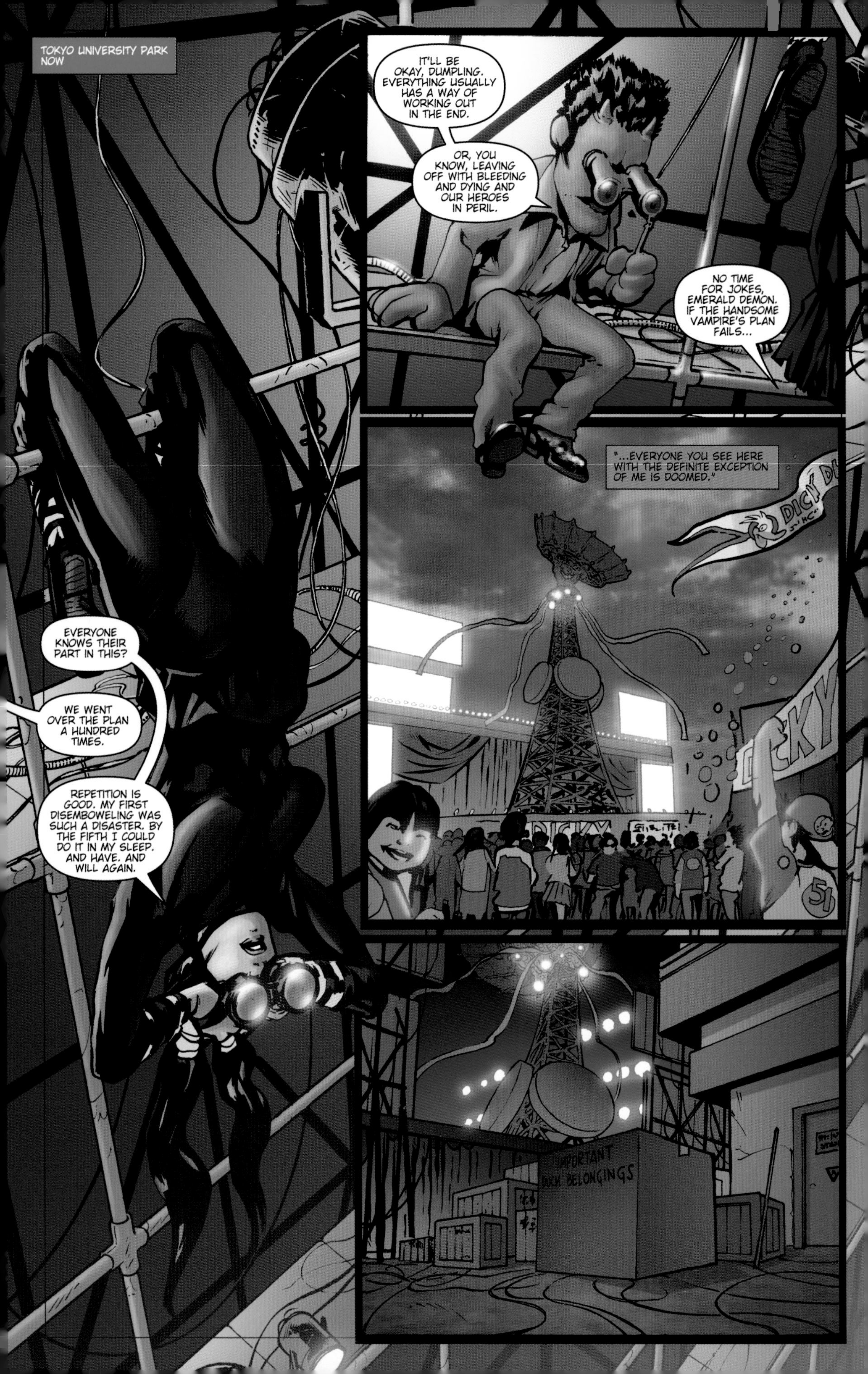
TOKYO UNIVERSITY PARK
NOW
IT'LL BE OKAY, DUMPLING. EVERYTHING USUALLY HAS A WAY OF WORKING OUT IN THE END.
OR, YOU KNOW, LEAVING OFF WITH BLEEDING AND DYING AND OUR HEROES IN PERIL.
NO TIME FOR JOKES, EMERALD DEMON. IF THE HANDSOME VAMPIRE'S PLAN FAILS...
EVERYONE KNOWS THEIR PART IN THIS?
WE WENT OVER THE PLAN A HUNDRED TIMES.
REPETITION IS GOOD. MY FIRST DISEMBOWELING WAS SUCH A DISASTER. BY THE FIFTH I COULD DO IT IN MY SLEEP. AND HAVE. AND WILL AGAIN.
"...EVERYONE YOU SEE HERE WITH THE DEFINITE EXCEPTION OF ME IS DOOMED."
DICKY
IMPORTANT DUCK BELONGINGS

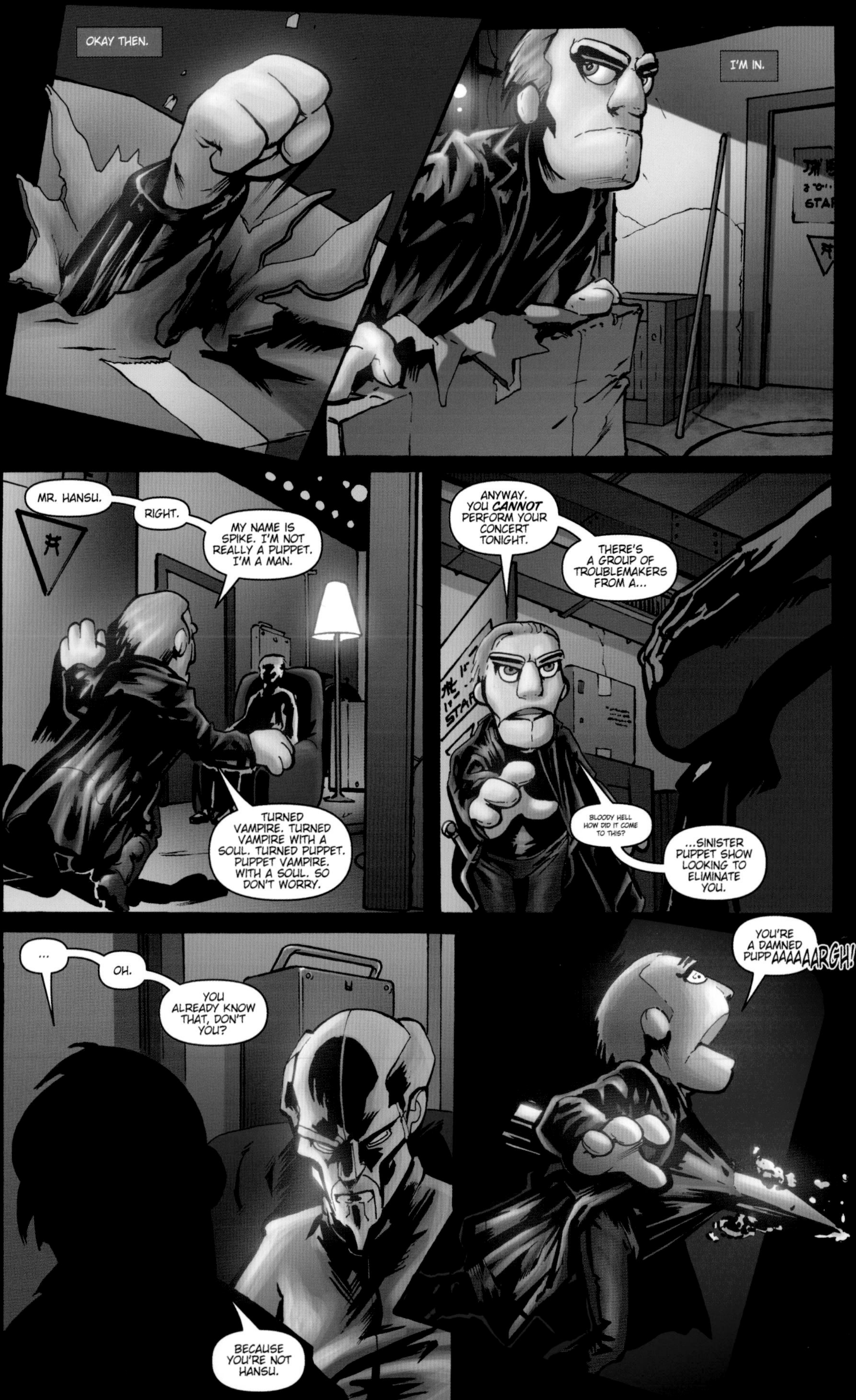
OKAY THEN.
I'M IN.
MR. HANSU.
RIGHT.
MY NAME IS SPIKE. I'M NOT REALLY A PUPPET. I'M A MAN.
TURNED VAMPIRE. TURNED VAMPIRE WITH A SOUL. TURNED PUPPET. PUPPET VAMPIRE. WITH A SOUL. SO DON'T WORRY.
ANYWAY. YOU CANNOT PERFORM YOUR CONCERT TONIGHT.
THERE'S A GROUP OF TROUBLEMAKERS FROM A...
BLOODY HELL HOW DID IT COME TO THIS?
...SINISTER PUPPET SHOW LOOKING TO ELIMINATE YOU.
...
OH.
YOU ALREADY KNOW THAT, DON'T YOU?
BECAUSE YOU'RE NOT HANSU.
YOU'RE A DAMNED PUPPAAAAAARGH!

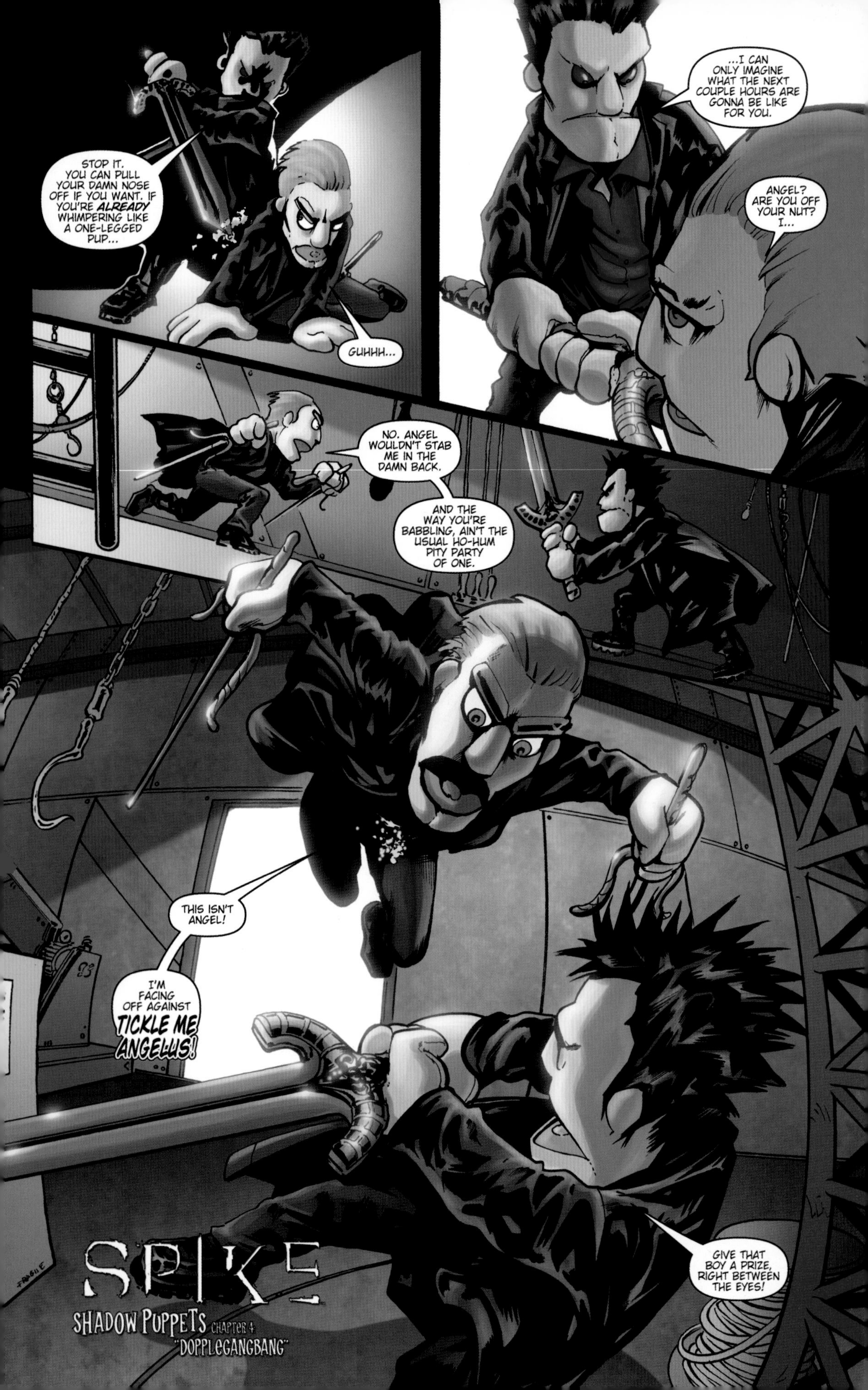
STOP IT. YOU CAN PULL YOUR DAMN NOSE OFF IF YOU WANT. IF YOU'RE ALREADY WHIMPERING LIKE A ONE-LEGGED PUP...
...I CAN ONLY IMAGINE WHAT THE NEXT COUPLE HOURS ARE GONNA BE LIKE FOR YOU.
GUHHH...
ANGEL? ARE YOU OFF YOUR NUT? I...
NO. ANGEL WOULDN'T STAB ME IN THE DAMN BACK.
AND THE WAY YOU'RE BABBLING, AIN'T THE USUAL HO-HUM PITY PARTY OF ONE.
THIS ISN'T ANGEL!
I'M FACING OFF AGAINST TICKLE ME ANGELUS!
GIVE THAT BOY A PRIZE, RIGHT BETWEEN THE EYES!
SPIKE
SHADOW PUPPETS CHAPTER 4 "DOPPLEGANGBANG"

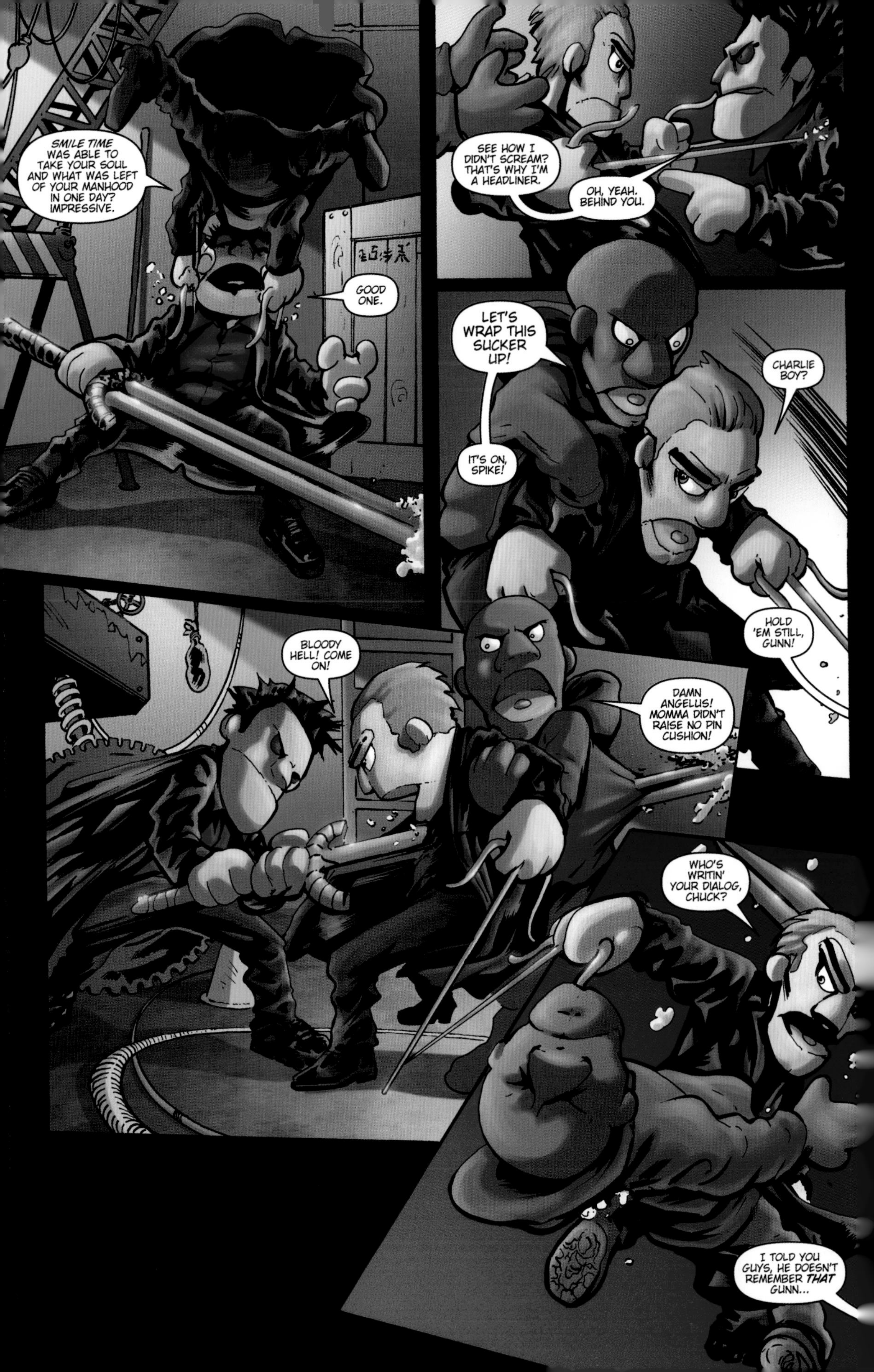
SMILE TIME WAS ABLE TO TAKE YOUR SOUL AND WHAT WAS LEFT OF YOUR MANHOOD IN ONE DAY? IMPRESSIVE.
GOOD ONE.
SEE HOW I DIDN'T SCREAM? THAT'S WHY I'M A HEADLINER.
OH, YEAH. BEHIND YOU.
LET'S WRAP THIS SUCKER UP!
IT'S ON, SPIKE!
CHARLIE BOY?
HOLD 'EM STILL, GUNN!
BLOODY HELL! COME ON!
DAMN ANGELUS! MOMMA DIDN'T RAISE NO PIN CUSHION!
WHO'S WRITIN' YOUR DIALOG, CHUCK?
I TOLD YOU GUYS, HE DOESN'T REMEMBER THAT GUNN...

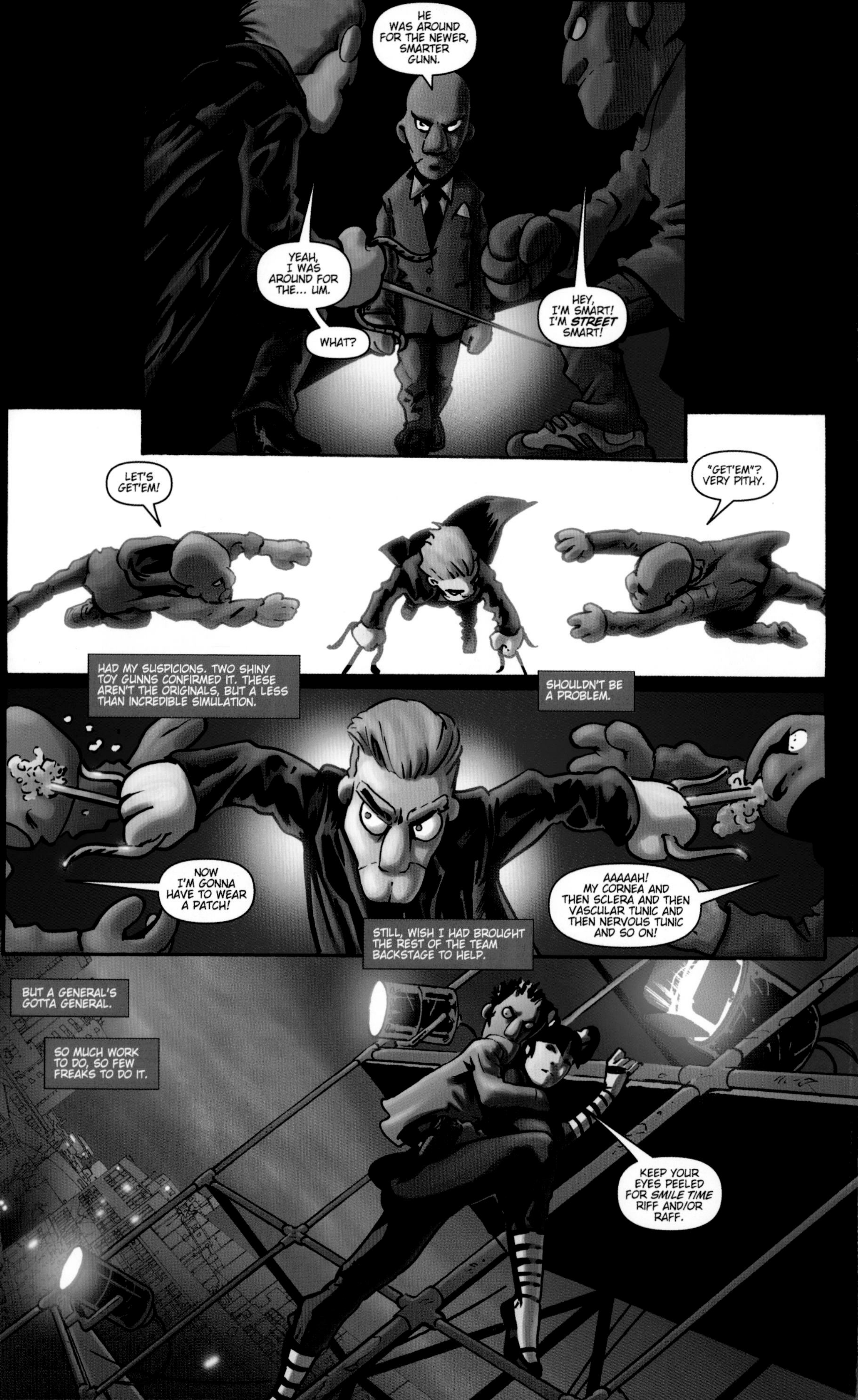

HE WAS AROUND FOR THE NEWER, SMARTER GUNN.
YEAH, I WAS AROUND FOR THE... UM.
WHAT?
HEY, I'M SMART! I'M STREET SMART!
LET'S GET'EM!
"GET'EM"? VERY PITHY.
HAD MY SUSPICIONS. TWO SHINY TOY GUNNS CONFIRMED IT. THESE AREN'T THE ORIGINALS, BUT A LESS THAN INCREDIBLE SIMULATION.
SHOULDN'T BE A PROBLEM.
NOW I'M GONNA HAVE TO WEAR A PATCH!
AAAAAH! MY CORNEA AND THEN SCLERA AND THEN VASCULAR TUNIC AND THEN NERVOUS TUNIC AND SO ON!
STILL, WISH I HAD BROUGHT THE REST OF THE TEAM BACKSTAGE TO HELP.
BUT A GENERAL'S GOTTA GENERAL.
SO MUCH WORK TO DO, SO FEW FREAKS TO DO IT.
KEEP YOUR EYES PEELED FOR SMILE TIME RIFF AND/OR RAFF.

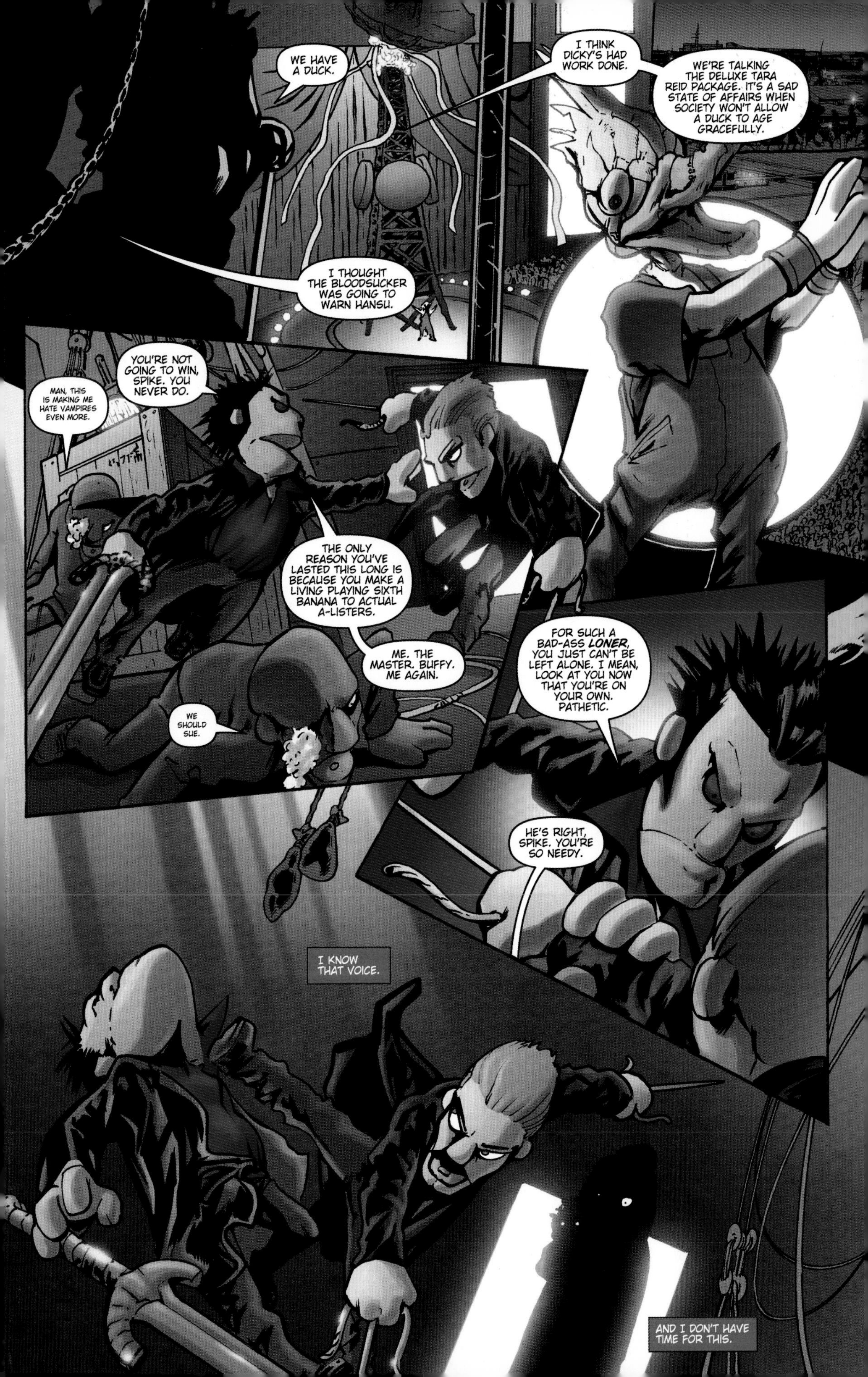
WE HAVE A DUCK.
I THINK DICKY'S HAD WORK DONE.
WE'RE TALKING THE DELUXE TARA REID PACKAGE. IT'S A SAD STATE OF AFFAIRS WHEN SOCIETY WON'T ALLOW A DUCK TO AGE GRACEFULLY.
I THOUGHT THE BLOODSUCKER WAS GOING TO WARN HANSU.
MAN, THIS IS MAKING ME HATE VAMPIRES EVEN MORE.
YOU'RE NOT GOING TO WIN, SPIKE. YOU NEVER DO.
THE ONLY REASON YOU'VE LASTED THIS LONG IS BECAUSE YOU MAKE A LIVING PLAYING SIXTH BANANA TO ACTUAL A-LISTERS.
ME. THE MASTER. BUFFY. ME AGAIN.
WE SHOULD SUE.
FOR SUCH A BAD-ASS LONER, YOU JUST CAN'T BE LEFT ALONE. I MEAN, LOOK AT YOU NOW THAT YOU'RE ON YOUR OWN. PATHETIC.
HE'S RIGHT, SPIKE. YOU'RE SO NEEDY.
I KNOW THAT VOICE.
AND I DON'T HAVE TIME FOR THIS.

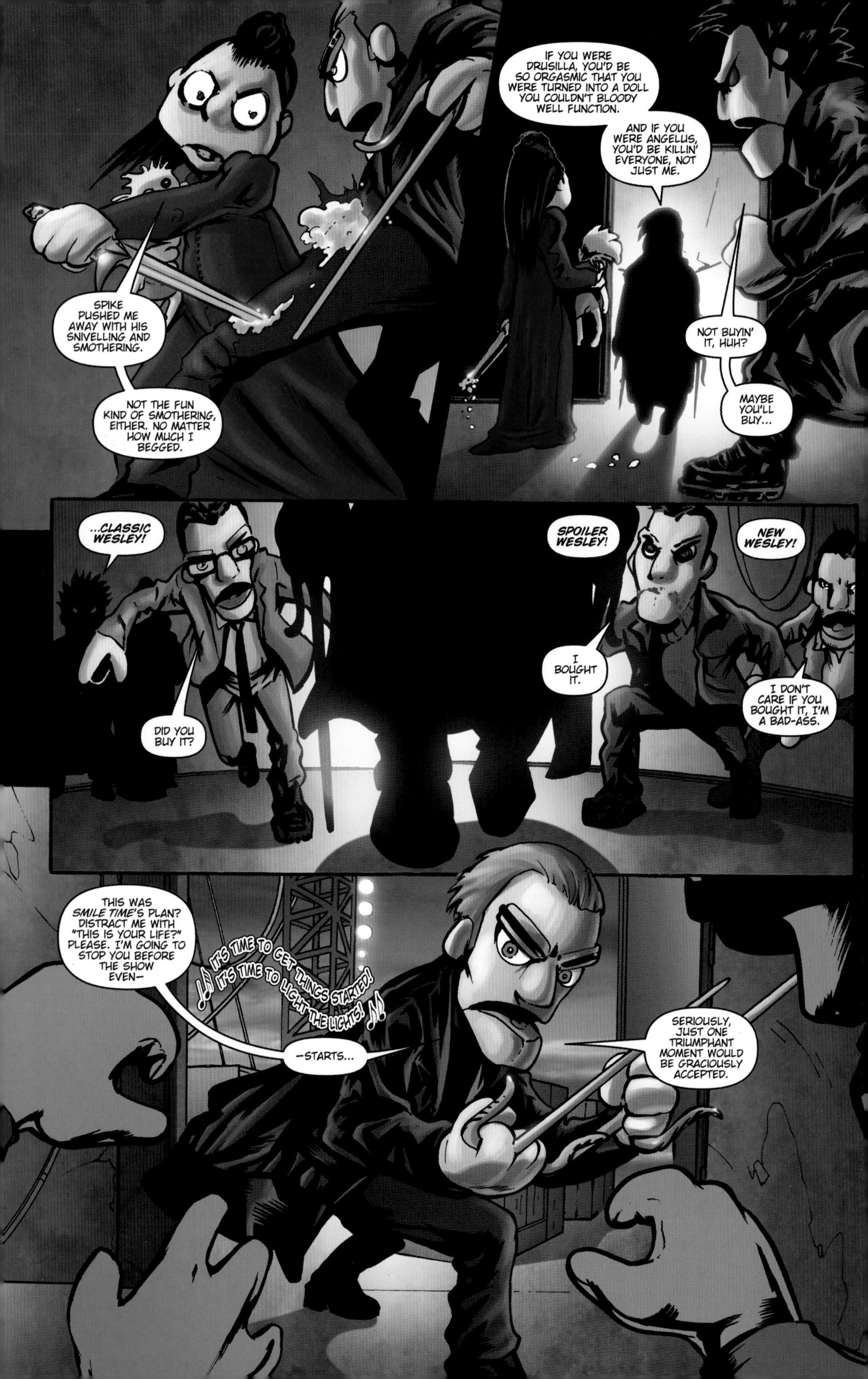
SPIKE PUSHED ME AWAY WITH HIS SNIVELLING AND SMOTHERING.
NOT THE FUN KIND OF SMOTHERING, EITHER. NO MATTER HOW MUCH I BEGGED.
IF YOU WERE DRUSILLA, YOU'D BE SO ORGASMIC THAT YOU WERE TURNED INTO A DOLL YOU COULDN'T BLOODY WELL FUNCTION.
AND IF YOU WERE ANGELUS, YOU'D BE KILLIN' EVERYONE, NOT JUST ME.
NOT BUYIN' IT, HUH?
MAYBE YOU'LL BUY...
...CLASSIC WESLEY!
DID YOU BUY IT?
SPOILER WESLEY!
I BOUGHT IT.
NEW WESLEY!
I DON'T CARE IF YOU BOUGHT IT, I'M A BAD-ASS.
THIS WAS SMILE TIME'S PLAN? DISTRACT ME WITH "THIS IS YOUR LIFE?" PLEASE. I'M GOING TO STOP YOU BEFORE THE SHOW EVEN—
IT'S TIME TO GET THINGS STARTED! IT'S TIME TO LIGHT THE LIGHTS!
—STARTS...
SERIOUSLY, JUST ONE TRIUMPHANT MOMENT WOULD BE GRACIOUSLY ACCEPTED.

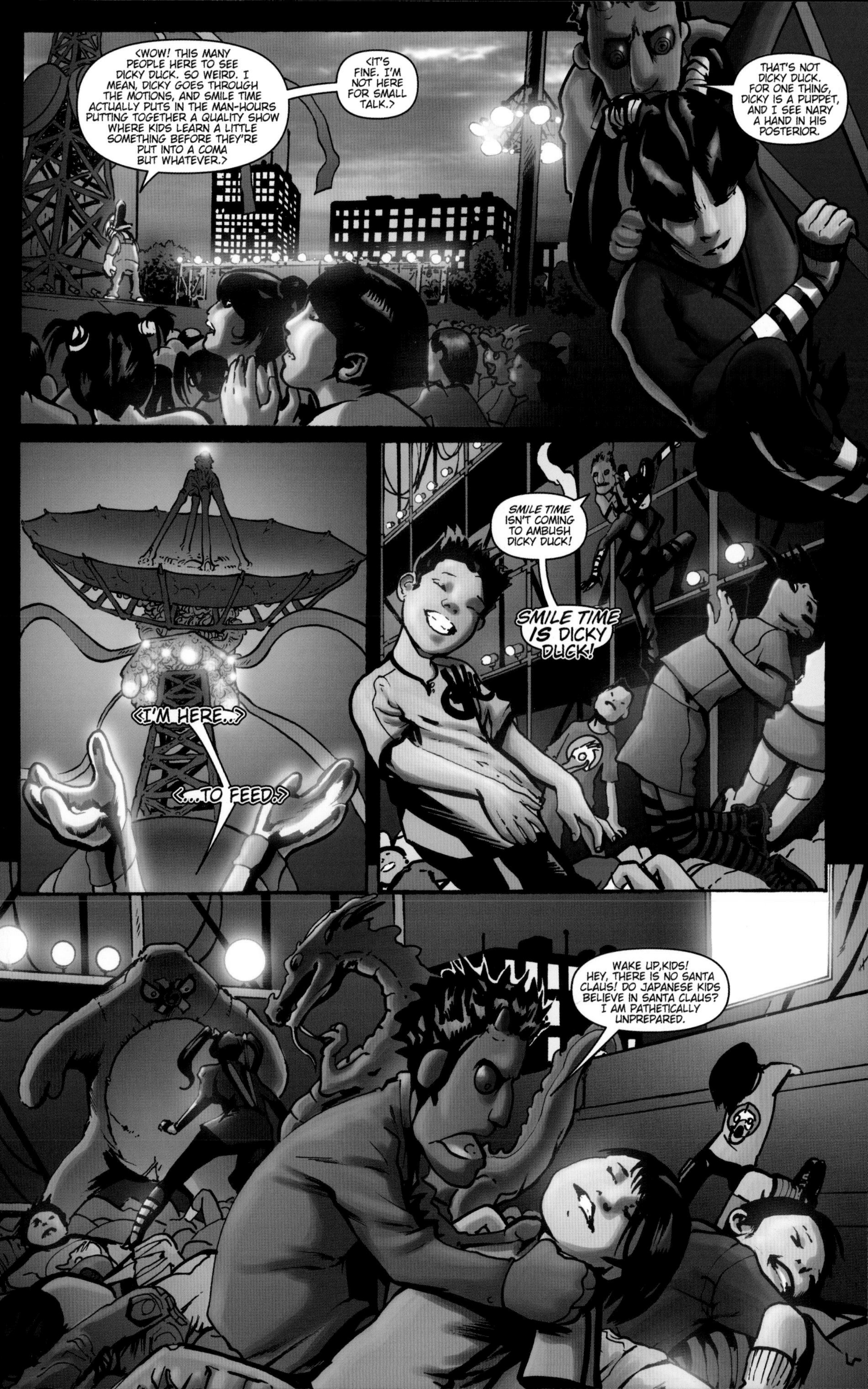
<WOW! THIS MANY PEOPLE HERE TO SEE DICKY DUCK. SO WEIRD. I MEAN, DICKY GOES THROUGH THE MOTIONS, AND SMILE TIME ACTUALLY PUTS IN THE MAN-HOURS PUTTING TOGETHER A QUALITY SHOW WHERE KIDS LEARN A LITTLE SOMETHING BEFORE THEY'RE PUT INTO A COMA BUT WHATEVER.>
<IT'S FINE. I'M NOT HERE FOR SMALL TALK.>
THAT'S NOT DICKY DUCK. FOR ONE THING, DICKY IS A PUPPET, AND I SEE NARY A HAND IN HIS POSTERIOR.
<I'M HERE..>
<...TO FEED.>
SMILE TIME ISN'T COMING TO AMBUSH DICKY DUCK!
SMILE TIME IS DICKY DUCK!
WAKE UP,KIDS! HEY, THERE IS NO SANTA CLAUS! DO JAPANESE KIDS BELIEVE IN SANTA CLAUS? I AM PATHETICALLY UNPREPARED.

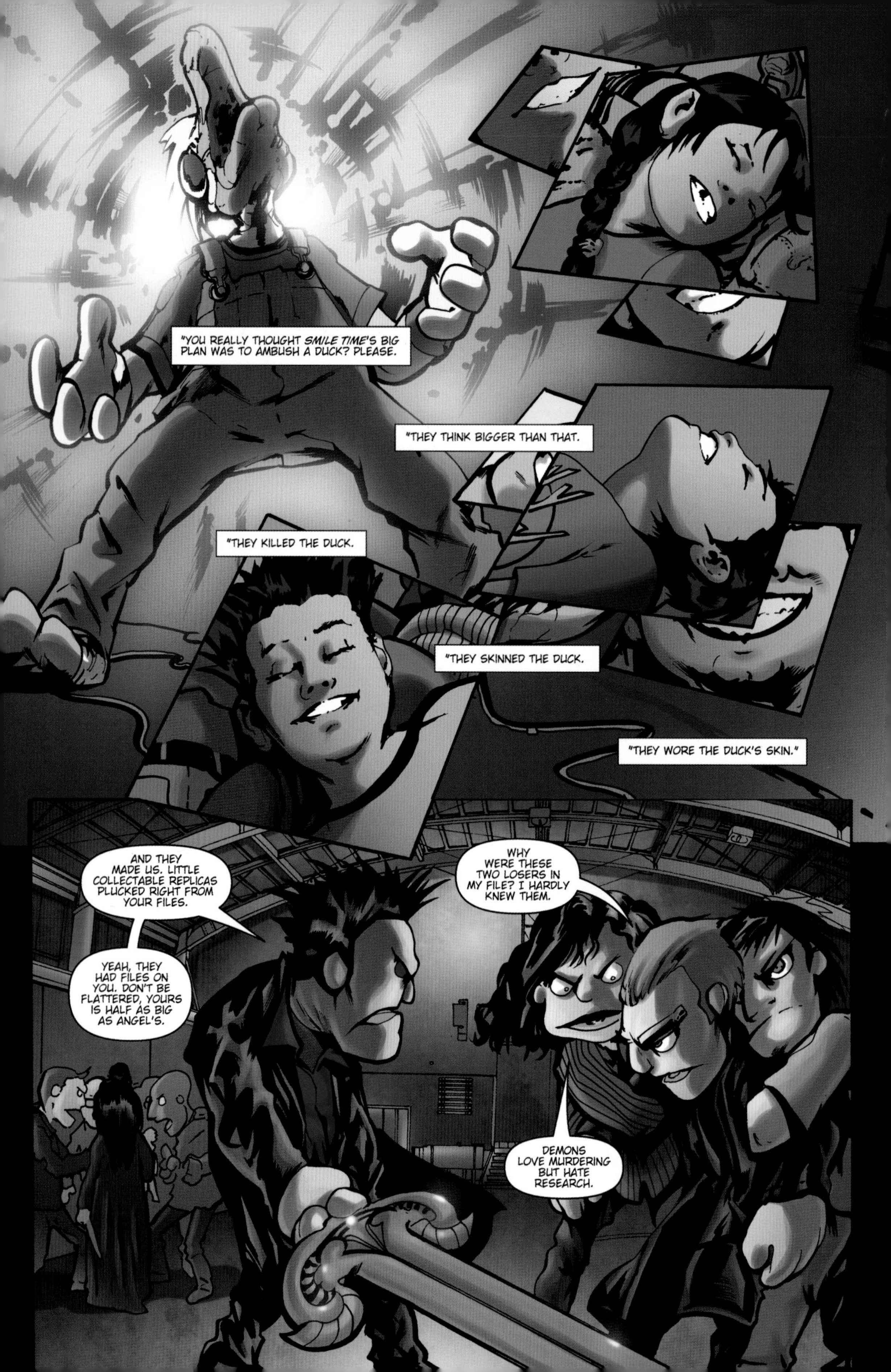
"YOU REALLY THOUGHT *SMILE TIME*'S BIG PLAN WAS TO AMBUSH A DUCK? PLEASE.
"THEY THINK BIGGER THAN THAT.
"THEY KILLED THE DUCK.
"THEY SKINNED THE DUCK.
"THEY WORE THE DUCK'S SKIN."
AND THEY MADE US. LITTLE COLLECTABLE REPLICAS PLUCKED RIGHT FROM YOUR FILES.
YEAH, THEY HAD FILES ON YOU. DON'T BE FLATTERED, YOURS IS HALF AS BIG AS ANGEL'S.
WHY WERE THESE TWO LOSERS IN MY FILE? I HARDLY KNEW THEM.
DEMONS LOVE MURDERING BUT HATE RESEARCH.

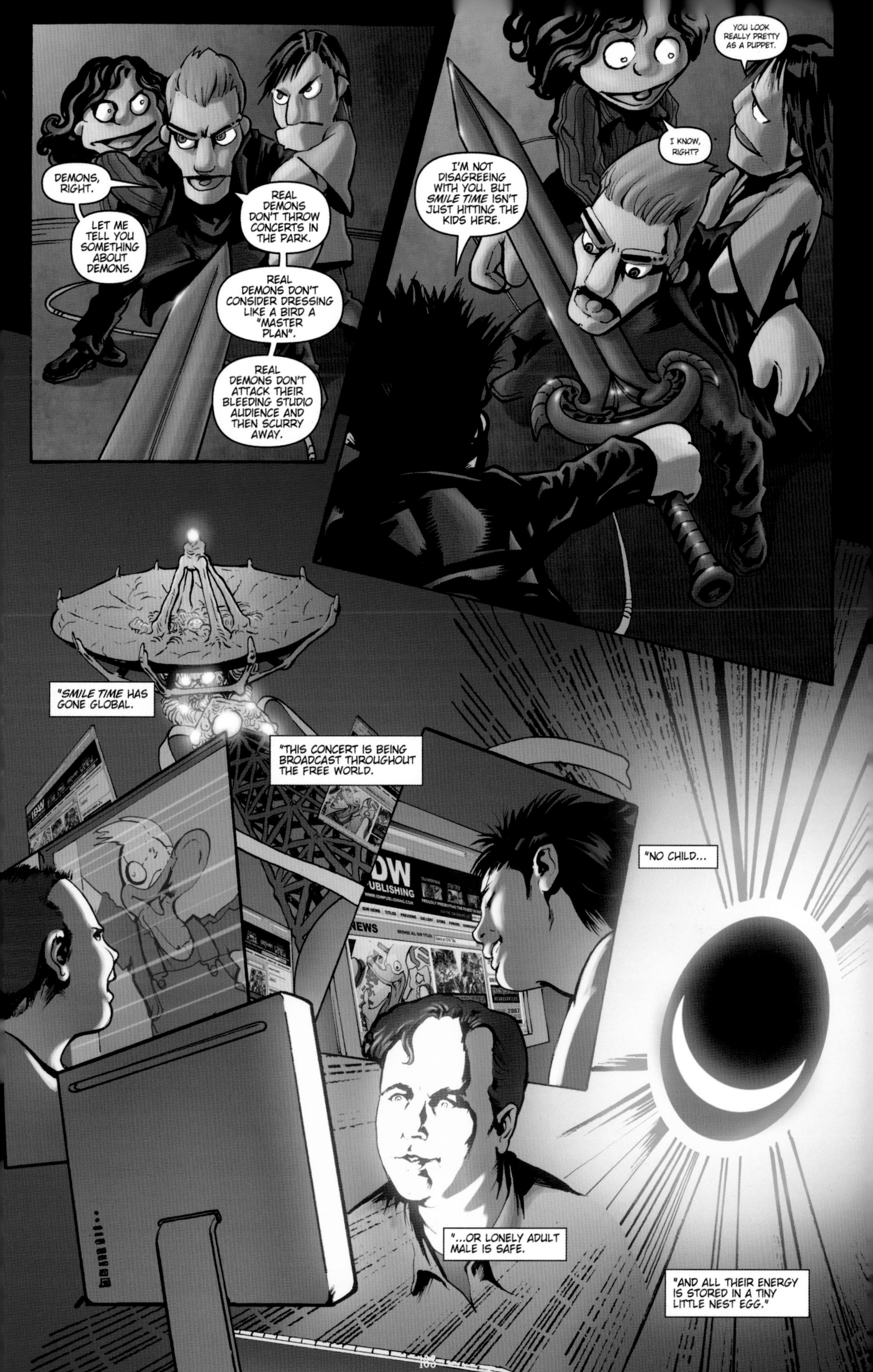
DEMONS, RIGHT.
LET ME TELL YOU SOMETHING ABOUT DEMONS.
REAL DEMONS DON'T THROW CONCERTS IN THE PARK.
REAL DEMONS DON'T CONSIDER DRESSING LIKE A BIRD A "MASTER PLAN".
REAL DEMONS DON'T ATTACK THEIR BLEEDING STUDIO AUDIENCE AND THEN SCURRY AWAY.
I'M NOT DISAGREEING WITH YOU. BUT SMILE TIME ISN'T JUST HITTING THE KIDS HERE.
YOU LOOK REALLY PRETTY AS A PUPPET.
I KNOW, RIGHT?
"SMILE TIME HAS GONE GLOBAL.
"THIS CONCERT IS BEING BROADCAST THROUGHOUT THE FREE WORLD.
"NO CHILD...
"...OR LONELY ADULT MALE IS SAFE.
"AND ALL THEIR ENERGY IS STORED IN A TINY LITTLE NEST EGG."

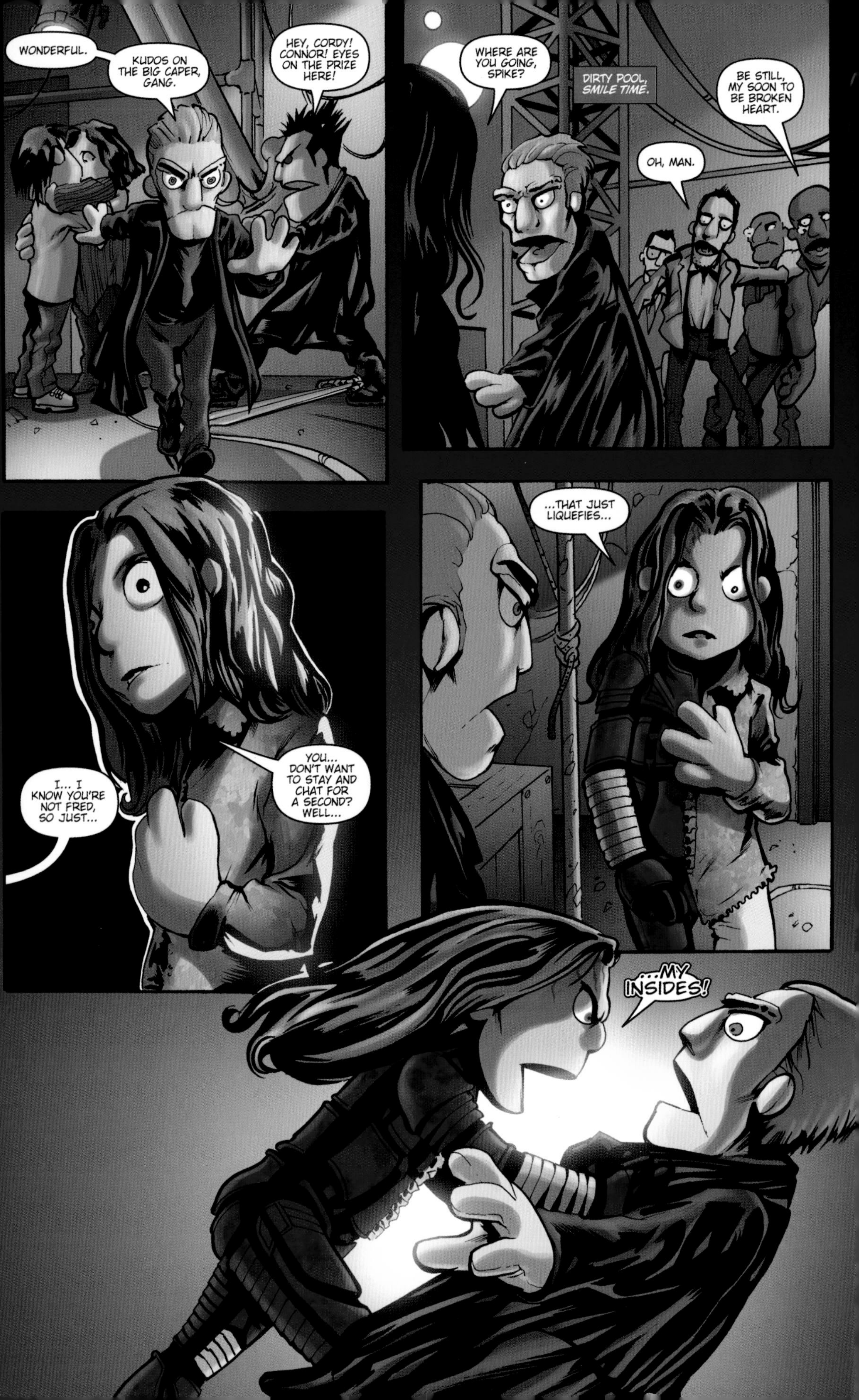
WONDERFUL.
KUDOS ON THE BIG CAPER, GANG.
HEY, CORDY! CONNOR! EYES ON THE PRIZE HERE!
WHERE ARE YOU GOING, SPIKE?
DIRTY POOL, SMILE TIME.
BE STILL, MY SOON TO BE BROKEN HEART.
OH, MAN.
YOU... DON'T WANT TO STAY AND CHAT FOR A SECOND? WELL...
I... I KNOW YOU'RE NOT FRED, SO JUST...
...THAT JUST LIQUEFIES...
...MY INSIDES!

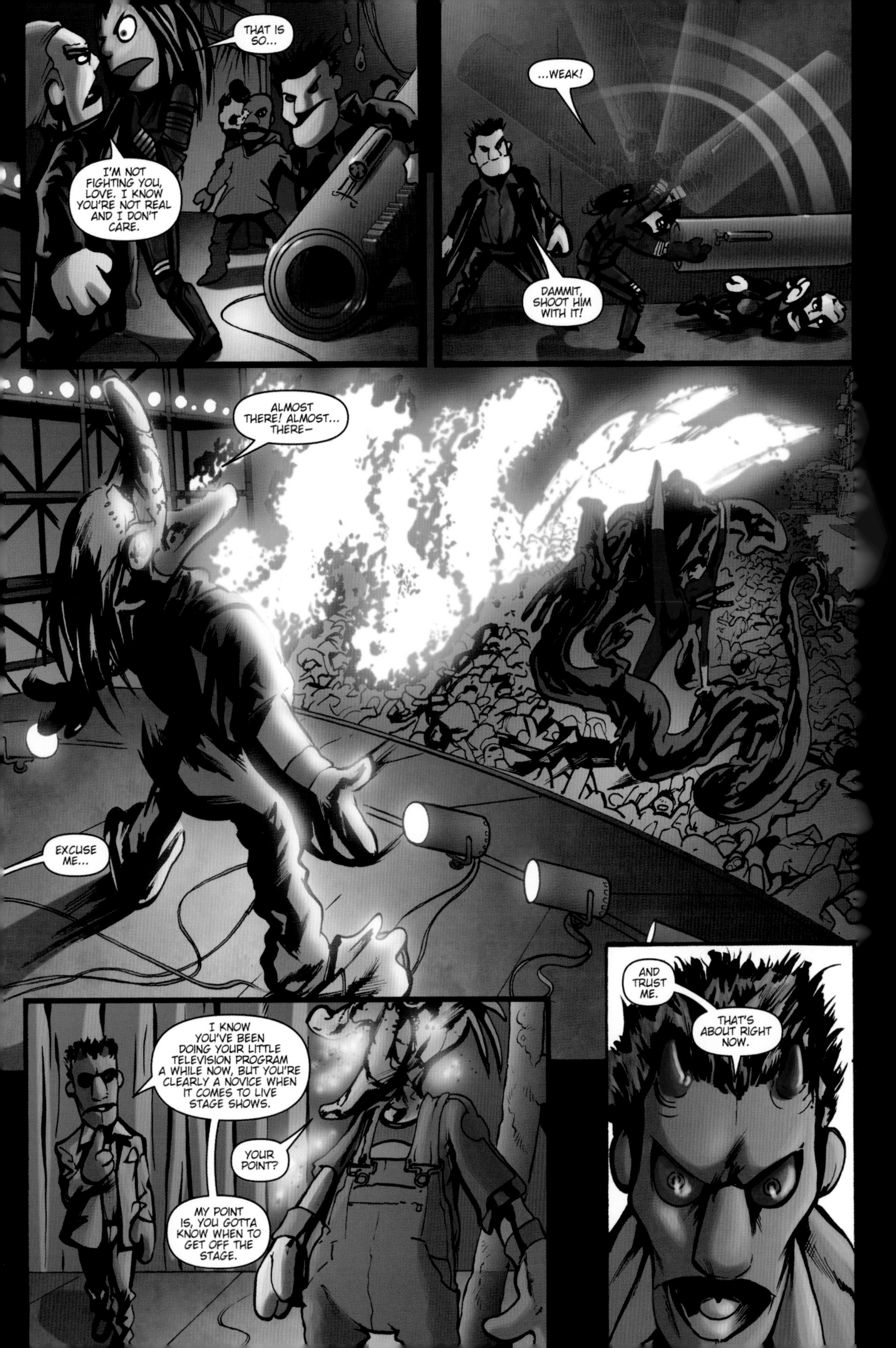
THAT IS SO...
I'M NOT FIGHTING YOU, LOVE. I KNOW YOU'RE NOT REAL AND I DON'T CARE.
...WEAK!
DAMMIT, SHOOT HIM WITH IT!
ALMOST THERE! ALMOST... THERE–
EXCUSE ME...
I KNOW YOU'VE BEEN DOING YOUR LITTLE TELEVISION PROGRAM A WHILE NOW, BUT YOU'RE CLEARLY A NOVICE WHEN IT COMES TO LIVE STAGE SHOWS.
YOUR POINT?
MY POINT IS, YOU GOTTA KNOW WHEN TO GET OFF THE STAGE.
AND TRUST ME.
THAT'S ABOUT RIGHT NOW.

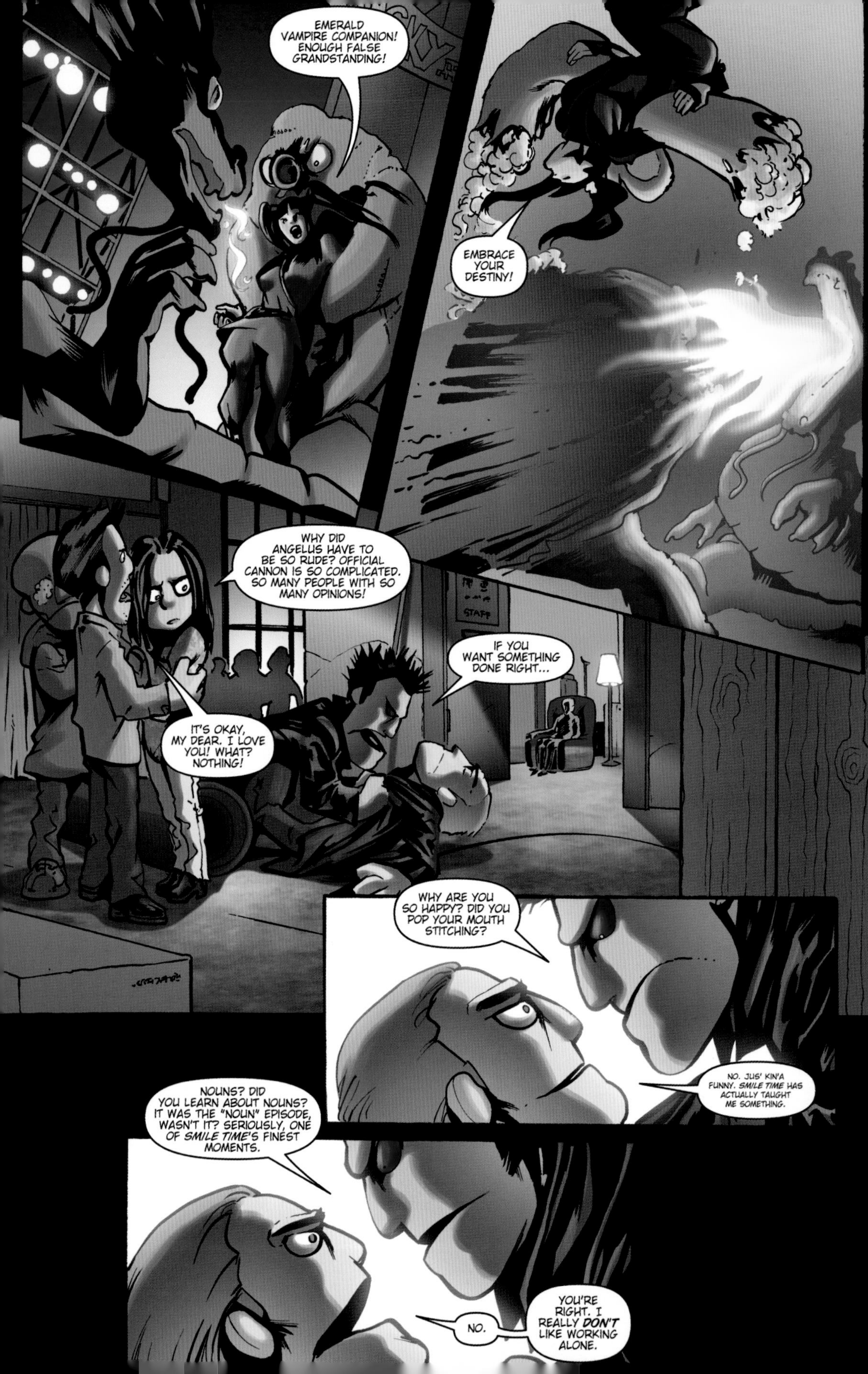
EMERALD VAMPIRE COMPANION! ENOUGH FALSE GRANDSTANDING!
EMBRACE YOUR DESTINY!
WHY DID ANGELUS HAVE TO BE SO RUDE? OFFICIAL CANNON IS SO COMPLICATED. SO MANY PEOPLE WITH SO MANY OPINIONS!
IT'S OKAY, MY DEAR. I LOVE YOU! WHAT? NOTHING!
IF YOU WANT SOMETHING DONE RIGHT...
STAFF
WHY ARE YOU SO HAPPY? DID YOU POP YOUR MOUTH STITCHING?
NO. JUS' KIN'A FUNNY. *SMILE TIME* HAS ACTUALLY TAUGHT ME SOMETHING.
NOUNS? DID YOU LEARN ABOUT NOUNS? IT WAS THE "NOUN" EPISODE, WASN'T IT? SERIOUSLY, ONE OF *SMILE TIME*'S FINEST MOMENTS.
NO.
YOU'RE RIGHT. I REALLY ***DON'T*** LIKE WORKING ALONE.

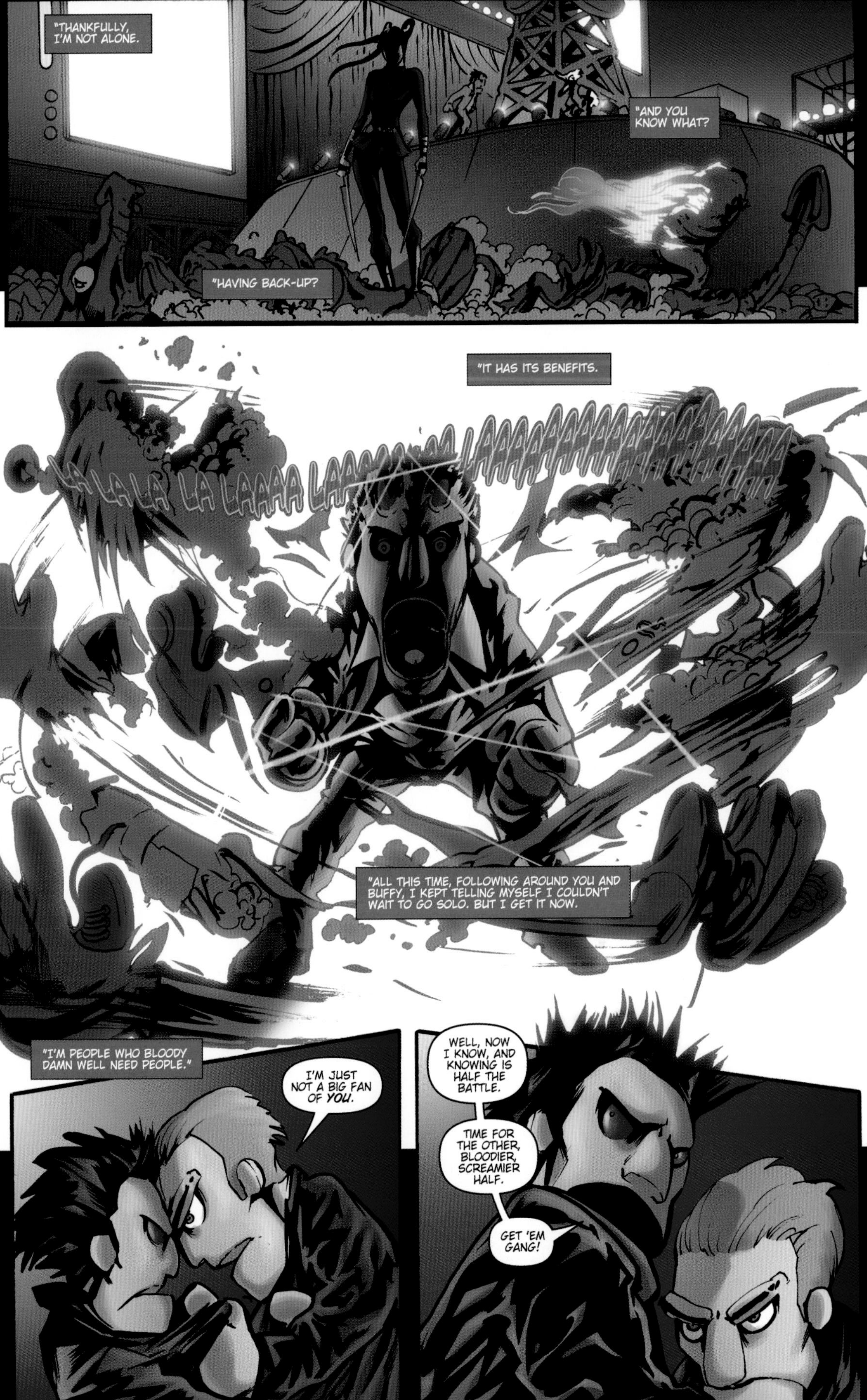
"THANKFULLY, I'M NOT ALONE.
"AND YOU KNOW WHAT?
"HAVING BACK-UP?
"IT HAS ITS BENEFITS.
LA LA LA LA LAAAA LAAAAAAAA LAAAAAAAAAAAAAAAAAAAAA
"ALL THIS TIME, FOLLOWING AROUND YOU AND BUFFY, I KEPT TELLING MYSELF I COULDN'T WAIT TO GO SOLO. BUT I GET IT NOW.
"I'M PEOPLE WHO BLOODY DAMN WELL NEED PEOPLE."
I'M JUST NOT A BIG FAN OF YOU.
WELL, NOW I KNOW, AND KNOWING IS HALF THE BATTLE.
TIME FOR THE OTHER, BLOODIER, SCREAMIER HALF.
GET 'EM GANG!

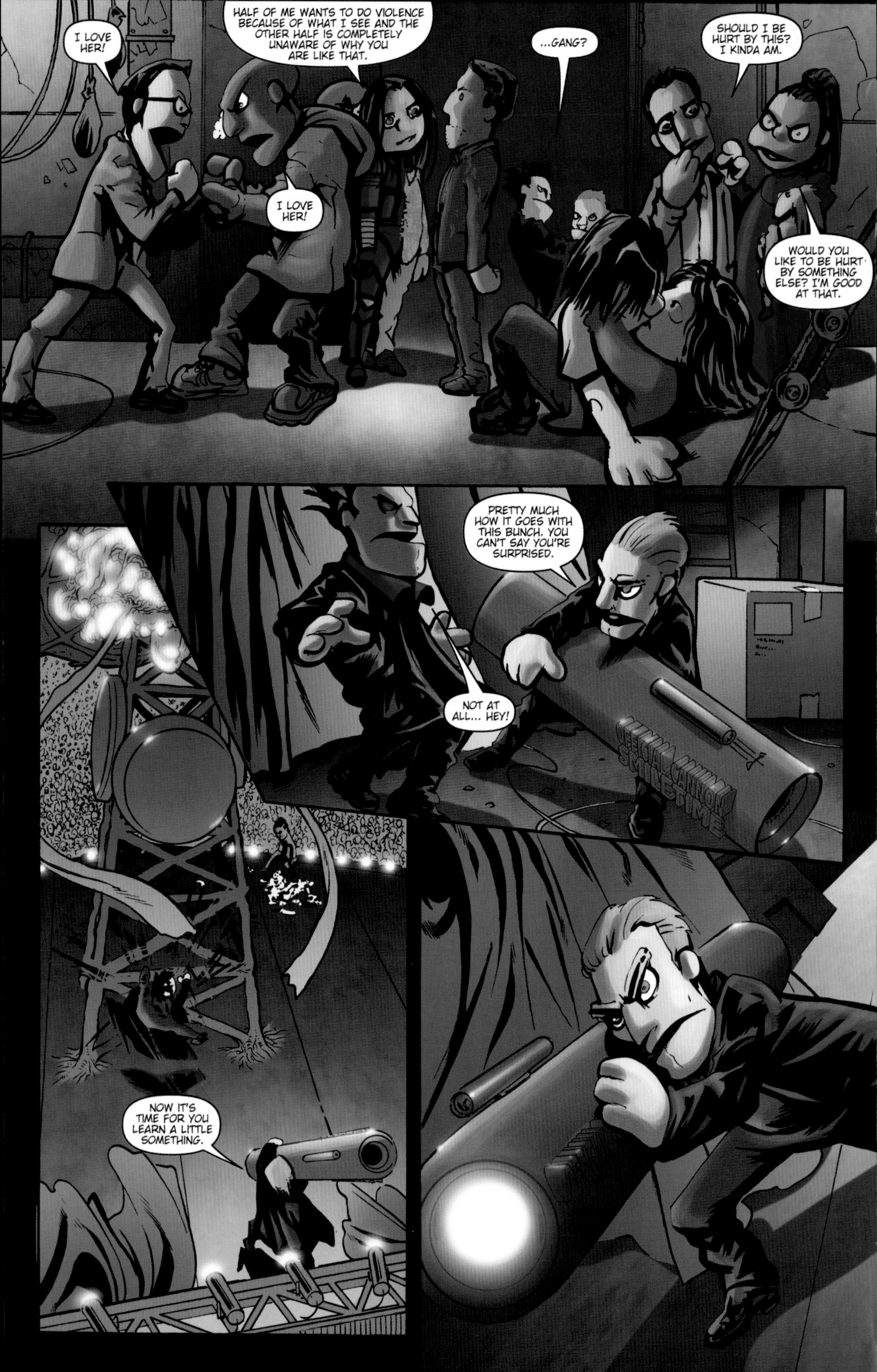
I LOVE HER!
HALF OF ME WANTS TO DO VIOLENCE BECAUSE OF WHAT I SEE AND THE OTHER HALF IS COMPLETELY UNAWARE OF WHY YOU ARE LIKE THAT.
I LOVE HER!
...GANG?
SHOULD I BE HURT BY THIS? I KINDA AM.
WOULD YOU LIKE TO BE HURT BY SOMETHING ELSE? I'M GOOD AT THAT.
PRETTY MUCH HOW IT GOES WITH THIS BUNCH. YOU CAN'T SAY YOU'RE SURPRISED.
NOT AT ALL... HEY!
OFFICIAL CANNON SMILE TIME
NOW IT'S TIME FOR YOU LEARN A LITTLE SOMETHING.

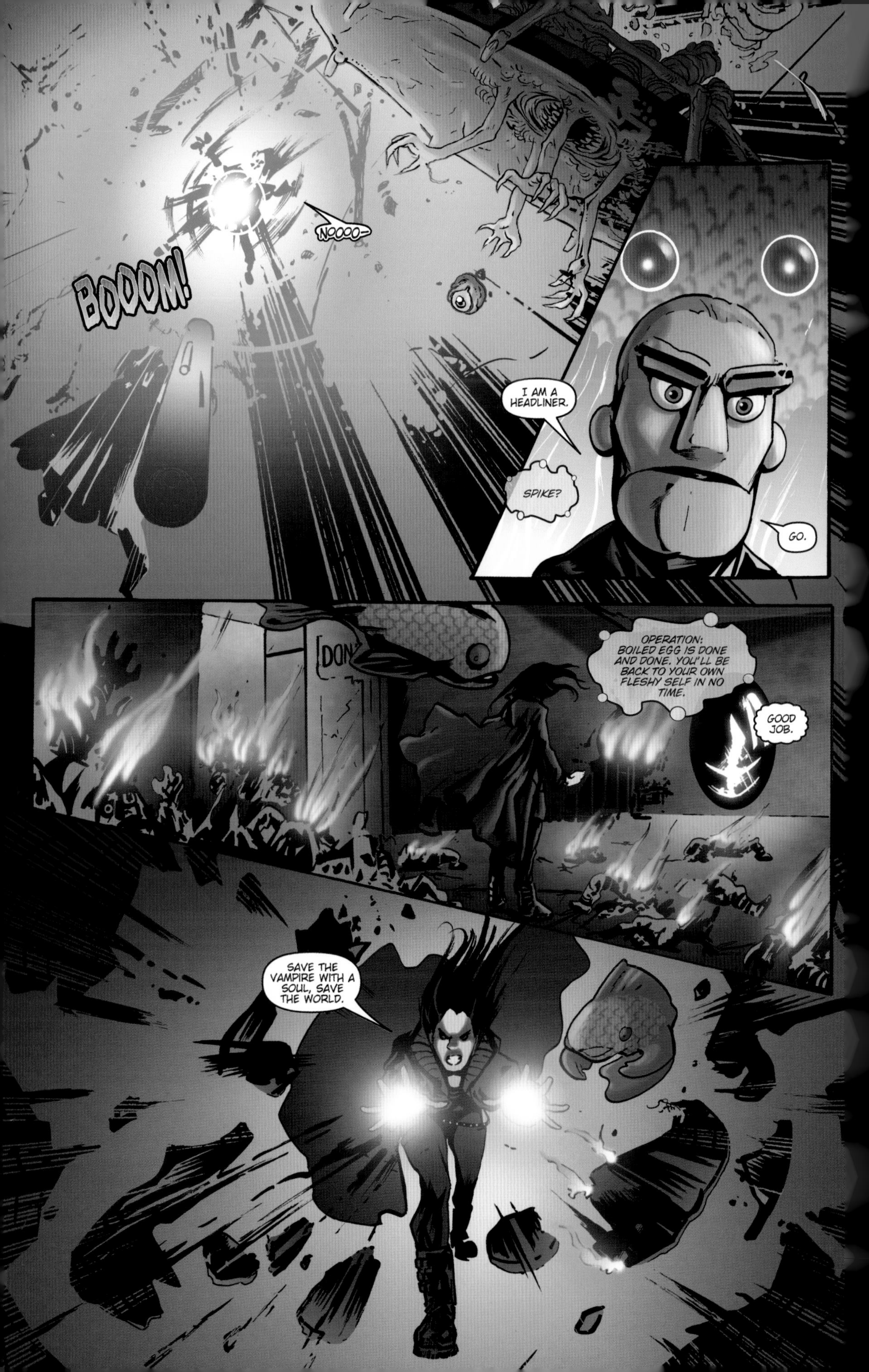
BOOOM!
NOOOO—
I AM A HEADLINER.
SPIKE?
GO.
OPERATION: BOILED EGG IS DONE AND DONE. YOU'LL BE BACK TO YOUR OWN FLESHY SELF IN NO TIME.
GOOD JOB.
SAVE THE VAMPIRE WITH A SOUL, SAVE THE WORLD.

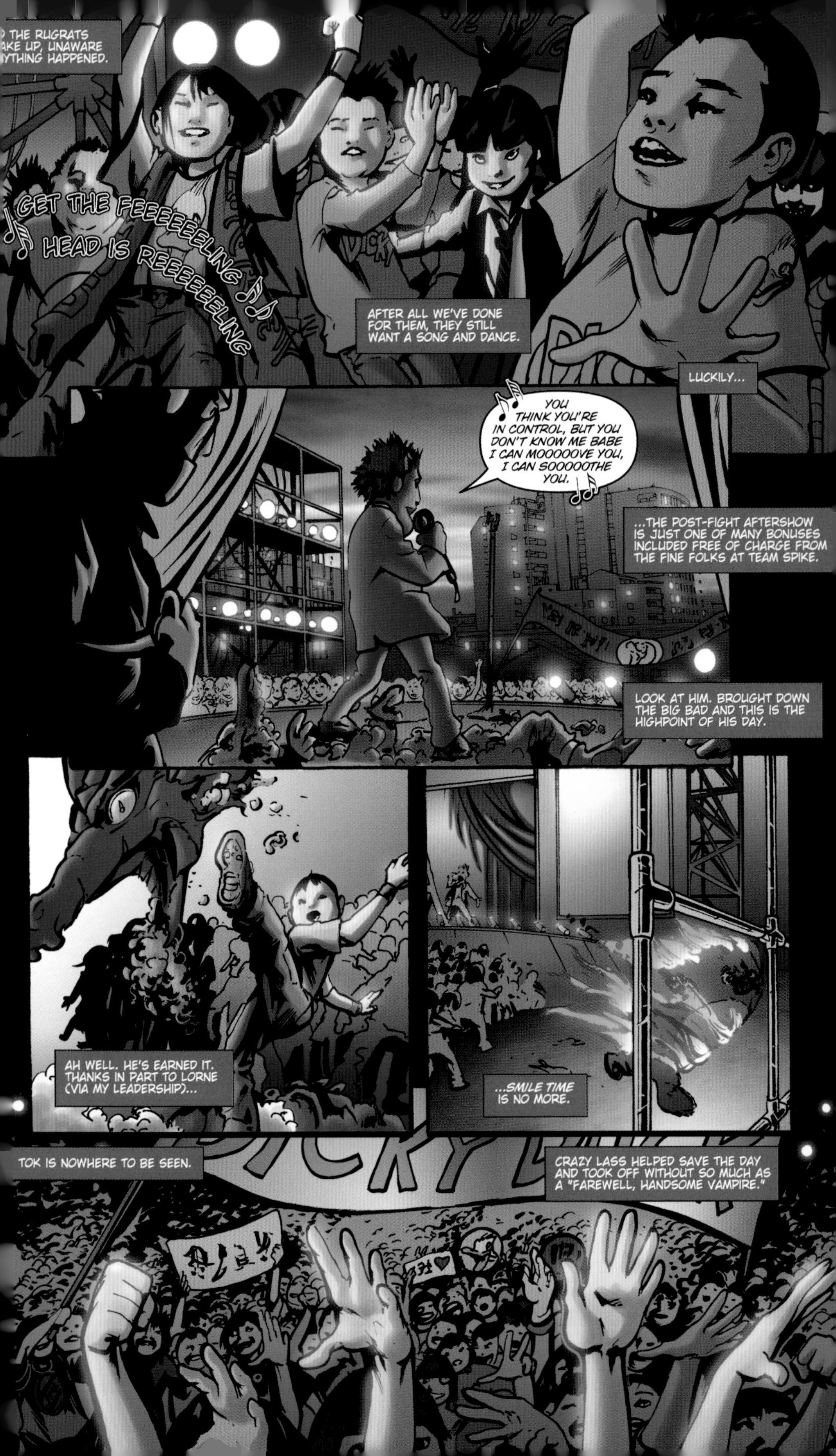

D THE RUGRATS AKE UP, UNAWARE YTHING HAPPENED.
GET THE FEEEEEEELING HEAD IS REEEEEEELING REEEEEEELING
AFTER ALL WE'VE DONE FOR THEM, THEY STILL WANT A SONG AND DANCE.
LUCKILY...
YOU THINK YOU'RE IN CONTROL, BUT YOU DON'T KNOW ME BABE I CAN MOOOOOVE YOU, I CAN SOOOOOTHE YOU.
...THE POST-FIGHT AFTERSHOW IS JUST ONE OF MANY BONUSES INCLUDED FREE OF CHARGE FROM THE FINE FOLKS AT TEAM SPIKE.
LOOK AT HIM. BROUGHT DOWN THE BIG BAD AND THIS IS THE HIGHPOINT OF HIS DAY.
AH WELL. HE'S EARNED IT. THANKS IN PART TO LORNE (VIA MY LEADERSHIP)...
...SMILE TIME IS NO MORE.
TOK IS NOWHERE TO BE SEEN.
CRAZY LASS HELPED SAVE THE DAY AND TOOK OFF WITHOUT SO MUCH AS A "FAREWELL, HANDSOME VAMPIRE."

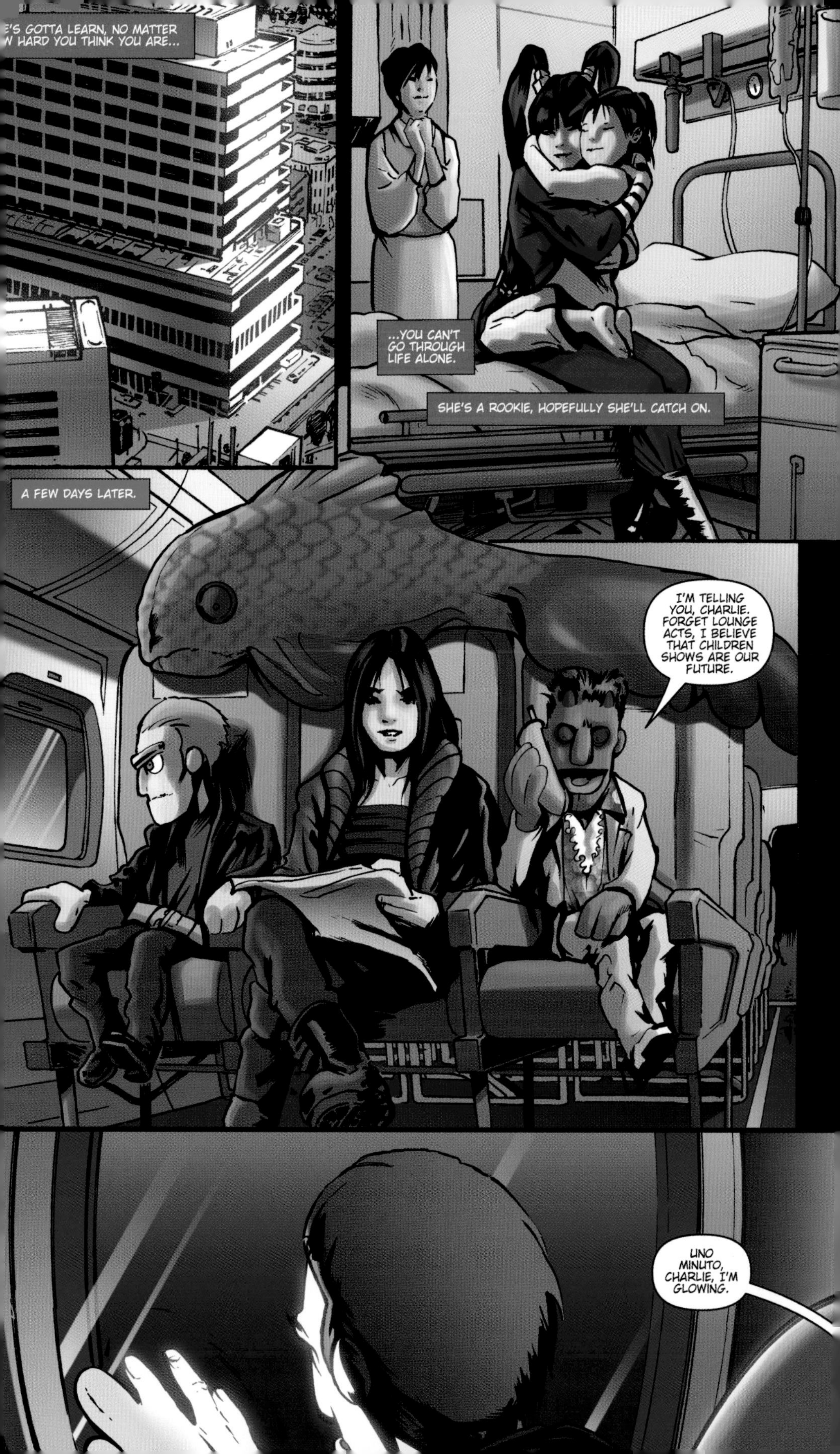

E'S GOTTA LEARN, NO MATTER
W HARD YOU THINK YOU ARE...
...YOU CAN'T GO THROUGH LIFE ALONE.
SHE'S A ROOKIE, HOPEFULLY SHE'LL CATCH ON.
A FEW DAYS LATER.
I'M TELLING YOU, CHARLIE. FORGET LOUNGE ACTS, I BELIEVE THAT CHILDREN SHOWS ARE OUR FUTURE.
UNO MINUTO, CHARLIE, I'M GLOWING.

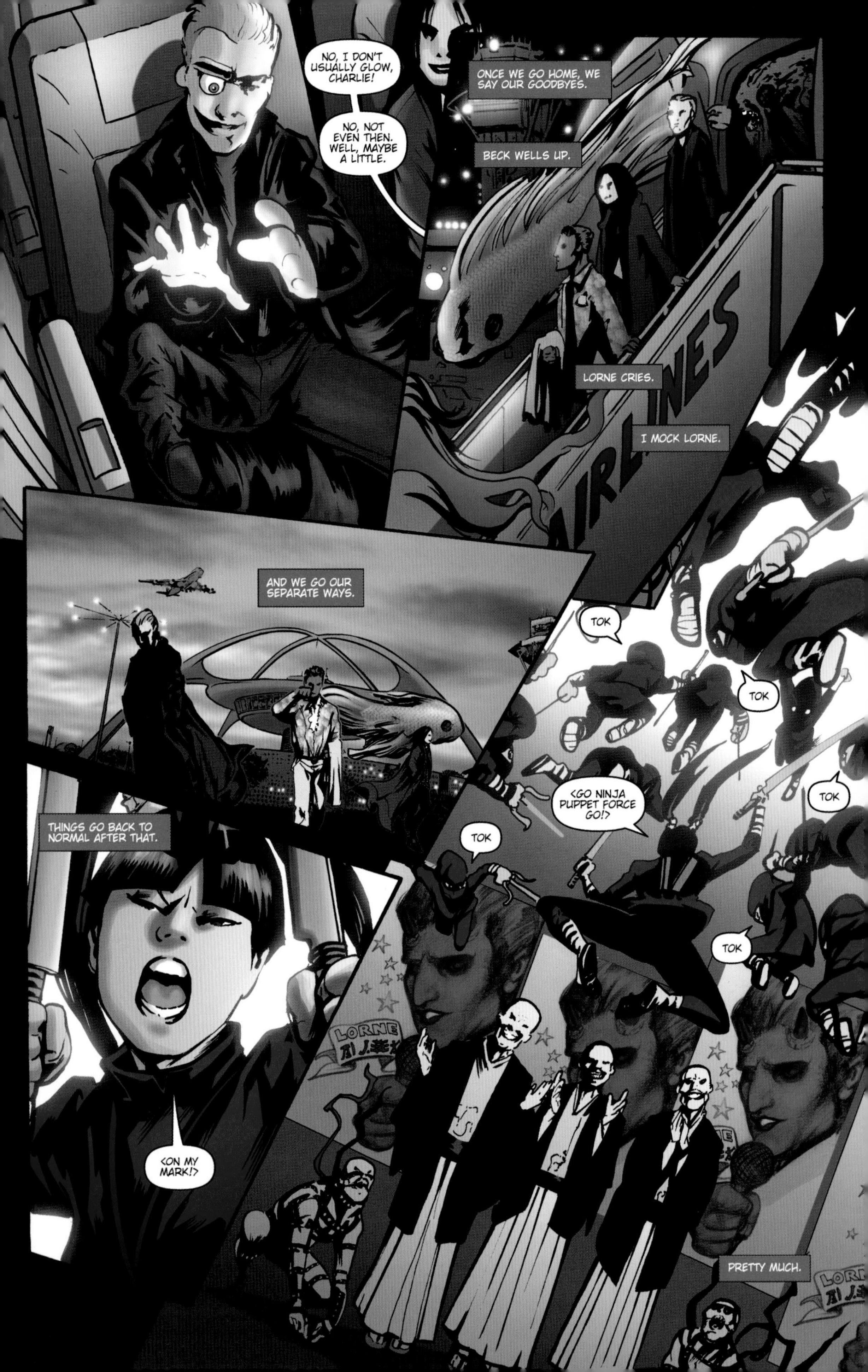

NO, I DON'T USUALLY GLOW, CHARLIE!
NO, NOT EVEN THEN. WELL, MAYBE A LITTLE.
ONCE WE GO HOME, WE SAY OUR GOODBYES.
BECK WELLS UP.
LORNE CRIES.
I MOCK LORNE.
AIRLINES
AND WE GO OUR SEPARATE WAYS.
THINGS GO BACK TO NORMAL AFTER THAT.
<ON MY MARK!>
TOK
TOK
<GO NINJA PUPPET FORCE GO!>
TOK
TOK
TOK
LORNE
PRETTY MUCH.

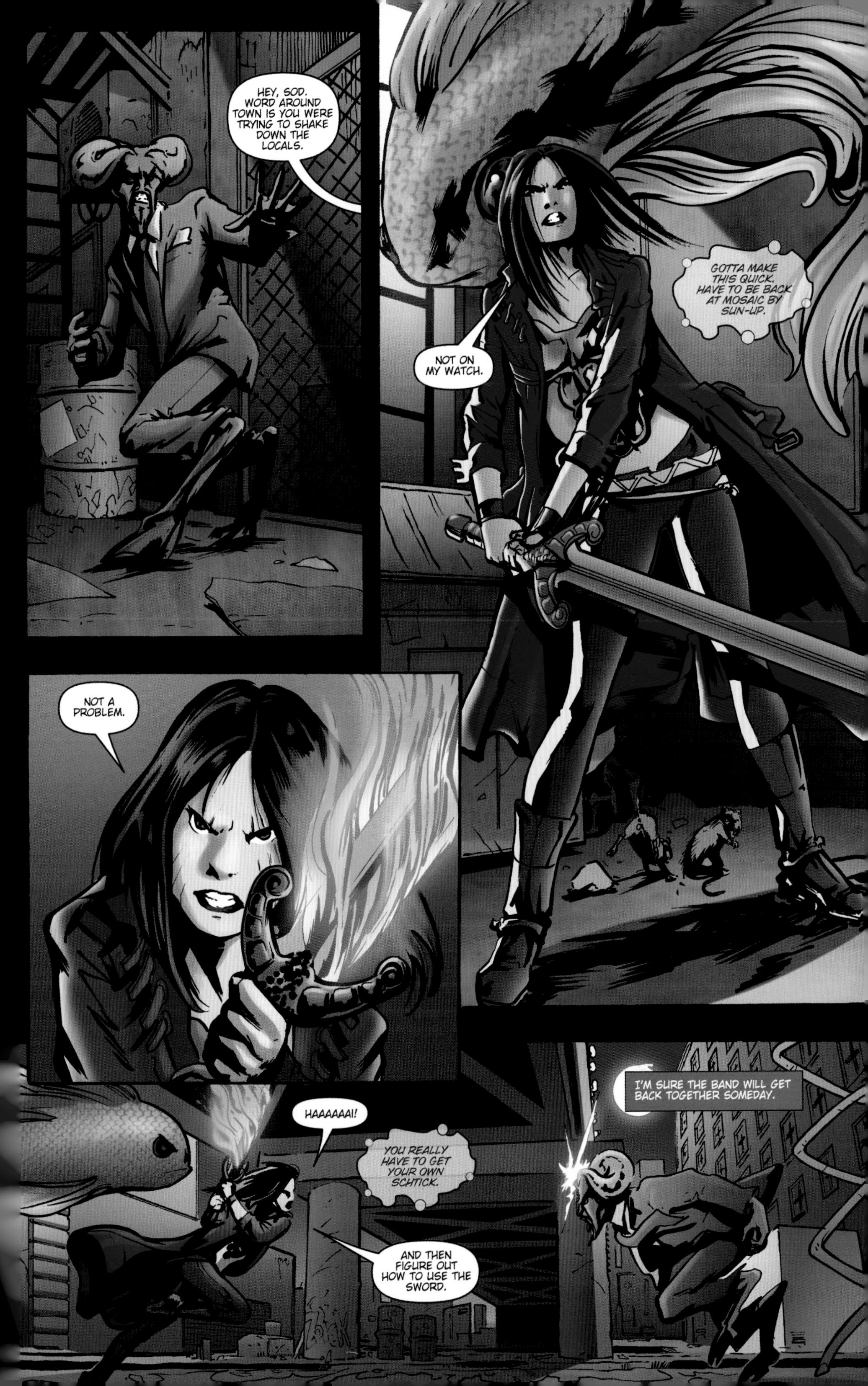
HEY, SOD. WORD AROUND TOWN IS YOU WERE TRYING TO SHAKE DOWN THE LOCALS.
NOT ON MY WATCH.
GOTTA MAKE THIS QUICK. HAVE TO BE BACK AT MOSAIC BY SUN-UP.
NOT A PROBLEM.
HAAAAAAI!
YOU REALLY HAVE TO GET YOUR OWN SCHTICK.
AND THEN FIGURE OUT HOW TO USE THE SWORD.
I'M SURE THE BAND WILL GET BACK TOGETHER SOMEDAY.

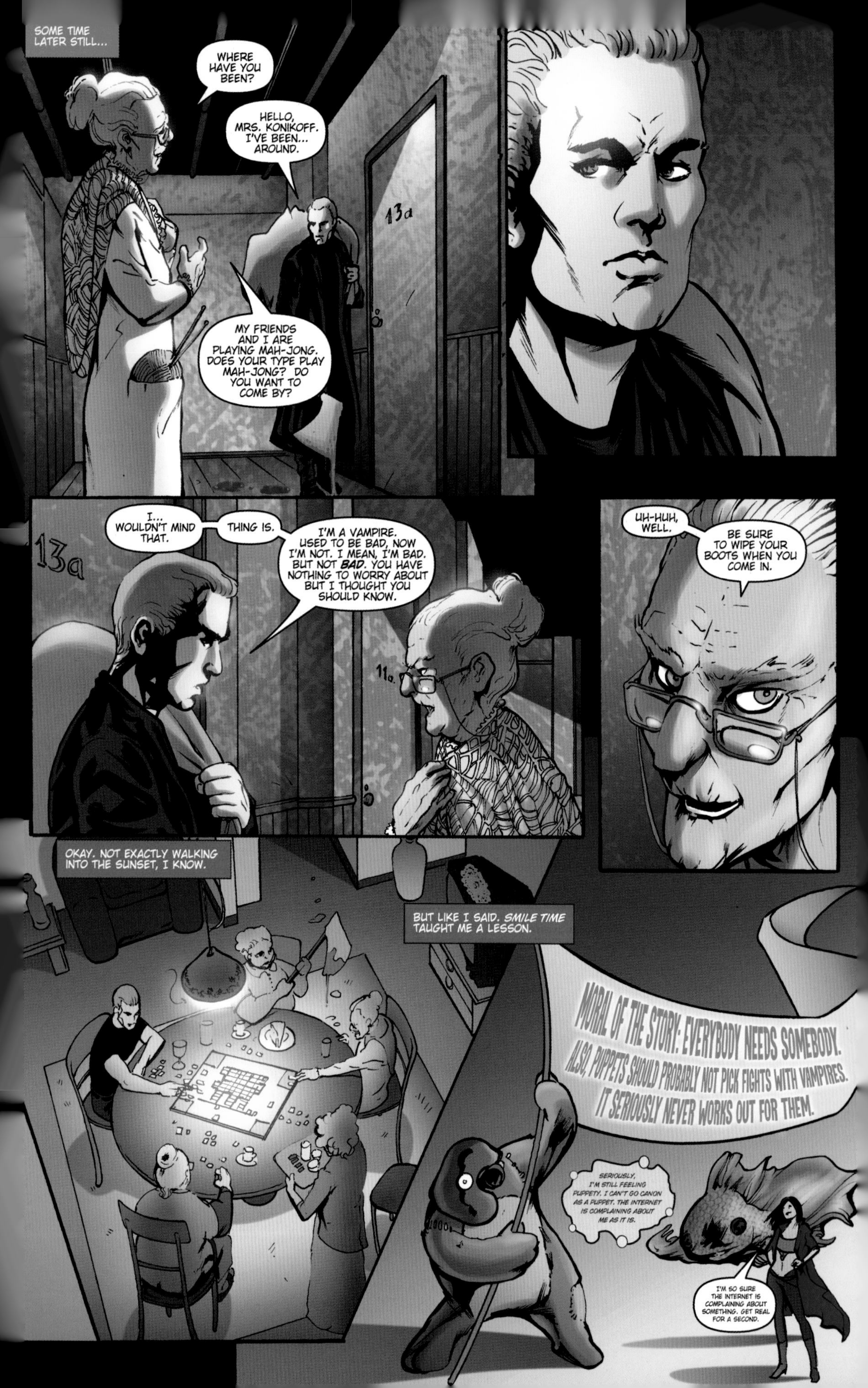
SOME TIME LATER STILL...
WHERE HAVE YOU BEEN?
HELLO, MRS. KONIKOFF. I'VE BEEN... AROUND.
MY FRIENDS AND I ARE PLAYING MAH-JONG. DOES YOUR TYPE PLAY MAH-JONG? DO YOU WANT TO COME BY?
13a
I... WOULDN'T MIND THAT.
THING IS.
I'M A VAMPIRE. USED TO BE BAD, NOW I'M NOT. I MEAN, I'M BAD. BUT NOT ***BAD***. YOU HAVE NOTHING TO WORRY ABOUT BUT I THOUGHT YOU SHOULD KNOW.
UH-HUH, WELL.
BE SURE TO WIPE YOUR BOOTS WHEN YOU COME IN.
OKAY. NOT EXACTLY WALKING INTO THE SUNSET, I KNOW.
BUT LIKE I SAID. *SMILE TIME* TAUGHT ME A LESSON.
MORAL OF THE STORY: EVERYBODY NEEDS SOMEBODY.
ALSO, PUPPETS SHOULD PROBABLY NOT PICK FIGHTS WITH VAMPIRES.
IT SERIOUSLY NEVER WORKS OUT FOR THEM.
SERIOUSLY, I'M STILL FEELING PUPPETY. I CAN'T GO CANON AS A PUPPET. THE INTERNET IS COMPLAINING ABOUT ME AS IT IS.
I'M SO SURE THE INTERNET IS COMPLAINING ABOUT SOMETHING. GET REAL FOR A SECOND.

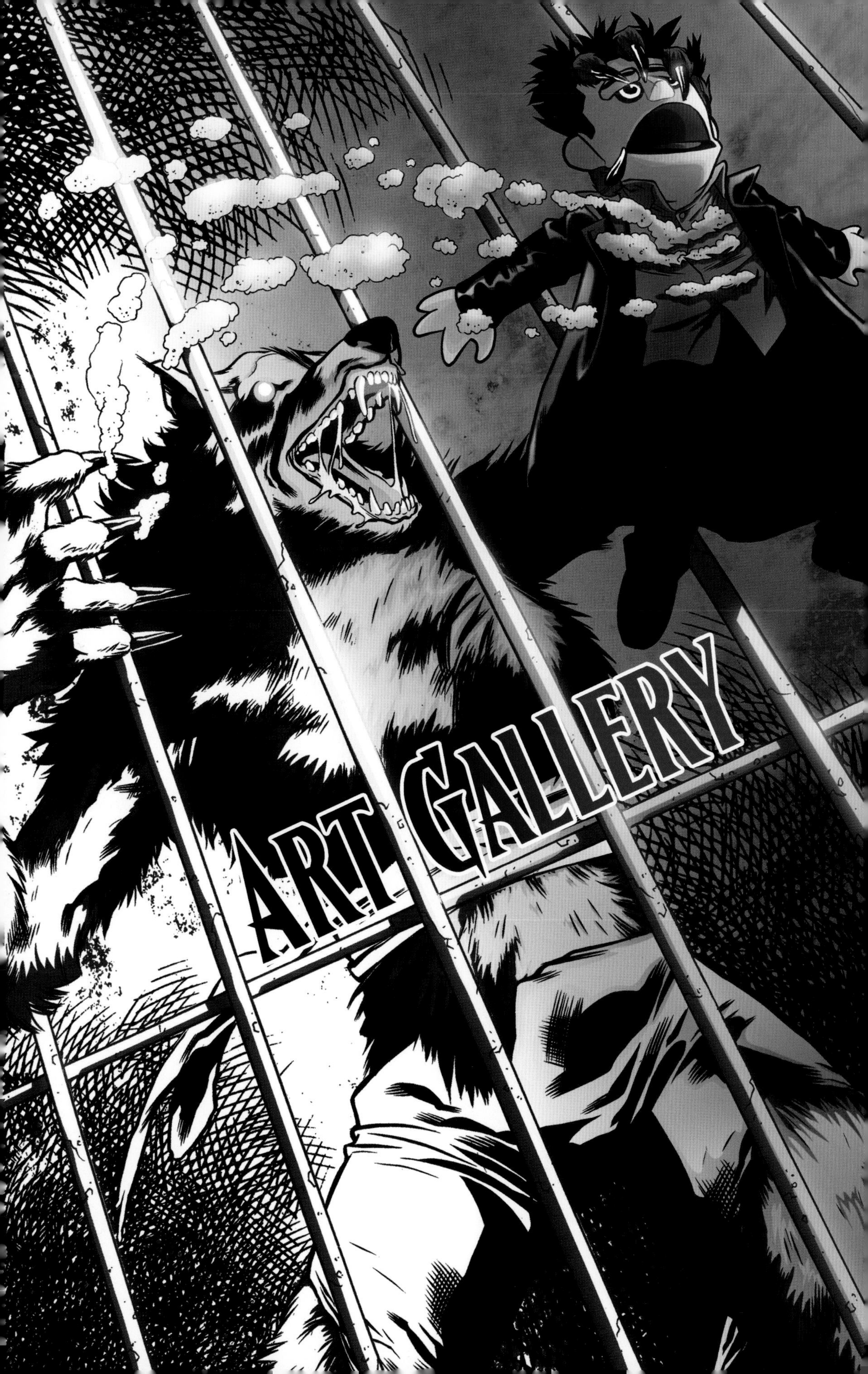
ART GALLERY

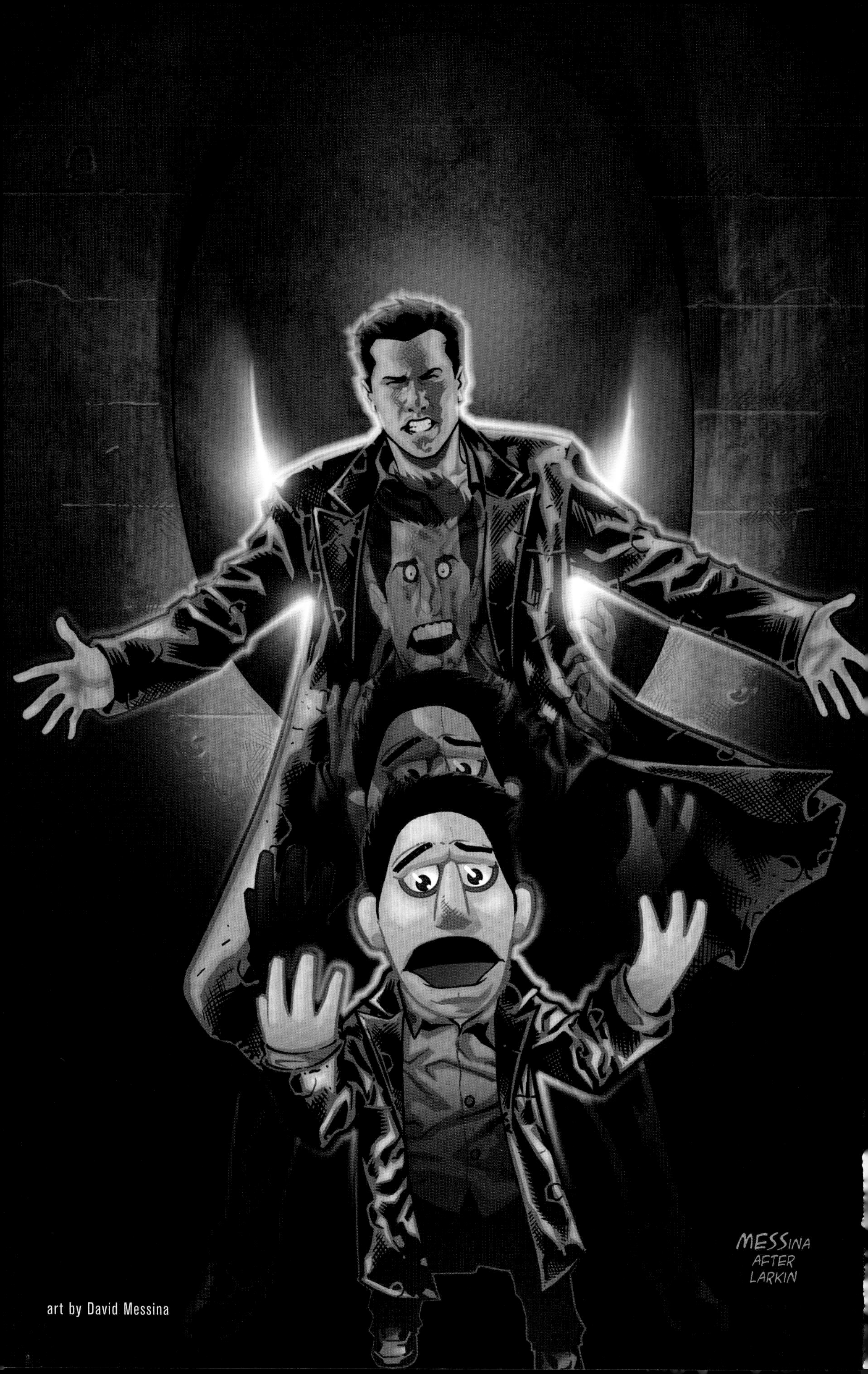
MESSINA
AFTER
LARKIN

art by David Messina

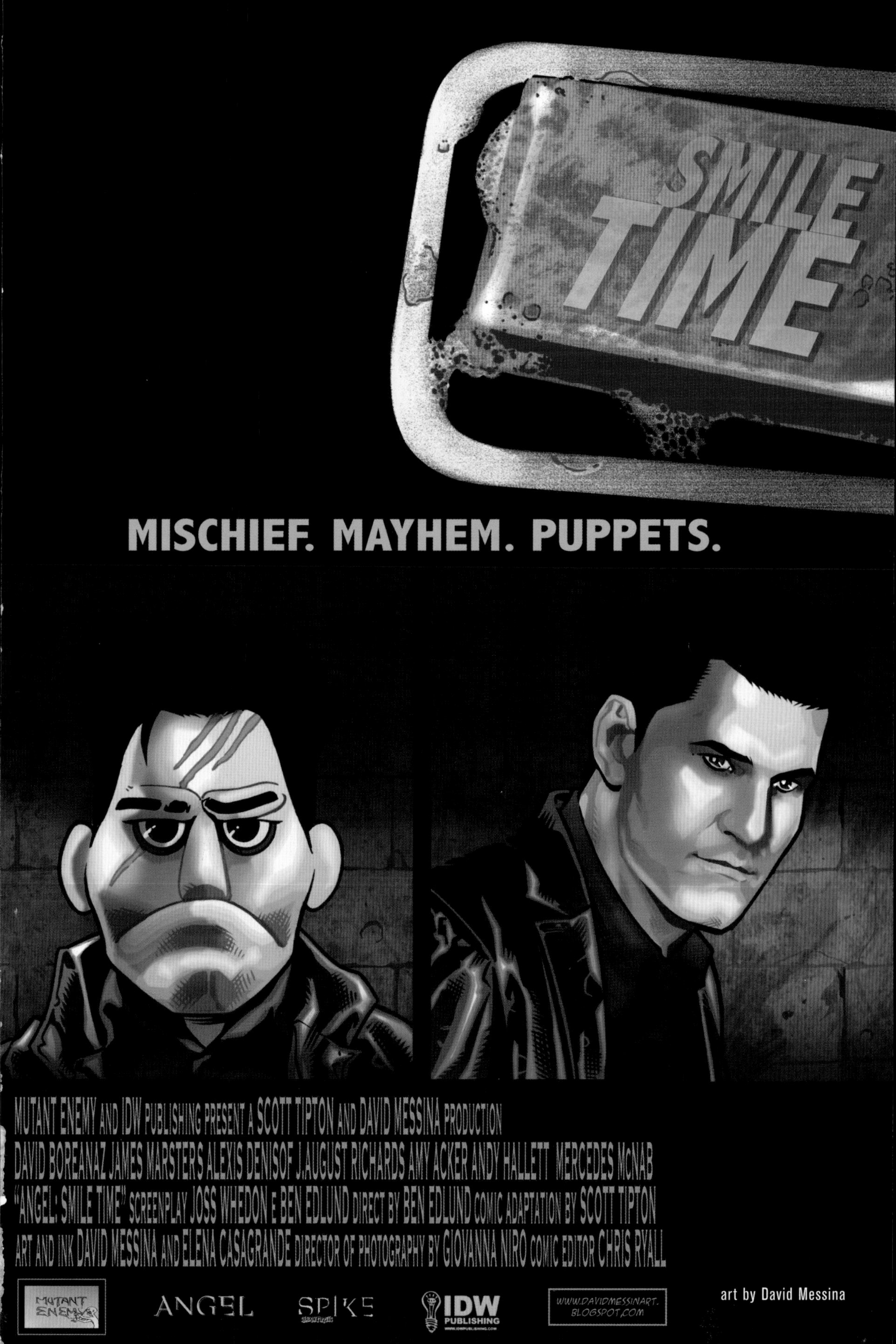
SMILE TIME
MISCHIEF. MAYHEM. PUPPETS.
MUTANT ENEMY AND IDW PUBLISHING PRESENT A SCOTT TIPTON AND DAVID MESSINA PRODUCTION
DAVID BOREANAZ JAMES MARSTERS ALEXIS DENISOF J.AUGUST RICHARDS AMY ACKER ANDY HALLETT MERCEDES MCNAB
"ANGEL: SMILE TIME" SCREENPLAY JOSS WHEDON E BEN EDLUND DIRECT BY BEN EDLUND COMIC ADAPTATION BY SCOTT TIPTON
ART AND INK DAVID MESSINA AND ELENA CASAGRANDE DIRECTOR OF PHOTOGRAPHY BY GIOVANNA NIRO COMIC EDITOR CHRIS RYALL
MUTANT ENEMY
ANGEL
SPIKE
IDW PUBLISHING
WWW.DAVIDMESSINART.BLOGSPOT.COM
art by David Messina

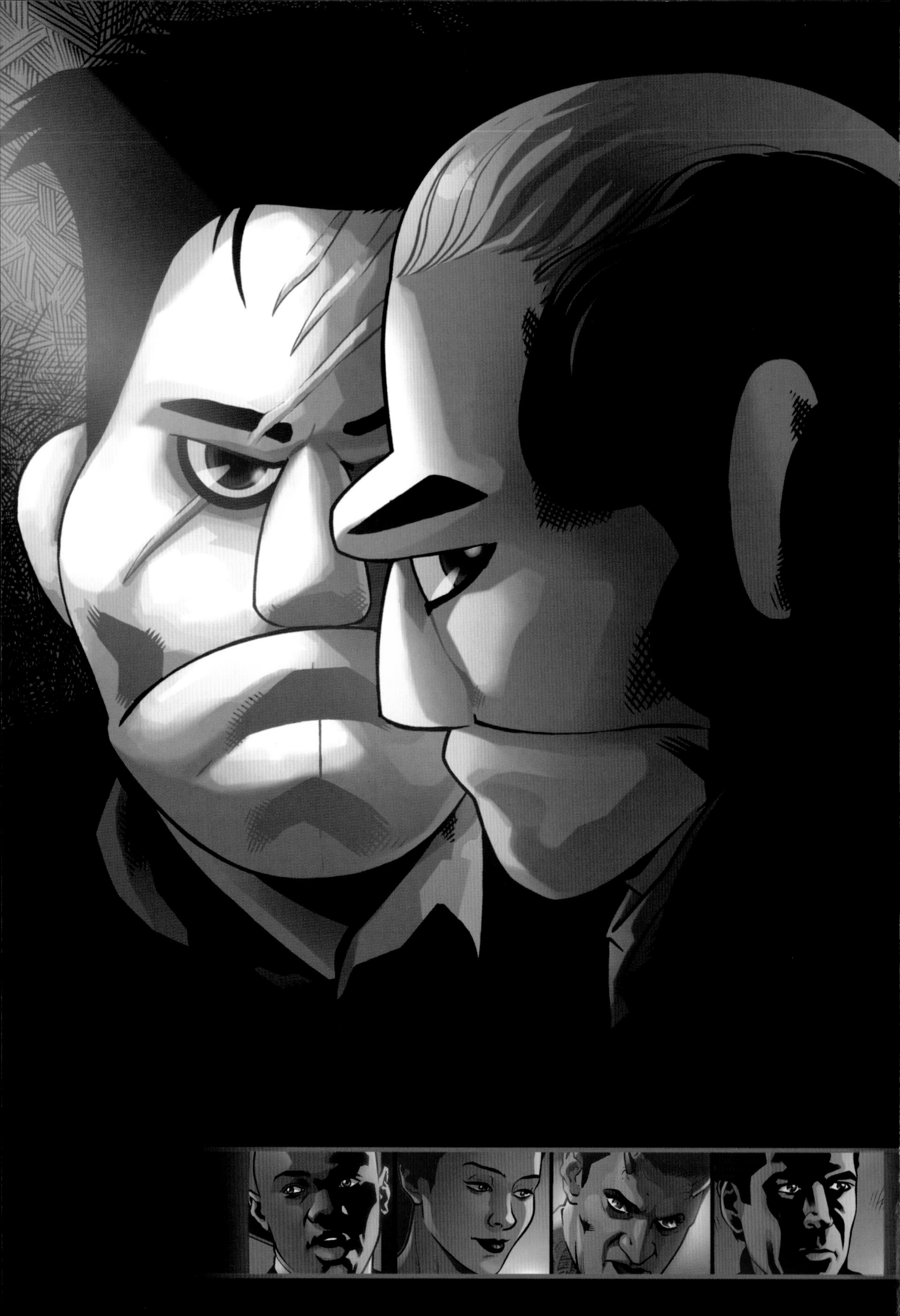

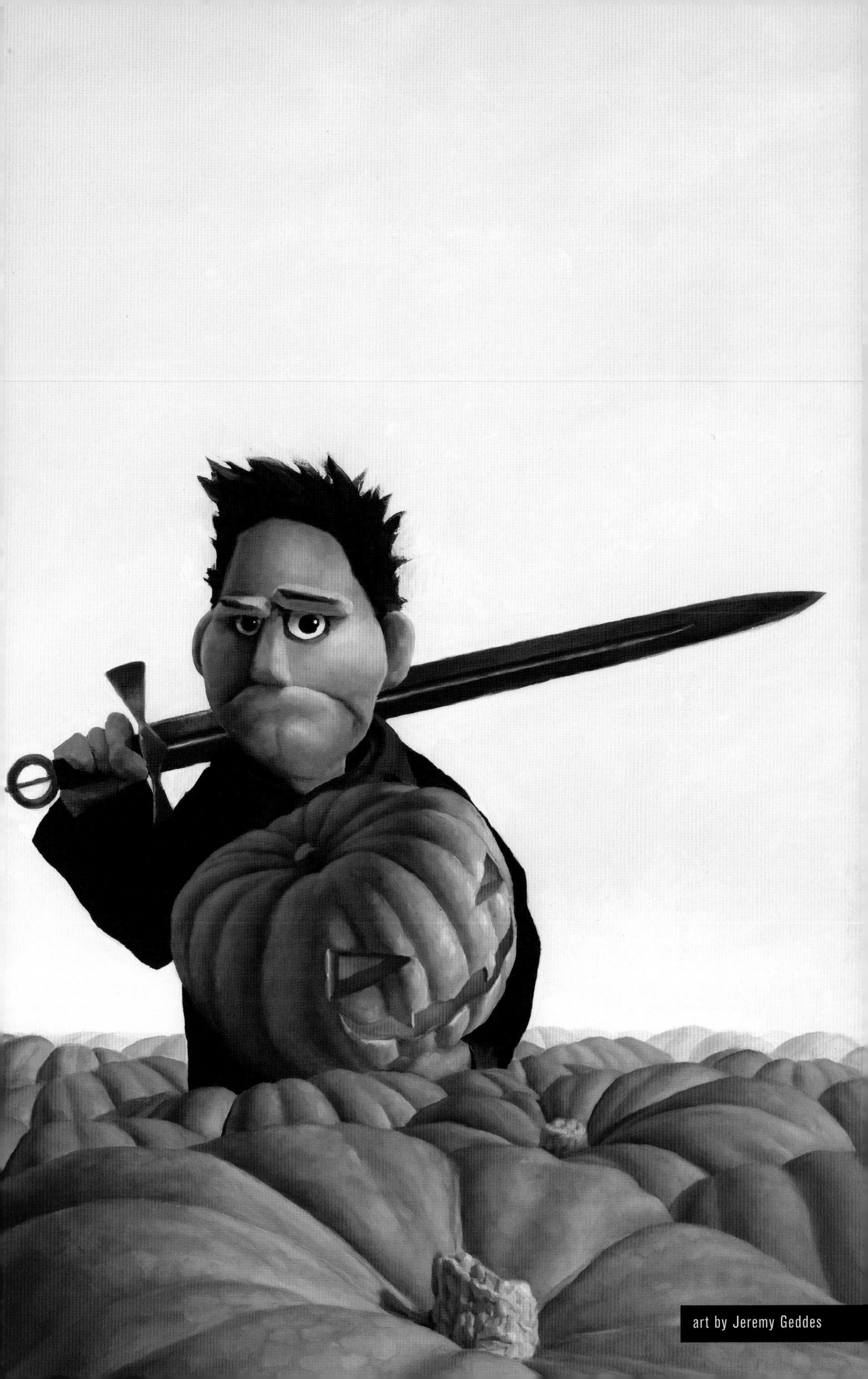

art by Jeremy Geddes

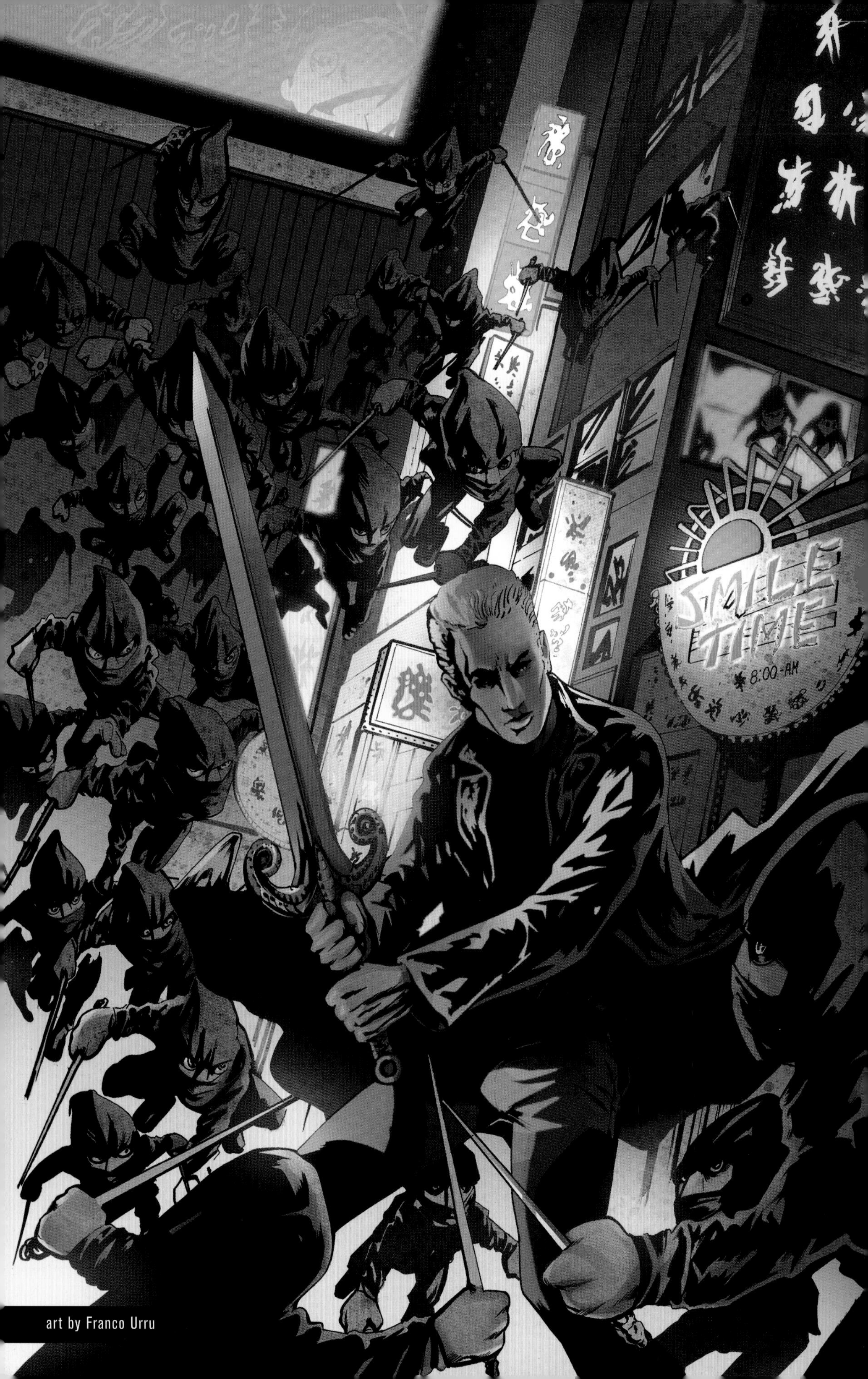
SMILE TIME
8:00-AM

art by Franco Urru

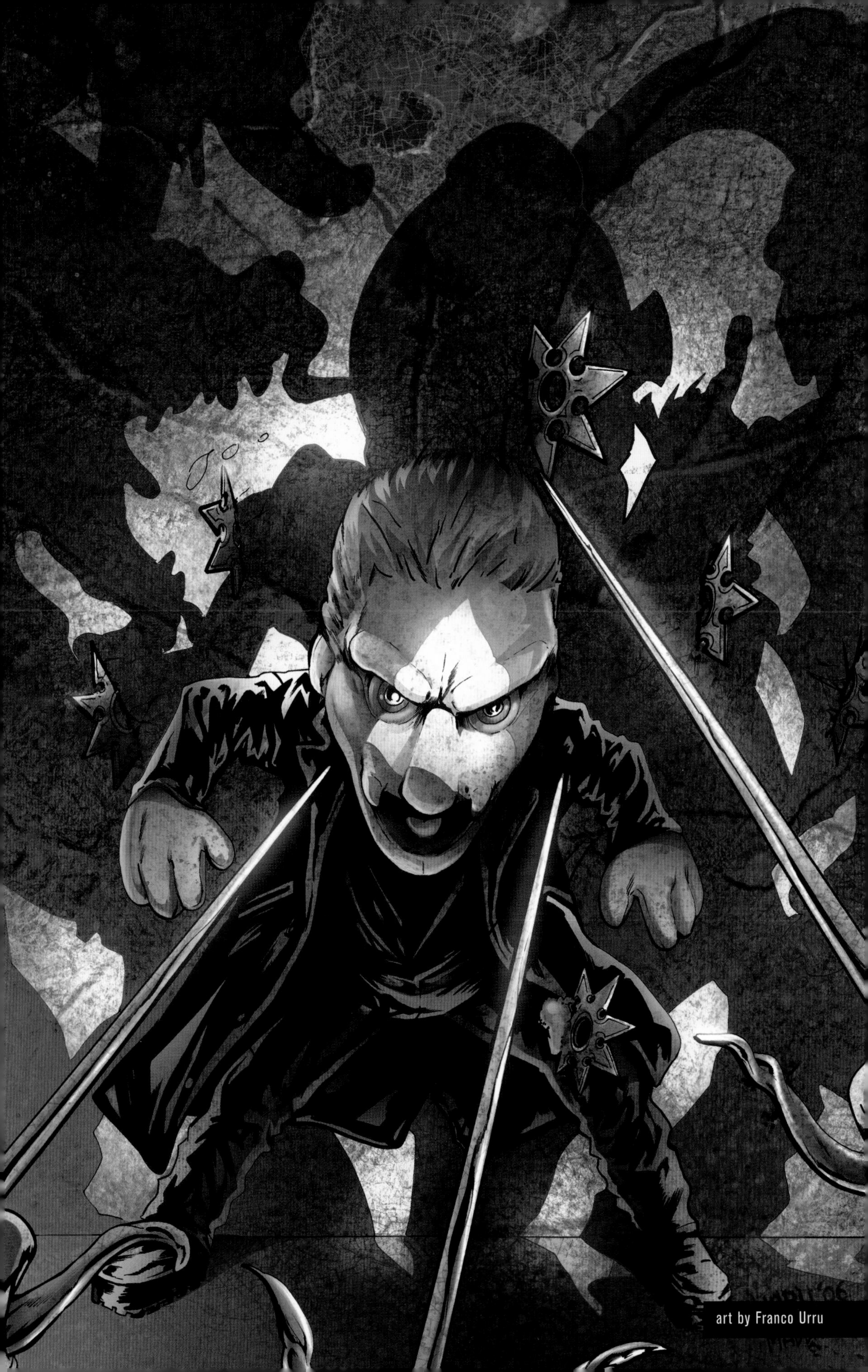

art by Franco Urru

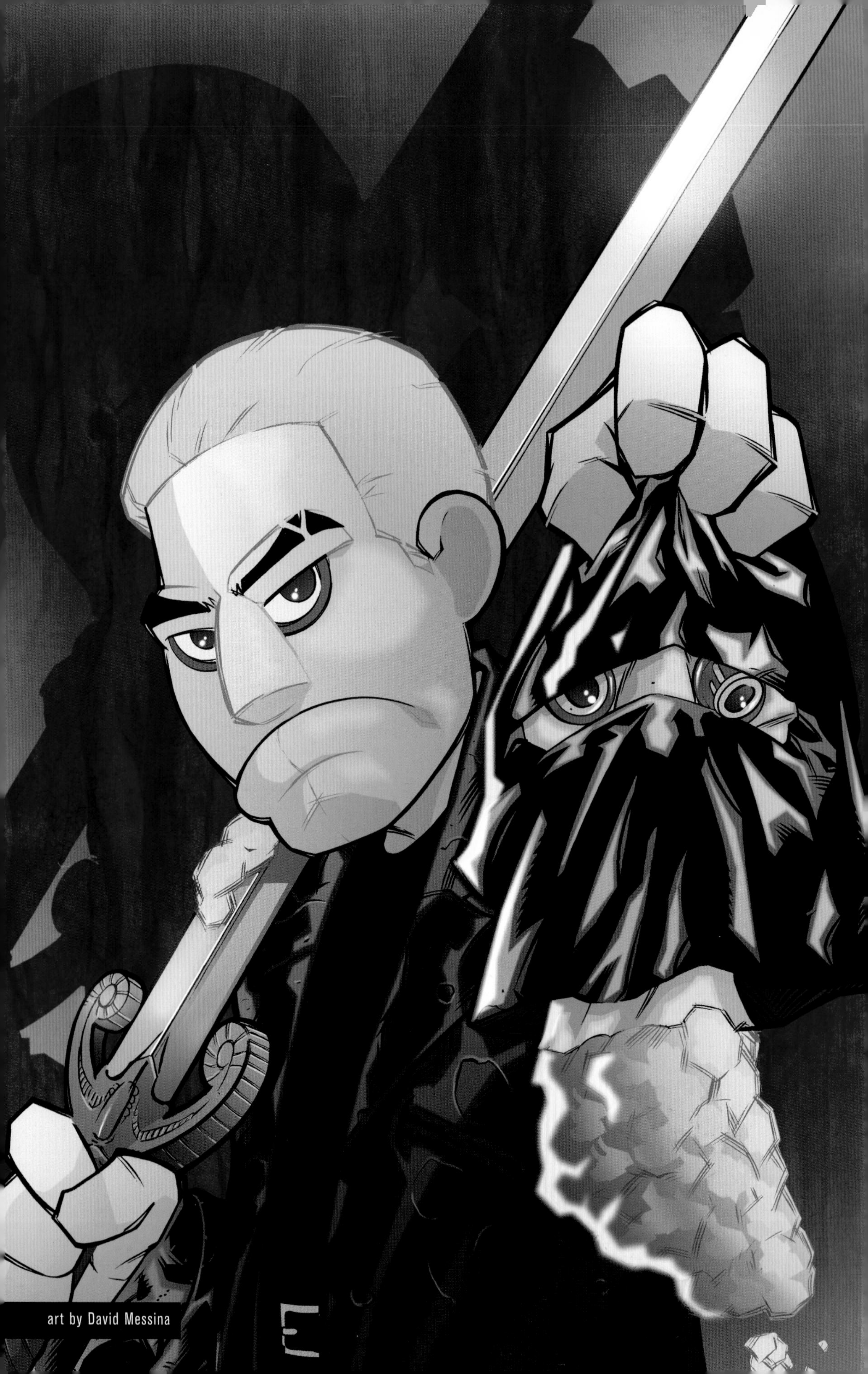

art by David Messina

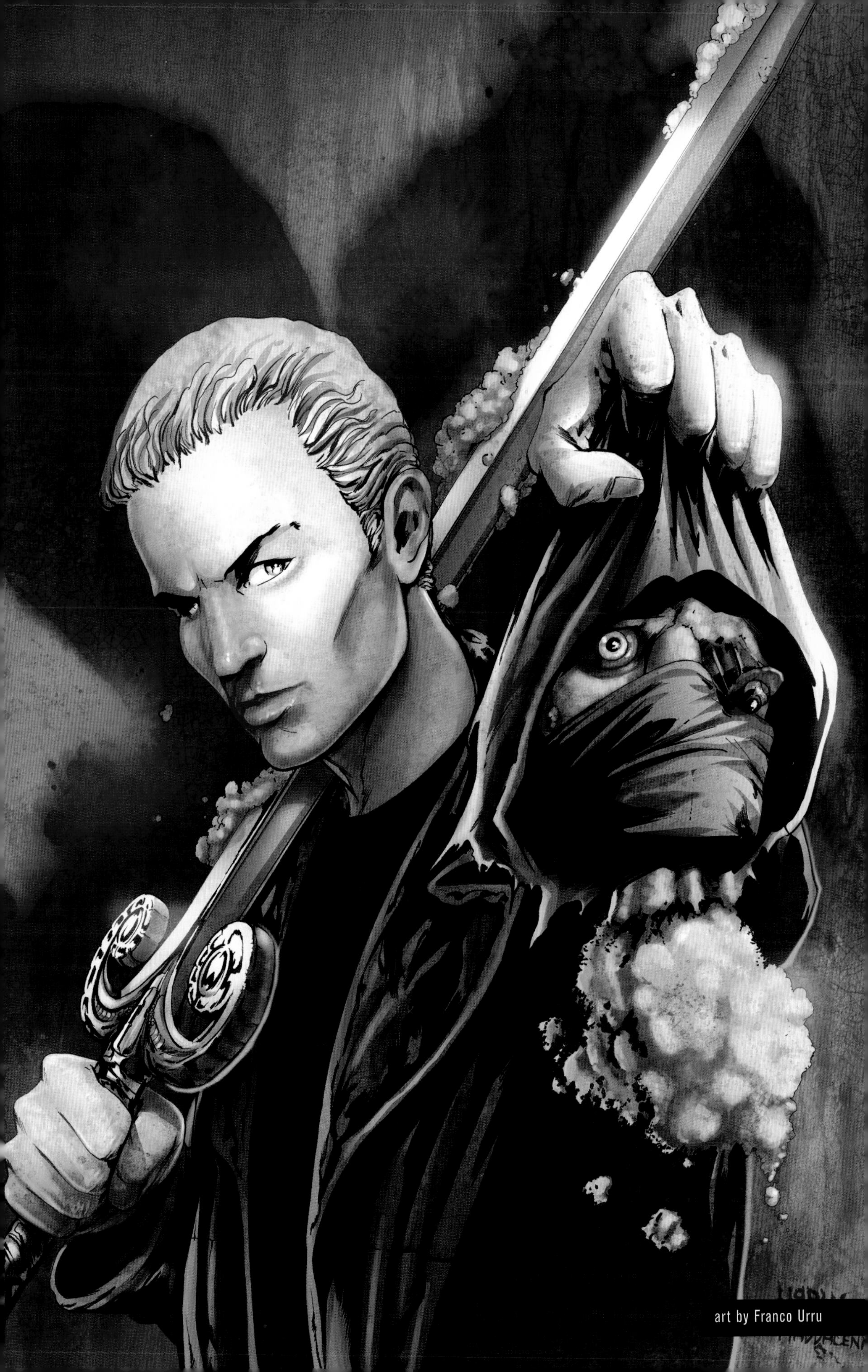

art by Franco Urru

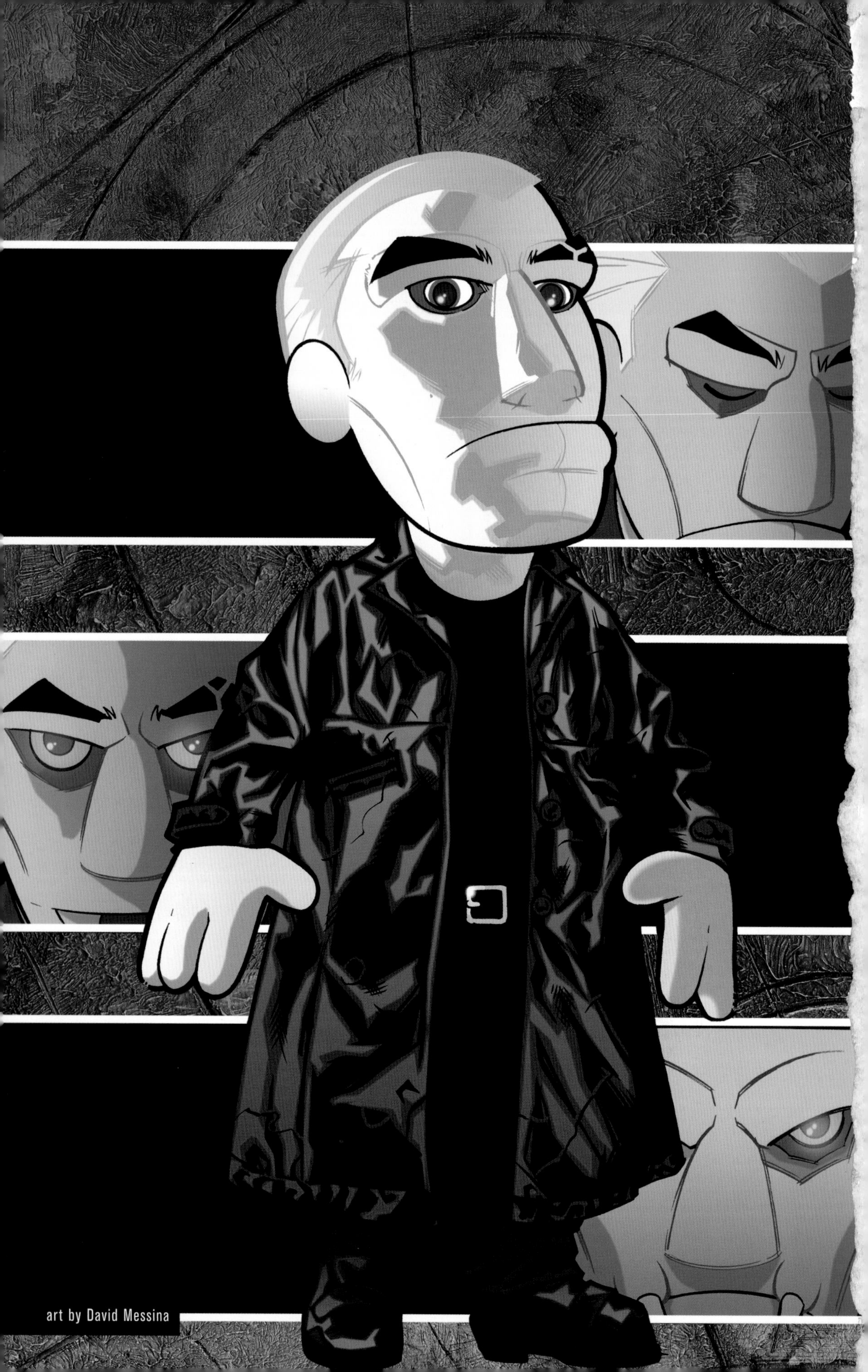

art by David Messina

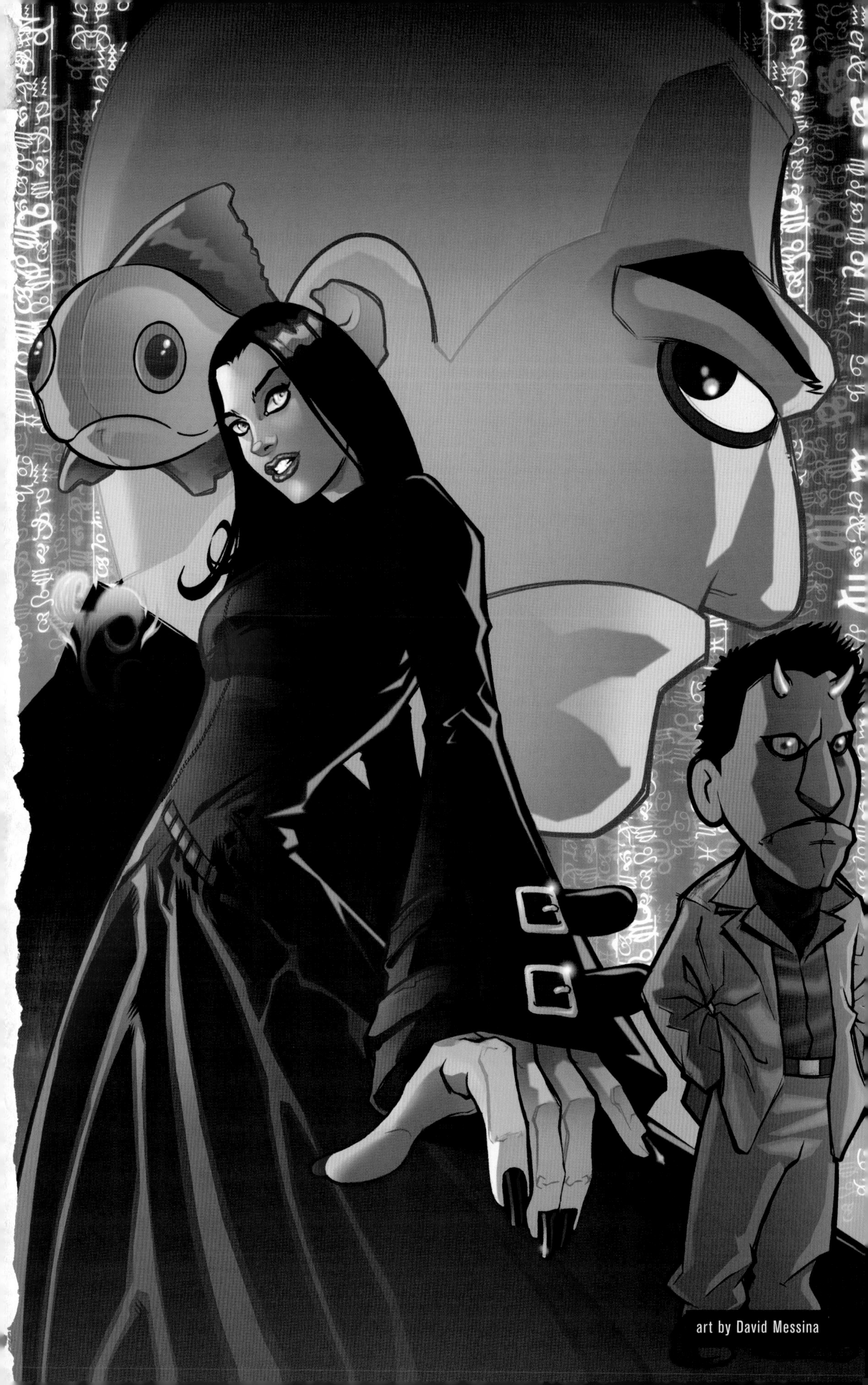

art by David Messina

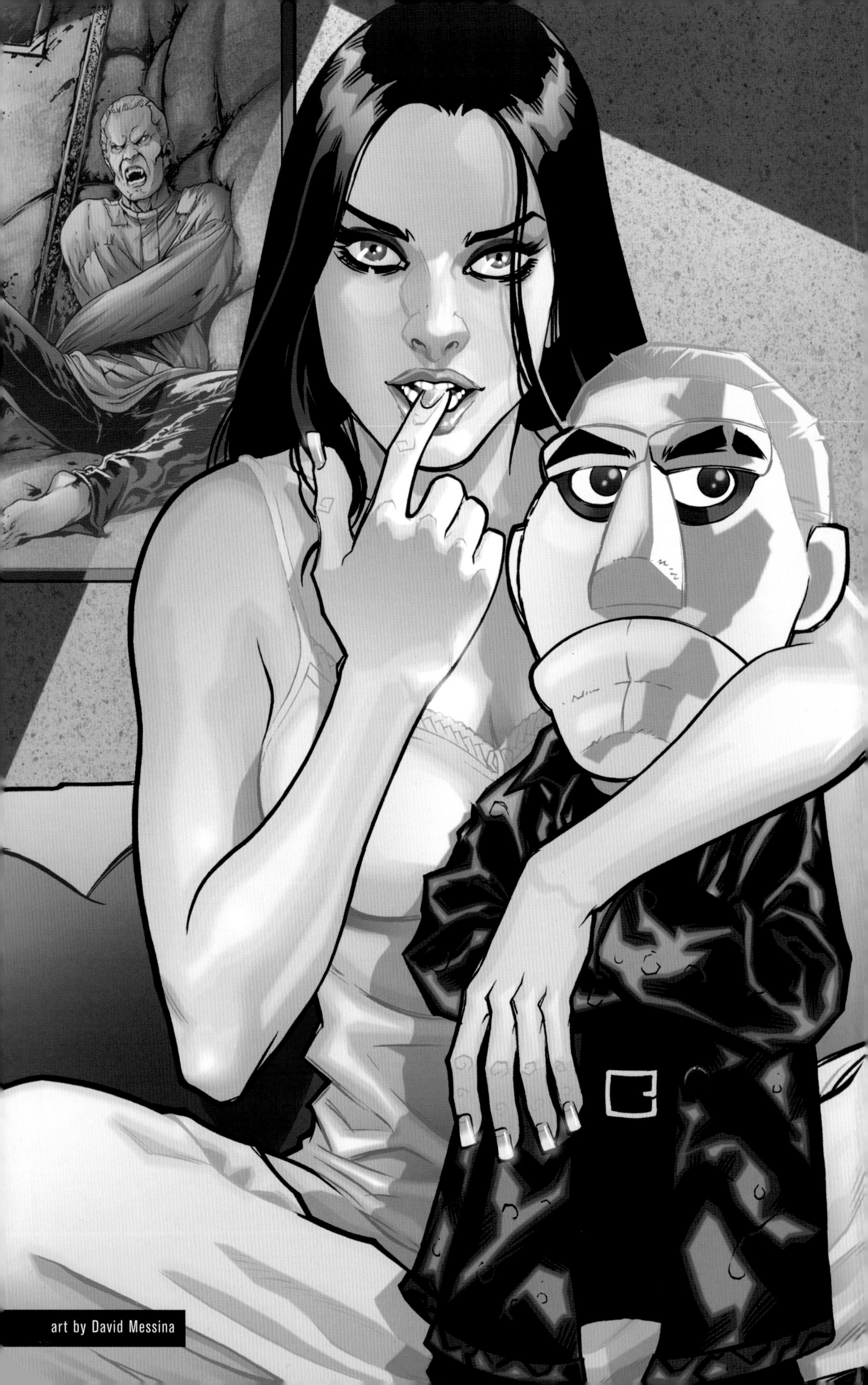

art by David Messina

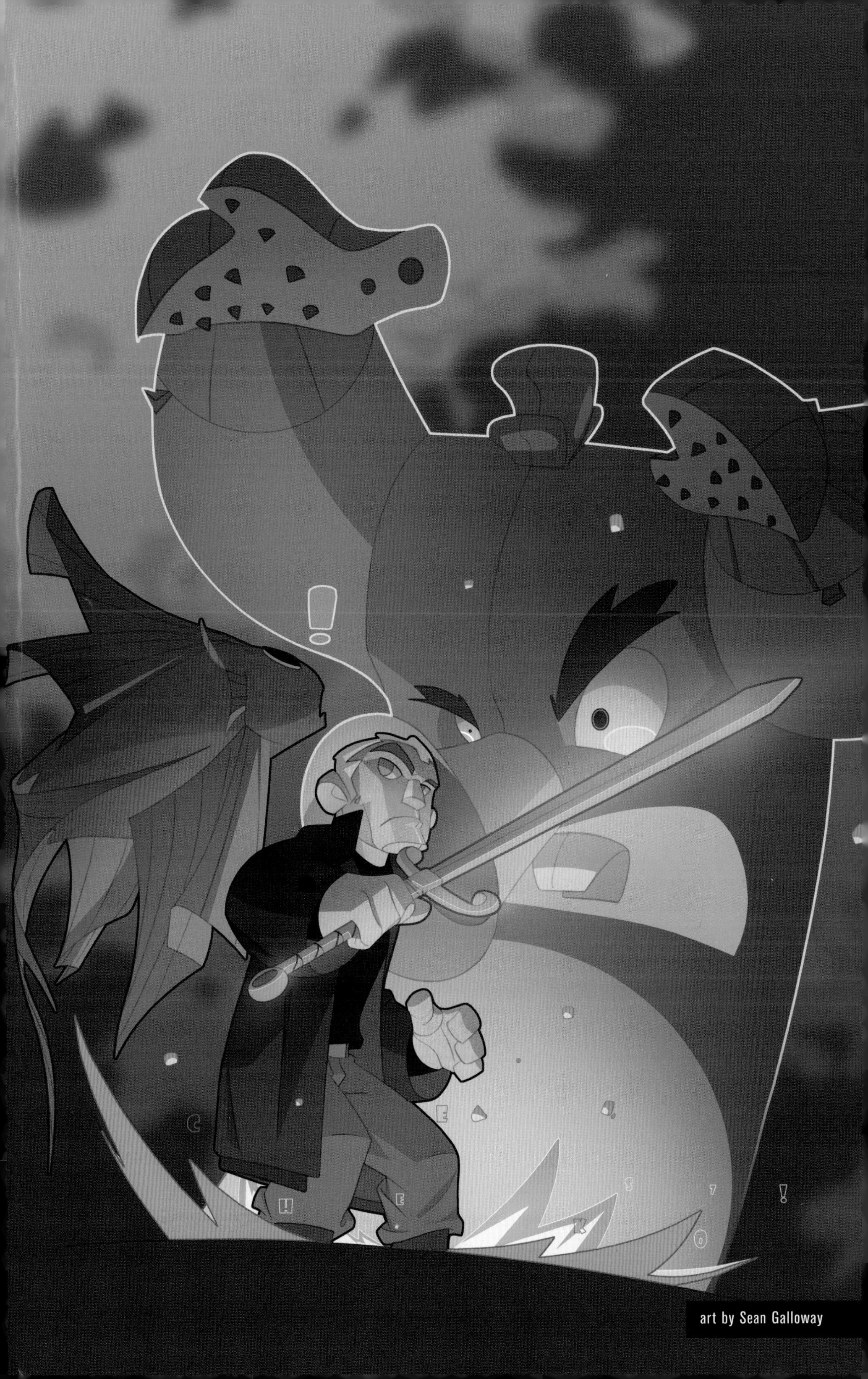

art by Sean Galloway